MAIER'S

COCAINE ADDICTION

Prof. Dr. Hans W. Maier
1882-1945

MAIER'S

COCAINE ADDICTION

(Der Kokainismus)

Translated and Edited by

ORIANA JOSSEAU KALANT

ADDICTION RESEARCH FOUNDATION
Toronto

Originally published in 1926 as *Der Kokainismus—Geschichte/Pathologie Medizinische und behördliche Bekämpfung*

Translated into French by Dr. S. Jankélévitch
La Cocaine—Historique.—Pathologique.—Clinique.—Thérapeutique. —Défense Sociale.

An introduction, with references, has been added to this abridged translation of the original work by Oriana Josseau Kalant

Canadian Cataloguing in Publication Data

Maier, Hans W. (Hans Wolfgang), 1882-1945.
Maier's Cocaine addiction (Der Kokainismus)
Translation of: Der Kokainismus, Geschichte, Pathologie, medizinische une behördliche Bekämpfung.
Bibliography: p.
Includes index.
ISBN 0-88868-160-7
1. Cocaine habit. 2. Cocaine habit—History. 3. Cocaine–Physiological effect. 4. Cocaine–Psychological aspects. I. Kalant, Oriana Josseau, 1920- . II. Addiction Research Foundation (Ont.). III. Title. IV. Title: Cocaine addiction (Der Kokainismus).
HV5810.M3413 1987 616.86′3 C87-094186-0

TABLE OF CONTENTS

INTRODUCTION

> *Der Kokainismus by Hans Maier, published in 1926, is still the best book to consult with regard to the history and development of cocaine dependence.*
>
> *B. Holmstedt and A. Fredga, 1981*

Why Is This Book Necessary Now?

During the past 15 years the non-medical use of cocaine has increased markedly in North America and elsewhere. For example, a report from the National Institute on Drug Abuse (NIDA) indicated that in 1979 nearly 10 million people in the USA had used the drug at least once (*The Journal*, 1982). One informal estimate puts the number of regular users at three million in the USA at present.

At first the popular press tended to glamorize cocaine use, as exemplified by a 1974 article in *The New York Times Magazine* entitled "Cocaine—The Champagne of Drugs" (Crittenden and Ruby, 1974). This was partly because, at that time, the drug was very expensive and therefore used primarily by wealthy and glamorous people, such as entertainers, professional athletes and other style setters. Such popular articles often gave the impression that the drug was essentially harmless. Dr. Robert Petersen, formerly of NIDA, has referred to "the optimism that accompanies all use" of drugs, especially of new or rediscovered ones (*The Journal*, 1982). At the same time, although the scientific literature contained a great deal of information on the pharmacology of cocaine, including its dependence liability in experimental animals (Mulé, 1976), the clinical literature had virtually ignored for more than half a century the consequences of cocaine use by humans.

However, as the extent of use increased, larger numbers of serious clinical complications began to be observed. These include deaths from cocaine overdose (Finkle, 1972; Smith, 1983) and large numbers of adverse effects on physical and mental health, including psychological malfunctioning (Washton et al., 1983).

This course of events was greeted with bewilderment and alarm. There were many statements to the effect that very little was known about this "new" drug and therefore that research was required urgently. Experimental studies with modern techniques are obviously necessary for further understanding of the mechanisms by which the drug produces its effects and complications. However, sound and detailed clinical observations of the syndromes occurring in heavy cocaine users had already been published many decades earlier and subsequently were largely forgotten. To a considerable extent, this may be due to the fact that most of the relevant literature was published in German, French and Italian, and knowledge of these languages among English-speaking clinicians and researchers has fallen drastically since the Second World War.

Perhaps the best monograph on clinical aspects of cocaine dependence from that earlier period was Hans Maier's *Der Kokainismus*. The cost of forgetting this knowledge includes the waste of time and effort needed to rediscover it and failure to respond adequately to present-day problems because of ignorance and neglect of the past. In one of the most widely misquoted statements, George Santayana (1954) said "Those who do not remember the past are condemned to repeat it." The purpose of translating and publishing Maier's monograph now is to help prevent these unnecessary costs.

Cocaine Problems—the Rise and Fall of Knowledge

Cocaine, an alkaloid contained in the leaves of the Andean coca bush (*Erythroxylon coca*), was isolated and identified chemically by the German chemist Albert Niemann in 1860. Not very much was done with the pure compound for the next two decades or so. However, two major developments occurred in 1884. The first was Freud's review of the existing literature on coca and cocaine, which led him to study the subjective and objective effects of cocaine and to recommend it in the treatment of depression, alcoholism and morphine addiction (Byck, 1974). The second was Carl Koller's discovery and clinical use of the local anesthetic effects of the drug on the cornea (Koller, 1884).

The early enthusiasm for these applications soon waned. Experts on alcohol and morphine addiction quickly realized that their patients, when treated with cocaine, transferred their addiction to it. Surgeons also soon found out that the drug, if absorbed systemically from injection sites, could have dangerous and even lethal effects (Mayer, 1924). Despite the early awareness of these hazards by physicians, the public had already learned about the euphoriant effects of cocaine and illicit use and dependence quickly became widespread. At first, the main route of administration was hypodermic injection, and the material used was pure cocaine obtained from pharmacies. Not surprisingly, many of the early addicts were health care professionals or their patients. In the early part of this century, the practice of sniffing cocaine appeared, apparently originating in the USA, and it soon largely replaced subcutaneous injection. Concomitantly, an illicit traffic developed, including adulteration with various inert or potentially toxic materials.

As a result of the public alarm created by these practices, many western governments legislated controls over the availability and use of cocaine. Frequently this was done by including it under measures directed primarily against opiates, such as the Hague Convention of 1912 and the *Harrison Act* in the USA in 1914. By the mid-1920s, its use was illegal in most western countries, except as a local anesthetic. By that time, the non-medical use of cocaine had diminished markedly, except for a small number of intravenous users of heroin who mixed it with cocaine to make the "speedball."

Shortly afterwards, the amphetamines, which had been synthesized many years earlier, were tested for their pharmacological properties and possible therapeutic applications (Bett, Howells and Macdonald, 1955). They were found to have vasoconstrictor and pressor effects and to be potent central nervous system stimulants which produced euphoria, prolonged wakefulness and suppression of appetite. Therefore they were soon employed as nasal decongestants, antidepressants, appetite inhibitors and as antihypotensive agents during surgical anesthesia. Amphetamine free base, which is volatile, was used in over-the-counter inhalers for the relief of nasal congestion due to colds and hay fever. It soon became popular knowledge that these inhalers provided an inexpensive and legally available "high," and their abuse led to their withdrawal from the market.

However, therapeutic use of the non-volatile salts of amphetamine continued for another three decades, principally in the management of narcolepsy, hyperkinesis in children and obesity. During this period, numerous case reports of adverse effects, including physical and psychiatric illness and dependence, were published. These were reviewed in three major monographs published during the 1950s and 1960s (Bonhoff and Lewrenz, 1954; Connell, 1958; Kalant, 1966). Though a few German and Swiss clinicians, writing in German, made passing reference to the similarities between the effects of cocaine and those of the amphetamines, the point was not generally appreciated (Gardner, 1969). Indeed, the two major monographs in English (Connell, 1958; Kalant, 1966) did not even mention cocaine. One of the first clear statements of the essential similarity between cocaine and the amphetamines was that made by

Bejerot (1970), who wrote: *In my opinion synthetic central stimulants have the same relationship to the natural product cocaine as morphine substitutes have to morphine.*

Major outbreaks of intravenous use of amphetamines occurred in Japan in the 1950s and in North America and some European countries during the late 1960s and early 1970s. These were associated with major medical and psychiatric problems and numerous deaths by violence (Kalant and Kalant, 1976). As a result of the ensuing publicity, the drug fell into disfavor even among regular drug users. This coincided in time with the revival of cocaine use among the wealthy and glamorous, as noted above. Although many basic scientists, including cardiovascular and behavioral pharmacologists and neuropharmacologists, were well aware of the close similarity in actions of the two drugs, the expert clinicians and social scientists who had been knowledgeable about cocaine were by now largely gone from the scene. The younger ones were, as pointed out earlier, unacquainted with the relevant older literature. It was, therefore, as if one started with a blank page. In the last few years this deficiency has been corrected to a considerable degree. However, all of the problems encountered in the past two decades could have been anticipated, and possibly prevented, if the experience and knowledge of earlier generations had not gone into oblivion.

The Author and the Book

Hans Wolfgang Maier was a Swiss psychiatrist who became the chief physician of the Burghölzli Psychiatric Clinic affiliated with the University of Zürich. He carried out pioneer work on hallucinations and paranoia, for which he received a professorship and ultimately became chairman of the Department of Psychiatry at Zürich. He had a major interest in alcoholism and drug dependence, as well as in child psychiatry, outpatient treatment and medico-legal questions. He died in 1945 at the age of 63. According to his obituary in *Archiv für Neurologie und Psychiatrie* (Klaesi, 1946), *Der Kokainismus* is his best known published work.

This book was published in 1926 in German, and in a French translation by Jankelevitch in 1928. The French translation unfortunately contains innumerable errors. The original work contained sections on the history of coca and cocaine, analytical methods for the measurement of cocaine, the physiological and psychological effects of the drug, an extensive review of the literature on patterns of use, toxicity and dependence, differential diagnosis of cocaine psychoses and other complications, prognosis, treatment, epidemiology and control measures. The most important section, however, consists of the detailed case histories of 35 patients, selected from 100 seen by Maier and his colleagues over a period of years. They were chosen to illustrate the most salient syndromes from the mildest to the most severe. Observations of this kind are invaluable because ethical considerations preclude the experimental administration of massive doses of drugs of this type to human subjects. One of Maier's patients, for example, is reported to have taken 19 g of pure cocaine in one night. Our knowledge of the effects of such huge doses rests exclusively on case histories which are regrettably dismissed by some writers as "anecdotal" (presumably untrustworthy) accounts.

Maier's classification of the psychiatric complications of heavy cocaine use is, by modern standards, belabored and unnecessary. He has divided the cases into too many categories which modern psychiatry would view as parts of a continuum. This probably reflects the Kraepelin tradition in German psychiatry of that period, with its excessive emphasis on phenomenological description and classification, in contrast to the modern emphasis on pathogenetic mechanisms. However, this section has been translated verbatim and the reader who wishes to do so can reclassify the cases according to modern practice. In the case reports, Maier makes frequent use of the terms "Psychopath" and "psychopathisch." It is important to note that in the German-language psychiatric literature of the early part of this century, the term "Psychopath"did not have the same connotation that it has in modern English usage. It did not necessarily imply antisocial behavior or defective superego function. Rather, it was intended as a non-judgmental term to include a rather wide variety of disturbances otherwise labelled as "neurasthenia," "cyclothymic personality," and so forth (Schneider, 1958). In the present translation it has been rendered as "personality disorder," as used by Kevin Standage (1979).

Another very valuable section is the chapter on the diffusion of cocaine use within European and other countries. Despite the passage of more than 60 years and of the absence at that time of radio, television and other modern means of communication, the social groups involved in cocaine use show many similarities to their present-day counterparts.

The present translation is selective. The first three chapters of the original text have been omitted because the history of the coca plant has been well described in many other books, and the sections on chemistry and analytical methods are now obsolete. Portions of chapters VI and VII, dealing with medico-legal aspects of treatment and legal measures to control the spread of cocaine addiction, have also been omitted because they are of only local relevance to

Switzerland in the 1920s. Everything else has been translated in full, including Maier's comprehensive bibliography, which has been verified to the extent possible and rewritten according to contemporary usage. Bibliographic standards were evidently less rigorous in Maier's time, and the original had numerous inconsistencies with respect to authors' initials, abbreviations of article and journal titles, and details of volume and page numbers and year. To the extent possible, these inconsistencies have been corrected. Many of the authors mentioned in the text by Maier were not listed in his bibliography. Some of these have been located by other means and have been added to the list of references. However, those names which are not followed by year references in parentheses have remained unidentified. Some references in the bibliographic list were not cited in the text; however, they have been retained because they may be of interest to present-day readers.

Some Highlights in Maier's Book

Maier, as well as several of his predecessors, realized through their clinical observations that addiction to stimulants was quite possible. It had been known for a long time that addiction to depressants, such as alcohol, barbiturates and opiates, was a reality in heavy users, but cocaine was the first well identified stimulant to be investigated or noticed in this respect. This continued for a long time to be a bone of contention, because a World Health Organization (WHO) Expert Committee stated as late as 1964, that only the depressants produce, upon long-term use, a true addiction. Again, this attitude prevailed for about three decades after the introduction of amphetamine (Leake, 1958). The argument hinged on whether or not these drugs produce a severe physical withdrawal syndrome (Kalant, 1966). The important question, however, is whether the drugs do or do not induce behavioral dependence. In experimental animals, cocaine and amphetamines are highly effective reinforcers of drug self-administration (Thompson and Unna, 1977). There is no longer any question that stimulants such as cocaine and amphetamines do produce, in heavy users, strong psychological dependence. Maier must be credited with having understood and reported this fact most lucidly. He referred to chronic heavy cocaine users as "cocaine addicts."

A closely related question is whether or not cocaine produces tolerance. Maier noted that most of his patients had increased their dosage markedly. He recognized that this, as Joël and Fränkel (1924) had stated, did not prove the existence of tolerance. However, a number of the patients on very large doses had only minor or no subjective symptoms. Therefore, Maier's own view was that tolerance does actually develop. This is in keeping with modern experimental findings indicating tolerance to at least some of the effects of cocaine and of amphetamine (Fischman and Schuster, 1980; Leith and Barrett, 1981; Branch and Dearing, 1982; Vee et al., 1983). At the same time, Maier cites the work of Bravetta and Invernizzi (1923) showing that animals receiving repeated large doses of cocaine lost their tolerance and became more sensitive to the drug. This also has been confirmed by the work of many later investigators (Post, 1981).

Most of Maier's patients were multiple drug users. Their histories indicate heavy use of alcohol, morphine and other drugs. Many of them had a pattern of use characterized by prolonged "runs" or binges, during which they rapidly escalated their dosage and experienced extended states of intoxication, insomnia and anorexia. This foretold the behavior pattern of the "speed freak" of the 1960s (Kramer et al., 1967), and of some of today's generation of cocaine users (*Medical Letter,* 1984).

Among the most serious physical complications noted in Maier's patients were chronic rhinitis and septal perforation in those who sniffed cocaine, and seizures, cardiac arrhythmias, respiratory arrest and death in those who took high doses by any route. The case histories also record a high frequency of violent behavior under the influence of the drug, including murder and suicide. With the exception of the perforated nasal septum, this is exactly the pattern of physical and behavioral complications which was described 50 years later (Kalant and Kalant, 1976) in heavy users of amphetamine, and recently again in cocaine users (*Medical Letter,* 1984). Maier also recorded the lesser problems associated with unsterile injection techniques, such as abscesses and venous thromboses, which are also well known in today's drug users.

Maier devoted his greatest attention, however, to the psychiatric complications of cocaine use, especially to the cocaine psychosis characterized by paranoid delusions, hallucinations (especially tactile) and stereotypy. He also noted the difficulty of differentiating between this condition and schizophrenia, alcoholic hallucinosis and a large number of states produced by other drugs, including morphine, mescaline, cannabis, muscarine and atropine. This question of comparison of drug effects, both subjective and objective, was investigated experimentally years later by Isbell's group at the Addiction Research Center in Lexington (Haertzen, 1966). Maier also noted the characteristic sequence of disappearance of these symptoms after the drug had been discontinued. All of these attributes of certain drug-induced psychoses, which were often confused with schizophrenia or alcoholic hallucinosis, were rediscovered years later in relation to amphetamine abuse (Connell, 1958; Kalant, 1966).

One must not expect Maier to have anticipated every feature of cocaine use and abuse in our own era. There are some significant differences between today's practices and those of Maier's patients. Most of the latter used pure cocaine of licit manufacture (even if adulterated with inert materials), while today's drug traffic is in illicit and relatively crude material that is often heavily adulterated with other active drugs. Moreover, Maier had no knowledge of the present practice of free-basing (Siegel, 1982).

Conclusion

Despite the limitations noted above, Maier's book is a classic and outstanding contribution to the clinical knowledge of cocaine dependence and its complications, but has not been available in English until now. Because it has a great deal to offer, it should be read with great care by clinicians and investigators.

Knowledge of this material at the right time might have foretold all of the problems associated with the amphetamine epidemic and with today's cocaine revival. Perhaps most importantly of all, it might have prevented the false glamorization and too easy acceptance of cocaine by the mass media that have probably contributed to the creation of a "new" drug fad.

To some extent, this error is now being rectified. In the last two or three years, the mass media have reported a number of deaths by cocaine overdose, and other accidents associated with the use of this drug, among sports and entertainment celebrities. However, the use of cocaine by high school students in the United States and some parts of Canada is still increasing rapidly, while that of most other drugs such as heroin and cannabis is either stable or decreasing (Johnston et al., 1985; Smart et al., 1986). These events appear to have produced a sharper perception of the dangers of cocaine, among government authorities and the public-at-large. However, the erroneous image of cocaine as a safe drug need not have arisen in the first place, if older knowledge and experience had been heeded.

Newer developments in this field have included the widespread use of cocaine free base, most recently in the form known in North America as "crack" (*Medical Letter,* 1986). Again, this is being treated by the media as though it were a new drug. A knowledge of the classical literature on the pharmacology of cocaine would avoid such misconceptions by providing the context in which these variants of cocaine use can be understood.

References

Anonymous. Adverse effects of cocaine abuse. *Med. Lett.* 26: 51-52, 1984.

Anonymous. "Crack." *Med. Lett.* 28: 69-70, 1986.

Bejerot, N. A comparison of the effects of cocaine and synthetic central stimulants. *Brit. J. Addiction* 65: 35-37, 1970.

Bett, W.R., Howells, L.H., and Macdonald, A.D. *Amphetamine in Clinical Medicine: Actions and Uses*. Edinburgh: E. & S. Livingstone, 1955.

Bonhoff, G., and Lewrenz, H. *Über Weckamine*. Berlin: Springer, 1954.

Branch, M.N., and Dearing, M.E. Effects of acute and daily cocaine administration on performance under a delayed-matching-to-sample procedure. *Pharmacol. Biochem. Behav.* 16: 713-718, 1982.

Bravetta, L., and Invernizzi, G. Il cocainismo. Osservazioni cliniche—Ricerche sperimentali e anatomo-patologiche. *Note Riv. Psichiat.* 11: 179-245, 1923.

Byck, R. (ed.). *Cocaine Papers by Sigmund Freud*. New York: Stonehill Publishing Co., 1974.

Cocaine Today. *The Journal*. July 1, 1982, pp. 7-10.

Connell, P.H. *Amphetamine Psychosis*. London: Chapman and Hall, 1958.

Crittenden, A., and Ruby, M. Cocaine—the champagne of drugs. *The New York Times Magazine*, 1974. Reprinted in *Addictions* 21(4): 62-74, 1974.

Finkle, B. Cocaine fatalities. *Bulletin*, International Association of Forensic Toxicologists 8(3-4): 8-9, 1972.

Fischman, M.W., and Schuster, C.R. Acute tolerance to cocaine in humans. *NIDA Res. Monogr. Ser.* 34: 241-242, 1980.

Gardner, R. Psychotomimetic effects of central stimulants. In F. Sjoqvist and M. Tottie, eds., *Abuse of Central Stimulants*, pp. 113-139. Stockholm: Almqvist and Wiksell, 1969.

Haertzen, C.A. Development of scales on patterns of drug effects using the Addiction Research Center Inventory (ARCI). *Psychol. Rep.* 18: 163-194, 1966.

Holmstedt, B., and Fredga, A. Sundry episodes in the history of coca and cocaine. *J. Ethnopharmacol.* 3: 113-147, 1981.

Joël, E., and Fränkel, F. Der Kokainismus. Ein Beitrag zur Geschichte und Psychopathologie der Rauschgifte. *Ergebn. der Innere Medizin* 25: 988-1096, 1924.

Johnston, L.D., Bachman, J.G. and O'Malley, P.M. *News Release: News and Information Service*. University of Michigan, November, 1985.

Kalant, O.J. *The Amphetamines: Toxicity and Addiction*. Toronto: University of Toronto Press, 1966.

Kalant, O.J., and Kalant, H. Death in amphetamine users: causes and estimates of mortality. In R.J. Gibbins, Y. Israel, H. Kalant, R.E. Popham, W. Schmidt, and R.G. Smart (eds.), *Research Advances in Alcohol and Drug Problems*, Vol. 3, pp. 317-357. New York: John Wiley & Sons, 1976.

Klaesi, J. Prof. Dr. Hans W. Maier [obituary]. *Arch. Neurol. Psychiat.* 57: 1-6, 1946.

Koller, K. Über die Verwendung des Cocaine zur Anaesthesierung am Auge. *Wiener medizinische Wochenschrift* 34(43 and 44), 1884.

Kramer, J.C., Fischman, V.S., and Littlefield, D.C. Amphetamine abuse: pattern and effects of high doses taken intravenously. *J.A.M.A.* 201: 305-309, 1967.

Leake, C.D. *The Amphetamines—Their Actions and Uses*. Springfield: Charles C. Thomas, 1958.

Leith, N.J., and Barrett, R.J. Self-stimulation and amphetamine: tolerance to *d* and *l* isomers and cross tolerance to cocaine and methylphenidate. *Psychopharmacology* 74: 23-28, 1981.

Mayer, E. The toxic effects following the use of local anesthetics. *J.A.M.A.* 82: 876-885, 1924.

Mulé, S.J. *Cocaine: Chemical, Biological, Clinical, Social and Treatment Aspects*. Cleveland: CRC Press, 1976.

Petersen, R. Quoted in *The Journal*, March 1, 1982, p. 4.

Post, R.M. Central stimulants. Clinical and experimental evidence on tolerance and sensitization. In Y. Israel, F.B. Glaser, H. Kalant, R.E. Popham, W. Schmidt, and R.G. Smart (eds.), *Research Advances in Alcohol and Drug Problems*, Vol. 6, pp. 1-65. New York: Plenum Press, 1981.

Santayana, G. *The Life of Reason*. New York: Charles Scribner's Sons, 1954.

Schneider, K. *Psychopathic Personalities*. Translated by M.W. Hamilton. London: Cassell, 1958.

Siegel, R.K. Cocaine Smoking. *J. Psychoactive Drugs* 14: 271-359, 1982.

Smart, R.G., Adlaf, E.M. and Goodstadt, M.S. Alcohol and other drug use among Ontario students: an update. *Can. J. Publ. Health* 77: 57-58, 1986.

Smith, D. Quoted in *The Journal*, November 1, 1983, p. 3.

Standage, K.F. The use of Schneider's typology for the diagnosis of personality disorders—An examination of reliability. *Brit. J. Psychiat.* 135: 238-242, 1979.

Thompson, T., and Unna, K.R. Prediction of abuse liability of stimulant and depressant drugs. Washington, D.C.: Natl. Acad. Sci.—Natl. Res. Council, 1977.

Vee, G.L., Fink, G.B., and Constantine, G.H., Jr. Anorexic activity of cocaine and coca extract in naive and cocaine tolerant rats. *Pharmacol. Biochem. Behav.* 18: 515-517, 1983.

Washton, A.M., Tatarsky, A., Benitez, E.F., and Freedman, A.M. Cocaine abuse: adverse effects on health and psychosocial functioning. Proc. 45th Annual Scientific Meeting of CPDD, 1983.

W.H.O. Expert Committee on Addiction-producing drugs: Terminology in regard to drug abuse. *W.H.O. Tech. Rep. Ser.* 273: 9-10, 1964.

Acknowledgments

I wish to thank Dr. Harold Kalant for help with the original German text, for extensive discussions of its content and for verification of the references in the original version. This translation was checked in detail against the original German by Dr. Brigitte Kalow, to whom I am greatly indebted. I am also grateful to Ms. Lise Anglin for copy-editing the first draft, and especially to Ms. Barbara Fulton for a very thorough editing of the final draft; to Dr. Karin Woodruff for compiling the index; to Professor Luigi Manzo, Università di Pavia, for kindly providing photocopies of the papers by Bravetta and Invernizzi; and to Mrs. Valdemira Cabral for careful typing of the manuscript. It is also a pleasure to thank Prof. P. Kielholz, of the University of Basel, and Prof. J.-P. von Wartburg, of the University of Bern, for their help in obtaining the photograph of Hans Wolfgang Maier, that was graciously provided by his son, Prof. Conrad Maier, of Stäfa, Switzerland.

Maier's Original Table of Contents

*Designates sections not included in this translation.

Maier's Foreword

The preliminary work leading up to this book dates back to the year 1916, when the first group of cases of habitual cocaine sniffing in Switzerland were observed. Even at that time, I had the impression that this illness was a particularly dangerous form of drug addiction because the special effects of the alkaloid could become more ominous than those of morphine. This fear has, unfortunately, proven justified: especially in the post-war years, an increase in cocaine abuse was seen in almost all countries. In some areas it was reduced again, but in others it has continued to the present day. Public authorities began, with good reason, to become uneasy about it, especially when in some cases, there was a connection between the drug use and particularly dangerous kinds of criminal behavior. Many of my own observations and investigations on this subject during the last nine years have been confirmed by the publications of colleagues, especially in Germany, France and Italy, that have appeared during this time. In the course of my practical trials of social hygiene measures for combating cocainism outside the clinic and the medical office hours, I learned by experience that the spread of cocainism can be quite effectively halted by the combined action of the police, the public guardian's office and the physician, if the necessary legal infrastructure is in place. Since this has now, or will shortly, come about in most countries, in relation to the so-called Hague International Convention on Opium of 1912, or its extension in 1925, I felt that the time had come to put together all the collected material on the subject. In so doing, it seemed to me to be most important to set out, in addition to the medical pathology of this disease, its historical development. Apart from its general cultural interest, this approach seems to me to be important for really protecting against the present-day manner in which the addiction arises and for being able to make it disappear again, if possible. During the violent upheavals that have marked this era, drug addiction has become a much more serious phenomenon among certain sectors of the population, especially in our large cities, than it used to be. We must therefore keep in sight the possibility that other, no less dangerous, drugs might spread in place of cocaine, the more we succeed in eliminating the latter. However, the devastation wrought by cocaine, that is readily visible in the case material assembled here, makes clear that it is simply not acceptable to give up the struggle for that reason. On the contrary, we are forced to conclude that with all new intoxicants that are capable of being misused for hedonistic purposes, we must find the necessary preventive measures right at the outset. Certainly one of these is attracting our youth to a natural pleasure in life, averse to all drug use; but that alone cannot suffice against the influence of suggestion that unfortunately emanates from these very strong intoxicants. An addiction such as that to cocaine must be thought of in the same way as an infectious disease, the spread of which we cannot manage to control without the use of official governmental measures. A portion of the older literature, that seems to me to be necessary for an understanding of the whole issue, is not readily accessible; I have therefore quoted in their original form those parts of it that seemed to me to be of greatest importance.

The exposition of the subject is done in such a manner, I hope, as to enable not only the physician but also the jurist, the police officer and the administrator to find in it whatever they need for their knowledge and participation in society's moves to combat this phenomenon.

Since cocaine addiction is no longer combined with morphine addiction, as it usually was in earlier decades, but occurs in the pure form of cocaine sniffing, it has in my opinion a heightened medical interest not only for the elucidation of clinical questions, but also for the general field of psychopathology. Particularly interesting parallels are offered with respect to the simultaneous excitatory effect on the brain and the sympathetic nervous system, which are both very strongly affected by cocaine. It would surely be of great value in this connection if the clinician could present his collected clinical experience to the physiologist.

I extend my thanks to a great many Swiss colleagues for their generous permission to use material from cases observed in their institutions, but above all I thank the Director of our clinic, Herr Professor Bleuler, for the friendly interest he displayed in these studies. In addition, I should like to make special mention of the sympathetic help that was provided to me by the Zürich police authorities in the study of the social relationships of cocainism and the attempt to combat it.

Hans W. Maier
Zürich, 15 November 1925.

IV

THE PHYSIOLOGICAL ACTION OF COCAINE

According to the evidence reviewed by Poulsson (1890, 1920, 1922), the primary action of cocaine on any living organism is to produce excitation or an increase in excitability. If more concentrated solutions are applied, inhibitory phenomena always appear immediately or shortly afterwards. According to Grasset (1885), cocaine has a mild antiseptic action on bacteria and it inhibits fermentation. Molds, on the contrary, grow well, even in concentrated solutions. Poulsson, as well as Cloetta (1919) and Biberfeld (1919), has reviewed the literature on the effects of cocaine on lower animals. Poulsson summarizes his conclusions as follows:

> The first comprehensive investigations concerning the action of cocaine on lower animals appear to have been performed by Aducco. He observed inhibition of the contractile protoplasm of amebae and other protozoa, lower plants (Chara, Nitella) and muscle cells, and inhibition of the movement of ciliated epithelium and spermatozoa. Albertoni has also noted the rapid elimination of protoplasmatic movements of all sorts under the action of a 0.5% cocaine solution. The rapid twisting movements of lepidoptera larvae stop immediately under the action of a 0.25% cocaine solution, and are only partially restored when the larvae are transferred to fresh water. Spermatozoa of rabbits, guinea pigs and frogs show a marked decrease of motility a few minutes after being placed in a cocaine solution, and stop completely after 30 minutes or longer. The mucus glands of the nictitating membrane of the frog are inhibited following application of cocaine to the eye, so that they do not react normally to electrical stimulation (swelling of the secretory cells, and obstruction of the lumen). The following experiment is very interesting: charcoal particles placed on the palate of a frog fixed in the supine position with its mouth open are rapidly propelled towards the esophagus by the ciliary movements. This phenomenon is inhibited one minute after the application of a 0.5% or stronger cocaine solution. A 0.25% solution, on the other hand, clearly stimulated the propulsion of the carbon particles. This is an example of excitatory action on the protoplasm.
>
> Many investigators have paid special attention to infusoria, particularly the vorticella, a tulip-shaped animacule whose bell- shaped body contains pulsating vacuoles and very actively vibrating cilia, and ends in a peduncle which, when stimulated, coils up in a cork-screw shape. The first stage of the action of cocaine on these animacules is easily observed. According to Schürmayer, application of weak solutions is

followed first by stronger movements and then by deep and lasting inhibition. At the same time, the body of the cells becomes markedly vacuolated and swollen, the contractile elements stop in diastole, bleb formation occurs, the nucleus of the cell disintegrates, and the whole organism falls apart. From a quantitative point of view, it has been found that amebae placed in a 1:100,000 solution remain motile for only 30 to 40 minutes, after which they contracted into the shape of vacuolated spheres. Paramecia were less sensitive, and remained alive after half an hour in a 1:10,000 solution. Stentoria are capable of remaining alive for more than an hour in even more concentrated solutions (1:2,000). They do, however, show toxic signs after 15 to 20 hours even in very dilute solutions (1:1,000,000).

According to Ostermann, who has reported in great detail the reactions of vorticella to a large number of drugs, dilute solutions of cocaine produce effects comparable to contractures in higher animals. The works of Korentschewsky and of Charpentier contain further information about the inhibitory action of cocaine on protozoa.

Danilewsky, who has experimented with a great variety of marine animals, found that the sensitivity to cocaine varied markedly from species to species. Here is a brief summary of his results. **Coelenterates:** when Actiniaria are placed in an aqueous solution of cocaine (1:1,000 to 1:500), the whole animal is anesthetized, the tentacles retract, the whole body contracts and all movements, both spontaneous and reflex, disappear. The animals recover quickly when they are replaced in fresh water. Isolated tentacles retract and become motionless when placed even in quite dilute solutions. Sections of Gorgonia provided with briskly mobile polyps are less sensitive and do not become anesthetized unless they have stayed for many hours in 1:500 to 1:1,000 solutions. Various Echinodermata are equally resistant, and some of them have even shown evident signs of excitation (curvature of the rays, and restless motion) during the first stages of cocaine action. **Worms:** worms react in various ways to the action of cocaine. Some become motionless and totally anesthetized even in dilute solutions, while others become very excited and show violent movements even in comparatively concentrated solutions. This is gradually followed by inhibitory phenomena. **Arthropoda:** in weak solutions (1:3,000 to 1:5,000) small arthropods at first appear very agitated and jump energetically but within 15 to 20 minutes they become weak and unreactive. **Mollusca:** a subcutaneous injection of 60 mg of cocaine into a medium-sized common octopus, together with addition of the drug to the water, first inhibits the function of the chromatophores, giving a pale grey coloration to the skin, and then produces complete anesthesia with motor weakness and slowed respiration. The animal, however, recovers quickly when placed in fresh water. The isolated tentacles of this animal become paralyzed when placed in cocaine solutions of 1:2,000 to 1:3,000. The embryos of *Sepia* *officinalis* just removed from the egg first show violent excitation and then, after two or three minutes, become completely paralyzed when placed in cocaine solutions of 1:500 to 1:1,000. Small fish (Syngnathidae and Ammodytidae) and *Amphioxus lanceolatus* are very sensitive to cocaine. A few minutes after being placed in a 1:4,000 cocaine solution they became weak and anesthetized and were dead within 25 to 30 minutes. When placed in weaker solutions, fish first show marked reflex excitability and contractures.

Vulpian and Richard have also experimented with several classes of animals but apparently only with strong paralyzing doses. Their results are therefore rather uniform. Injections of 3 mg of cocaine in snails produced cardiac arrest in diastole, but the animals recovered after a few hours. An injection of 25 mg produced inhibition of all spontaneous movements, but even after such a colossal dose considering the body weight of these animals, the signs of poisoning disappeared within a few days. An injection of 6 mg into the middle portion of earthworms produced local paralysis of the injected section of the body, while the rest of it remained mobile. An injection of 12 mg weakened all movements, but after 24 hours all signs of intoxication had disappeared. Fresh water bryozoans became weak in a 1:1,000 cocaine solution and were totally unreactive in a 1:750 solution. Crustaceae were still quite active after 20 minutes in a 0.3% solution, quickly became sluggish in a 0.5% solution, but did not become paralyzed until they had spent more than 24 hours in this solution. In a brief communication, Nagel reports that *Bereo ovata* shows contractions when a cocaine solution is applied to the body.

According to Lendenfeld, sponges are comparatively resistant and do not show any reactions in relatively weak solutions (1:1,000 to 1:15,000). Strong solutions produce constriction or total closure of the epithelial pores, as well as narrowing of the pore canals of the subdermal spaces and of the superficial afferent canals.

The extensive research carried out by O. and R. Hertwig on the action of drugs on the fertilization and division of sea urchin eggs has shown that even under the influence of a weak solution of cocaine (1:4,000) for five minutes, the non-fertilized egg loses the ability to resist more than one spermatozoon, leading to polyspermia or overfertilization with all the consequent abnormalities.

Magnus has provided a detailed analysis of the effects of cocaine on *Sipunculus nudus* which, because of the simple structure and ready visibility of its muscles, nerves and central nervous system, lends itself admirably to pharmacological investigations. For this marine worm, cocaine is a strongly paralyzing poison. Through its action on the ganglia of the ventral nerve cord and on the central and peripheral sensory apparatus, cocaine produces a flaccid general paralysis. With stronger solutions or longer exposure, the conductivity of the ventral nerve cord and motor nerves is abolished, and there is paralysis of the muscles. The author makes no reference to excitatory phenomena.

However, the doses used were quite high, i.e., injection of 0.25 to 0.5 cc of a 2% cocaine solution in sea water, or immersion of the animals in the same solution.

Concerning chicken embryos, Féré has reported that injection of 5 mg cocaine into the eggs does not produce any effects. Following injection of 40 mg, he obtained only 8.3% normal embryos, as opposed to 58.3% in the controls, and an injection of 50 mg inhibited development completely.

Mosso has noted the favorable action of weak cocaine solutions on *Phaseolus vulgaris*. Germination is very rapid in cocaine solutions no stronger than 0.01%. In this case the radicles were twice as long as those of the control samples. Germination was retarded, on the other hand, by a 1% solution, and totally arrested by a 2% solution.

Concerning the action of cocaine on higher animals, it should be noted that the neurotoxicity of the drug is greater the higher the organism is on the evolutionary tree. The drug then exerts its effects not only on the central nervous system but also on the conductivity of the axonal fibers of peripheral nerves as well as on numerous nerve endings, particularly those of afferent nerves. Nevertheless it acts most strongly, that is, in the lowest concentrations, on the central nervous system. Its action is not exerted through the intact skin of higher animals and man, but through open wounds, mucosae, subcutaneous tissues, serosal membranes, etc. It inhibits the sensory nerve endings, producing analgesia and anesthesia. The disappearance of the drug and of its effects is quicker the greater the local circulation in the area involved. Cocaine salts are very soluble and enter the tissues and cells more easily and rapidly than the salts of other alkaloids. According to Gros (1910, 1911), the hydrolysis of these salts into lipid-soluble bases contributes in large measure to this rapid absorption of cocaine[1]. The weaker the acid, and therefore the faster the hydrolysis of the salt, the more intense is the action of cocaine. Thus, for example, the bicarbonate of cocaine exerts an action five times stronger than that of the hydrochloride. According to Traube (1912), the action of cocaine on the tadpole is enhanced by adding an alkali. Braun (1898, 1903, 1905) has shown that below a concentration of 1:20,000, cocaine has no effect on man. The duration of action depends on the concentration. When very weak solutions are used, the effects are limited to the wheal produced by

[1] Ed. note: This is now known to be incorrect. The salt is not hydrolyzed. Rather, it is either ionized or unionized, depending on the pH of the tissue fluid. The unionized form, being more lipid-soluble, enters the cell membrane more readily.

the injection. As the concentration increases, an increasingly large surrounding area becomes anesthetized or semi-anesthetized. When the cocaine solution used is not very concentrated and is osmotically neutral, its effects disappear without trace. This is not the case with many cocaine substitutes.

Drawing especially on the writings of Goldscheider (1886), Poulsson emphasizes particularly the fact that in localized intoxications there is a stage during which temperature sensitivity is abolished and thermal stimuli produce marked pain rather than a sensation of heat. This has led to the conclusion that at first cocaine stimulates rather than inhibits the receptors sensitive to pain. According to the same author, the sensitivity to tickling and to heat disappears first, being followed by the loss of sensation of pain, touch and smell.

In 1884, Laborde and Charpentier were the first to call attention to the localized action that cocaine exerts on the nerve trunks. This observation served as the basis for the use of cocaine as a nerve blocker.

In 1886, Koch found that when cocaine is applied to a mixed nerve, sensory conductivity disappeared first and motor conductivity only later.

In 1892, Franck established that cocaine inhibits not only nerve endings, peripheral nerves and the nerve centers, but also muscle and glandular cells, the ciliated epithelia, white blood cells and microbes. He also established that cocaine acts upon the nerve trunk as though it caused a physiological transection, that is, that it abolishes function without causing any anatomical alteration. In these cases the inhibition is always preceded by a short-lasting increase in excitability. The central nervous system is more sensitive to cocaine than the peripheral, and the sensory organs more sensitive than the motor ones. This difference is not due to the sensory fibers being more accessible to the action of drugs, but to their greater affinity for cocaine.

Between 1885 and 1888, Corning was the first to use cocaine to produce experimental lumbar anesthesia in dogs. The procedure was systematically applied and studied in man by Bier in 1889. He succeeded in producing conduction block anesthesia on the grand scale: a dose of 5 mg was sufficient to anesthetize two-thirds of the body for 45 minutes. He observed that sensitivity to pain disappeared first, while tactile sensitivity remained unimpaired.

But this method did not acquire major practical importance until less toxic substitutes for cocaine became available. When comparatively large doses of cocaine were administered by lumbar puncture, there was not only inhibition of sensitivity, but also motor paralysis of the lower limbs, bladder and large intestine.

According to Sicard (1899), local application of cocaine to the brain surface produces a purely central reaction within a few minutes. This includes excitation, hallucinations, contractures and epileptiform seizures.

In 1903, Braun showed that adrenaline, which by itself is not an anesthetic, reinforces the anesthetic action of cocaine markedly when the two substances are used simultaneously. This is due to the fact that adrenaline produces marked vasoconstriction which, in turn, prevents cocaine from being removed by the circulation, thus increasing its intensity and duration of action. There is no doubt that the main feature of this combination is the effect that adrenaline has on the circulation. The resulting ischemia facilitates the action of cocaine by making the tissues less resistant to the action of the drug. The same results can be achieved by proximal constriction of the limb to be anesthetized.

Cocaine does not act simultaneously on all tongue sensations. The feeling of pain is lost first and this is followed in turn by loss of sensitivity to bitter, sweet, salty and acid tastes, and finally to the feeling of touch. But the speed and intensity of the action of cocaine on the tongue varies considerably among individuals.

The action of cocaine on the sense of smell consists of initial stimulation followed by transitory loss of sensitivity to smells.

In either weak or strong solutions cocaine acts on the blood vessels by producing marked arterial contraction followed later by marked dilatation. This effect can give rise to post-operative hemorrhages which can often be very unpleasant.

The action of cocaine on the tongue of the frog is quite different. Krüger(1885) has observed arterial vasoconstriction of short duration only after the application of very weak solutions, while the application of strong solutions produced an immediate dilatation. In cats, constriction is of very short duration, and is quickly followed by strong dilatation. Generally speaking, the observations of different authors on this phenomenon are quite varied. Constriction predominates in living tissues, while dilatation is more commonly seen in isolated organs.

According to Poulsson, the conditions in the eye are the most suitable for the effects of cocaine to be seen. Instillation of a few drops of a 2 to 3% solution produces first a slight burning sensation followed by a feeling of cold and of dryness. Within five minutes the conjunctiva and the cornea are completely anesthetized, and the iris partially so. At the same time, the eye becomes pale. After 10 to 20 minutes there is partial dilatation of the pupil. This begins to diminish after one hour and disappears completely in six to eight hours. Simultaneously with this effect there is protrusion of the eye ball and dilatation of the palpebral fissure as a result of the contraction of Müller's muscle. All these phenomena occur in the frog as well as in higher animals and man. Proof that these reactions are due to stimulation of the sympathetic nervous system lies in the fact that they do not occur after removal of the superior cervical ganglion and the consequent degeneration of the fibers it supplies, or in individuals suffering from paralysis of the sympathetic innervation. If the effects of adrenaline and cocaine on the eye are compared, it is still uncertain whether cocaine acts by actively stimulating the sympathetic nervous system, or indirectly, by paralyzing a normal inhibitor of the dilatation processes. A pupil dilated by cocaine is still capable of reacting to light, accommodation and convergence. While atropine produces pupillary dilatation by inhibiting the oculomotor nerve, cocaine can produce active dilatation. Therefore, the pupillary effects of atropine and cocaine are mutually reinforcing. Cocaine often produces an alteration of accommodation, probably due to effects on the blood vessels and on the blood pressure. Concerning the intraocular pressure, the ischemia produced by cocaine results in a diminution of aqueous humor production, but the thickening of the iris slows down its drainage. This latter effect can precipitate an attack of glaucoma in a susceptible patient.

It is known that cocaine is rapidly absorbed in the body and that it is split into compounds as yet unknown. This makes detection of the alkaloid in the body difficult. According to Poulsson, we still lack specific color reactions for cocaine and, because of its ready decomposition, special precautions are needed during its isolation. In 1868, Moreno y Maiz demonstrated that the urine of a guinea pig which had received 40 mg of cocaine had an action analogous to that of cocaine itself. Among more recent authors, Wiechowsky showed in 1901 that the drug undergoes nearly complete destruction in the body. The urine of guinea pigs intoxicated with cocaine did not contain any, and not even ecgonine. The urine of dogs that had received very large doses contained 5.1% of the administered cocaine. But the investigations of Rifatwachdani in 1913 gave different results. In fact this author found 42 to 85% of the administered cocaine in the urine of intoxicated rabbits. Based on clinical studies we know that the urine of cocaine addicts may or may not contain cocaine. Therefore negative urinalysis is of no diagnostic value. Future research done on larger samples will no doubt provide an explanation for these differences. The toxicity of cocaine diminishes rapidly if the drug has been allowed to act on a particular area for only a short time. This statement is supported by common experience in surgery, as well as by experimental evidence in animals obtained by Braun (1898, 1903, 1905), Kohlhardt (1901) and Fischer (1904). This inactivation of cocaine is a vital process because it does not occur in dead organs.

It is generally believed that when cocaine has not been applied locally, but circulates freely in the blood, it does not exert an anesthetic action. This is based on the concept that circulating cocaine is too diluted to act locally. Apparently contradicting this view, however, cocaine users claim that after sniffing the drug they experience anesthesia of certain zones of the body. Such a possibility should be kept in mind, but since it is based on purely subjective reports, caution should be exercised until systematic objective investigation has been conducted. Joël and Fränkel (1924) state, for example, that a sufficiently large dose of cocaine is capable of producing general analgesia even after systemic absorption. They feel that this is confirmed by the state of general ischemia of the skin that occurs simultaneously. This argument is incorrect because the ischemia is due to sympathetic stimulation of central origin.

According to Poulsson, cocaine, like atropine, acts on the various sections of the central nervous system in descending order. The higher the animal is on the evolutionary scale, the greater is the relative importance of the psychological stimulation produced by cocaine. This is particularly true in man, in whom the stimulation of the motor areas of the brain gives rise successively to restlessness, compulsive movement, convulsions and epileptiform seizures. There are, in addition, disturbances of coordination, peculiar and bizarre behaviors and impulsive automatic motor manifestations. During this stage there are also palpitations, rapid respiration, vasoconstriction and ocular symptoms, confirming that the action of cocaine has spread to the *medulla oblongata* and the sympathetic nervous system. This picture is soon complicated by exaggeration of reflexes and contractures of special origin. If the state of intoxication continues, inhibitory phenomena appear in the same sequence as the excitatory phenomena just described. When the inhibitory phenomena become marked and reach the *medulla oblongata*, death occurs as a result of inhibition of the respiratory center. It is important to note, however, that the distinction between the excitatory and inhibitory stages is not as clear-cut as the above schematic description would suggest; there are many transitional phases between them. The simultaneous presence of both excitatory and inhibitory phenomena produces a very complex symptomatology in cocaine intoxication, particularly following the intake of large doses.

There is also a big difference between the pictures of cocaine intoxication in hot- and cold-blooded animals. In the latter, inhibitory phenomena predominate while excitation and contractures are of very minor importance.

Poulsson observed that the administration of small doses to frogs produced a stimulation of jumping, motor weakness with exaggerated reflexes and contractures. Larger doses provoked very marked inhibitory phenomena followed by motor excitation six to eight hours later.

Anrep (1880) has also observed marked motor excitation in rabbits following cocaine administration. Larger doses first produced motor inhibition of the hind limbs and then of the front limbs accompanied by chewing movements and tremors of the extremities. Guinea pigs rapidly develop seizures. Dogs are much more sensitive to cocaine than the other species mentioned, particularly with respect to the behavioral manifestations. They appear happy and inebriated, move about endlessly and dance on their hind legs. A dog undergoing chronic cocaine intoxication, which I had the opportunity to observe personally, showed an initial stage of euphoria followed by a very pronounced state of anxiety during which he barked in apparent fear at spots on the floor where there was nothing in particular to be seen. One had the impression that this was due to small visual hallucinations. His respiratory rate was increased and the pupils were dilated. When the intoxication was more marked there were disturbances of body balance, motor inhibition and persistent spasms.

In 1922, Bravetta and Invernizzi reported some experimental findings which are particularly interesting from a psychiatric point of view. Following chronic cocaine intoxication in rabbits, these authors have observed marked increase of the respiratory and cardiac rates. During the inhibitory stage they observed clonic seizures of the extremities, which occurred either spontaneously or in response to the slightest stimulus. Later the respiration became very slow but the heart continued to beat very rapidly. The eyelids were widely separated. If the cocaine dose was diminished, the inhibitory phenomena decreased while rhythmic head movements accompanied by myoclonic phenomena reappeared. In their experiments with dogs these authors administered such large doses that the psychomotor excitatory phase was practically bypassed, and the inhibitory phenomena appeared rapidly and dominated the picture. Lowering of the dosage was sometimes followed by a state of depression lasting several hours. But in some cases the authors observed a phase of true inebriation which they described thus: "Immediately after the injection the animal shows marked motor excitation, jumps and runs around the room, and twists and turns around as though he were drunk. This is followed by incoordinated and confused movements and then, immediately, the animal starts jumping with wide-open eyes, as if under the influence of hallucinations. If a finger is placed in front of his eyes he closes them, but he does not respond to his name and rejects all food." The same facts have been mentioned in descriptions of other experiments: the animals give the impression of being under the influence of visual hallucinations, while at the same time they are almost totally indifferent to environmental stimuli. They do not, for example, pay the slightest attention to the presence of another dog of the same breed. In comparatively strong states of intoxication there are spontaneous muscular twitches. For example, 27 myoclonic movements of a duration of one second each were counted in one weakened hind leg in the space of one minute. The rhythmic movements of the head are reminiscent of those of a ram charging against an obstacle with its horns. During the intervals between twitches, the limbs are not spastic. Bravetta and Invernizzi (1922/23) note the interesting fact that tolerance to cocaine develops from the beginning of the intoxication in dogs, so that progressively increasing doses are required to obtain the same effects. In more severe intoxications the sensitivity to cocaine increased[2] again. Considering that the experiments were repeated every 24 hours, the authors conjecture that in some cases there may have been cumulative effects because the dose administered in the preceding experiment had not been disposed of completely. It appears, however, that this exaggerated sensitivity to cocaine manifested itself particularly in fasted debilitated dogs, whereas the well-fed dogs were less sensitive.

Birds offer a significantly greater resistance to the action of cocaine. Pigeons show bizarre pendular movements of the head with contractures and opisthotonus.

Administration of 10 mg/kg of body weight to horses produces mild excitation. A dose of 50 mg/kg makes them fearful and provokes diarrhea and attacks of frenzy. A dose of 20 mg/kg[3] often

[2] Ed. note: The original German text says "decreased," but this was evidently an error. The paper by Bravetta and Invernizzi (1923) states clearly that after the initial development of tolerance, the drug effect begins to increase again. They attributed this, as Maier noted, to accumulation of unmetabolized drug. However, modern evidence indicates that it was more likely the result of central nervous system sensitization (Post, 1981).

[3] Ed. note: Original says 20 mg/kg, but in view of the previous sentence, possibly it should be 200 mg/kg.

provokes seizures and respiratory difficulties ending in the animal's death. The temperature rises 2-3°C or more.

The first symptoms of acute cocaine intoxication in man are either those related to stimulation of the sympathetic nervous system (precordial discomfort, nausea, increased pulse rate, lassitude, vertigo and syncopes) or mental excitation reaching the level of hallucinations and delirium. In general, there is a variable mixture of these two types of symptom. Very high doses may produce immediate death through collapse and respiratory arrest. Because of large individual variation in sensitivity to cocaine it is impossible to state a single lethal dose with any accuracy (see below).

Experiments in animals show that, with the exception of tetanus, the seizures originate in the cerebral cortex. Decerebrated animals respond to cocaine without showing an irrepressible tendency to movement, and do not show typical seizures. Newborn dogs, whose motor cortex does not become excitable until the tenth day, do not show seizures following cocaine administration.

If the medulla is sectioned at the level of the sixth thoracic vertebra, there are contractures of the forelimbs, but not of the hind limbs. Langlois and Richet (1895, 1898) have prepared a table showing that in animals the ease and frequency with which cocaine produces seizures increase in proportion to the relative weight of the brain. Rolling seizures and the pendular movements suggest that cocaine acts strongly on the labyrinth and the semi-circular canals.

The view that cocaine exerts an hemolytic action on the blood is far from being well documented. In any case, the cyanosis seen in severe cases of intoxication is due to respiratory disturbances rather than to hemolysis.

On the other hand, it has been well demonstrated that cocaine exerts an inhibitory action on the white blood cells *in vitro*. Alkaline solutions of cocaine exert a much more destructive effect on the blood than acid solutions. In any event, strong cocaine solutions must exert a marked effect on the blood, because only this can explain the very frequent production of emboli. We should add, however, that Maurel's early theory, according to which the white blood cells shrink and clump together in the bloodstream, is not in accordance with the complexity of the facts.

The phenomena related to the autonomic nervous system are explainable as excitation of the sympathetic nervous system, changing to inhibition at high doses. In most animals, there is stimulation of gastrointestinal motility, increase in intestinal tone and strong contractions of the uterus, vagina, bladder and the *vas deferens*.

In mammals, small to moderate doses of cocaine produce a significant and prolonged increase in the blood pressure and increased pulse rate, whereas high doses lead to a marked fall in blood pressure and death. These phenomena are due to initial stimulation and subsequent inhibition of the sympathetic cardio-accelerator nerves, of the vasomotor centers, or of both. Vasoconstriction is very clear in man. Thus, Mosso (1890, 1891, 1894, 1897) has observed a marked decrease in the volume of the forearm by means of the plethysmograph following the systemic administration of 10 mg of cocaine. In 1922, Wolfer studied the effect of 2 mg of cocaine on the circulation of animals subjected to deep narcosis and therefore not subject to the control of the brain. Although the results were extremely variable, it was possible to classify them into three groups: 1) acute toxic inhibition with fall in blood pressure, small, slow and irregular pulse, flaccid and dilated heart and a fatal outcome; 2) abrupt fall of the blood pressure, slowing and dilatation of the heart and rapid recovery; 3) small or no effect on the circulation, slight increase in the pulse rate and a mild rise or fall in the blood pressure. The author emphasizes the extremely high variability of these effects and refers to Schapiro's data on 21 human fatalities following cocaine intoxication. In seven cases, very large doses had been taken, six individuals were in a very weakened state, and in the remaining eight cases death occurred in healthy and strong subjects following the intake of moderate doses. The respiration is accelerated as a result of stimulation of the respiratory center. At higher doses, the respiratory movements become shallow and decrease steadily until complete arrest is reached. The local action of cocaine on the intestinal glands results in inhibition of their secretion. This effect has scarcely been investigated in cases where cocaine has been absorbed systemically, but on the basis of clinical reports it appears that, in man, cocaine inhibits the secretion of saliva and gastric juice. At very high doses, on the contrary, there is stimulation of secretion. Cocaine intoxication in animals most frequently produces enlargement of the liver. The organ looks pale and studded with hemorrhagic spots. According to P. Ehrlich, microscopic examination shows cellular degeneration accompanied by vacuolation and fatty infiltration in the peripheral portion of the lobule.

We are particularly indebted to Mosso (1890) for the careful investigation of the action of cocaine on skeletal muscles. This information is of particular interest in relation to the claims of South American coca chewers and of the explorers who have visited this continent. Mosso concluded that a dose of 100 mg of cocaine taken by mouth exerts a very favorable action on the performance of voluntary muscles. Following such a dose, an already fatigued muscle can increase its work output several-fold. These experiments have shown that, following cocaine, the performance of voluntary muscles improves markedly, as opposed to the very mild increase produced by electrical stimulation. This effect is evidence that the action of cocaine is central and that its direct and peripheral action on muscles is highly questionable. On the other hand, following rapid absorption of rather large amounts of cocaine, for example, by subcutaneous rather than oral administration, muscular work output falls by half. These effects were also observed in frogs, just as in man.

Based on information provided by the Indians, it was formerly believed that the coca leaves themselves had nutritional value, or at least that they spared the need for food by slowing down the metabolic processes. It is known today, however, that the ability of cocaine to lower the apparent need for food is due solely to anesthesia of the gastric mucosa, which results in inhibition of the sensation of hunger. The experiments of Underhill and Black (1912) have shown conclusively that small doses of cocaine have no effect on metabolism, while larger doses produce an abrupt diminution in strength. Men and animals to whom cocaine has been administered often have glycosuria and occasionally pentosuria.

In man cocaine most often produces elevation of body temperature. This is due in part to stimulation of the thermoregulatory center and in part to cutaneous vasoconstriction. This effect is also seen in dogs (as much as 5.8° C rise), horses and cows. It is less marked in rabbits and cats. On the other hand, there is a lowering of body temperature in guinea pigs and in chickens and other birds. Aliphatic chain hypnotics, such as chloral hydrate, effectively counteract the rise in body temperature produced by cocaine in man.

Information concerning the lethal dose is quite contradictory. It is certain that the lethal dose varies according to the mode of administration (subcutaneous or intravenous injection), and hence to the speed of onset and to the peak concentration attained. Thus, in man, the lethal dose varies from 1.6 mg to 1 g, while in other mammals it ranges from 30 to 100 mg per kilogram of body weight. The frog can withstand doses of up to 500 mg/kg.

When man uses cocaine for pleasure, there is generally a rapid increase in the dosage. It is not rare for the clinician to meet individuals who began using 100 mg per day and, in the space of a few weeks, increased it to several grams daily. Intakes of 12 to 18 g per day are occasionally seen in long-standing cases of cocaine addiction. The physiological basis of such apparent tolerance is still unknown. Some authors, particularly Joël and Fränkel (1924), have recently questioned whether this phenomenon can be considered as true tolerance. It is best to leave the question open for the time being. Chronic intoxication in animals is always followed by rapid loss of weight. Loss of body weight ranging from 20 to 30 kg in the space of a few months can also sometimes be seen in man. This is almost the rule in cases of combined cocaine and morphine addiction. There are other equally heavy cocaine users, particularly sniffers, who do not lose weight. This is particularly so in cases of intermittent sniffers who ingest and assimilate large amounts of food during the drug-free intervals.

It is known that cocaine is composed of a methyl and a benzoyl group and ecgonine. These constituents have the following physiological actions.

Ecgonine, a nitrogenous base, has weak physiological effects and does not possess anesthetic properties. However, it produces dilatation of the pupils, increased reflex activity and tetanus. As has been emphasized by Adolf Oswald (1922, 1924), the ecgonine ring structure does not produce local anesthesia except when it is coupled with a benzoyl radical. It is the ecgonine ring that confers on cocaine its central and sympathetic stimulant properties and produces mental excitation and convulsions. The methyl group itself does not have any specific action and can easily be replaced by ethyl and propyl radicals without any loss of the anesthetic action of cocaine. All these cocaine homologues can have properties similar to those of cocaine. Although ordinary cocaine is levorotatory, it is possible to obtain a dextrorotatory isomer. According to the most recent work of Gottlieb (1923, 1924), the *d*-isomer administered subcutaneously is only half as toxic in the central nervous system as the natural *l*-isomer, but twice as effective in producing conduction anesthesia. In view of its weak central action, it can be considered as a reinforced novocaine. As an anesthetic it is more active when injected subcutaneously than when applied topically. Once absorbed, it loses its toxicity very rapidly, possibly due to the fact that, as opposed to natural cocaine, it dilates the vessels more rapidly. The author believes that, generally speaking, the *d*-isomers of the cocaine series are more easily metabolized by the tissues than the *l*-isomers. This would be in accordance with the fact that the optical isomers show different degrees of reactivity toward equally active but optically opposite constituents of the cells and the enzymes which control metabolism. The same author has found that the anesthetic potency is parallel to the lipid solubility, and hence to the degree of affinity of the drug for the lipids of the nervous system (lipid theory of narcosis). The lipid solubility of the dextrorotatory pseudo-cocaine is greater than that of natural cocaine. It is true, however, that chemical and physico-chemical processes also play a role. The lipid theory may well be sufficient to explain the peripheral action of cocaine, but the concentrations capable of producing central effects are often too low to be relevant to this theory. It is probable that physico-chemical factors play a role here, but it is not known whether this is an alteration in the relationship between ions and oxidative metabolism, or other processes. It would be, of course, of the greatest interest to obtain more precise knowledge on this point so that a truly rational treatment of central intoxication by cocaine could be instituted.

The work of Gottlieb summarized above is based on research done in the laboratories of Merck in Darmstadt and on the chemical investigations by Willstätter (1924). The latter has recently published a detailed history of the synthesis of cocaine. He writes that, of the three methods of synthesis explored (in 1901-2, in 1914-17 and in 1920-23), the last was the most important from a practical point of view. This work also indicated that the dextrorotatory pseudo-cocaine which Gottlieb submitted to such detailed study in the paper just cited, would be the most valuable compound pharmacologically. It was put on the market by Merck under the name of "psicaine" (an abbreviation of pseudo-cocaine). It is a very effective anesthetic of apparently low toxicity.

Gottlieb's later work indicated that psicaine is the acetate of the dextrorotatory pseudo-cocaine. It can be easily sterilized since it can withstand a temperature of 110° C. Gottlieb believes that if extensive research confirms that psicaine is detoxified rapidly in the tissues, it will be a major step in combating cocaine addiction, since there will be no risk of central effects. The difficulties related to the slight vasodilatation can easily be overcome by adding adrenaline. In this respect, the experiments of Beringer and Wilmanns (1924) at the psychiatric clinic of Heidelberg should be cited. They compared the effects of cocaine and psicaine on an admittedly small number of students. With psicaine they never experienced euphoria or intoxication, only occasionally a feeling of lassitude. Equally, there were no cases of nausea or collapse. While cocaine raised the blood pressure by as much as 30 mm in most cases, psicaine often lowered it by 10 mm. Because these experiments were performed in a small number of subjects and only under laboratory conditions, it is advisable to leave open the question of whether or not psicaine is truly inoffensive from a psychological point of view, or capable of producing a type of dependence similar to cocaine addiction. If subsequent research eventually confirms that psicaine is psychologically harmless, this substance would assume an importance of the first order because it would make it possible to stop completely the therapeutic use of cocaine of natural origin, which is mentally so dangerous. Otologists such as Brodt and Kümmel (1924) and urologists such as Völcker (1924) have claimed that psicaine is as valuable as other substitutes, and that it is particularly suited to replace cocaine for purposes of mucosal anesthesia.

Psicaine has received a detailed description here because of its practical and theoretical interest, but it would be redundant to go into detail about other cocaine derivatives and their chemical relation to cocaine, particularly since we have already made reference to them while discussing the chemical constitution of cocaine. Many of these derivatives can readily replace cocaine for purposes of local anesthesia. Their only shortcoming is that their action is weaker and less lasting when used topically on the mucosae or periosteum. Thus in such cases, conscientious physicians, especially in otolaryngology and ophthalmology, still use cocaine[4]. It would represent real progress if psicaine should fill this gap and at the same time prove to be virtually harmless to the central nervous system. It should be remembered in this respect, however, that although at first procaine was also considered harmless, it has produced unfortunate accidents when administered intravenously, for example. Eucaine has the disadvantage of producing an excitatory effect on the brain when it is administered in large doses. I am familiar with patients who tried to withdraw from cocaine by substituting eucaine and who, for the reasons just stated, developed a true eucaine addiction with its corresponding abstinence symptoms.

This is why caution should be exerted even in the use of cocaine substitutes. Their use in the treatment of cocaine addiction would be not only a fundamental mistake psychologically, but a serious therapeutic risk.

In his work *Chemical Constitution and Pharmacological Action*, Adolf Oswald (1924) dedicates a special chapter to the tropine derivatives and pays particular attention to the difference in pharmacological action between cocaine and atropine. Cocaine produces mainly a state of inebriation, while atropine is much more likely to produce hallucinations. Both drugs produce involuntary movements of the fingers and hands and epileptiform seizures. On the other hand, cocaine does not produce the tonic spasms of the jaw muscles and the rotatory movements of the body around its longitu-

[4] Ed. note: Sixty years after Maier wrote this, cocaine is still used as a local anesthetic in otorhinolaryngology, because of its rapid penetration of the mucous membrane and its vasoconstrictor action.

dinal axis, which are seen after the administration of atropine. Atropine produces inhibition of the parasympathetic nerve endings, while cocaine inhibits sensory nerve endings and stimulates those of the sympathetic nerves. According to Oswald, the peripheral action of cocaine occurs directly on the site of application rather than via the bloodstream. Atropine inhibits the circular muscle which constricts the pupil, while cocaine stimulates the radial dilator muscle. Oswald believes, however, that the latter action is not, properly speaking, stimulation but, rather, a suppression of inhibition. It is in fact known that cocaine increases the sensitivity of the dilator muscle to adrenaline. The author also leaves open the question of whether the dilatation of the palpebral fissure produced by cocaine is actually due to sympathetic stimulation or to removal of some inhibitory influence. Since the rest of Oswald's discussion of atropine derivatives has only a theoretical connection with the problem at hand, I refer interested readers to his book.

In an appendix to his book, Oswald discusses the fate of organic compounds in the body and adds, in this respect, that we are almost totally ignorant about the fate of cocaine in the organism.

V

DEVELOPMENT AND GEOGRAPHICAL DIFFUSION OF COCAINE-RELATED ILLNESSES

The medical as well as the recreational use of cocaine began to spread around the world in 1860, the year of its discovery. A description of the factors, often quite strange, which have contributed to the expansion of cocaine use and of its varied forms, would constitute, from a medical point of view, a most interesting chapter in the history of our civilization. Because this is still an ongoing process, it is important to describe here the evidence available, much of which is not readily accessible. Because of the large number of articles on this topic, many of which cover the same ground, this description is necessarily incomplete, and limited to a mere citation of titles more often than I would have liked. I hope, however, that I have not missed the most significant relevant works.

After Samuel Percy suggested in 1856 that, because of their anesthetic effects, coca leaves might have medical applications, Bibera, in 1857, began to investigate the mechanism through which coca influences physical performance, including an increased capacity to work and enhancement of endurance.

Two years later, Mantegazza (1859) published the enthusiastic work already cited, in which he recommended the use of the drug for the treatment of the psychoses and of toothache. He apparently succeeded in having his views put to practise in Italy, because in 1865 he published another monograph on the treatment of mental illness by this means. In 1865 Rossier (1861) and Gosse (1861) reached similar, although more conservative, conclusions.

Immediately after the discovery of cocaine, Niemann (1860), a chemist, called attention to the fact that the salts of this alkaloid produced a loss of sensitivity of the tongue followed by a feeling of cold. In 1862, Schroff carried out experiments on himself, in which he found that cocaine produced mental depression and a slackening of intellectual performance. He therefore warned against the use of the drug.

In a thesis defended in Paris in 1868, Moreno y Maiz recommended the therapeutic use of the new drug, and the following year Fauwel suggested its application in laryngology. But astonishingly, despite all these reports, the practical application of cocaine as an anesthetic did not make any progress for more than 15 years, during which the subject is hardly mentioned seriously in the literature. It was not until 1884, following the work of Koller, that general interest in the topic was renewed.

Some interest in cocaine had indeed been rekindled in 1878-79 by reports from North America in which it was claimed that 16 cases of morphine addiction had been successfully treated by injections of cocaine. Bentley (1878, 1880), an American physician, published an enthusiastic article on this type of treatment. A method was then adopted which consisted of injecting 0.1 g of cocaine every time the patients showed morphine withdrawal symptoms. This method was apparently adopted by all the private clinics of North America, but it did not give rise to any significant publications until Hammond (1886) and Brower (1886) drew attention to the dangers involved.

Boudouy (1885) then published an article on cocaine addiction stemming from the use of this method in the United States, and considered by him to be much more serious than either morphine addiction or alcoholism. The same opinion was expressed by Lore (1885), and by Brower (1886), who reported a case of cocaine psychosis in a physician who had formerly been a morphine addict and who prescribed cocaine so indiscriminately that he became a real public danger.

Similar reports by Shaw, Kennicot, Bauer, Merriman, Spear and Everts appeared in the United States in 1885, demonstrating how serious the problem had become in that country. In the meantime this method had very few enthusiastic supporters in Europe, and it took several years before the danger of it was recognized.

In 1880 Coupard and Borderau had again noted, on the basis of experiments in animals, the anesthetic effect of cocaine on the cornea. But it was not until 1884 that this action of cocaine had a practical application in ophthalmology, following Koller's report (1884) to a meeting of ophthalmologists in Heidelberg. He stated in this paper that a few drops of a 2% solution were sufficient to produce moderate dilatation of the pupil, complete anesthesia of the conjunctiva and the cornea and vasoconstriction with ensuing decrease in intraocular pressure.

At the same time, cocaine began to be used as a local anesthetic in general surgery, but the frequent cases of poisoning and death that occurred following its use quickly dampened the initial enthusiasm. Thus, attempts were made to use weaker and weaker solutions, and some time later, on Bier's suggestion (1889), efforts were made to diminish or eliminate the systemic action of the drug by the administration of large amounts of fluids and by the use of a tourniquet to prevent the drug from reaching the general circulation. These precautions, however, did not fully succeed in preventing toxic accidents, and during the following decades all efforts were directed at finding a non-toxic substitute which, while having the same peripheral action of cocaine, would be devoid of its central effects.

During the autumn maneuvers of 1883, Aschenbrandt, an army physician, administered cocaine in oral doses of 0.01 to 0.5 g to the troops, and claimed that it had a refreshing and fortifying effect. In himself, he found that cocaine eliminated the desire to sleep, and stated that he had obtained excellent therapeutic results in cases of jaundice, constipation, diarrhea and disturbances associated with the drinking of contaminated water.

During the same year Sigmund Freud, the renowned psychotherapist, who was then an assistant physician at Vienna's General Hospital (*Allgemeines Krankenhaus*) experimented with the effects of cocaine on himself and others, and published his results first in the *Zentralblatt für die gesamte Therapie* (1884). The next year he published an enlarged version of the same work as a separate pamphlet. The following is a brief summary of his results:

During a mild state of depression due to overwork the author took 0.05 g of cocaine hydrochloride as a 1% solution in water. A few minutes later he felt suddenly happy and nimble. His thumbs and lips felt woolly at first and then warm. The respiration became slower and deeper. This was followed by a feeling of lassitude and by repeated yawnings. A state of euphoria, preceded by repeated belching, appeared after a few minutes. As the author repeated the experiments the toxic effects became increasingly less prominent and were replaced primarily by feelings of well-being, self-assurance and increased strength and capacity to work. The author was capable of prolonged mental work without becoming tired or experiencing any need to eat or sleep. Moreover, the insomnia was not at all trying. The effects of cocaine lasted for three to five hours, and occasionally longer, while quite frequently the feeling of elation would persist overnight. Freud cites the favorable effects obtained by E. Morselli and G. Buccola (1882) following the systematic administration of cocaine for several months to depressed patients. He distinguishes the purely stimulating effects of cocaine from those it exerts in cases of dyspepsia where it counteracts gastrointestinal disturbances, and considered it to be a tissue-sparing agent in cases of cachexia. Further, he shared the opinion, widely held at the time, that cocaine was invaluable in the treatment of morphine addiction and alcoholism. He also considered cocaine as an excellent remedy against mountain sickness, and thought it fair to conclude from the evidence available to him that cocaine could enhance sexual potency, without specifying, however, whether this applied to men, women or both. Generally, he believed that if this alkaloid was administered as indicated above, it was remarkably effective, that in human beings very large doses were required to produce toxic effects, and that, regardless of the dose, it was never fatal.

The following year (1885), Freud published another paper on cocaine, drawing the same favorable conclusions and in which he reported the results of experiments dealing with the exact action of cocaine measured by means of the dynamometer, and with the measurement of reaction time. He performed these experiments on himself because the other experimental subjects available to him did not respond consistently to the drug. But he confirmed the results by checking them against those obtained on other subjects, mainly his own colleagues.

The first experiment with the dynamometer was performed on both hands. Injection of 0.1 g of cocaine hydrochloride produced euphoria and an average increase of pressure of from 63 to approximately 75 pounds, while the maximum pressure rose from 67 to 82 pounds. This effect, confirmed in another experiment, lasted five hours. Although the absolute values obtained on different occasions varied considerably, cocaine consistently produced an increase in pressure. The author believed that this action was not due to a direct effect of cocaine on the muscles, but rather to an indirect action related to the general stimulating effect of the drug. Evidence for this was the fact that this effect of cocaine appeared quickly and simultaneously with the feeling of euphoria, but before complete absorption of the drug. Furthermore, this action was more pronounced in debilitated individuals with a weakened motor system. The results on reaction time, shortened by cocaine, were not as easily interpretable. Freud believed that when a reduction occurred it was also related to the general state of stimulation rather than to a direct effect. (Since both the experiments on muscle strength and on reaction time were only two in number, and performed on different days, no clear-cut conclusions are warranted.)

It is evident that Freud eventually came to appreciate the dangers of this drug, so highly praised by him at the beginning. He never referred to it again in his subsequent writings on psychology and psychotherapy. But his paper of 1884 aroused a great deal of interest. Since, furthermore, it coincided with the introduction of cocaine to ophthalmology by Koller, the result was that cocaine was adopted as a therapeutic agent by a number of German psychiatrists eager to test for themselves the earlier experiences of North American psychiatrists. In his paper of 1884, Freud himself had reported on a case of morphine addiction treated by the administration of cocaine.

At the meeting of the Berlin Psychiatric Association on December 8, 1884, Richter (1885), having adopted Freud's ideas, enthusiastically recommended the new method. During the discussion Blumenthal felt obliged to warn his colleagues against all the excitement about the drug, stating that, all things considered, cocaine was simply a new source of intoxication which could, in some circumstances, become very dangerous. But during the following year Walle (1885) published in the *Deutsche Medizinnalzeitung* an enthusiastic endorsement of the alkaloid which he considered a true gift of nature whose medicinal powers would restore hundreds of patients to health, or at least considerably improve their condition.

Even Obersteiner, a physician of high critical judgment, saw fit to recommend cocaine for the treatment of morphine addiction in 1884. But in 1886, he reported a number of cases of psychosis caused by this treatment showing characteristic tactile hallucinations of small animals crawling over the body. In 1885, Smidt and Rank published similar reports and gave a good description of a case of psychosis due to cocaine, without, however, realizing the connection between the condition and the administration of cocaine. Thus they reached the conclusion that cocaine is "an invaluable remedy which facilitates and shortens the detoxification of morphine addicts, a simply indispensable drug without any detrimental effects worthy of note."

In 1885, Jäckel reached the same conclusion and proudly declared that "soon after the commencement of the treatment his patients lost all interest in morphine and demanded only pure cocaine," and with this treatment "they remained fit for normal social life."(!)

It is unnecessary to list here all those who, during this period, extolled the virtues of cocaine and lacked the critical judgment necessary to recognize its drawbacks, dangers and disadvantages. To do this would require a review of all the medical literature of those years, country by country. Suffice it to say that since 1886, Pichon had eagerly recommended cocaine for the treatment of morphine addiction in France. But the alarm was soon sounded, and it came not only from the psychiatrists but also from ophthalmologists who used cocaine topically. Furthermore, in 1886 Billeter, in the *Korrespondenzblatt für Schweizer Ärzte*, drew attention to the sudden and occasionally alarming states of sexual arousal following the administration of cocaine to women whom he had seen in his dental practice. However, in an article on cocaine published by Emmert in the same journal during the preceding year (1885), there is no mention of such reactions. Still, in 1886, and in the same Swiss journal, Bühler described the cases of two morphine addicts who, following the "therapeutic" use of cocaine in doses of 2 to 2.5 g daily, experienced visual and cutaneous tactile hallucinations. The author did not recognize the etiological connection between cocaine and the hallucinations until the day when the drug was discontinued and the hallucinations disappeared immediately. During the same year Laubi observed a delusional state of two days duration accompanied by visual, auditory and gustatory hallucinations and fear of poisoning following an injection of cocaine for a dental operation. It should be noted, however, that in this case other factors may have been involved.

In 1886 Bornemann described six cases of cocaine addiction, calling attention in particular to the fact that the hallucinations experienced by these patients could give rise to dangers resulting from their impulsive behavior. In the same year Comanos Bey noted the same danger. A morphine addict receiving 1.5 g of cocaine daily during morphine withdrawal developed a delusional state during which he fired shots at imaginary objects, and insisted that his servant had a street lamp in his mouth which he wanted to extract forcibly. A paper by Haupt (1886) called attention, more particularly, to the dangers of cocaine toxicity. It reported the case of a female morphine addict, who became a cocaine addict while attempting to give up morphine. She also turned her 14-year-old son into an addict to whom she would give up to 3 g a day by injection. At the end of three months, the poor boy was both a physical and a mental wreck. It did not take long before he showed a paretic-like picture with nocturnal hallucinations and anxiety. Despite all these reports Smidt did not hesitate to praise the harmlessness and advantages of the use of cocaine in morphine addiction at a meeting of German natural scientists and physicians in 1886. The same treatment was recommended by Hammond (1886), who had injected himself over several days with cocaine in doses of up to 1.08 g. He experienced feelings of well-being and euphoria after each injection, but also a loss of consciousness at times. According to Hammond, cocaine was not habit-forming and he felt it was particularly indicated for the treatment of depression and masturbation.

Credit is due to the German scientist Albrecht Erlenmeyer for having called to the attention of all serious and responsible physicians the psychological dangers of the use of cocaine so indiscriminately adopted at that time, and thus checking the spread of a danger which was beginning to assume alarming proportions. He first raised the question in a paper published in 1885, and returned to it in the third edition of his extensive monograph *Morphine Addiction and Its Treatment* (1887, pp. 154 et seq.) where he dealt with the subject in great detail and depth, and reviewed all the relevant literature available at the time.

He began the chapter on *treatment by cocaine* with the following: "This therapeutic procedure has lately been publicly trumpeted and praised as a veritable salvation. But the greater the fuss made about this 'absolutely precious' and 'totally indispensable' route to health, the less efficacious it proved to be. These claims were made not only in the medical but also in the popular press, a current practice which, at the risk of offending our profession, I must highly condemn. It was simply a question of propaganda expounded by individuals without any truly scientific experience, as an objective analysis of the question easily demonstrated. But they persisted despite the warnings and ended up with the sorry and frightening result that use turned into abuse. The genies that they summoned up to help them turned into furies bearing misfortune and disaster."

The author himself tested the drug experimentally on eight morphine addicts and on a number of non-addicted psychiatric patients, administering a total of 236 cocaine injections. He observed an increase in pulse rate in all these cases, but none of the favorable effects claimed by others. He opposed the view that cocaine is a morphine antidote and saw it, rather, as an inferior substitute whose psychological effects are of short duration and capable of producing serious cardiac disturbances. He states that the proponents of cocaine therapy may have been led into error by misinterpreting the cocaine psychoses as morphine withdrawal symptoms.

Erlenmeyer then goes on to describe the actions of cocaine as known at that time, when these actions were always seen in individuals who were also addicted to morphine. He stresses rapid loss of weight, insomnia, impotence and hallucinations, gradually followed by a general state of mental weakness, loss of memory and paranoid psychoses. He describes a curious type of visual hallucination, the patients claiming to see, especially over white surfaces, innumerable black dots and spots while their visual field becomes sieve-like, probably due to the presence of small scotomata, which the patients interpreted as thousands of fleas or the like. This author was equally struck by the diffuseness of speech manifested by cocaine addicts in their conversation. As symptoms of withdrawal, he noted vasomotor disturbances and marked apathy. Discontinuance of the drug is followed by a quick disappearance of hallucinations and of clouding of consciousness, while the ideas of persecution and especially suspiciousness and jealousy persist much longer. The author advises abrupt discontinuation of the drug when the daily dose is no more than 1 g. Otherwise, and in cases of pure cocaine addiction, he recommends the administration of large doses of alcohol and a little morphine internally. In cases of combined cocaine and morphine addiction, the morphine dosage should be unaltered, while the dosage of cocaine should be gradually decreased and eventually stopped altogether. The prognosis in cases of combined morphine and cocaine addiction is less favorable than in uncomplicated morphine addiction, and requires hospitalization for a minimum of four to six months. The author concluded his chapter on cocaine in the following words: "The picture I have just described is dismal, and yet I do not think it is somber enough. Anyone who has witnessed the rapid and devastating physical, mental and moral breakdown of a cocaine addict cannot but be most pessimistic with respect to the effects of this drug. I know of only one substance whose effects are as disastrous as those of cocaine, and that is alcohol. Such are the consequences of the treatment of morphine addiction by cocaine. Should this method be recommended? Our answer should be easy to guess: Absolutely not! And one would add that it should be the duty of the competent authorities to forbid the oral and subcutaneous administration of cocaine."

In 1887 Thomsen also warned against the use of cocaine for the treatment of morphine addiction because it would do nothing except introduce further dangerous complications. At the same time Ring (1887), an American physician addicted to cocaine, reported his own case, providing an excellent illustration of Erlenmeyer's warning. To give an idea of the degree to which cocaine was abused in the United States, we cite an editorial which appeared in the *New York Medical Record* of May 29, 1886: "There is no other example of a drug which so shortly after its introduction has claimed so many victims. We fear that cocaine addiction has nothing but a dismal future. It is a habit more easily acquired than morphine dependence, and its physical and mental effects are much more disastrous than those of the latter drug. We make these remarks in connection with an unfortunate incident which was observed in a city in upstate New York. A physician and his daughter had gone to a hotel where they behaved in a maniacal fashion as a result of cocaine abuse. It was established that both had been taking enormous subcutaneous doses of cocaine for some time."

During the following years, reports of serious cases of acute cocaine poisoning occurring in relation to the use of the drug as an anesthetic in surgery were published. Even fatalities following the administration of relatively small doses were recorded. For example, in 1887 Schnyder described a case of poisoning following the administration of 0.1 g of cocaine. The subject exhibited loss of sensitivity of the upper and lower limbs, tremors, increased pulse rate, dryness of the mouth and intense thirst.

The case of Kolomin is well-known. Forty-five minutes after curettage of tubercular ulceration of the rectum, under local anesthesia with cocaine, the patient developed cocaine poisoning and died. As a consequence, the physician committed suicide. In 1889 Dufournier provided statistics which included a large number of cases illustrating the ill effects of cocaine. He recommended extreme caution, even in the practice of surgery, because of individual variation in response and unpredictable idiosyncratic reactions.

Credit is due to French authors for later research on the psychological effects of cocaine intoxication. Combined addiction to morphine and cocaine had become so frequent in Paris also that in 1889 Magnan stressed the point by presenting three typical cases to the Biological Society. His report should be considered a classic because it contained the first detailed description of the tactile hallucinations of cocaine addicts which, for this reason, are known as the "Magnan symptom." Here is the report of the French investigator:

> "I have recently observed three cases of mental disturbances following the chronic use of cocaine. As you will see from a fourth case, I have been able to apply the information gathered from these three cases.
>
> 1. Since 1876 a 48-year-old businessman had resorted to injections of morphine to alleviate the pain produced by renal colic. For many years he was able to use the drug very moderately, being able to discontinue its use totally from time to time. Between 1878 and 1886, he injected 0.3 g daily without experiencing any problems except, as is always the case, withdrawal symptoms during periods of abstinence. In 1886 he resorted to cocaine as a substitute but, as usual in such cases, he ended up by using both drugs every day. He reached a daily dose of 0.5 g within a few weeks, and eventually 1 g per day. After each injection he experienced a marked feeling of well-being and a remarkable facility to work. Two months after the beginning of the addiction the first disturbances appeared. They consisted of visual

hallucinations (all objects around the patient appeared to be in motion), auditory hallucinations (he would hear frightful knockings on his door every night) and tactile hallucinations (he had the sensation that his tongue was covered with small black worms). He also experienced muscular contractures and cramps. All these phenomena disappeared when the patient stopped the cocaine, while the use of morphine was continued. After six months he renewed the use of cocaine taking daily doses of 1.5 to 2 g. Three months later he again experienced very pronounced hallucinations. He could see dancing shadows, he felt surrounded by a swarm of bees and a turtle made gestures at him. All these objects, including horses and dogs, looked to him smaller than in reality. He claimed that he was forced to breathe a foul-smelling gas. He was constantly tapped on the shoulder, and foreign bodies crawled over his skin. There was a marked decrease in sensitivity to pain. He inserted needles, keys and a knife into his anus in order, as he put it, to breathe a bit, because his body was full of gas. There were tremors and contractures of individual muscles, and later nocturnal seizures with biting of the tongue.

2. In 1884 a 44-year-old pharmacist, subject to attacks of migraine, began to take morphine by injection to alleviate the pain of biliary colic. For three years he took 0.4 to 0.5 g of morphine daily without any serious problems. In 1887 he decided to resort to cocaine in order to get rid of his morphine habit. He reduced the daily dose of the latter drug to 0.1 g and ended up injecting 2 g of cocaine a day. At first each injection was followed by a feeling of well-being, but later he experienced over-stimulation and insomnia. He attempted to alleviate these symptoms by again using large doses of morphine. Some months later muscular contractures entered the picture, and in April of 1888 he suffered the first epileptic seizure, followed by another one in May. In June and July he experienced a series of seizures as well as sensory hallucinations.The patient claimed to be covered with vermin, that his clothes, the air and all the objects around him were full of microbes, and he excoriated his skin and probed into his wounds with nails or needles searching for microbes. When cocaine was discontinued in August all these symptoms disappeared quickly.

3. A 39-year-old physician began to use morphine in 1872 to alleviate persistent headaches. Despite a daily dosage of 1 g he had no serious problems until 1887, when, in order to withdraw from morphine he began to use cocaine parenterally. He succeeded in reducing the morphine dose to 0.1 g, but was soon taking 2 g of cocaine per day. Visual and auditory hallucinations appeared within a few months. The patient would hear his name being called, and could see people on the street looking at his windows and attempting to break into his house. He would then awaken his wife who, of course, could see nobody. He could also see heads which alternately would increase and decrease in size. He felt cocaine "crystals" under his skin. He scraped his tongue

and excoriated his hands and face to get rid of the crystals. At the same time there was hypalgesia and occasionally cramps in the calves.

In all three cases, the most important symptom consisted of the localized sensations under the skin. The three patients exhibited sensory hallucinations characterized specifically by the perception of foreign bodies under the skin. The first patient scraped his tongue hoping to find small black worms, and dug into his abscesses looking for the bacilli of cholera. The second excoriated his skin and looked for microbes in his wounds. The third, a physician, simply contented himself with looking for cocaine crystals. A patient described by Jennings also looked for worms under his skin. In our three cases the hallucinations related to cutaneous sensations appeared first, and were followed by visual, auditory and olfactory hallucinations. Although the hallucinations can be large in number, they do not give rise to the state of agitation seen in excessive use of alcohol or absinth. Morphine rarely produces hallucinations and, when it does, we are mostly dealing with highly disturbed patients in whom many other factors play a contributory role. In general, all three patients exhibited a moderate degree of analgesia, especially obvious in specific areas. The first two patients showed epileptic seizures but, as is the rule in seizures of toxic origin, they disappeared once the state of cocaine intoxication was over.

I have recently had the opportunity of making use of the knowledge acquired concerning the sensory hallucinations seen in cocaine abuse.

A nervous and irritable 35-year-old woman had been suffering from multiple skin abscesses for several months. The severe pain caused by the abscesses had been treated by the application of compresses soaked in a solution of cocaine. When I was called to see her, I found her anxious, sighing deeply, complaining about some black stains which she had discovered around her nails and which she strenuously attempted to get rid of. She claimed they were insects implanted under her skin which were biting her. She picked at the smallest black threads misplaced on her clothes. I inquired as to whether the patient was receiving injections of cocaine. The answer was negative but I was told that the patient was receiving cocaine compresses."

On February 25, 1889, Saury reported another three cases of hallucinatory delirium of toxic origin in cocaine users to the Medico-Psychological Society. He emphasized the similarities between these states and those produced by the use of absinth. In all three cases, as in those reported by Magnan (1889), tactile hallucinations were the most prominent symptom. They were followed in order of frequency by visual, auditory, olfactory and gustatory hallucinations. During the discussion, Seglas recalled that, several years earlier, Erlenmeyer had already reported similar observations which Seglas cited in detail. Agreement was reached to the effect that these paranoid hallucinatory states were due exclusively to cocaine addiction, in which the simultaneous use of morphine played no causal role whatsoever. Only Pichon (1886) was of the opinion that either morphine or alcohol was a necessary etiological factor to make the appearance of the syndrome possible.

On June 24, 1889, Henri presented another paper on cocainism to the same Society. During the discussion, Seglas noted that, with respect to the motor disturbances seen in cocaine addicts, a distinction must be made between those which accompany the state of intoxication itself and those of hysterical nature, since it is often the case that hysteria precedes drug use in cases of cocaine addiction. Saury (1890) then called attention to the fact that the withdrawal phenomena seen in cocaine addiction are milder than in comparable cases of morphine addiction.

During the years that followed, numerous publications on cocainism appeared in the English medical literature. In 1892, Norman Conolly published a monograph in which he stated that cocaine is much more dangerous than alcohol or morphine, and in which he reported three cases of cocaine addiction. They were characterized by the presence of visual hallucinations (which had only partially disappeared at the time of publication of the report), exaggerated sexual excitation with perverted manifestations, followed by impotence and loss of memory for dates. In the same year Smith published a paper in which he reached similar conclusions.

The psychological disturbances due to cocaine, observed almost exclusively in cases of combined cocaine and morphine addiction, were the subject of some thorough research in Germany at this time. Thus in 1895, Wilhelm Ihlow, under the direction of Jolly, published a thesis in Berlin on a paranoid hallucinatory state produced by abuse of cocaine. It referred to a female patient who had been injecting 0.5 g of morphine and 0.25 g of cocaine daily for a long time. She eventually developed an anxiety state, visual hallucinations of a paranoid nature, marked loss of weight, incontinence of urine and a peculiar type of motor excitation reminiscent of chorea. Six days after the withdrawal of cocaine the hallucinations and the ideas of persecution disappeared and four weeks later her menstrual periods, which had been absent for three years, reappeared. One week later she again experienced auditory hallucinations with clouding of consciousness, and motor seizures. This state, which lasted five days, was most likely related to the extremely slow withdrawal of morphine. From then on the patient began to recover. The morbid picture sometimes was quite similar to that of general paresis and, since the patient was exposed to lead in her work, the possibility of simultaneous lead poisoning cannot be excluded.

In 1897, Zangger published a typical case in the Swiss literature. Three years earlier, a physician in the Riviera had prescribed topical application of a cocaine solution to a 30-year-old woman who suffered from gingival ulcerations. It did not take long before she became an addict, using 30 to 40 g of the solution topically every day, that is, the equivalent of 1.5 to 2 g of pure cocaine. A state characterized by an abnormal sensitivity to sounds, loss of memory, alternating periods of energy and apathy, depression, and occasional periods of excitement with visual hallucinations soon developed, which the patient failed to recognize as abnormal. The author discontinued the cocaine gradually and replaced it with ammonium bromide which has the same taste. A withdrawal reaction, with violent vomiting and a right hemiparesis lasting 24 hours, developed. The mental picture improved rapidly, but the patient, having changed physicians, soon relapsed.

In 1898, Crothers published a paper that gives an idea of the considerable degree to which cocaine addiction had spread in North America at that time. In the space of a few years the amount of cocaine imported from Germany had increased sevenfold, while the price of the drug had been cut to half. Most cocaine addicts used the drug parenterally and the habit was frequently complicated by morphine addiction and alcoholism. The acute psychotic reactions associated with cocaine use were often mistaken for alcoholic psychoses. The author also refers to sudden cases of nymphomania appearing among female cocaine addicts.

By 1899, the dismal psychiatric results of the therapeutic use of cocaine 14 years earlier had been so completely forgotten in Germany that Leudesdorf could write, in the *Zeitschrift für praktische Ärzte*, that the administration of an infusion of coca leaves was the best treatment for the withdrawal syndromes of alcoholics and smokers, and for disturbances associated with arteriosclerosis. In 1901, Norris, an American, reported that 30% of cocaine addicts in the United States were physicians and dentists. He had successfully treated the addiction by substituting sulfonal for cocaine.

The first publication concerning the spread of cocaine addiction in India appeared in 1902. In this country, the population became acquainted with the drug as a result of the proximity to Ceylon and the Dutch Indies, where the coca plant is cultivated. The description of the characteristics of cocaine intoxication given by the Indian physician Kailas Chunder Bose agree in numerous respects with the present-day observations in Europe, and demonstrate clearly that the spread of this habit is in general identical among the most diverse races. Some of his observations are cited verbatim below:

> Besides the use of cocaine hydrochlorate as a therapeutic agent its consumption as a drug for intoxication is so great in Calcutta that unless stringent measures be adopted to control its sale, I have reason to fear that its demoralizing effects will soon spread amongst the juvenile members of respectable families, and that at no distant date special asylums will be required for the safety and treatment of cocaine inebriates.
>
> Fortunately, however, the cocaine habit is at present confined to people who are more or less addicted to opium, ganja, or alcohol, but we occasionally come across cases where the victims have contracted the habit *de novo*. We do not know how the people of Calcutta have obtained their knowledge of the intoxicating property of a costly drug which has hitherto been only handled by medical men, but facts tend to show that they have got it from Bhagalpore, where cocaine has become a social necessity amongst the less thoughtful. Inebriates say that the hilarity it produces is almost instantaneous,and is followed by no deleterious results. Novices as a rule take it quite secretly during the early hours of the night, whilst confirmed and veteran eaters consume it during all hours of the day. It is generally taken in the form of tablets or powder and chewed with betel leaves (*Pan*, piper betel) and slaked lime.
>
> Unlike ganja or bhang it requires no special preparation. The habit once acquired cannot be easily given up. The first symptom experienced by the victim after he has taken a dose of cocaine is loss of sensation in the tongue and lips, followed by dryness of the mouth and fauces. A thermometer placed under the tongue does not indicate any rise of temperature. The approach of the so-called hilarity is announced by a feeling of heaviness of the head, throbbing of the arteries of the neck, and palpitation of the heart. The pulse becomes slightly full and quick, but never exceeds 110. At this stage the inebriate likes to be left alone; he firmly closes his lips and avoids talking, lest, in his attempt to do so, the saliva flows out of his mouth. His ears become hot and red, whilst his cheeks become pale; the tip of the nose becomes cold, perspiration soon breaks out on the forehead and neck, and the height of intoxication is marked by coldness of the finger ends and dilatation of the pupils. This stage lasts from 30 to 45 minutes, after which the victim longs for a fresh dose, and unless he gets it he feels lifeless and dejected. This depression of spirits is more imaginary than real, for I have not noticed any fall of temperature or slowness of the pulse, but the respiration becomes slightly hurried.

The tongue and lips now become moist again, and perspiration on the forehead ceases altogether, but the pupils remain dilated. The physiological effects of cocaine are most marked upon novices. The teeth and tongue of confirmed cocaine eaters turn jet black, and this is probably due to the chemical change produced by the action of lime and saliva upon cocaine.

The craving for an increase of the dose becomes irresistibly great, and in one case the dose was raised from 1 gr. to 12 gr. within the short space of a month. Unlike opium, it brings on insomnia and anorexia, soon followed by dyspepsia and diarrhoea. The dyspepsia of a cocaine inebriate is very obstinate and does not readily yield to treatment. Its prolonged use brings on some deafness. The quantity of urine is diminished, but in none of my cases was albumen detected. Delusions and hallucinations often occur, and cause dejection and dread. In some cases cocaine brings on acute mania, which is not amenable to treatment. Amongst numerous other cases I select the following in which the deleterious effects of cocaine upon the system were most marked.

CASE I: Cocainism Following the Use of Opium and Bhang: Gradual Increase of Dose: Diarrhoea: Convulsions: Death.— L.B.M., a promising boy, aged 20, very respectably connected, fell into bad company and contracted the habit of taking opium and bhang in their various forms. His friends remonstrated with him, and he gave up the opium habit altogether and took a fancy to try the effects of cocaine. A friend of his offered him 1 gr., and its effect, as the young man said, was simply pleasant. He continued to take 1 gr. daily for some time with apparent benefit to his physical health. He then began to take 2 gr. twice daily, and he went on increasing the dose until it was raised to 30 gr. a day. The demoralizing effect of the drug was soon marked upon him: he now avoided society and became solitary. He was honest and truthful before, but now he became a liar and a pilferer. He was fair and strong, but he soon became weak and dark. He suffered very badly from insomnia, and hypnotics failed to give him rest and sleep. He would take nothing for his food except milk in very small quantities. His heart beat was strong, but his hands and feet were cold and clammy. His pupils were dilated, and the conjunctivae looked pale and bloodless; his tongue and teeth were black. Obstinate diarrhoea supervened and carried him off. He had convulsions before death.

CASE II: Confirmed Cocainism: Plus Sulphonal: Ruined Life.

S.B., aged 45, a Sanscrit scholar, and versed in Hindu philosophy, consulted me for insomnia, the result of the cocaine habit. As a priest he said he had to fast at least three days in a week. About a year ago he had occasion to go to Bhagalpore, where he met a learned Pundit, who advised him to take cocaine, which possessed remarkable power of sustaining vigour and life without food, and enduring fatigue of all kinds. This induced him to take cocaine. At the commencement he derived benefit from its use. Thinking he might further improve his health he raised the dose from 1 gr. to 3 gr. He felt weak and giddy, and consulted another cocaine eater, who advised him to take it twice daily and in pretty large doses. He raised the dose to 5 gr., which he took regularly for three months, when unpleasant symptoms began to make their appearance one after another. He soon felt himself dispirited and miserable; he suffered from anorexia and obstinate insomnia; he lost his memory, and became dull and stupid. I strongly advised him to give up his cocaine altogether. He promised to do so. After a few weeks he returned to me again and asked for a harmless drug which would act as a substitute for cocaine, as he regretted he could not resist the temptation and had to use cocaine, although he knew well he was poisoning himself. I noted the following symptoms: Temperature, 97° F.; pulse, 110, soft and compressible; heart sounds feeble, regular, no *bruit*; tongue and teeth jet black; sight impaired, lachrymation, photophobia, pupils dilated but respond to light; considerable wasting of the muscles of the body. I gave him 20 gr. of sulphonal to take with milk at bedtime. The next day he reported that he had slept a little, and felt easy. I gave him another dose, and the effect was satisfactory. Now, I hear, he takes sulphonal daily, and has kept up his usual dose of cocaine. He has given up his priestly duties, and mixes freely with low-class people. He lives entirely upon the charity of his neighbours.

CASE III: The Cocaine Habit Acquired through the Medicinal Use of the Drug: Its Tenacity and Ruinous Power.

G.A., aged 45, has been using cocaine for the last eighteen months. He was subject to facial neuralgia, and had several of his teeth extracted. He was advised by a cocaine eater to chew cocaine with betel leaf, and he did it with excellent results. This induced him to use it daily, and he thus acquired the habit. At present he takes 8 gr. twice daily. He wished to discontinue its use as he had no further neuralgia, and as the process was very expensive, but he could not do it. The following symptoms were recorded: Pulse 100, intermittent; respirations, 18; temperature, 97°F.; pupils dilated; general weakness of the body, anorexia, insomnia, constipation; mind clear; occasional vertigo and headache; tongue moist and clear, slightly tinged black; has lost all his virile power. To ascertain whether the craving of cocaine inebriates was more imaginary than real, I gave him 8 gr. of sulphonal, telling him that it was cocaine of the very best quality, and more exhilarating than the inferior kind of bazaar cocaine, and did not require any special preparation to produce the desired effect. He called again the next morning, and reported that the new drug had no effect upon him, and he had to take his bazaar cocaine, which gave him instant relief. He is impoverishing himself in order to procure his daily dose.

CASE IV: The Cocaine Habit in an Opium Eater: Delusions.

S.L., Burman, aged 52, a confirmed opium eater, used to take 30 gr. of crude opium twice daily, but has now reduced his daily ration to 10 gr. He contracted the cocaine habit two years ago. He first took it for the relief of pain which he was subject to. From 2 gr. he has increased his daily dose to only a few grains less than 2 drachms. He prefers to take it in the crystal form; says he can take two drachms with perfect safety. He gets his supply from a *panwalla* (betel leaf vendor) to whom he pays Rs. 2½ every day. When he cannot procure money by honest means he robs his wife and children of their jewellery. He was stout and strong before, but now looks pale, thin, and anaemic. He constantly feels a dull heavy pain on the head, and a sense of heat all over the body; perspires freely and suffers from insomnia, for which he sought my advice. Whilst giving the history of the case he suddenly stood up and looked bewildered; he walked to and fro for a few minutes and then sat down. He remained seated for about twenty minutes, and then hastened to hide himself behind an *almirah* which stood near. His friends, who accompanied him, stated that they had noticed this change in him for about a fortnight. I closely watched his behaviour, and did not allow anybody to disturb his movements. He soon came out and sat quietly on the floor. When questioned, he replied that for the last ten or twelve days an evil spirit had taken possession of him, and when he forgot to pay him his due he got annoyed and tried to kill him. He remained with me for more than an hour and a half and then left the place. His pupils were slightly dilated, pulse 86 good, respiration normal, tongue dark black, pretty moist, cannot distinguish salt from sugar, muscles of the body flabby, tendon reflexes diminished. His urine was analysed, but nothing abnormal was detected.

CASE V: Physical and Moral Degeneracy.

B.L.M., aged 33, has been using cocaine in 30 gr. doses twice daily during the last twelve months. He gets his supply from dispensaries. He was stout before, but has now lost his weight; suffers from anorexia; has not taken any food for the last four days; says he can tolerate fatigue very well; no constipation; absolute insomnia; disturbs his neighbours during night; talks too much, but coherently. Pulse 100, intermittent and feeble. Respirations normal. Hepatic dullness slightly increased. Tongue black; pupils normal; has lost all sexual appetite. At the commencement he was told by his friends that cocaine was a powerful aphrodisiac, but experience has taught him otherwise. He was a broker before, and at one time enjoyed the confidence of his clients. He has now brought ruin upon himself. He takes cocaine daily, about Rs. 2, and this amount he candidly confesses he raises by unfair means. He cannot give up the cocaine habit, although he is fully aware of its baneful results.

CASE VII: Cocaine in the Zenana.

A healthy-looking young Hindu girl, aged 16, contracted the cocaine habit under peculiar circumstances. An elderly woman living in the same house advised her to take cocaine to get rid of dysmenorrhea, which she was subject to. She also cited instances where cocaine proved a sovereign remedy for removing sterility. The foolish girl followed her advice, and took cocaine every day clandestinely in 1-gr. doses for six weeks. She then increased the daily dose, and one day she took 10 gr. Half an hour after she had taken the dose she complained of a choking sensation, and soon became unconscious. At this stage I was summoned to see her. The patient had all the symptoms of hysteria, and I prescribed for her accordingly. When I was about to leave the place the patient had a fit of convulsions, and the anxious father invited me to notice it. She had twitchings of the muscles of the face and general tremor of the body. The fit lasted for nearly three minutes, and was then followed by another after a pause of about ten minutes. It lasted for about three minutes and then left her altogether. Her pulse was 92, pretty good; temperature 99°F.: respirations shallow, 18; tongue, lips, and mouth dry. Pupils slightly dilated. The dryness of the mouth made me a little inquisitive, and I enquired whether she had taken bhang (leaves of cannabis indica) and the reply I received was in the negative. My next question was whether she had had any similar kind of fit before, and the reply was also in the negative. I examined her pulse again and found it to be soft and quiet. Profuse perspiration soon broke out on the forehead and neck and then gradually over the trunk and extremities. Her condition did not improve much and she remained unconscious till the next morning. At about 10 a.m. the following morning marked improvement was noticed in her general condition. She could now understand questions and answer them correctly. Her bladder was full and had to be relieved by catheter. Her pulse and respiration improved and she appeared a different person altogether. At about 1 p.m. she became very cross and wanted to go to the adjoining room where she had her box containing betel leaves and spices. As her friends did not allow her to move she became very irritable. At this time the elderly woman came up and offered her a prepared betel leaf which she chewed; she then became absolutely quiet. During the evening she became again irritable and she herself sent for the old woman, who responded to her call and gave her another prepared betel leaf which instantly calmed her down. This roused suspicion in my mind, and next day when she became worse and wanted to see the old woman, her movements were closely watched. Her husband, under instructions from me, received the prepared betel leaf and made it over to me. On opening the folded betel leaf cocaine was discovered, and then on being questioned the girl made a clean breast of the whole thing, and further said that there were three more girls under the same roof who were taking cocaine in pretty large doses. The enormity of the mischief which cocaine has done and is likely to do can be better imagined than described. The old woman was turned out and the young ladies have ultimately recovered, but one of them has become a confirmed opium eater.

CASE VIII: Complete Moral and Physical Decadence and Death.

J., aged 21, a promising young Brahmin boy, living with his relatives, suffered from spermatorrhoea, and on the advice of a quack contracted the cocaine habit. He commenced with a very small dose, and gradually raised it to half a drachm. The pernicious effect of the drug was most vividly marked upon his countenance. He was fair and pretty healthy before, but under the influence of cocaine he became dark and greatly emaciated. He suffered from obstinate dyspepsia and insomnia, for which he sought my advice. He confessed that he had tried but failed to reduce his daily ration, and at last became desperate and determined to resign himself to his fate. His brother, who was his guardian, confined him to a room in his house, and stopped his cocaine altogether. The boy sold his wearing apparel to corrupt the domestic servants in order to get his regular supply through them. He was ultimately turned out of the house. He lived for some time upon the charity of friends. He lost all his energy and intelligence. He suffered from obstinate diarrhoea which did not yield to medicine. He was reduced to a skeleton, his voice was hoarse, pulse soft and quick, heart sounds extremely feeble. Respirations 32, hurried; no *rales* or rhonchi were detected. Conjunctivae pale, and pupils widely dilated; suffered from vertigo and noises in the ears. Slightly deaf, no inclination for any kind of food. He still takes cocaine, and says his generous relatives out of compassion supply him with funds. Every attempt was made to reform him, but none proved effective. The unfortunate boy eventually died.

CASE IX: Chronic Dementia Caused by Cocainism.

H., aged 29, an intelligent man, lost his situation by contracting the cocaine habit. He has been addicted to its use for the last five months. Can now take half a drachm of cocaine without feeling any inconvenience. Says he can endure fatigue very well, and walk for miles without fatigue, or any kind of food or drink. Pulse 100, intermittent; tongue jet black. Says the excitement of cocaine is only temporary, and is not worth the expense and trouble. To quote his own words, "To eat cocaine is to court misery." He repents of his folly but cannot resist temptation. He cannot govern his ideas, and loses the thread of his conversation. Dread of being chased by the police maddens him.Whilst loitering on the streets, should he see any white powder he would carefully pick it up and put on his tongue and then throw it down, saying it is not the thing he wanted. He plucks flowers from plants and puts them on his head. He now lives entirely upon the charity of others.

To attempt to break the cocaine habit by substituting sulphonal or chloral is to induce the inebriates to consume both. The only remedy lies in locking inebriates up in asylums, and stopping their cocaine altogether. My friend, Babo Brojo Lall Dey, Superintendent of the Metropolitan Institution and College, Calcutta, informs me that he knows instances where students of tender age, belonging to private schools, have become addicted to cocaine, and got so demoralized that they were ultimately expelled (from) the institution. He also mentioned that two brothers, aged 14 and 18 respectively, and belonging to a very respectable Hindu family, contracted the cocaine habit, and indulged to excess. Both of them became insane; the father locked them up and stopped cocaine altogether. In course of time they recovered, and joined their class.

Information has also reached me that women dealing in fancy goods, who have access into private houses, carry cocaine clandestinely, and sell it to girls, who take it in very small doses with betel leaves. The time has come where measures ought to be taken to put a stop to the illicit sale of cocaine.

In 1901 Mortimer published an original monograph on the history and the phenomena seen among South American coca chewers. The author specifically emphasized the fact that the action of coca leaves on the nervous system was not due to cocaine alone, but to other substances which are, moreover, very volatile. Indeed, the coca leaves used in this fashion were claimed to have a relatively low cocaine concentration and to contain, in addition, a large number of other stimulants which were little known at the time.

During this period cocaine addiction in North America had reached alarming proportions and, judging by the literature, the drug was primarily sniffed. Thus, two accounts in the *British Medical Journal* of 1902 referred to laws passed in Ohio and Kentucky forbidding pharmacists to sell cocaine except by prescription, the penalties for infraction consisting of heavy fines or imprisonment. In Cincinnati alone the estimated number of cocaine addicts was then 10,000, the vast majority being sniffers. It is fair to say that the true beginning of the use of cocaine by inhalation through the nose occurred at about this time. In 1903 Simonton noted an increase in the prevalence of cocaine addiction among the blacks of Pittsburg. During this period the wealthy took cocaine subcutaneously, while the poor resorted to sniffing. The same author suggested a method, already propounded by others, for the differential diagnosis of cocaine addiction by subcutaneous injection and by sniffing. Individuals belonging to the first category presumably showed a brown discoloration around the injection sites. We know today that this sign was of no significance, the discoloration in question being simply due to the use of impure preparations. Simonton further adds that there is a large individual variation in the sensitivity to cocaine, and that the period of detoxication must last from six months to a year to diminish the chances of relapse which, however, cannot be altogether eliminated.

In 1905, Léquyer published in France the case of a young girl who, after taking 161 g of cocaine applied to the nasal mucosa in the space of a year, had lost an enormous amount of weight, had become irritable, did not sleep at all, but did not present visual or auditory hallucinations. Abrupt withdrawal of the drug was carried out without any problems. In the same year, Claude Farrère published a novel entitled *Les Civilisés* which contains a very good description of the symptoms of addiction to cocaine sniffing. These included photophobia, perforation of the nasal septum, loss of sensitivity to heat (which is an asset in tropical countries) and sexual hyperexcitation in women.

The rhinological literature contains a report by Albert Stein in 1904 of a case of perforation and collapse of the nasal septum (saddle nose) following chronic inhalation of cocaine. In 1908, Lubet-Barbons of Paris reported perforation of the nasal septum in a cocaine addict and, during the same year, Kasparjantz of Moscow reported two similar cases. Cocaine addiction appears to have been more widespread in Russia than in Central Europe at that time, since Poprokoff had been able to collect numerous case histories in 1904-1905. He expressed the view, which we do not share, that there is a diagnostic difference between cocaine addiction originating from some initial therapeutic use and that derived from the simple desire for intoxication. The latter would have a less favorable prognosis and would require treatment in specialized institutions. Furthermore, the author was against abrupt withdrawal.

In 1906 Bouardel published a comprehensive review of the symptomatology of cocainism as it was known at the time. Lubet-Barbons believed that the perforation of the septum was due to the vasomotor action of cocaine which, giving rise to ischemia, would seriously affect the viability of the tissues, eventually leading to gangrene. In Paris, Hautant (1909) published a paper on chronic cocainism by nasal inhalation. One of his female patients had reached a dose of 10 g per day. This had resulted in ulceration of the nasal septum without perforation, which healed spontaneously when the drug was discontinued. In 1908 in North America, Gordon analyzed 171 cases of cocaine and opium addiction and concluded that cocaine very often, though insidiously, leads to dementia.

Between 1902 and 1910 cocaine addiction had spread so widely in North America and India that it had become a real public danger, but cocaine use in Central Europe was still limited to certain segments of the population of the large cities, particularly to decadent artistic circles in Paris, Berlin, London and Munich. In addition, there were a few physicians and pharmacists who had become habituated to cocaine, most of whom had begun with the abuse of morphine and heroin. It was therefore very difficult, and often impossible, to determine the relative role of these alkaloids in the toxic effects observed.

The following are some of the psychiatric studies published during this period:

In 1910 Sollier and Arnaud described the case of a patient who became successively addicted to morphine, heroin, cocaine and alcohol and who, in addition, presented a pathological picture of syphilitic origin. These authors, who had had the opportunity to examine 350 drug addicts, had never seen delusional states among patients who used only morphine or heroin.

During the same year, Sollier, on the basis of results obtained in two cases, declared himself in favor of abrupt withdrawal in cocaine detoxication. He had successfully used this method, first in the case of a physician addicted to morphine who had been taking 8 to 10 g of cocaine daily for 15 years and who suffered from insomnia, ideas of persecution and sensory hallucinations and, secondly, in the case of a cocaine addict who presented with convulsive seizures. Also in 1910, Barbé and Bénoit, from the Ballet Clinic, having observed sensory disturbances in seven patients who used large doses of morphine, heroin or cocaine, reached the following conclusions:

> Disturbances of various types of sensory function are much more marked in cocaine and heroin addicts than in morphine addicts [*sic*].There is large individual variation in the symptoms observed; they do not bear a direct quantitative relationship to the amount of drug used, and are independent of the mode of administration. It appears, however, that sensory disturbances are more frequent and more easily provoked when the drug is used subcutaneously. They are also more frequent in beginning users than in cocaine addicts of long standing. The simultaneous use of various drugs does not intensify sensory symptomatology. In the vicinity of abscess scars, sensory disturbances are more frequent and more marked than in normal skin, and are predominantly located in the lower limbs. The most frequent symptom consists of a slowing and decreased acuity of pain sensation. Disturbances in the sensitivity to temperature are rare and trivial, while according to most authors, deep sensation is not affected. Discontinuation of the drug is followed by a complete disappearance of all these sensory alterations.

Also in 1910, Higier published in Germany the case of a dentist who, following the daily injection of 5 g of cocaine, suffered from insomnia, tremors, paresthesias, anxiety states with flight of ideas, fits of destructive violence and ataxia. A diagnosis of alcoholism was originally made. This author attributes the sensation of foreign bodies under the skin, known as Magnan's symptom, to somatic hallucinations rather than to neuritis, and in this respect he particularly emphasizes a case of Korsakoff's in which the hallucinations disappeared after 14 days of abstinence, while the neuritis persisted. According to him, pure cocaine addiction was then comparatively rare in Germany, cocaine addicts accounting for only 2% of all cases of addiction. He also believes that the frequency of relapse in cocaine addiction is not very high.

In 1911 Wildenrath published a paper on the medico-legal aspects of cocaine intoxication and emphasized the difficulties associated with the identification of cocaine in the body. He cites a report by Edmund Falke (1890) concerning 176 cases of cocaine intoxication gathered from 1890, and which included 10 fatalities. The autopsies performed by this author in two cases of cocaine intoxication with epileptiform seizures revealed numerous congestive lesions, especially in the brain. Falke reported a fatal case following a dose of 0.4 g, while in other instances doses of 1.5 to 5.0 g were tolerated without any serious symptoms.

In 1913 Briand published a report of cocaine addiction in a monkey, but I have, unfortunately, been unable to locate this report. In the same year Bose (see above) reported on the increase and steady spread of cocaine addiction in India, as well as on the tendency to criminal behavior produced by cocaine. He stated that the consequences of cocaine addiction become more serious as the habit spreads. While he had not seen a single fatal case during the previous 27 years, he had observed three during the last six months.

In 1913 Heilbronner published his classic paper *On Cocaine Psychoses* based on a medico-legal inquest. It is evident in retrospect that in the case reported by this author both cocainism and schizophrenia were implicated. While the author strongly emphasized the role of an endogenous factor, he was incorrect in making the generalization that a toxic psychosis does not occur in the absence of a psychotic predisposition. In the case in question, which had been the object of a coroner's inquest, the patient obtained the drug from pharmacists in small bottles containing 0.3 g each. Over a period of 10.5 years she had obtained 8771 bottles, amounting to a total of 2.6 kg of cocaine. One of the pharmacists involved, who would send her 40 bottles at a time, stated in self-justification that he understood cocaine was used only externally by inhalation, in which case there was no maximum dose to be considered. The patient developed a paranoid psychosis with marked schizophrenic elements, and auditory hallucinations of such magnitude that she had to be hospitalized twice, in 1906 and in 1912.

In his expert testimony, Heilbronner expressed the opinion that the frequency of cocaine addiction diminished as the awareness of its dangers increased, and he questioned the existence of a *chronic* psychosis following the use of cocaine. He acknowledged that the mental status of the patient was probably pathological prior to the use of the drug, but considered it unlikely that cocaine intoxication had eventually seriously aggravated her state. He wondered whether the moral degeneration of morphine and cocaine addicts did not have more to do with the premorbid psychopathological characteristics of the patient than with the action of the drug. He compared the psychoses seen in cocaine addiction to the chronic alcoholic psychoses which are increasingly viewed, as knowledge accumulates, as due primarily to endogenous factors, and in which the intoxicant plays a comparatively secondary role.

Cocaine sniffing began to spread between 1912 and 1914, particularly in Paris, where the habit assumed considerable proportions. It is for this reason that we owe the first and most important works on this subject to French authors.

In 1914, Vallon and Bessière published a very comprehensive study of the mental disturbances associated with cocaine addiction in the journal *Encéphale*. Based on their own observations they distinguished two phases in cocaine intoxication, i.e. a stage of stimulation characterized by marked logorrhea and motor excitation, and a dreamy stage requiring physical repose interrupted now and then by abrupt and violent body movements. In chronic cocainism they observed a rather rapid slowing down of intellectual functioning and loss of memory, especially for time and dates. Concerning hallucinations, the authors distinguished acute, subacute and chronic stages, the latter eventually developing into the systematized delusional states of cocainism. Illusions and hallucinations appeared first, followed by delusions of persecution and finally of jealousy. Although the patients misinterpreted external reality, their idea of self remained intact. The delusional states, often accompanied by anxiety, last for five to 10 days after withdrawal of the drug, and are more frequent than cocaine psychosis proper.

We are indebted to the neurologist Georges Guillain for a thorough study of cocaine intoxication originally published in 1914. He demonstrated that there is a large individual variation in sensitivity to the action of cocaine and claimed, on the basis of his own observations, that the origin of cocaine addiction is based on imitation in the vast majority of cases, as opposed to morphine addiction whose origin is most frequently iatrogenic. He confirmed the claims of other authors to the effect that since 1912 half the prostitutes of Montmartre had become cocaine addicts, and that the habit was equally frequent among homosexuals. Following the inhalation of cocaine, the author observed a rise in body temperature of up to 40°C. He emphasized the similarities between the hallucinations produced by cocaine and alcohol. Both are characteristically unstable, they are related to the profession of the subject, and in both cases the patients frequently claim to be seeing non-existent animals. But the hallucinations produced by cocaine differ from alcoholic hallucinations in that they are more vividly colored, their content is more often artistic in nature and they are less frightening. Furthermore, cocaine affects auditory phenomena more markedly than alcohol. While the disturbances of the senses of taste and smell are less frequent than in alcoholism, those affecting the sense of touch play a predominant role. Cocaine itself plays an important role in the hallucinations, occasionally assuming in them the proportions of a true personality. Ataxic phenomena are very rare.

Guillain cites a case, reported by Marfan, of a father of four children. The first, conceived before the subject began to use cocaine, was normal in every respect. The second, conceived some time after the beginning of the addition, was of normal intelligence although constitutionally weak. The last two, conceived at the height of the addiction, were mentally retarded for the rest of their lives, and one of them was microcephalic.

Based on the results of experiments in animals, the author

claimed that application of cocaine to the region of the fourth ventricle is quickly followed by paralysis of the respiratory center with accelerated cardiac action. He confirmed previous observations according to which local application of cocaine to the tongue first abolishes the sensitivity of pain, then to bitter, sweet and salty taste, and finally the sensitivity to touch and thermal stimuli. Injection of 4 to 5 mg of cocaine (in solution) into the abdominal cavity of a frog whose spine had been sectioned at the level of the fourth thoracic vertebra produced abolition of reflexes in the segment above the section, while those of the caudal segment remained intact. Therefore, the drug acts on the central nervous system rather than on the peripheral nerves. The higher resistance of animals to the action of cocaine when the drug is injected into the portal vein is probably due to the detoxifying function of the liver. Gley has found that a dose of 0.02 g of cocaine is fatal if injected into the general circulation, but that twice as much is required to obtain the same effect if the drug is injected into the portal vein. The author conducted experiments designed to determine the lethal dose according to the mode of administration. Intracerebral injections of cocaine to guinea pigs caused immediate death in doses of 0.02 to 0.04 g, in five minutes after administration of 0.005 g and in 15 minutes with a dose of 0.002 g. When the drug was administered intraperitoneally the lethal dose was, by contrast, 0.05 g, while a dose of 0.025 g produced no effect. It must therefore be concluded that the toxicity of the drug is 25 to 30 times higher by the intracerebral than by the intraperitoneal route, the difference being due to the detoxifying action of the liver. Furthermore, the intracerebral administration of the drug produces only depressant effects, whereas the predominant effects following intraperitoneal or intravenous administration are generalized convulsions.

Guillain also attempted to establish the site and mode of action of cocaine on the nervous system. For this purpose, he injected into frogs aqueous extracts of the brains of rabbits and guinea pigs previously treated with cocaine, but the results were negative. He explained this negative result, quite plausibly, by postulating that, as soon as cocaine reaches the brain, it becomes bound to lipids, and that there is no procedure yet available to identify this compound.

For the treatment of acute cocaine poisoning, the author suggests that the patient be laid with the head down, and recommends administration of chloral, or of chloroform or ether by inhalation to control the seizures. He also recommends the administration of caffeine, ether, or oil of camphor by injection, and considers an alkaline solution of tannin as the most effective remedy against poisoning by the oral route. In states of chronic intoxication he recommends abrupt withdrawal, while gradual discontinuation of the drug would be indicated only in the case of debilitated patients presenting with cardiac or renal symptoms. The primary method of prevention should relate to legislative measures. The most serious factor contributing to the spread of the drug is not the pharmacist, but the small trafficker.

As one might have expected, the years following the war of 1914-1918 saw a marked increase in the frequency of psychopathological phenomena among the masses of the population. This happened in Switzerland on an even larger scale than elsewhere because during the war many of the casualties on both sides of the conflict were hospitalized in this country, while at the same time it served as a refuge to those who, for whatever reasons, felt obliged to leave their own countries, and as the headquarters for a bunch of unsavory individuals engaged in spying and counter-espionage.

The first cocaine sniffers, the majority of whom were women, appeared in Switzerland in 1915-1916 and came primarily from Paris. Cocaine-sniffing groups soon appeared in our cities and in our most sought-after resorts. But as the popularity of the drug increased it became increasingly difficult to obtain. The main source of cocaine in Europe at the time was the German pharmaceutical industry. But export prohibitions, even against neutral countries, made trade in the drug difficult, while commercial relations between Germany and its enemies were totally cut off. Thus, smuggling between France and Germany through the neutral countries, especially Switzerland, soon acquired very significant proportions. The traffickers made exorbitant profits, further increased by adulterating the drug, especially by adulterating it with boric acid. The chemical industry of the neutral countries, which had grown considerably during the war, increased its production of alkaloids, and thus large amounts of Swiss and Dutch cocaine appeared on the market. The methods used for smuggling were quite elaborate, including for example, the use of automobile tires or of alabaster statuettes. Moreover, the dangers of this type of traffic had not yet been fully appreciated and there were no adequate laws to counteract it. Because of the complex political situation that prevailed, some of the methods used—for example, transporting cocaine in sealed diplomatic bags—were especially difficult to control.

Since the cocaine addicts were obviously not eager to be located or discovered, it was some time before our clinics and psychiatric institutions began to recognize the consequences and manifestations of this new form of drug addiction. I first became aware of the existence of a group of cocaine addicts in Zürich in July of 1916, and I was able to establish that the habit was rampant among the large clientele of a hotel catering primarily to artists. Not all the cocaine used was illicit, since the addicts were able to get as much as they wanted from an accommodating and unscrupulous pharmacist. Legal action against him was taken on our initiative, but he got out of trouble lightly by paying a ridiculously small fine considering the size of his profits. Shortly afterwards, I had to treat a female member of one of these circles who became seriously ill. From then on, I was able to study the whole range of the symptomatology of cocaine addiction in Zürich and other Swiss cities with the help of the authorities and with the information provided to me by my colleagues in Geneva, Bern, Lausanne and Lugano. My first report on the results of my investigations was made in November of 1916 to the Congress of the Association of Swiss Psychiatrists, and I have since had many opportunities to make further contributions in this area.

In the meantime, the abuse of cocaine had also spread considerably in France, Spain, England and Italy. A special law against the abuse of cocaine was passed in France in 1916. The countries of Central Europe were originally spared the problem of cocaine abuse. It is significant in this respect that an authority in this field as competent as Friedländer, in his *Handbuch der Therapie des Nervenkrankheiten*, published in 1916, deals exclusively with simultaneous addiction to morphine and cocaine and other similar combinations, and considers that addiction to cocaine alone is very rare. According to recent reports by Joël and Fränkel, cocaine addiction was then widely spread in the Russian army. But Paris always remained the center of cocaine use.

It is therefore not surprising if, once again, we are indebted to the French psychiatrists for the first detailed descriptions of the characteristics of the intoxication that appeared during the war. First, a committee was organized in Paris with the purpose of studying the ill effects of drugs (cocaine, opium, ether, etc.), and the measures to combat them, and soon afterwards (1918) Courtois-Suffit and Giroux published a monograph entitled *La Cocaïne* sponsored by Dupré who was then the director of the Psychiatric Hospital of Paris. In a foreword for the monograph, Dupré emphasized the need to fight against this new disease. The authors described the properties of the drug, the extent of its use among the various classes of the population of Paris and the characteristics of the illicit traffic prevalent at the time. On the basis of 13 cases, mostly their own, the authors described the symptomatology of cocaine addiction and noted the differences between the acute and chronic states of intoxication. Finally, they deal with the methods required to do research on cocaine, and describe the evolution of the French laws designed to counteract the use of narcotics.

In 1919, Piouffle, a physician at a private clinic in the suburbs of Paris, where many cocaine addicts were treated, published a monograph entitled *Les Psychoses cocainiques*. Although not as critical as the work by Courtois-Suffit and Giroux, it is nevertheless very valuable because of the detailed description of seven cases, including samples of their handwriting.

Piouffle classified cocaine intoxication into six types: inebriation, acute psychosis, chronic delirium, systematized psychosis (equivalent to what we call cocaine madness), cocaine paresis and cocaine dipsomania. We shall return to this point in the section dealing with the clinical picture of cocaine psychoses.

We also know, through personal communications, that cocaine addiction spread widely in the United States as well as in England and Spain during the war and post-war years. Clubs of cocaine addicts were founded in Madrid and Barcelona while the Spanish government, just like many others, felt obliged to adopt special legislative measures. In Italy the habit spread alarmingly and its consequences were described in detail in 1920 by Tirelli, the director of the insane asylum at Turin. He insisted upon the fact that Italians had not acquired the habit in the battlefield but as a result of their contact with nationals of the allied countries. In some circles the sniffing of 4 or 5 g of cocaine a day was considered quite fashionable. Although cocaine use was most frequent among prostitutes and pimps, there was no social stratum free from it.

Foreign sailors were responsible for a brisk traffic in cocaine in Italian ports. Of the 41 drug addicts the author had the opportunity to study, 10 were addicted to cocaine alone; eight, to both morphine and cocaine; and their average age was 31 years. Most if not all had a pre-addiction psychopathological predisposition. Under the influence of cocaine, one of the patients dropped in weight from 95 to 45 kg and died of cardiac arrest in the bathtub.

In 1921 Coronedi published a parallel account in the Italian literature of the ravages produced by cocaine. He makes the interesting observation that although in France the majority of cocaine addicts are women, in Italy they are mostly men between the ages of 30 and 40 years. Based on his own experience, the author is quite pessimistic with respect to the effect of treatment in these cases. An improvement in the situation can be expected only from preventive measures, especially incumbent upon the authorities to adopt, and from a rigorous implementation of anti-narcotic laws which had been passed in Italy in 1916.

Another article on the frequency and characteristics of cocaine addiction by inhalation in Italy was published by Sabatucci in 1922. His observations are generally in agreement with those of others. He considers that illusions and hallucinations are rare in the acute intoxication, while many patients experience, on the other hand, a sense of "detachment from reality." The author observed marked fine tremors which sometimes, particularly in the morning, resembled intention tremors, following the inhalation of large doses. The general exaggeration of reflex activity was almost always accompanied by inhibition of the pharyngeal reflex. The pupils were often unequal and also insensitive to light, and some patients presented a transitory amaurosis. The author has also confirmed a decrease in sexual potency in men which occasionally reached the level of impotence and is often accompanied by perversions. In women, on the other hand, he has seen sexual over-stimulation which, in the later stages, is replaced by a loss of libido. There were no cases of chronic cocaine psychoses or of cocaine paresis among his patients.

Trisolini (1921), another Italian author, emphasizes the importance of cocaine as a factor in social pathology, although his paper contains no new information on the purely medical aspects of the problem.

Bravetta and Invernizzi, on the other hand, published a work in 1922 that describes the results of one of the most comprehensive and thorough studies ever made in relation to the cocaine problem.

After a detailed historical account, the authors described their observations of 24 patients, three of whom were women and 21, men. They included a laborer, two prostitutes, four officers, two artists, four business clerks, two down-and-out aristocrats, four students, one pharmacist, one businessman and three individuals without any profession. Four of the subjects had become cocaine addicts accidentally, following the therapeutic use of the drug. The origin of the addiction was by contagion in all the other cases. During their illness six of the patients had committed criminal acts, including one manslaughter and five instances of swindling. Twelve were pure cocaine addicts while the others also used alcohol, morphine, ether and benzol concurrently. All the patients had been hospitalized at the Mombello asylum near Milan. The authors experimented extensively in animals, making important anatomical observations to which we shall return. They also described the equally interesting results of an autopsy performed by Bravetta on a chronic cocaine user who died following the intake of a very large dose.

In Germany and Austria, the revolutionary period of the years 1918-1919 was particularly favorable to the propagation and spread of cocaine addiction by inhalation for two reasons. In the first place, the psychopathological state which affected all segments of the population, especially in the large cities, constituted a favorable terrain and gave rise to the need for drugs, a fact further confirmed by the enormous increase in the consumption of alcohol which took place despite the very poor economic conditions. Secondly, the chaos that prevailed in the distribution of army stocks had made available to the population a large number of pharmaceuticals, especially alkaloids, the trade in which was soon totally beyond control. It goes without saying that, at the time, the authorities were in no position to present a common front against the social disorganization that prevailed. It is interesting to note that in response to a request for information that I made to the central bureau of hygiene of one of these two countries, I was told that pure cocaine addiction was practically unknown there, while I knew the opposite was the case from information given to me by many patients. Furthermore, at the same time that public health officials were denying the fact, the police authorities of one district of the capital city in question were informing me that the spread of cocaine addiction was becoming alarming, and it was going to be necessary to organize a body of officials especially charged with the fight against this evil. Considering the lack of concerted action that prevails among the various administrative bodies, it is not surprising that the public health authorities are unaware of the existence and magnitude of this problem.

To my knowledge, credit is due to Glaserfeld (in the *Deutsche medizinische Wochenschrift*, 1920) for first calling attention to the dangerous level of expansion of the illness in Berlin. According to the information available to him, cocaine was primarily distributed by the drug stores. He knew patients who had been able to obtain enormous amounts of up to 1 kg. They had to pay seven to eight marks per gram instead of the official price of one mark, and even at that the drug was often adulterated. In addition, cocaine was sold at night by street dealers under such whimsical names as "koks" or "gramophone records" in packets of 1 to 6 g. The street dealers adulterated the drug extensively, and for this reason the users differentiated clearly between a gram and a "street gram." A certain number of the author's patients had taken part in the war and had fought in areas which had been invaded by German troops. He makes particular mention of a lieutenant in the air force who, in 1915, had fought in the north of France. Glaserfeld makes the important observation that by no means all his patients showed signs of psychopathology and that, on the contrary, many were perfectly healthy young people who had become cocaine addicts, and subsequently ill, in order to conform to the mores of their social circles. Even when the patients were admitted to sanatoria, detoxification was not always possible because, as a result of the social disorganization that prevailed, the staff was easy to corrupt and provided the patients with the drugs they demanded.

In 1921 Leppmann, a forensic psychiatrist in Berlin, published a paper on the medico-legal aspects of cocaine addiction based on the fact that during those years cocaine addicts were often involved in criminal activities. He presents two typical cases of cocaine psychosis in an unmarried couple and refers to four cocaine addicts who were found guilty of swindling, robbery and keeping a gambling establishment. All of the accused had shown psychopathic traits prior to cocaine use, and some were homosexuals. The fact of cocaine use should not be considered as an attenuating circumstance with respect to the responsibility of the individuals concerned. Leppmann gives a specific example to illustrate the care that must be taken in order to establish the criminal responsibility of addicts.

In 1920, Mayer-Gross published the autobiography of a cocaine addict which we shall describe in some detail because of its particular value from a phenomenological point of view.

The subject was a young physician with a clear family history of mental illness, unquestionable artistic inclinations and mild emotional instability of a cyclical nature. He became a morphine addict following a bout of dysentery that he suffered during the war, towards the end of 1916. In order to withdraw from morphine, he resorted to increasing doses of cocaine between October and December of 1917. Following the development of mental disturbances he decided to give up cocaine and succeeded in doing this without much difficulty. He resumed the use of both morphine and cocaine in November of 1918 and soon experienced insomnia, nocturnal restlessness, some feelings of depersonalization (his soul was somewhere else) and overpowering logorrhea. He consequently decided to enter the psychiatric hospital at Heidelberg. On admission, he was in a state of anxiety interrupted now and then by fits of gaiety; he talked incessantly, describing all sorts of animals which had supposedly entered his room; believed that he was now in one city and then in another; and his state of agitation knew no respite.

After a few days, he admitted that after swallowing 0.1 g of cocaine he had been injecting a solution of cocaine with some morphine added to it. As a rule the effects appeared in three minutes and lasted 20 minutes and consisted of physical and mental stimulation without euphoria and flight of ideas similar, according to his own comparison, to the effects of caffeine. He said that one night in 1917, he had auditory hallucinations of burglars breaking into his house, and that since then he had experienced a state of anxious expectation every evening. The interpretation of noises was systematized, but he was aware of the unreality of his visual hallucinations.

Some weeks after admission, he had a relapse of short duration during which he decided to record all his symptoms. Following some cocaine injections in gradually increasing doses of up to 2 g, there was heaviness of the head, increase in the rate and fullness of the pulse, the respiration was shallow and accelerated and the patient felt increasingly excited. After 30 minutes the pulse became slower and weaker. Association of ideas and fantasies were speeded up from the beginning, his idea of self was sharper, and he experienced a certain kind of euphoria. Between the fifth and the 30th minutes there was a feeling of torpor similar to the one that accompanies drunkenness, soon followed by a state of dissatisfaction, irritability and anxious suspiciousness. He feared auditory stimuli most of all, being extremely sensitive to the slightest sound, and eventually developing auditory hallucinations for which, at the beginning, he was more or less able to compensate. But after some time he could not do this and would anxiously wait for the burglars with a gun at the ready for hours on end. The hallucinatory episodes would sometimes last for 12 hours. Visual hallucinations were rarer and did not appear until a more advanced phase of the intoxication. He stated that, in his case, dependence on cocaine had developed very rapidly and that he had been compelled to increase the dose 10-fold in the space of 14 days. After starting cocaine, the patient lost his sexual potency, and as the addiction progressed even his sexual desires disappeared. The euphoria induced by morphine is very sensual and physical in nature, giving rise to an overall feeling of well-being. The euphoria produced by cocaine, on the contrary, is determined by the more rapid flow of ideas, and the subject feels "more intelligent than normally." In the state of stimulation produced by cocaine the subject is very active, jumping from one task to another, as can happen in mild states of alcoholic intoxication. During all the psychotic episodes but one, the patient retained his orientation as to time and place. In this case, auditory as well as the visual hallucinations were essentially perceptual in character, and the patient never experienced cutaneous sensations. His sense of time was normal.

In 1922 Joël published a paper in which he showed, as had Glaserfeld (1920) before him, that cocaine addiction had assumed epidemic proportions in Berlin. But the case material reported by Joël, as opposed to that of Glaserfeld, dealt exclusively with degenerated, emotionally unstable individuals who had shown signs of psychopathology even before the advent of the addiction. The average daily dose ranged from 1 to 3 g. The author distinguishes two types of reactions. One is characterized by volubility and the other by a state of contemplative repose, which may, furthermore, alternate in the same individual. Joël, like so many other authors, was particularly struck by the fact that, despite their multiple sensory hallucinations, many patients were aware, at least partially, of what was abnormal in their state. In view of the psychological dangers associated with the use of cocaine, the author wondered whether the drug should not be abandoned altogether.

This opinion was shared by the pharmacologist Walter Straub, then professor at Freiburg in Breisgau, who wrote in 1919: "The dangers of cocaine intoxication are especialy serious when they affect the large sectors of the population which we consider the most ambitious and active. The present political restlessness of the masses, their comparative affluence and the scarcity of alcohol which can provide a reasonable means of escape have all paved the way for the dangerous and epidemic spread of cocaine addiction. What can be done? It would be naive to rely on information programs, and satisfactory results can be expected only from the official prohibition of the manufacture of cocaine. Some will say that it is impossible to prohibit the manufacture of a therapeutic agent, but this objection is without foundation.We shall succeed in developing a whole series of cocaine derivatives which will have all the therapeutic efficacy of this drug, but none of its abuse potential. In this way, medicine will not be hampered by the elimination of cocaine."

Simultaneously with Joël (1922), Fränkel became interested in cocaine addiction in Berlin and published the first results of his investigations in 1923.

He distinguishes three phases in the intoxication produced by the abuse of cocaine: a stage of euphoria, an hallucinatory stage and a depressive stage with general inhibition. Using the method of Liepmann, the author has been able to produce visions in cocaine addicts by exerting pressure on the eyeballs. Disturbances of consciousness are not necessarily present in cocaine addiction, but there is, rather, a splitting between the self that experiences the psychological effects and the self that observes and judges them. The states of anxiety that the subjects experience often force them to tidy things up, to clean or write without any reason or need to do these things. Most frequently the subjects are seized by a mania for searching. These are not obsessions in the strict sense of the term, but rather specific impulsive behaviors which the patients do not perceive in any way as abnormal.

In 1924 Joël and Fränkel published in collaboration a monograph on cocaine addiction in *Ergebnisse der inneren Medizin und Kinderheilkunde* based on their own observations in Berlin, and in which they describe the general symptomatology of the condition in greater detail than in their previous papers. In the chapter on cocaine dependence the authors conclude that the question of whether cocaine produces tolerance or increased sensitivity cannot yet be answered. They are strongly in favor of the adoption of administrative and legal measures designed to fight against this disease. An appendix presents 16 detailed and very well-described case reports including two dealing with women, the protocols of three cocaine experiments in patients and a few samples of the notes written by cocaine addicts.

In 1923, Norbert Marx, of the Herzberg Institute in Berlin, published a paper entitled *Beiträge zur Psychologie der Kokainomanie* (Contributions to the psychology of cocaine addiction) in which, following in the footsteps of Poprokoff, he made what, in my opinion, is a vain attempt at distinguishing between two types of cocaine addiction. Cocaine addiction would derive from the initial therapeutic use of the drug, and the second type would include "cocaine addicts" who from the beginning used the drug as a source of pleasure. From a biological point of view these two categories of individuals are indistinguishable. The author then reports the case of a cocaine sniffer who had to be hospitalized because he developed a paranoid reaction. The patient claimed that he could feel grains of sand under his skin and bits of glass in his chest, and that when he looked at himself in the mirror he could see large white lice with red eyes on his head. The morbid picture, however, was predominantly characterized by auditory hallucinations. The patient's sexual potency had diminished, and he showed homosexual tendencies, although he claimed that he had never been a homosexual before. Marx observed the latter symptom in other patients as well. The specific symptomatology of this patient, including the presence of auditory hallucinations, and the chronic evolution of the picture, suggest that this was not a case of uncomplicated cocaine intoxication. Fränkel (1923) had the opportunity of examining this same patient and confirmed that several months after complete withdrawal he still showed schizophrenic symptoms including serious dissociation of personality, ideas of reference and hallucinations. He therefore disagreed with the conclusions drawn by Marx based on this case.

Cocaine addiction in Belgium was described by Vervaeck in 1923. He classified cocaine addicts into four groups: intellectuals and artists who use cocaine to stimulate their productivity; individuals who suffer from a physical illness; emotionally unstable individuals who use the drug to escape their painful reality; and sensual women, especially prostitutes, who resort to the drug as a sexual stimulant. Based on his personal observations, the author claims that the dose required to achieve a pleasant subjective reaction varies from individual to individual according to constitution, degree of tolerance and mode of administration. The author distinguishes three stages of drug effects: a euphoric phase determined, on the positive side, by the pleasure that the individual experiences at being able to move freely and, negatively, by the absence of painful feelings; secondly, a phase characterized by the elimination of all unpleasant feelings and by the state of dependence that, from then on, the individual develops towards the drug; and the third phase characterized exclusively by this state of dependence. The author recommends prolonged hospitalization (many months) in serious cases.

At the 18th Medico-Legal Congress in France, Courtois-Suffit and Giroux (1918, 1921, 1922, 1923) presented a report on the international fight against drugs in general and cocaine in particular. They noted in this respect that cocaine addiction in France had already begun to spread among school children. On the 13th of July, the French parliament passed a law that provided a penalty of 10 to 15 years banishment to anyone found promoting or encouraging the use of narcotics. Pharmacists found guilty of this offence could have their stores closed. The fines would be in proportion to the profits made, and prison sentences were greatly increased.

During the discussion Bathazard called attention to the relationship between cocaine addiction and homosexuality, and Soul referred to criminal acts committed by cocaine addicts, including homicide, under the direct influence of the drug.

But the severe measures adopted in France did not succeed in totally eliminating cocaine addiction, judging by the well-documented book published by Cyril and Berger in 1924 under the title of *La coco*. The authors were not physicians and their amateur status facilitated their acceptance in certain social circles thus allowing them to conduct their investigation without the suspicion that is usually engendered by more or less official inquiries. Furthermore, they were able to use information provided to them by the famous "drug squad" of the Paris police. The following interesting data are taken from this book:

> Arrests for illicit traffic in cocaine in Paris numbered 21 in 1916, 52 in 1917, 82 in 1918, 69 in 1919, 157 in 1920, 212 in 1921 and 187 during the first nine months of 1922. During 1920 alone, 70 kg of cocaine had been confiscated. The most important areas of use were Montmartre and its night places of entertainment, the district of the Halles, the Latin Quarter where cocaine use was widespread among students, and some fashionable clandestine places in the neighborhood of the Champs-Elysées.
>
> The traffickers were of two types, i.e. professionals, and physicians and pharmacists of dubious reputation. The current retail price in Paris is 20 to 30 francs per gram. Since the trafficker pays four to 4.5 francs per gram for cocaine illegally imported from Germany, he can make millions if his volume of business is large. Cocaine is also known as "snow," "rice powder," "quinine," "inhalant" and "snuff," but the most common name is "cam," an abbreviation of camelot. A 1 g packet of cocaine is called a "bag," and one sniffing is referred to as a "pravouse." According to their investigations, the authors distinguish two types of cocaine addicts: the first group consists of those who seek and find in cocaine a means to obtain a state of euphoria and contemplative repose (Cieff). These are the "loners," the ones who use the drug in secret. The second group is made up of the "joiners" who do not experience pleasure unless they sniff in the company of others. This group can, in turn, be divided into extroverts and introverts, the latter experiencing states of agitation, intense anxiety, or developing ideas of persecution under the influence of the drug. The authors emphasize the frequency with which dissociation of personality occurs among cocaine addicts.
>
> The authors conclude that the present legislation, despite its recent increase in severity, does not permit an effective fight against cocaine addiction. The costs of a trial involving 50 pharmacists and physicians, which took place in Paris recently, amounted to over 100,000 francs. The only effective means would be to develop an international system of control beginning at the source, that is, at the level of the manufacturers, which could possibly be extended to include the harvesting of coca leaves. In the meantime the branches of the police forces in charge of the fight against cocaine should be reinforced. In Paris at the present time, this branch includes eight police officers, only two of whom are experts on cocaine problems. Drug store sales should be more closely supervised, and those stores that engage in illicit sales should be closed indefinitely. Physicians who give prescriptions indiscriminately should have their licences to practise revoked, and the penalties against traffickers, at present liable to a maximum of

> only two years in prison, should be increased considerably. The fines, amounting to a maximum of 10,000 francs at present, should also be raised and should be strictly in proportion to the actual or anticipated profits. We should not be more lenient against cocaine traffickers than against counterfeiters since they affect the health of the nation, a resource far more important than money.

In 1922, Viktor Heinemann, working in Zürich under the direction of Heinrich Zangger, submitted a thorough medico-legal analysis of Swiss data on cocaine intoxication. His numerous observations are in full agreement with my own. The author's aim was "to emphasize the medical and psychological experience and considerations in favor of drafting legislation against the abuse of cocaine." The author strongly stresses the fact that every cocaine addict must be considered affected by a contagious disease and, consequently, as a public danger. He must, therefore, be strictly isolated, this being the only means of protecting society from the contagion. The distribution of cocaine should be confined to official bodies which should be, in turn, under strict control because of the temptation arising from the large potential profits. A record should be kept of the amounts of cocaine distributed each year to the consumers, especially physicians and chemical laboratories. Permission to manufacture cocaine and other drugs should be given exclusively to licensed firms which would produce only the amounts required in medicine and scientific research. Special records would be kept from the time of manufacture of the drugs, in order to be able to trace the smallest amounts of the substance, and to establish the exact source of the amount incriminated in case of illicit sales. The acquisition, possession or delivery of cocaine without indicating the source would constitute a crime subject to legal prosecution. Clandestine dealers would be mercilessly tracked in order to prevent the drug from reaching the public under conventional and inoffensive names. To avoid the forgery of prescriptions, official forms should be used for particularly potent drugs, as is done in the United States. The legislation should include not only cocaine but all substances with similar injurious effects. In this respect it should not be forgotten, however, that there are numerous fundamental differences between cocaine and morphine, the latter being of much greater therapeutic importance. The fight against these toxic substances requires emergency legislation that will unavoidably be rather severe.

Heinemann (1922) emphasizes the deplorable fact that cocaine addiction is encouraged by individuals with knowledge of medicine and pharmacology, such as pharmacists, pharmacy and medical students, dentists and even physicians—in other words, by people who ought to be aware of the significance of their behavior. According to his observations, cocaine-related deaths are much more frequent in the large cities than is generally believed. One is often surprised by the discovery of cocaine in the immediate surroundings of people who have died, apparently inexplicably. The author's findings are in agreement with my own in yet another respect. He feels, as I do, that in addition to subcutaneous injections and inhalation, there are other modes of administration of no less significance from a practical point of view. They include cocaine ointments which are applied by rubbing on the mucosae, especially of the anus, syrups for oral use and cocaine tea. Dried coca leaves are used to prepare infusions, and also are mixed with cigarette tobacco and smoked, or chewed as is the custom in Peru. In 1897 Zangger had already noted the introduction of cocaine for topical application to the gums and Erben (1910) has reported topical application to the mucosa of the vagina. Heinemann reports that recently cocaine has often been used for the criminal purpose of seducing young girls. According to the author, there are numerous cases of death resulting from the inappropriate use of opiates for treating the excitatory symptoms of acute cocaine poisoning. Chronic cocaine users often end up committing suicide, either during a serious anxiety attack at night or during a period of intense depression. But cocaine itself is rarely used for such purposes. From a criminal point of view, cocaine addicts are much more dangerous than morphine addicts because their hallucinations are much more vivid, because of their intense activity and because of their delusions of jealousy. Cocaine stolen from the manufacturers of pharmaceutical products accounts for a considerable proportion of the illicit trade in the drug. According to the author, the amount of cocaine currently produced is 100 times as large as the amount required for medical and scientific purposes. He knows individuals who, passing themselves as physicians, or assuming other impressive and misleading titles, have been able to obtain up to 10 kg of cocaine directly from the manufacturers simply by writing an order on a piece of paper with a fictitious letterhead. It goes without saying that the drug thus obtained soon finds its way into the illicit market. In this connection one often finds newspaper advertisements like the following: "Young physician with spare time and free of prejudices needed to represent manufacturer of chemical products." In 1921, Zangger, adopting a point of view consistent with the invaluable contribution of Heinemann, called the attention of a Swiss meeting of public health physicians to the dangers and the growing dimensions of the current illicit trade in drugs in general and cocaine in particular.

In November of 1921, Cramer reported to the medical society

of Geneva on the propagation of cocaine addiction in Switzerland, and in Geneva in particular, where the authorities had been obliged to increase the severity of the legal measures already in existence. He concentrates specifically on the description of the illicit traffic that takes place mostly at night and which exploits the addicts by extorting from them prices that grow higher the later the hour of the night. He described the case of an amputee whose artificial leg was full of cocaine-containing boxes which could be reached directly through the pocket of his trousers. Another trafficker concealed cocaine in a jar over which there was always a sleeping cat. A street musician had devised a method to carry 1 kg of cocaine in his mandolin. In order to throw the police off the track, the traffickers often have several addresses. For example, one dealer in Paris had six residences. Cocaine is given fantastic code names, sufficient to fill a whole glossary.

The investigations in Geneva demonstrated that cocaine addiction had spread through all the social classes, even the most dispossessed, and that it was beginning to assume alarming proportions among school youth. Thanks to the strict measures adopted by the authorities following Cramer's (1921) report, the situation improved somewhat, but it would be premature to think that cocaine addiction has totally disappeared.

Also in November of 1921, I personally presented a report to the Swiss Psychiatric Association on the *Neue Beiträge zur Symptomatologie und Bekämpfung des Kokainismus* (New contributions to the symptomatology and control of cocaine abuse), at the end of which I presented the following resolution which was unanimously adopted and submitted to the government:

> The Swiss Psychiatric Association, having met on November 27, 1921, and heard the report of professor Hans W. Maier, is convinced that cocaine, manufactured by the chemical industry in large amounts, is a toxic substance whose habitual use soon results in very serious and dangerous harm to the physical health, but most particularly to the mental health, of the user. For some time now cocaine addiction has been spreading alarmingly in Europe, including Switzerland where it has already caused enough misfortune in various places. In our opinion the chances of spreading of cocaine addiction are in proportion to the number of addicts, each one representing a focus of infection, and to the prohibited and illicit cocaine trade which is a source of considerable profits. It is still possible to eradicate this evil before it spreads like an oil slick on the water. Those members of our association who have studied the question feel that the local fight in each canton against this evil is totally futile, since the traffic can shift from district to district with great ease. Therefore the fight

should be federal in scope, and there is, furthermore, need for an international agreement among the various states to cope with the solidly organized smugglers. We propose the following measures:

1. Cocaine addicts, who always represent a public danger, shall be officially confined to closed institutions.

2. Illicit traffickers, or individuals found in possession of cocaine without due authorization or justification, shall be subject to severe penalties, and not just to simple fines.

3. The production, importation and exportation of cocaine shall be subject to rigorous control by the official authorities.

The Swiss Psychiatric Association resolves to request that the Federal Council adopt immediately the required legislative measures, and that it enter into agreement with other countries (possibly becoming a signatory to the 1912 Opium Convention at the Hague, and seeking to improve it) with the object of preventing the spread of cocaine addiction, and of putting an end to it where it already exists. We invite it to create a special expert commission for these purposes which shall be charged with the responsibility of devising all measures capable of preventing the improper use of other toxic substances (opium, pantopon, morphine) whose effects are as harmful as those of cocaine.

The Swiss Psychiatric Association, considering that this is a matter of the greatest importance from a public health point of view, requests that the Bundesrat give consideration as promptly as possible to this resolution which it is also bringing to the attention of the presidents of the confederate councils and of the cantonal governments.

This initiative of the Swiss Psychiatric Association, following on the Geneva report by Cramer (1921) already mentioned, certainly accelerated Switzerland's consideration of the question of adhering to the Hague Convention of 1912, so that since 1924 this country has taken part in the international fight against the abuse of toxic and narcotic substances.

The developments that followed the events just described materialized from the start in the most vulnerable districts, where new special legislation against cocaine and similar substances was adopted. Legal experts also became more concerned with this problem than they had previously been, as witnessed by the publication in 1922 of Paul Logoz's paper in the *Schweizerische Zeitschrift für Strafrecht*. In this paper he discusses the stricter law adopted in the canton of Vaud on December 1, 1921, and analyzes the characteristics of the new resolution adopted in Geneva on March 15, 1922, according to which not only those who sell cocaine are subject to legal penalties, but also those who give it to others free, and those who barter toxic substances. In contrast to the cantonal law of Vaud, the Geneva law provided for the confinement of the addicts in closed institutions, instead of legal penalties. However, individuals who procure drugs without legitimate reasons, or by forging prescriptions, as well as physicians and dentists who prescribe toxic substances without legitimate medical reasons, are liable to legal penalties. These consist of a maximum of one year imprisonment or a fine of up to 10,000 francs, or both. Logoz regrets that the law did not include a minimun duration of imprisonment. Additional penalties include: deprivation of civil rights for one to five years; temporary or indefinite closing of the place of business of an owner who violates the law, including factories, pharmacies, and the offices of physicians and dentists; publication of the verdict in the newspapers at the expense of the convicted offender, and confiscation of the drugs even in cases of acquittal. The penalties can be doubled in the cases of physicians, dentists, veterinarians, pharmacists or any other professionals who commit a second offence. Those who incite to the crime or are accessory to it are liable to the same penalties as the major offenders.

In addition to the authors already cited, Hans Hunziker (1922) of Basel and Otto Binswanger (1924) of Kreuzlingen have also called attention to the dangerous spread of cocaine use in Switzerland, and have recommended the adoption of strict measures against the use of toxic substances. In his book *Diagnostische und therapeutische Irrtümer bei Vergiftungen* (Diagnostic and Therapeutic Errors in Cases of Poisoning), Zangger attaches particular importance to the differential diagnosis of cocaine intoxication, a point to which we shall return in a subsequent chapter.

The development of cocaine addiction and the fight against it in the United States are of particular interest. In 1912 Wilbert and Motter reviewed all the legal measures adopted to date concerning the possession, use, sale and manufacture of toxic substances, especially narcotics, in an official publication of the Public Health Office in Washington. According to this publication, the number of fatal cases of poisoning, excluding those due to alcohol, were then 5,000 per year, the majority being due to opium and cocaine.The first special law against the abuse of cocaine was passed in Illinois in 1897. By 1912, a large number of the states of the Union, exclusive of the territories of Alaska and Hawaii, had adopted special measures forbidding the dispensing of cocaine except on prescriptions issued by registered physicians and veterinarians. The federal government, in turn, had prohibited shipment of cocaine through the mails. The public schools of 14 states included courses on the harmful effects not only of alcohol, but also of opium, morphine and other drugs.

The civil laws of some states included clauses stipulating that cocaine and morphine addiction, as well as alcoholism, are grounds for divorce. Physicians and dentists are forbidden to issue cocaine or cocaine preparations to recognized cocaine addicts. Three states have prohibited the addition of narcotics to cigarette tobacco. To give an idea of the magnitude that the legislation against toxic substances had reached in the United States between 1897 and 1912, it is sufficient to say that the simple listing, without commentary, of all the pertinent laws occupied 209 printed pages of the work from which we have drawn all this information. But despite all these numerous legal measures the use of toxic substances continued to spread and intensify, so that it became necessary to resort to even more severe and centralized measures to fight against the abuse and the illicit traffic. The first step in this direction was taken in 1913 when the law No. 470 was passed. It makes the manufacture and sale of cocaine subject to the control of the government which can initiate the application of penal sanctions. A police inquiry, initiated after the promulgation of this law, revealed the unexpected dimensions of the abuse of cocaine and heroin. This finding was the stimulus for the organization of the so-called Vanderbilt Committee in New York in 1913-1914. It was composed of members of Congress, physicians and lawyers, and undertook the task of finding more effective means to combat the abuse of narcotic substances. A new law against narcotics was passed in the state of New York on July 1, 1914.

A propos of this new and more severe law, Collins said the following in an official publication of the Public Health Service of New York: "Thanks to this new law, the enormous proportions of the illicit traffic in toxic substances and of its disastrous consequences have been revealed. At the same time it throws light on the serious dangers to which all segments of the society are exposed." Furthermore, new resolutions designed to increase the severity of the penalties were adopted in January of 1915, and finally the Harrison Act became effective on the 1st of March, 1915. It included strict penalties concerning narcotics, and was applicable throughout the Union. Thus the illicit traffic became increasingly risky, giving rise to exorbitant profits and to the search for increasingly sophisticated methods to evade the law and escape prosecution. It was then established that 10% of the criminals referred to the courts owed their moral downfall to the use of opium and of cocaine. In the state of New York alone, the number of drug addicts was estimated at 100,000, and at 60,000 in Massachusetts. In 1918, a central office in charge of the control of narcotics was created in New York. The prescription of drugs was subjected to severe restrictions. By ordinary prescription, a physician could only issue a very small amount of cocaine. If larger doses were required, he had to write the prescription on official forms and report the specific purpose to the authorities. Special clinics for the treatment of drug addicts were created in the large cities. The patients could attend them voluntarily because they wished to be cured or because they were no longer able to obtain the drugs, or they were referred to them by the authorities. In 1919 Greenfield, under the auspices of the Public Health Office of Washington, published a widely distributed leaflet on the treatment of narcotic intoxication and which, in addition, informed the public of all the current laws concerning narcotics. It explained that, in accordance with the Harrison Act, drug addicts could, at the expense of the government, seek either gradual withdrawal under constant medical supervision in the clinics or be sent to special institutions.

In a paper published in 1919-1920, Copeland, then physician-in-chief of the Public Health Service of New York, states that on the 8th of April of 1919, for the first time, six New York physicians and four druggists had been arrested for illicit traffic in narcotics. A few hours later, hundreds of patients, no longer able to obtain their drugs, sought treatment from the authorities. To honor this request, the Public Health Service created a special clinic on the 10th of April which had looked after 7,000 individuals until January of 1920. The ambulatory treatment proved ineffective because the patients always succeeded in finding new sources of intoxication. The first group of 3,262 patients included 2,647 men and 615 women, and 2,802 whites versus 460 blacks. The origin of the abuse was therapeutic in only 429 cases. In the remaining cases, drug use had begun following association with users or had been provoked by curiosity, imitation, etc. This experience demonstrated that pure cocaine addicts rarely sought admission to the clinic. This is in full agreement with our own observations concerning the mildness of the withdrawal phenomena in this type of intoxication.

The types of drugs involved are shown in the following case statistics:

Cocaine	6 cases
Cocaine plus morphine	42 cases
Cocaine plus heroin	305 cases
Morphine	690 cases
Morphine plus heroin	41 cases
Heroin	2,178 cases

In only 211 cases the duration of the illness was less than one year. In the remaining cases it ranged from two to 10 years. Most patients ranged in age from 20 to 25 years and 908 were between 15 and 19 years of age. The treatment, especially of morphine and of heroin addicts, included three stages. The first, lasting about three days, was used to ascertain, as thoroughly as possible, the physical health of the patient, his type of addiction and the dosage. On the fourth day, the patient was purged by the administration of a mixture of rhubarb, ipecac, strychnine, atropine and a little calomel. This was followed by a reduction in the dose of the narcotic until the last one was administered on the morning of the seventh day. At noon, the patient was given 0.5 to 1 mg of hyoscine as a sedative, which was repeated as needed. The acidosis, which is the rule in similar cases, was counteracted by the administration of alkaline solutions. Insomnia, which was rare, was treated with chloral in the case of men and with trional in the case of women. In cases of combined addiction to alkaloids and alcohol, the alcohol was totally withdrawn, but in some of these cases paraldehyde proved to be therapeutically beneficial. Cardiac insufficiency and other complications were treated symptomatically. The patients remained in bed during the period of detoxification and one nurse was assigned to supervise every two patients. During the third period of the treatment, the patients, already detoxified, worked in the fields or repaired streets in the neighborhood of the clinic. Since most patients were also heavy smokers, they were only given four or five cigarettes per day. Arrangements were made to keep in touch with the patients after discharge. It is obviously impossible to make an accurate prognosis with respect to the probable duration of the cure. But it cannot be too pessimistic considering the fact that, as a result of the strict implementation of the law, former addicts find it increasingly difficult to obtain drugs and must pay prohibitive prices for them. Since the domestic production of narcotics is subject to the most stringent controls, the efforts of the American authorities to eradicate drug addiction were primarily hindered by the illicit international traffic.

A particularly interesting question concerns the influence that the prohibition of alcoholic beverages in the United States (1918) had on the use of narcotics. As we have already said, the official and vigorous fight against narcotics began in the state of New York in April of 1919, roughly coinciding with the advent of prohibition. Thus the increase in the number of hospitalizations cannot be attributed to an increase in the prevalence of morphine, cocaine and other addictions, but it appears to have been primarily due to stricter law enforcement.

In 1923, C.F. Stoddard published a paper on the influence of prohibition on the spread of use of other narcotic substances. Based on substantial statistics she concluded that, during 1921 and 1922, neither the number of hospital admissions nor the statistical data on causes of mortality, judicial proceedings or police activities warranted the conclusion that prohibition had had any influence on the development of the abuse of narcotics. In places where the authorities recognized an increase in the known number of addicts, the officials themselves claimed that the apparent increase was due to a more vigorous implementation of the law. However, since Stoddard carried out this investigation privately, and was a strong supporter of prohibition, her conclusion may have been biased and must be viewed with caution.

But a more recent publication (May 23, 1924) from the Public Health Service of Washington presents a most objective analysis of the extension of narcotic use in the United States and of the factors that influence it. The authors, both on the staff of the Public Health Service, were Kolb, a physician, and Du Mez, a pharmacologist. After critical analysis of the evidence available to them, they concluded that at around 1900 there was a maximum of 264,000 narcotic users in the United States. This figure did not include alcohol users. The number of narcotic users had certainly decreased since then. By 1924, and despite an increase in the general population, the number of narcotic users was probably 110,000, and certainly no more than 150,000. The average dose used by morphine or cocaine addicts was estimated at 0.4 g. In the majority of cases, the drug habit had been acquired through imitation, curiosity, bad influences, etc., and in only a small minority was the origin of the habit therapeutic in nature. Since the introduction of legislation five years earlier, opium addiction in all its forms had decreased markedly, but was partly replaced by the use of the pure alkaloids. The increase in criminal activity among addicts, despite the decrease in drug use, is probably due to the fact that precisely because of the new laws, a relatively higher proportion of drug use occurs among degenerated psychopaths, while mentally healthy individuals have tended to use drugs less and less. It can therefore be concluded that the fight against drugs by the authorities and the medical profession has been successful, and it is legitimate to hope that within a few years, once the illicit international traffic is eliminated, this serious danger to public health will have disappeared completely. Be that as it may, this publication contains no evidence whatsoever in support of the view that the use of narcotics increased following prohibition. The opposite is rather the case. It should be recalled in this respect that, during the first years of the war, Bonhoeffer (1925-26) established in Germany that a marked decrease in alcoholism had not been necessarily followed by an increase in morphine or other addictions. On the contrary, the increase in cocaine addiction in Germany coincided with an alarming increase in the rate of alcoholism, and there is no reason to believe that there is an inverse relationship between these two conditions any more in France than in Germany. The official American findings concerning this question are of particular importance because of the fierce controversy in the American popular press, where well-organized interest groups have repeatedly argued the opposite to the official statistics. This has usually been based on inadequate facts, or on biased and haphazardly selected statistical data. Many European authors (for example, Joël and Fränkel, 1924 in their monograph on cocaine), who undoubtedly had not had access to these official findings, have relied on this arbitrary and incomplete evidence to draw conclusions about cocaine addiction that they believed to be scientifically valid. This is not the place to argue for or against prohibition in the United States. But the question is too serious and important from a public health point of view to permit an attack on prohibition which, based on biased and ill-founded conclusions, claims that it facilitates and encourages the use of other narcotics.

American physicians, not all of whom are prohibitionists, have taken issue with this misconception. This opportunity arose as a result of unjustified statements in the press according to which physicians have contributed to the supposed increase in narcotic use by prescribing these drugs incautiously, indiscriminately and without regard to the consequences.

In a paper in the *Medical Journal and Record* of February 6, 1924, Knopf attacked the American press for such exaggerations as, for example, the claim that one million people in the United States, or 1% of the population, are users of narcotics (exclusive of alcohol) and that the majority of these addicts acquired their habit through the negligence and lack of caution of physicians. In this respect he states that according to Dr. D. Simon, a police official in New York, and an expert in the field, no more than 2% of morphine, cocaine and heroin addicts can claim to have become addicted as a result of medical prescriptions. Knopf suggests that official authorization to prescribe narcotics during the detoxification of addicts be given only to physicians reasonably conversant with the psychiatric complications of drug addiction. This policy would be an effective means to put an end to the possible misconduct on the part of some physicians, which is, fortunately, very rare. A special commission would inspect, from time to time, the records of these authorized physicians. Knopf is also in favor (see also his article in the *New York*

Medical Week of January 5, 1924) of an international agreement concerning the limitation of production of alkaloids and the supervision of their sales. To accuse American physicians of being indifferent in the presence of a national danger, and even of contributing to it, is most unjust. On the contrary, the American medical profession is quite prepared to take an active part in the national and international fight against this danger. The author does not say that alcohol prohibition has contributed to an increase in the incidence of drug addictions.

Simon wrote in the *New York Tribune* of January 28, 1924: "Contrary to statements made elsewhere, it should be emphasized that the abuse of narcotics has not shown any increase following alcohol prohibition. At this time, the authorities have conclusive data on this question available to them. While in 1921 the police had a list of 35,000 drug addicts, the figure has fallen to 9,000 at present." Dr. Simon, a member of the New York police force, and, since 1921, director of the special branch in charge of the drug problem, is better qualified than anyone else to know it in depth. In the space of three years, 10,553 drug addicts had been arrested. They included 1,635 patients who had submitted voluntarily to hospitalization. During the same period of time, 770 dealers in narcotics had been referred to the courts by the police. Of 9,637 arrested patients, 8,174 had previous convictions, 876 were opium smokers, 379 were morphine addicts and 6,892 were addicted to heroin or cocaine, or to both. The average age of the individuals arrested in 1921 was 25 years and 27 years for those arrested in 1923. In view of the seriousness and extent of the danger represented by these figures, it is not surprising that the American public and the Congress demanded as rapid and strict an implementation as possible of the Hague Convention of 1912. Based on these facts, the American Congress decided in 1924 that the United States would participate in the opium conference that the League of Nations had convened at Geneva for the 24th of November of the same year. The vigor with which the American delegation defended its point of view and its uncompromising attitude are well known.

At the end of 1924, L. Lewin, the noted Berlin pharmacologist, published a book entitled *Phantastica* which includes a comprehensive review of the effects of cocaine put in a historical perspective. He states that the effects vary considerably from individual to individual, and that, for example, a single injection into the gums may be followed by serious disturbances of brain function, including clouding of consciousness and sensory hallucinations, which may last more than a day. No other drug, he says, is used in such a variety of preparations as cocaine, including cocaine wine, cocaine champagne and cocaine cigarettes. One of Lewin's patients inserted cotton tampons soaked in a cocaine solution into the cavities of his teeth. The author concluded his chapter on cocaine with the following statement: "During recent years I have seen among men of science frightful symptoms due to the craving for cocaine. Those who believe they can enter the temple of happiness through this gate of pleasure purchase their momentary delights at the cost of body and soul. They speedily pass through the gate of unhappiness into the night of the abyss."[5]

I am indebted to Bonhoeffer (1925-26) for the following figures which give, even though indirectly, an idea of the extension of cocaine addiction in Germany and in Austria. Of 1,000 patients admitted to the psychiatric clinics of the universities, the proportion of cocaine addicts was as follows:

	Berlin	Vienna		Berlin	Vienna
1913	1.75	1.50	1919	1.25	1.00
1914	0.00	0.50	1920	7.50	2.00
1915	0.00	0.00	1921	10.00	0.75
1916	1.25	0.50	1922	6.25	1.00
1917	1.50	1.25	1923	7.00	3.00
1918	3.00	1.50	1924	13.00	9.75

This table clearly shows that the proportion of cocaine addicts has increased during recent years.

According to a personal communication from Mocchi of Cairo, cocaine addiction has had devastating effects in Egypt for some time, especially among the higher classes. It has been necessary to adopt severe measures which have not yet, however, produced very satisfactory results.

Before closing this historical account we should mention the attempts that have been made recently to elucidate two problems by means of some medical applications of cocaine which are independent of its anesthetic effects.

The well-known fact that cocaine frequently produces epileptiform seizures in animals suggested the idea of using the drug for research in epilepsy. The initial hypothesis was that the seizures produced by cocaine are due to its direct action on the cerebral cortex.

[5] Ed. note: The quotation in English has been taken from: L. Lewin. *Phantastica. Narcotic and Stimulating Drugs. Their Use and Abuse.* Wirth, P.H.A. (trans.). London, 1964. Routledge & Kegan Paul.

Sauerbruch produced experimental lesions of the cerebral cortex of a monkey by creating a depressed fracture of the skull, by a severe puncture wound, or by application of tincture of iodide, without provoking any seizures whatsoever. But the injection of cocaine in a dose much smaller than that usually required in the intact animal was immediately followed by seizures.

Attempts at using cocaine injections as a provocative test in man in cases of uncertain diagnosis have failed, in the sense that it was impossible to provoke seizures. This is not surprising, however, since cocaine-induced seizures are far less frequent in man than in animals, even in cases of severe intoxication. Furthermore, this method is not only unreliable but even dangerous, considering the large individual variation in sensitivity to cocaine and the often low doses at which the drug can be fatal.

Cocaine has lost its usefulness for this purpose since it is now possible to provoke seizures by means of a more physiological and infinitely less dangerous method based on more accurate knowledge of the relationship between the metabolism of sodium chloride and epileptic symptoms. This method consists of the abrupt administration of large amounts of sodium chloride after having saturated the body with bromide. In this context, we should warn against the danger of administering cocaine to individuals with chronic cerebral lesions such as those due to trauma, epilepsy or apoplexy. This warning is directed especially to dentists who, through long-standing habit, have not yet completely abandoned the use of this drug.

The second problem has been extensively studied experimentally by Berger. After accidentally observing the disappearance of a serious case of catatonic stupor following a single cocaine injection, the author repeated the experiment on a larger scale, and in 1921 published 11 case reports. In eight cases, cocaine injections diminished the severity of the catatonic stupor but the effect was of very short duration, sometimes no longer than one or two hours. He was also able to observe the stimulating action of the drug on the cerebral cortex by having two mentally depressed patients perform arithmetic exercises after the administration of cocaine injections. These results were confirmed by Becker during the same year in six catatonic patients. In one case the improvement lasted 20 hours and in another, three hours, but he never succeeded in producing a lasting effect. Hinsen (1922) tried the same procedure in two patients with organic brain damage (depression associated with paralysis and senile dementia), but the improvement lasted only 15 and seven minutes respectively.

In 1922 Bakody published a paper on the effects of cocaine on the autonomic nervous function of schizophrenics. He examined 50 patients and 13 controls. While cocaine produced an increase in blood pressure in the normal subjects, it often led to a fall in blood pressure in the schizophrenics and almost always in the catatonics. He attributed this effect to stimulation of the parasympathetic system. The blood pressure increased in the catatonics only when cocaine produced mental stimulation. While the controls showed an increase in pulse rate, it was slowed down in some schizophrenics, and particularly in the catatonics. In many cases the same effects occurred on the respiration. Cocaine stimulates the sympathetic nervous system of normal subjects and both the sympathetic and parasympathetic nervous systems in schizophrenics. The stimulation of the Aschner (oculocardiac) reflex in catatonics may be related to this effect.

Mosler (1922) observed only one reasonably clear positive effect after administering cocaine injections to 15 patients in catatonic stupor. He believes that it is unwarranted to generalize on the basis of this one positive outcome. In contrast, during his research on schizophrenia, Steck (1923) found only two cases who failed to respond following the administration of cocaine to patients in a state of stupor. Fleck (1924) obtained transitory improvement following the subcutaneous administration of doses of up to 0.2 g of cocaine in some cases of stupor of various origins constituting part of the symptomatology of diverse pathological states. He attributed these effects, as well as those observed in normal individuals, to strong central stimulation. He states that the personality of the individual, as well as the morbid state, must be taken into account to explain the lack of consistent effects of cocaine. He feels that these experiments sometimes provide the opportunity to get a glimpse into the mind of withdrawn patients. But he is also of the opinion that the therapeutic value of this procedure is trivial considering the short duration of action and the risk of dependence. He also experimented with cocaine on himself and experienced, following an injection of 0.1 g, a slight and pleasant feeling of warmth throughout his body and a subjective sense of stimulation accompanied by the need to talk, the effects lasting about half an hour. Administration of the same dose to another normal subject produced, in addition, a feeling of euphoria with motor excitation and the need to be active. Recently, Bychowski (1925) administered cocaine in doses of 0.1 to 0.2 g to 30 schizophrenics in a state of stupor. In two of them there was a weakening of heart function which assumed alarming proportions in one. This demonstrated the danger in the administration of such large doses, and the caution that must be observed in comparable cases. Generally the effects were short-lived and even in the most favorable cases the stimulation of the patients lasted only a few hours. In some cases, however, this transitory stimulation permitted the author to obtain important information on which to base the differential diagnosis.

In general, however, Bychowski concluded that his investigations had not yielded any practical results. He made the remarkable discovery that as the experiment was repeated in the same patient, the effects became clearly less marked. This was attributed not to any property of cocaine itself, but to the fact that the mental patient would become less responsive to psychic stimulation through familiarity with the experience. All these experiments can be compared to those of Claude who had attempted to devise a method of classifying schizophrenics based primarily on differential diagnosis through the use of ether.

In 1920, Agda Hofvendahl published a paper on the means to counteract the symptoms of acute intoxication in experimental animals, a question of particular importance to laryngologists and ophthalmologists. He concluded that death following a single administration of cocaine was due to the action of the drug on the cerebral cortex, resulting in respiratory arrest. The lethal action of a given dose of cocaine can be prevented by diminishing the excitability of the brain through the administration of an appropriate sedative. Sodium veronal was more effective than chloral or scopolamine, especially if administered quickly and intravenously. Morphine is contraindicated in these cases because it also exerts an inhibitory action on the respiratory center.

In another paper, Hofvendahl (1921) reported that Somnifen (a diethyl-diallyl-barbiturate derivative) is, at present, the most effective of the barbiturates in the treatment of acute cocaine poisoning. Four mL of a 20% solution (0.8 g), and even up to 1.25 g in grave cases, can be administered intravenously to man without danger. The author found that, in the monkey, the exact ratio of the antidote to the poison was 1:2 or, in other words, 1 g of Somnifen is necessary to counteract the action of 2 g of cocaine. As a preventive measure in local anesthesia he recommends the parenteral administration of 0.5 g of Sodium Veronal or the equivalent dose of Somnifen[6] half an hour before the administration of cocaine.

[6] Ed. note: Barbiturates, which were valuable sedatives and anticonvulsants in Maier's time, have now been almost completely replaced by benzodiazepines, which have much lower toxicity for the same degree of therapeutic effect.

In animal experiments conducted at the hospital for ear diseases at Basel in 1922, Karl Mayer demonstrated that calcium has an antagonistic action against cocaine. He therefore recommended the intravenous administration of calcium chloride in cases of cocaine poisoning.

VI

THE EFFECTS OF COCAINE IN MAN

A. General Symptomatology

We shall attempt to describe the general symptomatology of cocaine poisoning in relation to the use of this alkaloid as a local anesthetic, the side-effects varying according to the mode of administration. Cocainism associated with subcutaneous administration, which was very common in earlier days, is now seen only in old morphine addicts who use both drugs simultaneously, or have replaced morphine with cocaine. These subjects, who inject themselves with more or less care, show injection marks over the body, and occasionally signs of abscesses due to infection. It was believed, 30 or 40 years ago, that the injection scars in cocaine users had a brownish-yellow coloration, while those of morphine users were normal in color. This distinction has lost its significance at present because it has been established that the brownish-yellow coloration of the scars of cocaine addicts was due primarily to the absence of aseptic precautions.

Cocaine use by inhalation through the nose, which 20 years ago was a very rare phenomenon in Europe, has become, since 1915, such a common practice that today the vast majority of cocaine addicts are sniffers. Cocaine is generally used as a powder, either pure or adulterated with boric or salicylic acids. Depending on the social status of the users and on the manner in which they obtain the drug on a particular occasion, it is kept in snuff or candy boxes, or simply in packages of one or more grams each, which the users always have in their pockets. Habitual cocaine users always carry with them a small bone spoon, a thimble or some other small receptacle by means of which they introduce into each nostril an amount of cocaine of about 1/8 g which they sniff deeply while keeping the other nostril closed. Cocaine addicts who do not have any of these gadgets simply put the powder in the "anatomical snuff box," that is, the hollow which is formed on the radial side of the base of the hand when the extensor muscles of the thumb are contracted. When the user runs short, and does not have enough drug to sniff, he will put what is left over on the tongue or on the inner side of the lips. I have seen cocaine addicts lick the floor to rescue the last remnants of the powder.

Cocaine inhaled through the nose settles primarily on the

cartilaginous part of the nasal septum and on the inferior turbinate from which it is absorbed. The most important local effects following the inhalation of cocaine are a feeling of enlargement of the nasal fossae, followed by loss of the sense of smell and a cold sensation, not only limited to the nose but spreading also to the upper part of the mouth and particularly to the upper incisors. In addition, the sense of taste is often disturbed, especially at the tip of the tongue.

As the sniffing increases in frequency, an eczematous inflammation develops in a band of about 1/2 cm in width surrounding the nostrils. This sign often permits the identification of a cocaine sniffer. The eczema may spread in a butterfly pattern over the nose, around the eyes, and occasionally even beyond. The subjects attempt to conceal these lesions by covering them with a heavy layer of powder.

The nasal cavities remain dry for as long as the action of cocaine persists. But by contrast, during the intervening periods, the nasal mucosa secretes a copious and watery fluid referred to as the coryza of chronic cocainism. This is quite distressing and, together with the psychological symptoms acting in the same direction, forces the patient to seek amelioration by sniffing some more cocaine.

It is known that the unpleasant symptoms of the common cold can be quickly, although temporarily, alleviated by inserting into the nose tampons soaked in a solution of cocaine[7]. Thus, a large number of cocaine-based preparations against the common cold are available on the market. I have recently had the opportunity of looking after a very busy physician and a dentist who, too impatient to put up with the slightest discomforts, resorted to cocaine at the first signs of a cold. It did not take them very long to become dependent on the drug, reaching daily doses of 2 to 3 g in a space of six to eight weeks, and turning into true addicts. For this and many other reasons, I must strongly warn against the use of cocaine as a treatment for rhinitis.

Cocaine used in this fashion can produce, in a matter of weeks, a chronic atrophic rhinitis with crust formation. These atrophic

[7] Ed. note: When cocaine was placed under strict legal controls, this role was taken over by amphetamine, in the form of the Benzedrine® inhaler which contained the volatile free base of racemic amphetamine. This product was soon removed from the market because it had become too popular for euphoriant non-medical use. It has been replaced by a variety of preparations containing similar phenylethylamine derivatives with epinephrine-like vasoconstrictor effects.

lesions are seen not only on the mucosa of the turbinates, but especially on the cartilaginous septum where round ulcerations with well-defined and circumscribed edges are often formed. They become deeper and deeper until they eventually lead to a painless perforation of the septum. They are usually located on the middle third of the septum, at a distance of about 2 to 3 cm from the nostrils. The formation of the ulcers is frequently preceded and heralded by profuse nasal hemorrhages, following which the mucosa appears thinner and pale, and is surrounded by a rim with slightly raised edges. If this process continues, it leads eventually to necrosis of the ulcerated surface. Some earlier authors such as Albert Stein (1889, 1904) claim to have observed in some cases, necrosis of the upper segment of the nasal septum with ensuing collapse of the nose, giving rise to what is referred to as "saddle nose." I have never observed this phenomenon myself, nor have I seen it described in the literature of the last 10 years. It is therefore legitimate to ask whether those cases in which it occurred were not more likely instances of lesions of syphilitic origin.

The interesting symptom of septal perforation in cocaine sniffers was first described by Lubet-Barbons of Paris in 1908, and also by Hautant (1909) during the same year. In subsequent years it has been noted and described by Chevallier, Laignel-Lavastine (1924) and others. In 1915 Lichtenstein reported similar observations made among New York prison inmates.

An important and comprehensive report on this subject was published in 1924 by the Russian authors Leo Natanson and L. Lipskeroff. Between 1920 and 1924, they observed 74 cases of septal perforation caused by cocaine among patients from the venereal disease section of a Moscow prison hospital and among the inmates of two concentration camps and a correctional institution for minors. In 40 of the 74 cases, syphilis was not implicated, 28 were considered latent syphilitics, and in six there were overt syphilitic symptoms. The patients included office workers, mechanics, actors, lathe operators and day laborers. The majority of the women were prostitutes. The duration of the addiction to cocaine ranged from a few weeks to 10 years, and the daily dose from 0.5 to 1 g. In an institution for minors, the authors discovered 120 cocaine addicts, of whom 16 had perforation of the nasal septum and three had healed ulcerations; only one had a normal nose. The cocaine they used was usually adulterated with aspirin, boric acid or salicylic acid. Histological examination of the edges of the perforation revealed separation of the fibers of the hyalin cartilage with degenerative processes and proliferation of connective tissue, and a general picture of marked ischemia and lymphoid infiltration of the submucosal layer. The ulcerations observed by the authors, round at first, had become oval in shape with the longer diameter along a horizontal axis. Their size ranged from that of a pea to that of a 20 mark coin. The orifice of the perforation is often closed by a thick crust devoid of foul smell.

The high prevalence of perforation of the nasal septum in Russia is remarkable. This phenomenon is much rarer among us, occurring, to my knowledge, in about 25% of cases. It is possible that the high frequency of perforations in Russia is related to the particular contaminants of the cocaine used in that country, or to a lowered resistance of the body as a result of under-nutrition. Be that as it may, this question requires further study.

Bonvicini (1925) has recently published a detailed study of these phenomena. Among 32 cocaine sniffers he observed perforation of the nasal septum in 10, and simple ulceration in another 10.

The differential diagnosis must first take into account similar lesions found in tuberculosis. This is not very difficult because the perforations of a tubercular nature are more irregular in shape and their edges are more swollen and covered with thick granulations. In perforations of syphilitic origin the edges show radiating scars; furthermore, the loss of tissue involves the bone as well. Perforations of the nasal septum are also observed with relatively high frequency among burnishers who handle materials rich in chrome, among individuals subject to other types of occupational intoxications, as well as among bakers. However, it is easy to eliminate the diagnosis of cocaine addiction by simply establishing the occupation of the patient.

The main cause of perforation of the nasal septum in cocaine addicts is undoubtedly the vasoconstriction produced by topical application, as well as the tendency to formation of emboli as a result of the toxic action of the alkaloid on the protoplasm. Other contributory factors are neurotrophic processes, the small lesions caused by cocaine crystals and the larger lesions caused by inserting the finger into the nose and, finally, by the proliferation of the mucosal flora facilitated by all the preceding factors.

In connection with his investigations on septal perforation in cocaine sniffers, Bonvicini has made some interesting observations concerning the neurotrophic action of the drug. In this respect, he examined 20 hospitalized patients in Vienna and in a third of them he found short- or long-lasting hyper- or hypoexcitability phenomena, especially in the afferent section of the trigeminal nerve. These disturbances often lasted for several weeks after cocaine withdrawal. The signs of hyperexcitability almost always occurred in individuals who had been using the drug for comparatively short periods of time, while hypoexcitability was observed in chronic users who had relapsed many times. Hypoesthesia or anesthesia, with paresthesias, especially of the second and third branches of the trigeminal nerve, were observed in almost all cases of recent use. The regions affected showed decreased sensitivity to touch, pain and temperature and anesthesia of the sclera and cornea. There was absence of scleral, corneal, sternutatory and pharyngeal reflexes and the sense of smell and the sensitivity of the tip of the tongue were decreased, as well as the sense of taste of the front two-thirds of the tongue. In contrast, the motor branches of the trigeminal nerve were hyperexcitable, with evidence of contractures of the masseter and pterygoid muscles. The latter phenomena provide a physiological explanation for the trismus or lockjaw so often seen in cocaine sniffers, and for the abnormal tendency to chew and swallow observed in milder cases.

Under the influence of cocaine, the trophic branches of the trigeminal nerve undergo functional inhibition and this explains the atrophic phenomena observed, particularly in the nasal mucosa. In some instances the acne of the face, so common in cocaine addicts, can be traced to these trophic disturbances. It goes without saying that prolonged irritation of the nasal mucosa eventually affects the sense of smell.

When the effects of cocaine reach a certain level of intensity, the patients show muscular movements of the face which mimic a smile. Bonvicini, who observed this symptom twice, has labelled it "*risus sardonicus,*" and feels it is due to the simultaneous tetanization of the trigeminal and facial nerves. Cases of this type often show facial tics or fibrillation of the facial muscles, trembling of the lips and lateral deviation of facial muscles. Bonvicini has noted further that the lips become thinner, less mobile and incapable of fully covering the teeth, and that the corners of the mouth are drawn into a smile, pulled strongly towards the sides and slightly downwards, while the naso-labial folds are deepened (flat smile). The author, however, feels that these motor phenomena are not convulsive in nature but correspond, rather, to the psychological state of the patient.

Contractures probably also occur in the muscles supplied by the oculomotor, abducens and cochlear[8] nerves because patients

[8] Ed. note: *Sic*; the trochlear nerve is probably meant.

under the influence of cocaine often experience an obvious difficulty in moving their eyeballs and have to turn the whole head in order to look to the side.

All the phenomena related to the cranial nerves are very frequent in cocaine sniffers but are seldom or never mentioned in reports dealing with subcutaneous use of cocaine. It is known that once the drug enters the bloodstream, it becomes quickly inactivated. Therefore, it is possible that the specific peripheral effects seen in cocaine sniffers are due to local action around the cranial nerves while the cocaine concentration is still high enough to affect them.

It has been established through numerous observations that cocaine affects the function of the sensory nerves. Thus, for example, there is an increase in the sensitivity of the auditory nerve so that the subjects are able to perceive clearly the slightest sounds. Likewise, there is, according to many authors, an increase in sensitivity to weak light stimuli. However, chronic intoxication is reported to produce contraction of the visual field, especially for colors, as well as signs of amblyopia.

The decrease in sensitivity to taste and smell in cocaine sniffers has already been noted. It goes without saying that taste perception is also impaired in coca chewers.

In connection with cutaneous sensitivity, many cocaine sniffers show, some even after the first few doses and others not until later, abnormal sensations such as itching and the feeling that there are foreign bodies under the skin. These sensations in time take on a hallucinatory character and are then known as the Magnan symptom (see below).

According to some authors, cocainism produced either by sniffing or by subcutaneous injection can cause general anesthesia or, at the very least, a very distinctive state of hypoesthesia over the surface of the body. I have been unable to confirm these claims on the basis of my own observations which are, furthermore, inconsistent with the fact already mentioned that cocaine, once it enters the bloodstream, loses its ability to inhibit the peripheral endings of the sensory nerves.

Naturally what the subjects themselves say in this respect must be taken with a great deal of caution. A patient (R.F.) of Joël and Fränkel claimed, for example, to have felt no pain while undergoing suture of a deep wound which he had inflicted upon himself while under the effects of cocaine. This could well have been due, as often happens in alcoholic intoxication, to a central loss of sensitivity to pain.

It is possible, on the other hand, that once considerable amounts of cocaine have been absorbed and eliminated by the tissues, they may exert an anesthetic action on the areas through which it is eliminated. Indeed, the alkaloid can often be found in the gastric juice of individuals who have not taken the drug by mouth. For this reason, the appetite-impairing effect of cocaine, that is said to be an important reason for coca-chewing in South America, must be attributed to anesthesia of the gastric mucosa.

Epileptiform seizures are the most dramatic motor phenomenon produced by cocaine. In our review of the experimental evidence we have already called attention to the fact that this phenomenon is more marked in animals than in man. It is a curious fact that this reaction was relatively frequent in the cocaine addicts of earlier decades, who took the drug subcutaneously, while it is seldom seen in present-day sniffers. The experimental evidence is consistent with the hypothesis that these are true convulsions originating in the cerebral cortex. Further research is necessary to determine whether an epileptoid constitution is a necessary condition for the production of such convulsions in man, whether it is a simple instance of triggering, as is frequently the case in alcoholic convulsions, or of a true toxic effect. It is probable that epileptiform seizures are due to either of these mechanisms because we know of cases in which the abrupt intake of large doses of cocaine was followed by epileptiform convulsions, coma and fatal respiratory arrest, which there was good reason to attribute to a pure toxic reaction of the central nervous system.

However, the most characteristic symptoms are those caused by over-stimulation of the sympathetic nervous system. Inhibitory phenomena, which in some cases are life-threatening, appear only after very large doses. The most prominent sign is pupillary dilatation which is not extreme because subsequent administration of atropine can enhance it further. Reaction to light is diminished but not abolished. In addition, there is a clear-cut widening of the palpebral fissure and slight protrusion of the eyeballs. In summary, we are dealing with a typical Horner's syndrome[9]. Even small doses of cocaine cause an increase in the pulse rate of 20 to 30 per minute and, if the dose is large, of up to 100 per minute. This increase in the pulse rate is accompanied by a subjective feeling of palpitations and of pre-cordial pressure. The respiratory rate is also increased. In general, the blood pressure rises, but this effect may be absent in

[9] Ed. Note: *Sic*; this is actually a reversed Horner's syndrome.

some patients, or there may even be a fall in blood pressure. This is probably due to the fact that the threshold for the appearance of inhibitory phenomena varies from individual to individual. Cocaine intoxication is very often accompanied by an increase in body temperature of 2 to 3° C. This is probably due to stimulation of the thermoregulatory center, and is directly related to an increase in tonus of the sympathetic nervous system, a fact already observed in urticaria, and confirmed experimentally. Moreover, urticaria-like lesions of the skin are not infrequent in cocaine intoxication. But I have been able to observe, even more frequently, purplish blotches on the limbs which were cold to the touch and gave the patients a subjective feeling of cold. These are due to local circumscribed spasms of the vasoconstrictor fibers.

The phenomena described above, including the Horner's syndrome [*sic*], the elevated pulse rate, palpitations, increased respiratory rate and, frequently, an increase in blood pressure, are remarkably similar to the symptoms of hyperthyroidism in which, as is well known, enhanced sympathetic activity plays an important role. Furthermore, the facies of individuals intoxicated by cocaine, with their widely opened eyes and protruding eyeballs, dilated pupils and bright corneas, are astonishingly similar to those of hyperthyroid patients. Based on this comparison, Löffler and others have recently been partially successful in ameliorating the symptoms of this endocrine condition by attempting to decrease the activity of the sympathetic system through the use of ergotamine in the form of a preparation (Gynergen® Sandoz) with very little risk of toxicity. I have myself obtained very good results with this drug in cases of endogenous urticaria. It would therefore be of interest to investigate this type of therapy in severe cases of cocaine intoxication.

According to recent reviews by Laignel-Lavastine (1924) and others, the sympathetic symptomatology can be briefly described as follows:

The localized vasoconstriction of the limbs, already described, and giving rise to the cold, circumscribed, bluish spots in the skin, can be so marked as to remind one of Raynaud's disease. But it differs from the latter condition in that, together with the other signs, it disappears quickly once the state of intoxication is over. In chronic states of intoxication, on the contrary, there is often a picture of long-lasting acrocyanosis also seen in some schizophrenics. This sign tends to complicate the differential diagnosis, particularly when the mental symptoms also resemble those of schizophrenia. So far, I have not been able to observe the opposite phenomenon, that is, inhibition of vasoconstriction in various parts of the body resulting in pain and local elevation of temperature, as seen in the erythromelalgia of Weir- Mitchell. But on the other hand, localized paresthesias of the limbs and circumscribed or diffuse erythemas, which disappear under digital pressure and which are also likely due to sympathetic stimulation, are not rare. I have never observed localized irritation of the skin of the limbs. On the other hand, the red phase of the dermographic response is generally exaggerated. Among the other skin disturbances associated with cocaine dependence, we have already mentioned urticaria as well as the intense itching which often spreads over the whole body and gives rise to the well known cutaneous hallucinations induced by cocaine. Other disturbances associated with increased sympathomimetic activity include excessive perspiration commonly seen in cocaine addicts, seborrhea which is more rare and occurs only in advanced stages of the intoxication, and a slight appearance of goose flesh to the skin. I have never observed edema as a sign of cocainism. Although most patients experience loss of weight, there is, in some cases, a peculiar increase in the amount of adipose tissue. Whether or not this involves lipodystrophic phenomena of nervous and, more specifically, of sympathetic origin remains open to investigation. Other sympathomimetic symptoms observed in cocaine addicts include the fine tremors particularly visible in the limbs. They occur during, or immediately after, the state of intoxication.

The vasoconstriction of sympathetic origin that occurs in cocaine intoxication gives rise to localized symptoms such as constriction of the retinal arteries and cerebral ischemia accompanied by subjective or objective signs of dizziness. The marked brightness of the cornea, as well as the tendency to migraine and hypertensive attacks seen in cocaine addicts, have also been attributed to sympathetic over-stimulation due to direct action of the drug.

Recent research tends to establish with increasing certainty that the function of the sympathetic nervous system, directly related to the brain stem, has an equally strong connection with psychological, especially emotional, reactions[10]. It is sufficient to recall the *sequelae* of encephalitis, as well as the similarities and connections between the psychological disturbances of hyperthyroidism on the one hand, and psychoneurotic phenomena as well as some of the effects of cocainism, on the other.

10 Author's note: W.R. Hess (*Schweiz. Arch. Neurol. Psychiat.* 16, 298 et seq., 1925) in a study on the action of cocaine, has recently established beyond doubt the close relationship between increased sympathetic tonus and enhanced mental activity.

In summary, the most frequent symptoms following the intake of a single rather large dose of cocaine (and which are therefore of particular diagnostic value) consist of very intense palpitations which occasionally give rise to attacks of angina pectoris accompanied by intense anxiety, heaviness, a feeling of tension in the head and back of the neck, cold sensations in the limbs and a slight increase in the pulse rate. As the state of intoxication becomes more serious, the respiratory rate decreases rapidly. In some cases there is true Cheyne-Stokes respiration, fever, albuminuria and localized or generalized clonic and tonic seizures. Heinrich Zangger (1922, 1924) has even observed cases of anuria and yellow discoloration of the conjunctivae. Occasionally these symptoms lead to loss of consciousness and to death by respiratory arrest. The feeling of euphoria may be absent after the first few doses of cocaine. For this reason cocaine addicts who want to proselytize, and this unfortunately happens very frequently, always make sure of warning their victims that they will not experience pleasurable sensations until after four to six trials of sniffing.

The physical and psychological effects of cocaine on sexual function are of particular importance. According to my own observations, as well as those of many other authors, they differ radically from one sex to the other. In women there is, without exception, an increase in both the physical and psychological components of sexual drive. There is an exaggerated sensitivity to sexual stimuli with its concomitant desires and fantasies. Sexually, the subjects experience both pleasurable sensations and the need for satisfaction, and this applies even to young girls who have never had such feelings or needs before. The sense of modesty disappears and, with her critical judgment set aside, the woman often makes direct sexual advances to any man who happens to be present, regardless of his personality, of the circumstances and of the possible consequences. During sexual intercourse, orgasms, although of short duration, are multiple, and therefore sexual pleasure is greatly increased. This fact is often used to seduce young girls. In the case of women who have discovered this fact by chance, it can become the stimulus for the development of cocaine addiction. This is why, generally speaking, prostitutes or sexually licentious women are especially prone to like cocaine. Because of their intense libido and the response that they evoke in their sexual partners, women who are addicted to cocaine are specially sought out by men who associate with these circles. Through contagion, imitation or curiosity, these men, in turn, run the risk of becoming addicted to cocaine and of rapidly losing their sexual potency. The fact that, under the influence of cocaine, previously normal women often develop lesbian inclinations can, at least superficially, be explained thus: in the rather limited circles these women frequent, the men, who are also addicted to cocaine, are not able, because of their diminished sexual potency, to satisfy the women's libido which is further stimulated by the erotic fantasies provoked by the environment. Thus, substitute homosexual liaisons, capable of providing boundless erotic satisfaction, often develop among these women. But the lesbian relationships vanish rapidly once a normal man becomes available. It should be added, however, that in some cases, among both women and men (see below), cocaine, by diminishing normal inhibitions, can bring to the fore, either actively or passively, latent and unconscious perverted tendencies.

An academic, trained in psychology, has told me that, when he questioned a series of cocaine addicts on the influences of the drug on sexuality, the women unanimously felt that the effect was highly positive, while only two men gave the same answer. One of the latter, a homosexual, was quite emphatic, claiming that a single dose was sufficient to stimulate his sexual appetite. It goes without saying that this type of evidence does not allow for any firm conclusions as to the cause of the phenomena under discussion. Are we dealing simply with an elimination of the inhibitions normally present in the sober state, or is it necessary to invoke other factors? Here is what the same individual wrote to me about a sexual experience he once had with one of the most seductive female cocaine addicts of the place where he lived: "After a night of sexual prowesses, compared to which the seven labors of Hercules were a mere nothing, I fell asleep, only to be immediately awakened by the renewed demands of my insatiable partner. I was able to verify on myself the degree to which cocaine renders women incapable of achieving sexual relaxation. Orgasm follows orgasm, each one further increasing the intensity of the desire. The most sexually potent man must eventually give up the hope of being able to satisfy such a woman. There was nothing left to do but to flee in self- preservation."

In general, the effect of cocaine on the sexuality of the male is quite different. In this regard, men show, for the most part, a dissociation between the psychological and the physical factors of sexual function. Almost all patients state that, under the influence of cocaine, they experience a clear-cut diminution of sexual potency. At first, erection occurs fairly normally, but ejaculation time becomes very prolonged, sometimes reaching half an hour or even an hour. Accordingly, the patients claim to experience more prolonged pleasure and wrongly see this as an enhancement of their sexual potency. As the addiction becomes more deeply entrenched, the capacity for erection decreases and eventually disappears completely. But these patients are still able to ejaculate even in the absence of erection, following repeated and prolonged stimulation. Since coitus is not possible, this implies recourse to a great variety of perverted practices. The psychological component of sexuality remains, on the other hand, very active, and the patients often show a tendency to indulge in obscene fantasies which they share and match with each other. This must be seen as the source of the fantastic orgies which have so often been described. Some cocaine addicts indulge in this kind of orgy all alone by giving to their fantasies an hallucinatory reality of primarily optical character. They can do this with great ease. In this respect, an observant physician has given me the following description of his experiences under the influence of cocaine:

> In my imagination I let the doors open to allow in an extraordinarily beautiful woman to whom I first spoke (without having true auditory hallucinations; I had only visual and somatic hallucinations); I then undressed her, and finally had intercourse with her. During this repeated imaginary coitus I could vividly feel my penis entering the vagina and had a sensation of voluptuous pleasure in the loins and penis. This happened 30 times in one night although, of course, without ejaculation. My heart rate, already accelerated, would go up to 140 per minute after each imaginary coitus. At the same time, I would look at pictures and postcards and was able, at will, to enlarge the individuals represented in them, to identify them as friends or simple acquaintances, to have intercourse with them, or to make them have intercourse with each other. My hallucinations at that time never had a perverted content. As my states of cocaine intoxication became more frequent, my hallucinations became more limited to the sexual area, until one fine day the perversions also made their appearance. The feelings of voluptuousness became weaker and weaker, and the images followed each other more quickly than at the beginning. The sexual perversions finally reached such proportions that from then on I was able to see myself as a woman. I would see myself quite willingly as a prostitute having intercourse with several men at the same time, and I dreamed of nothing but sodomy, masochism and sadism. At a later stage, I was always seized by an attack of narcissism at the beginning of the intoxication, and I would stand in front of the mirror and dislocate my limbs in order to be able to practise fellatio on myself. At the same time, I was able to see at will in the image reflected in the mirror either a man or a woman and to have intercourse with either. I was at the time an attending physician in a hospital, and it often happened that when I was in one of these states

> the nurse on call would come to knock on my door to ask for advice or instructions. I would answer without opening the door, telling her to do this or that, to give an injection, for example, and to the extent that I was eventually able to check, my answers were appropriate and reasonable.

We can therefore conclude that, in general, the physical manisfestations of sexuality are stimulated in women and inhibited in men. On the psychological side there is generally an exaggeration of the libido and the erotic imagination is stimulated in both men and women. Finally, the latter phenomena are less consistent than the former due to large quantitative as well as qualitative individual variations in the psychological reactions to drugs. The difference between the sexes in the physical sexual response can be explained, in my opinion, as can most of the other physical symptoms already mentioned, on the basis of the selective stimulation by cocaine of the sympathetic nervous system.

It was Walthard who called my attention to this fact as a result of his studies on the relationship between the nervous system and the sexual organs of the female. According to W.H. Gaskell (1920), stimulation of the sympathetic system in man results in the constriction of the arteries of the *corpora cavernosa* of the penis, making erection impossible. We further know, from anatomical studies in animals, that there are muscle fibers innervated by the sympathetic system that make up a depressor muscle of the penis which actively prevents erection. It is likely that similar muscle fibers exist in man which, when the sympathetic system is stimulated, prevent the stiffening of the penis[11]. On the contrary, stimulation of the sympathetic system in women activates sexual function. The sensitivity of the whole clitoral region is increased, as well as the muscular reactivity of the uterus. This explains the more rapid and frequent attainment of orgasm at the slightest stimulus. Although it is true that cocaine prevents the blood from flowing into the erectile tissue of the female also, her sexual response is not significantly diminished because of the particular structure of the female genitalia. The action of the sympathetic system in this process is mediated by the inferior mesenteric ganglion. The same mechanism is responsible for the retention of urine often observed during the excitatory stage of cocaine intoxication. We know, in this respect, that the muscles of

[11] Ed. note: These concepts of the effects of sympathetic innervation on male sexual function are not fully in accord with present-day knowledge.

the sphincters of the bladder and anus are innervated by the sympathetic system while the antagonistic dilator muscles are innervated by the parasympathetic system.

Many authors, including myself, have been struck by the high proportion of homosexual men among cocaine addicts. As opposed to the effects of cocaine on heterosexuals, these individuals often experience enhancement of sexual excitation and potency in the physical sense. If this difference is real it could be interpreted, according to Steinach, by invoking the presence of gonads of the female type in homosexual men. Because of the importance of this question, I have endeavored to study it more closely by gathering the testimony of cocaine addicts. It is well known that we still lack solid evidence on the causes of homosexuality. Some workers believe that it is a type of neurotic manifestation produced during youth and reject the concept of a constitutional factor, while others attribute to the latter a fundamental role in the origin of this sexual anomaly. According to my own findings, the answer lies somewhere between these two extremes. In most cases, homosexuality, generally involving bisexuality, at least from a psychological point of view, would be due to some neurotic factor arising at an early age in individuals with a predominantly neurotic constitution. This includes some cases in which hereditary and other physical factors play an important role, and which are refractory to any attempt at therapeutic intervention. If what homosexuals tell us about the influence of cocaine is true, it would be in these serious constitutional cases where cocaine would produce an especially marked increase in sexual potency, while this would be rarer and less intense in the so-called intermediate or acquired neurotic types. But the evidence available to me, carefully analyzed from this point of view, has failed to confirm this hypothesis. Meanwhile Steinach's ideas, despite some confirmatory work, have proven inapplicable to intermediate cases. In this respect, attention should be called, for example, to the observations of Schinz and Slotopolsky (1925). It is known that, generally speaking, homosexuals are not very truthful and, when cocaine addiction is superimposed, their statements should be mistrusted even more. My own research in this area allows me to emphasize the role of a factor largely ignored till now. Confirmed sexual perverts are, for the most part, unable to give free expression to their impulses because of the psychological and social obstacles which they encounter in life. When they become cocaine addicts their situation improves, so to speak, in two ways. On the one hand, the internal inhibitions that previously prevented them from giving vent to their inclinations are eliminated and, on the other, they find among cocaine addicts, who, as opposed to morphine addicts, like to socialize, individuals who lend themselves more or less passively to the satisfaction of their sexual needs. This is why homosexuals are particularly attracted to cocaine-using circles, a fact which is quite independent of the psychopathology predisposing them to all sorts of deviant behaviors. If one is not satisfied with the vague statements of these patients with respect to the enhancement of their sexual potency by cocaine, and one probes more deeply, one finds that they achieve sexual satisfaction very rarely from coitus or similar acts. Instead, they resort to all sorts of perverted means which do not require erection as such. For all these and probably other reasons, it would be foolhardy, in the present state of our knowledge, to conclude that there is a real increase in sexual potency in homosexual cocaine addicts, and to derive from this evidence any support for Steinach's views.

These considerations lead to a phenomenon which has been observed by many authors including myself, to wit, that under the influence of cocaine homosexual tendencies and practices become manifest even in heterosexuals. This is very common among women under the effect of cocaine. We have already noted this fact and tried to explain it on the grounds that the men whom female cocaine addicts meet in their environment are unable to satisfy their exaggerated erotic needs and that this impels them to seek lesbian pleasures. Psychological observations on prostitutes have shown, moreover, that this type of substitute sexual satisfaction can occur without resort to intoxications of any kind.

Reference was made above, to the work of Norbert Marx (1923) in which he describes three cases of homosexuality occurring under the influence of cocaine and attributed to the suppression of inhibitions acting against this partial propensity. Fränkel (1923), on the other hand, claims that he has never seen a true change of direction of sexual inclinations. He believes that homosexual behavior in these patients is determined by their environment and suggestibility, being quite superficial and lacking deep psychological roots. Aschaffenburg (1925) has recently described the case of a 42-year-old man who had been using large doses of cocaine for five years, occasionally taking as much as 5 g a day, and whose history contained nothing abnormal with respect to his sexual behavior. The patient claimed that, a year after commencing the use of cocaine, his sexual potency began to diminish while his libido increased. He had all sorts of sexual fantasies preceded by erotic sensations in his genitals. He would then masturbate to relieve tension, without, however, achieving erections or ejaculations. Some years later the patient experienced an extension of the erotogenic areas, his buttocks and anus responding voluptuously to the touch. This was soon followed by homosexual fantasies always crude in content. Thus the patient would imagine himself in the company of a homosexual who masturbated him, or who would perform coitus *intra femora* on him. Mutual masturbation fantasies were rare. Frightened by the increasing frequency of these experiences the patient decided to consult a physician who supported him in his decision to give up the use of cocaine. All these phenomena disappeared from the moment that he discontinued the drug. Aschaffenburg believes that the enlargement of the erotogenic zone to the anus and beyond was related to the toxic stimulation of the peripheral nerves, and that it facilitated the appearance of homosexual fantasies involving this area of the body. This author also rejects Fränkel's view that, in cases of this type, one is dealing simply with superficial alterations of orientation of sex drive. He feels that this is not an adequate explanation, although it may apply to patients with bisexual tendencies.

Joël and Fränkel (1925) have often been told by their patients that their homosexual erotic inclinations appeared only after they truly began to abuse cocaine. These authors have also found among their cases examples of heterosexuals who, under the influence of cocaine, committed homosexual acts or showed sadistic, masochistic or voyeuristic tendencies.

According to my own observations, the interpretations of the deviant sexual behavior of cocaine addicts given by various authors are not mutually exclusive but, on the contrary, complementary to each other. Each applies to a particular group of cases, or accounts for some particular feature of a given case[12]. The oppressive atmosphere, full of erotic fantasies, in which cocaine addicts live, and the environment that renders men impotent to various degrees while enhancing their mutual suggestibility, provides an excellent medium for the development of every possible perversion of human sexuality. In addition, it is not unlikely that the phenomena of local and paragenital excitation, perhaps of neurotic origin, but most importantly the suppression of inhibitions under the action of the drug, also play some role. It is clear, nevertheless, that the characteristics of these cases tend to confirm to a certain degree Freud's concept, according to which even normal men have infantile perverted tendencies repressed by upbringing and by the influence of the social

[12] Author's note: Joël and Fränkel have recently published a paper (*Deut. Med. Wschr.* No. 38, 1925) in which, correctly in my opinion, they explore and develop the same concept.

environment. These tendencies come to the fore at the first opportunity provided by any type of morbid state. But the particular character that these tendencies will assume in any individual case cannot be determined except through a most detailed and thorough psychological examination. In summary, we are dealing with an obvious and visible manifestation of perverted latent and unconscious tendencies which have their counterpart in evidence provided by some types of alcoholics. It is evident, in any case, that at present there is no support for the hypothesis that cocaine is capable of actively creating homosexual tendencies through a specific action on endocrine or psychological functions. Aschaffenburg was correct in noting that the homosexual fantasies of his patient were crudely sexual and in no way represented the need for affection from others of his own sex which is so characteristic of a genuine homosexual predisposition. Schilder believes that toxic agents have affinity for specific psychic systems and produce changes in the libido, and that cocaine artificially reinforces the inherent homosexual components.

In his book on cocaine psychoses, Piouffle (1919) states that small doses of the drug taken in the initial stages of the addiction are capable of eliminating inhibitions that preclude normal sexual activity in patients suffering from anxiety, or obsessions and phobias. This would lead, even in males, to an apparent and transitory stimulation of sexual activity which, however, is soon followed by a decrease in sexual potency. Many cocaine addicts often rely on the initial effect to recommend the drug as an aphrodisiac and thus recruit new cocaine devotees. The same author refers to instances of exhibitionism caused by cocaine addiction. In these cases the exhibitionism did not take place indiscriminately and in public, but only during the orgies that take place in cocaine-using circles. According in Piouffle, this type of exhibitionism cannot be differentiated from similar behavior seen in alcoholics and in some cases of general paresis of the insane[13]. He has also reported a case in which sadistic tendencies became manifest following the abuse of cocaine. While under the effects of the drug, the subject, who had never before exhibited such behavior, would torture and kill small cats.

As we have already said, the use of cocaine has spread rapidly through the demimonde of all countries. Besides the aphrodisiac action of the drug on women, the need to forget and escape from painful and depressing reality has contributed to the propagation of the habit. Cocaine addiction is particularly common among both

13 Ed. note: A form of tertiary neurosyphilis.

men and women in artistic circles, and among female dancers in whom the drug stimulates psychomotor activity and eliminates feelings of fatigue and the need to sleep. Since, on the other hand, cocaine increases thirst, one often finds among these subjects cocaine addiction combined with alcoholism, leading to particularly complicated and serious states of intoxication. Cocaine addiction is considerably rarer among the inmates of houses of ill repute. For selfish and self-serving reasons the proprietors are strongly against the overt or covert introduction of the drug into their establishments. This is no doubt due, in part, to fear of the police but, above all, because prostitutes under the influence of cocaine lose interest in exploiting their clients financially. On the other hand, we know from recent reports that some prostitutes, particularly those of southern origin, have developed a technique consisting of applying a strong cocaine solution to the glans penis of their clients in order to prolong ejaculation time even in individuals exhibiting normal sexual potency. This procedure is apparently very effective since it can postpone ejaculation for one hour or longer, while at the same time heightening the psychological aspects of the man's libido. These "specialists" therefore gain special favor with their clients. It goes without saying that this is a dangerous procedure in that it can, in the case of some men, lead to a cocaine habit or to addiction if resorted to very frequently.

Among the other actions of cocaine on the genital organs we should mention the effects of the drug on menstruation. At first it is more copious but regular; only after prolonged intoxication does it become infrequent or stop completely. This is quite different from what happens in morphine addiction, in which amenorrhea is often observed from the beginning. On the other hand, pregnancy is very rare among women addicted to cocaine, even among those who do not resort to any contraceptive measures. If pregnancy occurs, it rarely goes to term, and miscarriages are very common among these women. This is why observations on the ill effects of cocaine on the newborn are very rare. I have never seen a case myself. I have already referred to a paper published in France concerning the offspring of a cocaine addict. The first child, born before the father began to use cocaine, was healthy. The second, born at the beginning of the addiction, although constitutionally weak, was of normal intelligence, while the last two, born at the height of the addiction, were mentally retarded. Even though degeneration of the germ cells can probably be caused by chronic cocaine use, a single case of this type is not enough to provide clear-cut evidence of such action. We need further data in this area which should not be very difficult to obtain in the large cities where cocaine addiction is always common.

At the beginning of the addiction the action of cocaine on the gastrointestinal tract, mediated via the sympathetic system, includes an increase in salivary and gastric secretion, and in motility[14]. The patients often complain of rumbling noises in the intestines and of a subjective sensation of pronounced intra-abdominal movements. The stools are soft and viscous as opposed to the vagotonic disturbances seen in other psychiatric patients. But after heavy chronic use of cocaine, one often observes, as in the case of other nervous conditions, sympathetic inhibition, with impairment of bowel movements or stubborn constipation. Difficulties in micturition, frequently seen in cocaine addicts as a result of contraction of the sphincter of the bladder, can lead to renal complications with polyuria or, in some cases, to anuria.

The peripheral nerve palsies, so frequently seen in alcohol intoxication and lead poisoning, do not occur in cocaine addiction. The tremors seen during the initial excitatory phase of intoxication are not accompanied, as is the case in alcoholism, by generalized ataxic phenomena. One generally observes, on the contrary, that the increased psychomotor activity is accompanied by a remarkable degree of motor dexterity. Individuals under the influence of cocaine are capable of balancing and acrobatic prowesses requiring a level of muscular tension and dexterity of which they are incapable in the normal state. One of my patients, while fully hallucinating, was able to climb up the front of a multiple-storey house with the facility of a cat.

Because of the absence of ataxic disturbances, the handwriting of these patients does not show evidence of tremors. During the state of intoxication the pressure of the pen on the paper diminishes, individual strokes become more widely separated, letters and words are left unfinished and, as the state of excitation increases, the patient covers the paper with illegible scribbles. The pattern of writing changes from moment to moment, the lines are slanted upwards and downwards and, as the patient continues to write, the letters become increasingly larger (manic excitability). In states of mental confusion the patients smear portions of the sheet of paper and intersperse illegible strokes with superficial and incomprehensible drawings. When persistent paralytic disturbances of central origin develop, the handwriting reveals signs of ataxia in addition to the features described above. Patients suffering from hallucinations and delusions of invention cover whole pages with the designs of

[14] Ed. note: *Sic*; intestinal motility and secretion are stimulated by parasympathetic innervation, not by sympathetic.

their complex inventions, followed by brief but totally inadequate explanations.

These disturbances are not, however, pathognomonic of cocaine intoxication per se but are, rather, manifestations of the patient's manic, confused, pseudoparetic or paranoid state.

Piouffle has collected a number of samples of handwriting of cocaine addicts which he reproduced in his monograph. I have borrowed four examples from his series and have added five of my own (see Figures 1-9).

The speech of cocaine addicts does not generally show any characteristic features. It is true that, during intoxication, it is often quick and precipitate, in keeping with the manic state of the patient, while it becomes slow and ponderous during the states of depression. In grave cases of intoxication with organic brain damage accompanied by paralytic phenomena, the patients sometimes are incapable of articulating syllables properly, giving rise to a certain amount of stammering. But omission of syllables, or other serious dysarthrias, are never observed.

1. Disturbances of Perception

General Comments on Sensory Illusions

Cocaine has the property of producing hallucinations of various sensory modalities in man. The observations made in experiments on dogs by Bravetta and Invernizzi (1922, 1923) and by myself warrant the conclusion that cocaine exerts the same action in higher animals. Following the injection of cocaine, dogs bark at specific ordinary spots of their surroundings with such intensity, and in such a state of excitation, that they convey a very strong impression of experiencing visual hallucinations. We know that drugs which have an effect on the nervous system, regardless of other similarities, differ essentially from one another with respect to the ease with which they can provoke hallucinations. Alcoholic intoxication, for example, seldom gives rise to hallucinations due directly to the alcohol itself. But when the prolonged use of alcohol gives rise to complex toxic disturbances such as *delirium tremens*, the picture presents the well-known sensory illusions accompanied by neuritic irritative phenomena, especially in the optic nerve. On the other hand, the tendency to auditory hallucinations seen in alcoholic psychosis must be attributed, at least in most cases, to the role of factors of schizophrenic nature. Although the opiates clearly stimulate the imagination, the fantasies that they produce are never perceived as real. It should be recalled in this respect that these drugs do not stimulate the sensory nerves. Atropine and mescaline, on the contrary, readily produce sensory illusions which differ from those produced by cocaine only in that they are accompanied by either more serious disturbances of consciousness or by more intense deliria than those seen in cocaine intoxication (Beringer, 1923; Morgenstern, 1923).

Delirium tremens and the hallucinatory states of hysteria can be considered, at present, as representing the two extremes of the phenomenon under discussion, corresponding to opposite causes. The hallucinations of *delirium tremens* have the origin in a toxic irritation of the visual organs. At first they are often of a rudimentary character and can be considerably enhanced by pressure on the eyeball. At the beginning they are small, very mobile and totally devoid of any catathymic characteristics (Maier, 1912). In other words, they are not closely related to any structured complex of visions with affective content. In cases where this occurs, as well as in those that present catathymic auditory hallucinations, it can be confirmed, once the delirium has disappeared, that one is in the presence of schizophrenic phenomena. Contrary to the hallucinations of alcoholic deliria, the sensory illusions of hysterical character always have a central psychic origin, are related to significant psychological content and are closely associated with the personality of the patient. Schizophrenic hallucinations can be placed between these two extremes and, although often related to a toxic process, this is much more complex and central than the process involved in patients suffering from alcoholic deliria.

What is characteristic of cocaine hallucinations is that, generally, at least at the beginning, they are produced by peripheral stimulation of the corresponding sensory organs which is recognized by the subjects and which can also be objectively demonstrated. Furthermore, like the hallucinations of alcoholic deliria, they can be provoked easily by suggestion originating either in other drug users who are equally prey to hallucinations or in the patient himself. The main difference between cocaine and alcoholic hallucinations is that, in the most typical cases of the former, the content of the sensory illusions is determined by psychological factors which have emotional tone. It is evident, therefore, that, in this respect, the hallucinations produced by cocaine lie somewhere between those of *delirium tremens*, which are of purely toxic origin, and those seen in hysteria, which are of exclusive psychogenic origin. This corresponds roughly to the combination of organic and psychological factors seen in schizophrenia. The role of the toxic factor is most clearly evident in the area of cutaneous sensitivity where the influence of psychogenic factors on the hallucinations is least likely to occur. From the point of view of content, the tactile sensations consisting of feelings of the presence of animals under the skin are highly primitive paresthetic phenomena. But, in the visual and auditory hallucinations, the psychological factors play a far greater role. Because the disturbances of consciousness in cocaine addiction, except in the most serious cases, are slight, and also because there is a marked increase in suggestibility, it is not surprising that the hallucinations can shift from one sensory area to another. The animals which at first are only felt under the skin, eventually become visible, and can even reveal their presence through sounds and noises. After some time these hallucinatory visions also begin to talk and sing and, in other cases, visual sensations are added to the original auditory hallucinations and illusions.

In general, the hallucinations produced by cocaine have all the characteristics of true perceptions. My patients invariably smiled condescendingly when I asked them whether they were sure that it was not, after all, simply a question of particularly vivid fantasies. Generally, the transition from paresthesia to hallucination is abrupt, without an intermediary pseudo-hallucinatory phase. It is a remarkable fact that, for as long as the patients retain some clearness of consciousness—and this is frequently the case even in severe states of intoxication—they can usually rectify their sensory illusions to some degree. But, while the patients state that they are morbid illusions which they do not hesitate to relate to the influence of cocaine under which they find themselves, they are still convinced of their reality, and behave according to their compelling nature. This is most likely a question of dissociation of consciousness. One of my female patients, for example, while walking by the station at Zürich one evening suddenly heard the voice of one of her friends telling her that a great misfortune had befallen her in Geneva and that she should go there right away. She admitted to an aquaintance that it was impossible to hear a voice at such a great distance, but this did not prevent her from getting on the first train to Geneva, without any luggage. Having arrived there, after taking large doses of cocaine during the trip, she suddenly started to hear and see people pursuing her on the street, to prevent her from getting to her friend. She went to a police station to ask for protection but was dismissed after she herself agreed that her ideas were unreal. Her imaginary persecutors appeared again very soon after she walked back into the street and, in order to avoid them, she jumped into the lake. This partial correction of the hallucination is particularly reminiscent of the behavior of some patients suffering from alcoholic psychosis in whom one must also recognize a combination of toxic and catathymic disturbances which is, in this case, of schizophrenic nature (Wolfensberger, 1923). When the cocaine intoxication reaches a certain level of intensity, this partial insight generally disappears, and the patient is totally dominated by the hallucinations.

Cocaine hallucinations are often characterized, at least at the beginning, by their extreme diminutiveness. This phenomenon, although less regular and less marked, is also seen in *delirium tremens*. This is unquestionably related to the paresthesias that affect the sensory nerves. The patients perceive the tactile hallucinations in the form of specks and of tiny animals located under the skin. In the case of visual hallucinations the patients see very small people and objects and even, in the case of auditory hallucinations, the sensations are very slight and hardly audible. As the intoxication becomes more vivid, the corresponding objects increase in volume, size and amplitude and often acquire, at the beginning of the withdrawal reaction, gigantic and frightening proportions. It is my impression that the progressive increase in dosage was slower when cocaine used to be taken subcutaneously than after the habit of snorting it was introduced. This difference, which may be due to purely extraneous reasons, perhaps explains the fact that the micro-hallucinations following the administration of moderate doses were described so often and in such large numbers in the case histories of the period of subcutaneous use. The patients of that era often made use of optical instruments in order to enlarge the micro-hallucinations. Since most of these patients were physicians, the microscope played an important role, which was either real when it was actually used to examine vision or the skin or when it was claimed that the phenomena could only be detected under the microscope. This was formerly described as "microscopic cocaine hallucinations." As a result of the general spread in the habit of snorting cocaine, our patients are no longer exclusively or, even mostly, physicians, and these phenomena have disappeared, but it is still not rare to encounter at least some descriptions of Lilliputian hallucinations occurring, especially at the beginning of the intoxication.

There are large individual variations in the speed of onset and in the frequency of hallucinatory phenomena. Some heavy chronic users of cocaine may develop disturbances of consciousness and states of hyper-excitation without hallucinations, while, in other cases, they may appear following two or three consecutive doses. The sensory area involved may also vary from case to case. Tactile hallucinations are almost always the first to appear in cocaine addicts who take the drug subcutaneously, while they are less frequent, and appear much later in the case of sniffers, among whom visual, and sometimes auditory hallucinations or sensory illusions are the first to develop. The patient of Mayer-Gross (1920) referred to above, for example, showed only auditory hallucinations despite being a heavy user, while the patient described by Aschaffenburg (1925) experienced no hallucinations at all. The explanation for these individual differences will no doubt have to await a thorough study of the constitutional psychological characteristics of a sufficient number of detoxified patients. Such studies have not been done to date. According to Schröder (1912), the hallucinations of alcoholics are in general not compatible with the picture of the world that they have in the normal state, and tend to substitute for it. The same does not appear to be the case among cocaine addicts, whose touch with reality remains normal and whose hallucinations are rigorously determined by it.

According to Schilder, hallucinations of color and of movement are frequent among cocaine addicts. The same author also claims that patients suffering from amentia often see colored surfaces stretching in space which bear no relationship to objects in the real world. Although I have never seen the phenomena described by Schilder among my own patients, I do not question that they may occur in some cases. If confirmed, this observation would be of considerable theoretical interest.

a) Visual Hallucinations

As already stated, the hallucinations, particularly at the beginning, are characterized in most cases by their diminutiveness. While the visions in alcoholic deliria are generally black or of rather indistinct color tone, cocaine addicts always claim that their illusory images are either normal or particularly vivid in color. Like those of alcoholics, however, at the beginning they usually occur at dusk or at night. Real objects assume bizarre shapes. The patient sees in a leaf, for example, the face of his beloved or of his mother, or he sees in the palm of his hand the image of a bear which, because of his childhood experience, he finds particularly frightening. Or again, he may see inscriptions in the form of advertisements on the back of his hand which evoke in him highly emotional states. Familiar heads, which never stop following him with their eyes, appear on the wallpaper. The visions of cocaine addicts, as opposed to those which occur in *delirium tremens*, are most frequently motionless and unchangeable, and reappear in subsequent toxic episodes in the same way and under the same guise. When the patient is in a state of psychomotor excitation, or when he is in the company of other cocaine addicts with whom he exchanges information and suggestions about their respective hallucinations, the latter eventually become mobile and follow the patient everywhere he goes. Finally, they stop appearing exclusively in the dark and can then also occur in the middle of the day and in the brightest of lights. The people in the street appear extremely small and the patient claims to know them and to detect on their faces pleasant or hostile expressions directed at him. Sometimes the whole scene, including the streets and everything that stirs in them, shrinks so that the patient receives from the world nothing but a Lilliputian image which he seems to find pleasant. Later, everything can become greatly enlarged. This change in the size of real objects suggests specific disturbances of accommodation which are independent of the effects of cocaine. This question deserves further study.

Based on the observation of numerous cases, Piouffle distinguishes several varieties of visual hallucinations, including stereotypic, cinematographic, microptic and megaloptic hallucinations. We have already referred to stereotypic illusions characterized by their immobility and unchangeability, as well as by the fact that they always occur at the same time and in the same place during different toxic reactions. Once they turn mobile, their movements immediately become very rapid and their shape changes in a very short time. The patients see them as disembodied shadows projected on the walls, for example, so that the subject has the impression of being in a motion picture theater, except for the fact that the images are in color. Sometimes they too are characteristically small. While the hallucinating cocaine addict is generally active and undergoing a state of marked psychomotor excitation, one can also observe, especially in chronic cases of intoxication, states in which the subjects feel physically trammelled and try to rest lying down in the greatest passivity. The oneiric visions then assume the character of unreal fantasy-like dreams which fit very aptly Piouffle's classification. It is because of this characteristic that microptic visions appear to be of particular interest to the patients who say that they have seen people they know being no more than 20 or 25 centimeters in height. We have already mentioned the opposite phenomenon.

The following examples illustrate how the visions originate in paresthesias. A patient could see isolated dots in the dark which got nearer to him as he fixed his attention on them. This was followed by the appearance of the most gorgeous shapes. All of a sudden, a point became luminous and lighted the whole scene when the patient could see a multitude of known people and objects. When, blinded by the light, he turned his head for an instant, everything disappeared. Another patient could see on the ceiling luminous electric signs which then turned into frightening visual phenomena. Another said that he could see butterflies, flames, the Lilliputian forms of known persons and snakes around his bed. It is of some interest that the patient who could see snakes was a very pronounced homosexual. Homosexual alcoholics in *delirium tremens* sometimes have this same content in their visions, a fact which is not surprising if one is familar with the characteristics of dreams described by Freud. A woman addicted to cocaine could see her mother, her lover or a well-known politician sitting in a tree which stood in front of her window at the clinic. These figures, none of which appeared to be more than 20 centimeters in height, spoke to her and answered her. The politician, whom she hated, would suddenly turn into a cow which bowed in front of her. She then saw, in the same place, a gigantic pair of shoes which she very much wanted, and next to it a woman whom she knew, who was looking in astonishment at the shoes, and a Saint Bernard dog. On a dark cloud she could see Mount Vesuvius in full activity and all its surroundings. Tea leaves in her cup would become the legs of flies which she believed she had had prescribed for her against the effects of cocaine. She could no longer go to the toilet because it was full of people spying on her. Another patient could see every night a non-existent very brilliant star which he could follow with his eyes and which would tell him that all the Rhinegold belonged to him and to his beloved. At night he could see beautiful yellow and green lights everywhere.

Among the hallucinations of cocaine addicts, the visions occur most frequently during the euphoric stage and generally have a sensuous flavor. But it goes without saying that they can also occur sometimes during the paranoid stages, when the symptoms of abstinence begin to develop, and that they can then become emotionally very unpleasant. Moreover, these hallucinations are the most susceptible to auto-suggestion or to suggestion from the environment. Some of our patients would say, for example: "Now I am going to see my mother, or my beloved," and the hallucination, with all the meaning of reality, would appear immediately and last for some time. During the acute intoxication, the physician can sometimes, as is the case with patients in alcoholic delirium (Liepmann's symptom), suggest hallucinations of this type by exerting slight pressure on the eyeballs.

b) Tactile Hallucinations

The transformation of cutaneous paresthesias into hallucinations, a phenomenon first described by Erlenmeyer (1886) and by

Magnan (1889, 1893), and referred to in the literature as "Magnan's symptom," has currently become, as already noted, a relatively rare occurrence. In my opinion, this is due to a change in the mode of administration from injections to sniffing. I have had under my care two physicians addicted to cocaine in whom the most marked symptoms were hallucinations of animals both over and under the skin. These patients, who had previously abused morphine, were in the habit of injecting cocaine all over the body. Despite the fact that Vallon and Bessiére (1914), among others, have never seen this symptom among their patients, I have clearly observed it in at least a third of mine. My observations are in agreement with the more recent reports of Piouffle (1919), Courtois-Suffit (1922) and Joël and Fränkel (1924). Erlenmeyer (1886) originally described cases with hallucinations of lice and bedbugs and we have observed the same phenomenon in cocaine sniffers. Piouffle (1919) has made the same observation in a patient who took cocaine by the rectum. Magnan's patients experienced first muscle twitchings and cramps, followed by sensations of tingling in the limbs, and of the pressure of little black worms on the tongue which they tried to remove with their fingers. Or, alternatively, they believed that their bodies were covered with microbes which swarmed all around them and they felt they itched so intensely that they scratched themselves until they pealed off the skin under which they claimed to find the stinging cocaine crystals. One of Piouffle's patients felt the presence of little bits of glass under his skin which he proceeded to dig out with needles and forceps. Another discovered under his skin the presence of "coccidia" whose characteristic mode of reproduction he proceeded to describe. Still another complained that he had fleas between the skin and the muscles, and foreign bodies in the nasal mucosa. Piouffle (1919) and Barbé and Bénoit (1911) relate all these phenomena to mild neurotic symptoms and feel that if one is observant enough, they can be seen, although perhaps less frequently, in states of intoxication produced by drugs other than cocaine. Recent studies on the *sequelae* of encephalitis, where neurotic elements are not rare, have revealed comparable phenomena in some cases. I have myself observed for a long time a case of post-encephalitic parkinsonism in which, following severe cutaneous itching, the patient came eventually to feel, and even to see, innumerable lice under his skin. Being a vagrant, he was thoroughly disinfected, despite the fact that an examination was negative. It was recognized only much later that the patient was suffering from hallucinations and he was then referred to a psychiatric hospital. The hallucinations disappeared once the itching was eliminated. One of my patients claimed that he, and many other cocaine addicts, experienced an unpleasant sensation as if the back of the neck were covered with crawling worms, following a few doses of cocaine. He was clearly aware that this sensation was unreal, and yet was unable to stop trying to remove with his hand the worms he felt were running over his skin. Another patient felt spiders running along the back of his neck and shoulders and kept on trying to chase them away with his hands. A physician experienced intense tickling under the skin, and having come to the conclusion that it was due to the presence of numerous larvae, he cut small pieces of skin, which, under microscopic examination, allowed him to see the larvae and the insects fly away. He discovered the same phenomenon in a large number of his own patients and, as he was a specialist in venereal diseases, he reached the conclusion that gonorrhea was due to the action of these insects and treated his patients by excising pieces of skin from various parts of the body. This remarkable method earned him considerable renown for a while. Besides the tactile hallucinations, this patient developed a systematized delusional picture and eventually a full-blown cocaine psychosis.

Further toxicological research will no doubt demonstrate if the type of tactile hallucination that we have just described occurs in intoxications due to other drugs. Be that as it may, we can conclusively say, based on the available evidence, that they occur more frequently in cocainism than in any other type of drug intoxication, although, on the other hand, they may be absent in severe states of cocaine addiction.

In my view, these hallucinations become easily associated, through auto-suggestion, with hallucinations of other sensory modalities: the patients soon see the supposed bugs under and on the skin, they hear them crawl, and one of my female patients suffered more from the smell than from the tactile sensations of her obsessive hallucinations.

c) Kinesthetic Hallucinations

It has been frequently observed that cocaine addicts make false judgments about the position of their bodies. While lying listlessly in bed, they feel they are walking around or believe they are flying. They feel the walls shifting in space, floors tilting, the body becoming lighter and lighter and the limbs becoming grotesquely elongated. I have personally experienced a brief state of cocaine intoxication, when a dentist gave me an injection of cocaine that must have penetrated a relatively major blood vessel. Together with alarming palpitations and dizziness, I had the sensation that my arms and legs had suddenly increased in length and were sticking out through the open window. Sensations of this type develop into the true feelings of depersonalization observed rather frequently in cocaine psychosis, especially of the oneiric type.

d) Sexual Hallucinations

These hallucinations, which are very frequent in schizophrenia and generally involve negative affect, are described by many cocaine addicts when asked about their subjective feelings. They are most frequently seen in men who present with an intensification of libido simultaneously with impotence. This constitutes a psychological state highly favorable for the appearance of hallucinations of this type, which occur when the subjects lie quietly in bed, even when they do not masturbate. From the consistent descriptions of numerous patients, I have come to the conclusion, however, that this is not always a question of purely imaginary sexual experiences. Rather, certain tactile stimuli applied to either primary or secondary erotogenic zones provoke very distinct sexual sensations and the patients experience an intense and often multiple orgasm accompanied by the corresponding body movements, but without erection or ejaculation. It may well be that, in these cases, local excitatory phenomena of a neurotoxic nature are responsible. Only one of my female patients described experiences of this type. Given the fact that sympathetic stimulation by cocaine produces different effects on sexual functions in men and women, it is not surprising that sexual hallucinations are far rarer in the latter than in the former.

e) Somatic Hallucinations of a Physical Nature

These hallucinations occur much more frequently in chronic cocaine users than do those due to sexual stimulation. I have been able to confirm their presence in many patients in whom medical examination both before drug use and after treatment rules out the possibility of schizophrenia. This fact is particularly important because such hallucinations are almost the rule in this type of psychosis. It is often possible to trace these hallucinations back to paresthesias, as in the case of the patient who first complains of tingling in the fingers, then of formication, and finally demands that the electric shocks be removed from his fingers. In connection with the latter sensation, the patient gradually gets to feel that an electric current has invaded his whole body and he attributes this to the hypnotic suggestion exerted upon him by his enemies. Somatic hallucinations generally disappear quickly following withdrawal and detoxication. One of my patients complained that the last moments he had left to live were being poisoned by torture with electric currents. He felt that his bed was in the middle of an electric field and he did not know where to go to avoid this torture.

f) Auditory Hallucinations

Auditory hallucinations, which generally begin as illusions, are very frequent in cocaine addicts. The level of auditory hypersensitivity in Mayer- Gross's patient was such that the cracking of a stick assumed the proportions of an explosion and the sound of the wind felt like the rumblings of a storm. The noise of a streetcar outside was at first perceived as such, but then suddenly turned into the sound of a marching multitude coming to attack him. He then heard with extraordinary vividness the front door of his house being battered down, then the sound of steps on the stairs, the attempts at breaking into his apartment and voices whispering to each other. The patient lay on guard for hours with a loaded revolver at the ready to shoot at the first intruder. But in many cases the hallucinations arise directly. At the beginning the hallucinations are rudimentary but, later, voices announce the news and the patient clearly distinguishes between male and female voices. Most often the voices belong to people he knows and whom he can name. Tirelli (1920) and Piouffle (1919) have observed patients who could hear dialogues as in the theater, a phenomenon that also occurs in alcoholic psychosis. I shall not question this claim even though, based on my own observations and on the literature, I believe that in most cases the "voices" talk directly to the patient about things of specific emotional meaning to him. These symptoms are, therefore, quite similar to those of schizophrenia from which they can hardly be distinguished, especially in severe cases of intoxication, even though some cocaine addicts are capable of a limited level of insight. The differential diagnosis can be established only after a detailed assessment of the morbid picture as a whole. The conclusion as to the possibility of a combination of cocaine addiction and schizophrenia can often be drawn with certainty only after the intoxication has been cured and a thorough evaluation of the pre-drug history has been made. The tendency to interpret, which is so frequently seen in cocaine addicts, is often illustrated by such assertions as that the walls and the roof of their house have been deliberately thinned out or perforated so that they can hear distinctly the voices of far-distant persons.

Isolated auditory hallucinations are more frequent than the

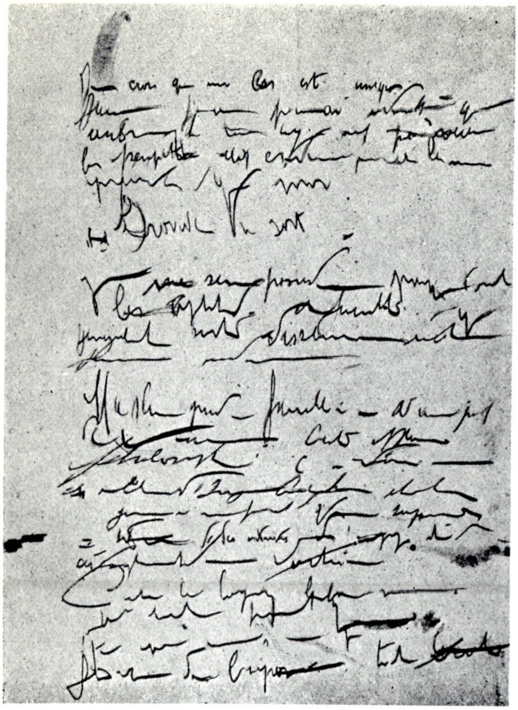

Fig. 1.
Handwriting of a cocaine user in a manic excited state, with obvious flight of ideas. With continuous writing, it became progressively more illegible. (From Piouffle, 1919).

Fig. 2.
Handwriting of the same patient as in Fig. 1, in a state of increasing mental confusion. (From Piouffle, 1919).

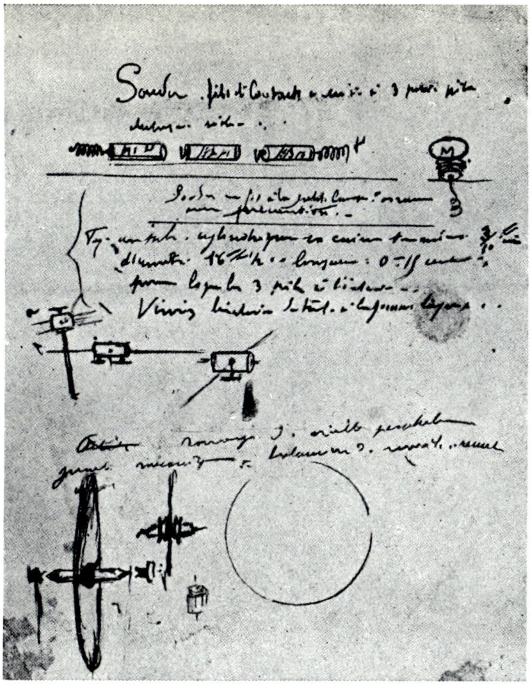

Fig. 3.
Document written by the same patient as in Fig. 1, in the stage of cocaine-induced delusions. It presents a device for annihilating enemy armies. (From Piouffle, 1919).

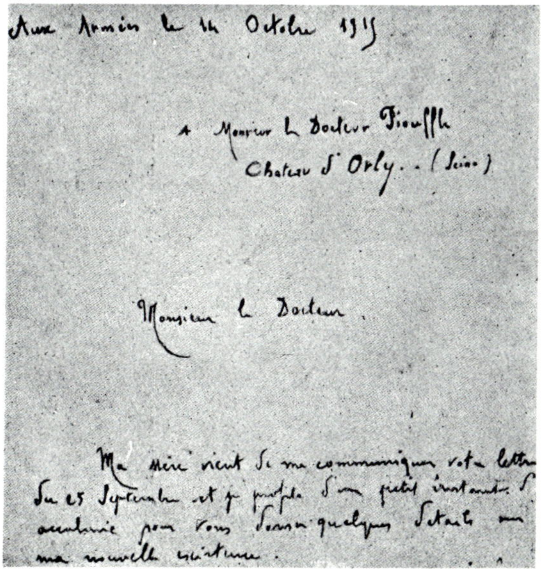

Aux Armées le 14 Octobre 1915

A Monsieur le Docteur Piouffle
Chateau d'Orly. (Seine)

Monsieur le Docteur.

Ma mère vient de me communiquer votre lettre du 25 Septembre et je profite d'un petit instant d'accalmie pour vous donner quelques détails sur ma nouvelle existence.

Fig. 4
Handwriting of the same patient as in Fig. 1, after recovery. (From Piouffle, 1919).

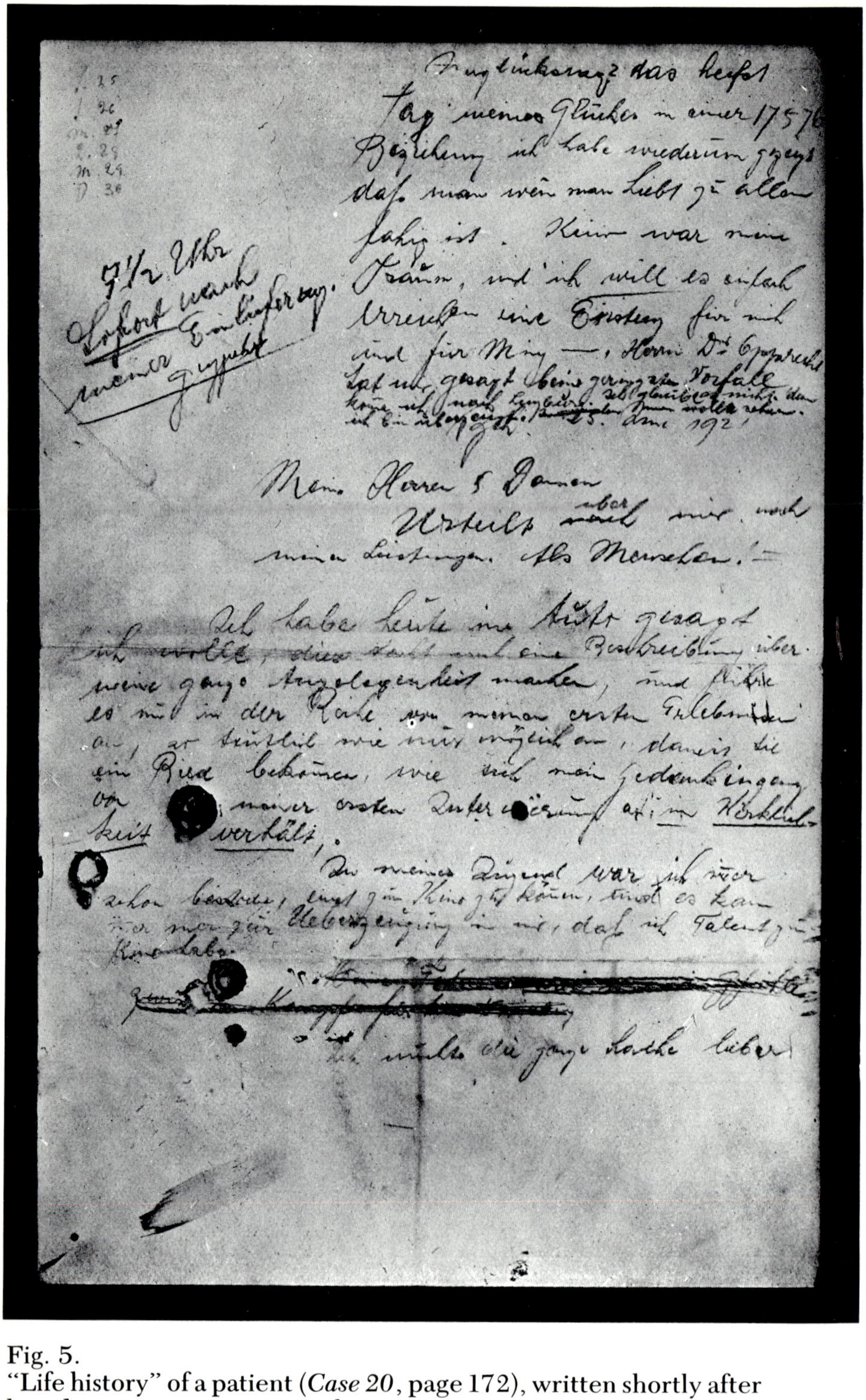

Fig. 5.
"Life history" of a patient (*Case 20*, page 172), written shortly after his admission in an acute euphoric manic state.

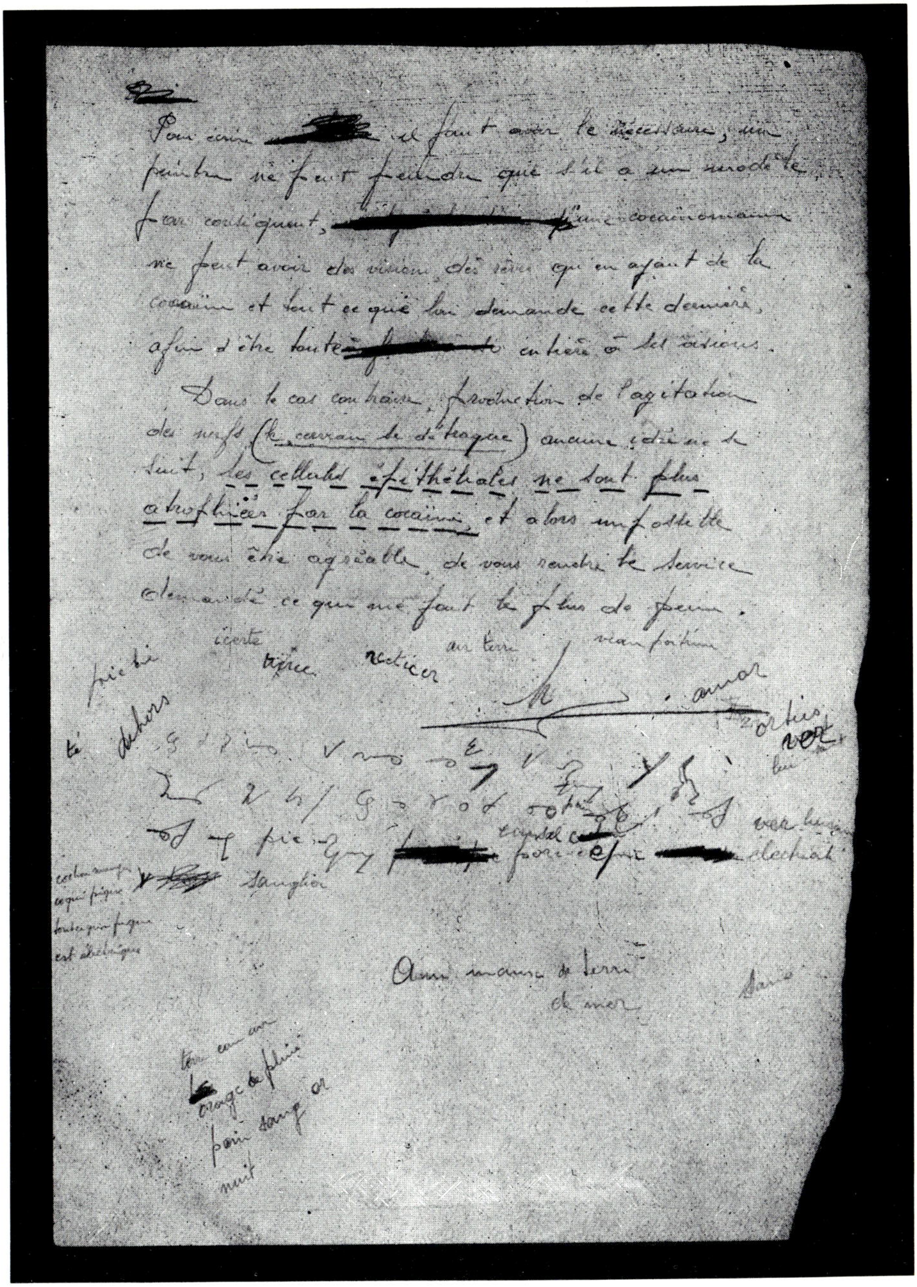

Pour ceci [redacted] il faut avoir le nécessaire, un peintre ne peut peindre que s'il a un modèle, par conséquent, [redacted] une cocaïnomane ne peut avoir des visions, des rêves qu'en ayant de la cocaïne et tout ce que lui demande cette dernière, afin d'être toute [redacted] entière à ses visions.

Dans le cas contraire, production de l'agitation des nerfs (le cerveau se détraque) aucune idée ne se suit, les cellules épithéliales ne sont plus atrophiées par la cocaïne et alors impossible de vous être agréable, de vous rendre le service demandé ce qui me fait le plus de peine.

Fig. 6.
"Life history" of a female cocaine addict (*Case 26*, page 186), written during a period of mild cocaine intoxication.

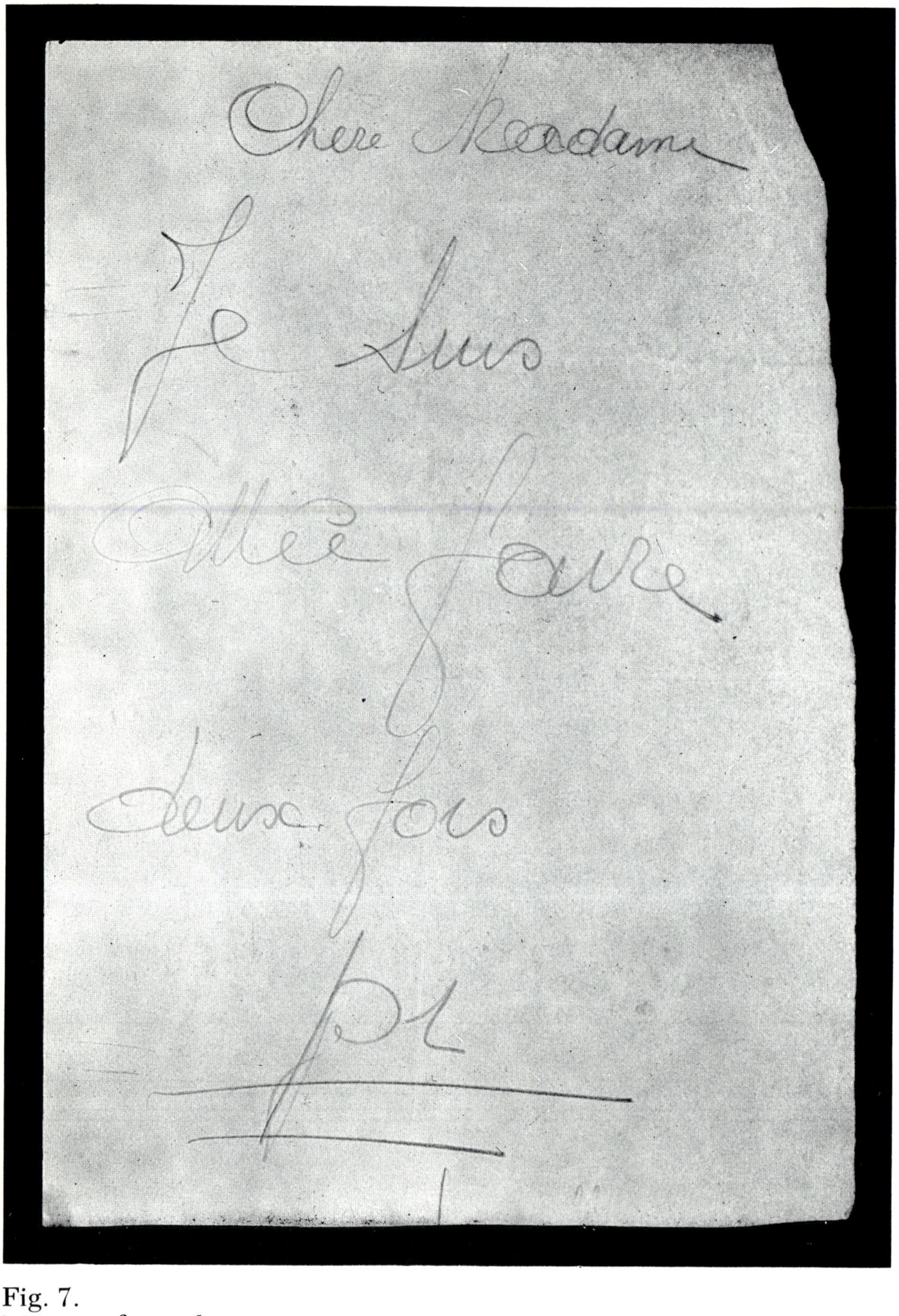

Fig. 7.
Message from the same patient as in Fig. 6 (*Case 26*), written to her guardian during a cocaine-induced episode of manic excitation. (Actual size of the sheet of paper: 34 x 23 cm).

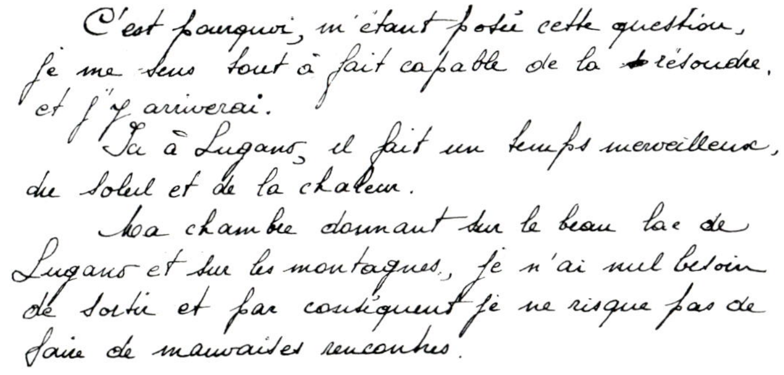

Fig. 8.
Handwriting of the same patient as in Fig. 6 (Case 26), after recovery.

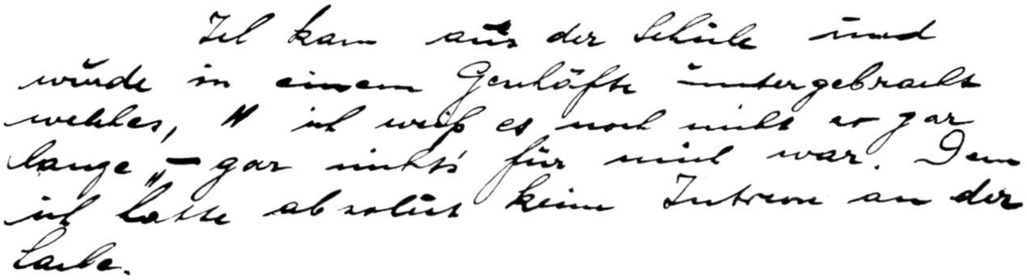

Fig. 9.
Handwriting of the same patient as in Fig. 5 (*Case 20*), after completion of withdrawal from cocaine.

Fig. 12

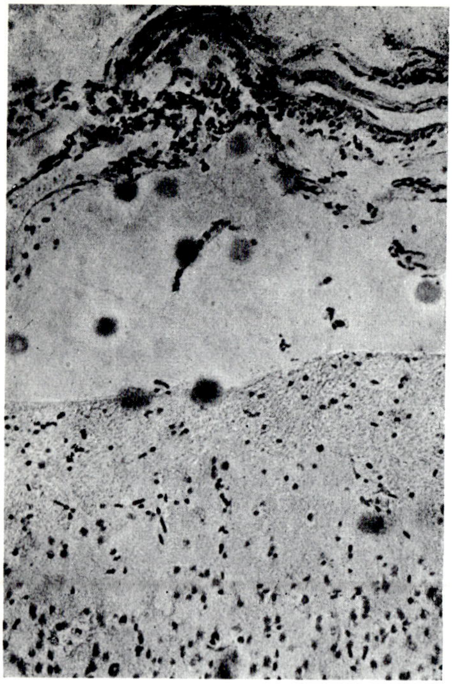

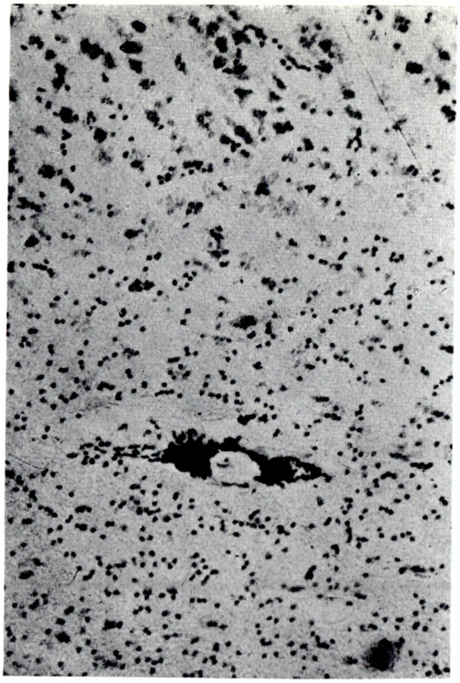

Fig. 13

Fig. 14

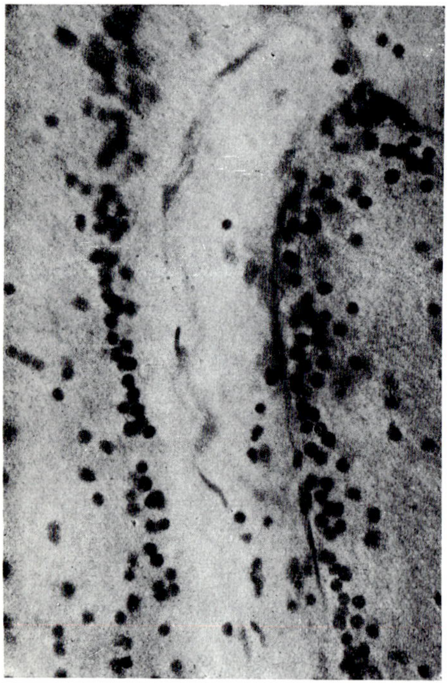

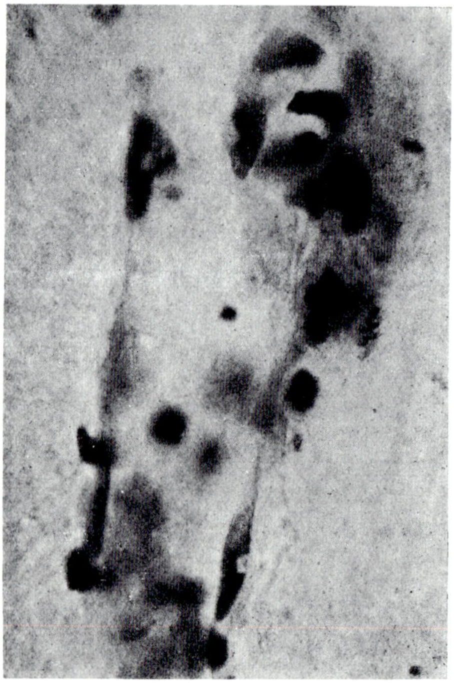

Fig. 15

Histopathological findings in a fatal case of cocaine poisoning (Bravetta, 1922).—Fig. 12. Oedema and lymphocytic infiltration of the *pia* (toluidine blue stain).—Fig. 13. Lymphocytic infiltration of the perivascular space surrounding a small vessel in the white matter (toluidine blue stain).—Fig. 14. Lymphocytic infiltration of the walls of a blood vessel in the white matter (methyl green stain).—Fig. 15. Fatty degeneration and vacuolation of the adventitial cells of endocerebral blood vessels (toluidine blue stain).

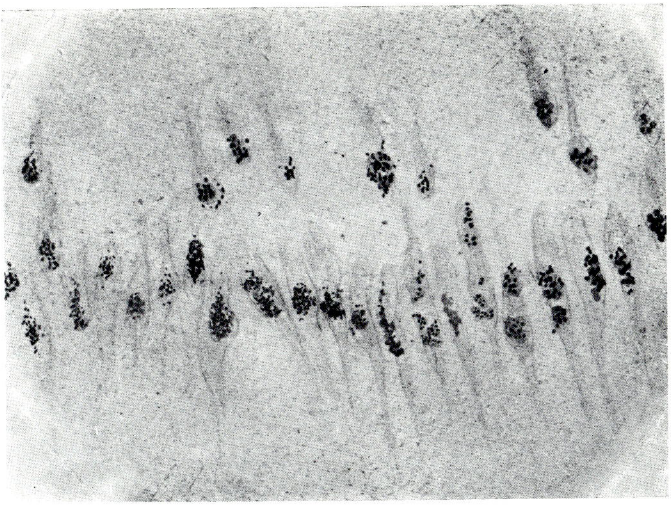

Fig. 16.
Fatty infiltration of pyramidal cells in Ammon's horn, in the brain of an animal exposed chronically to cocaine (Bravetta and Invernizzi, 1923).

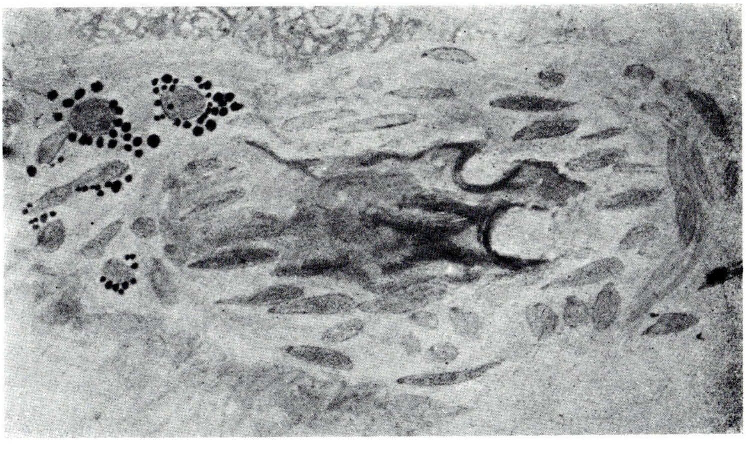

Fig. 17.
Red thrombus in a cerebellar vessel, with fatty degeneration of the adventitia (Bravetta and Invernizzi, 1923).

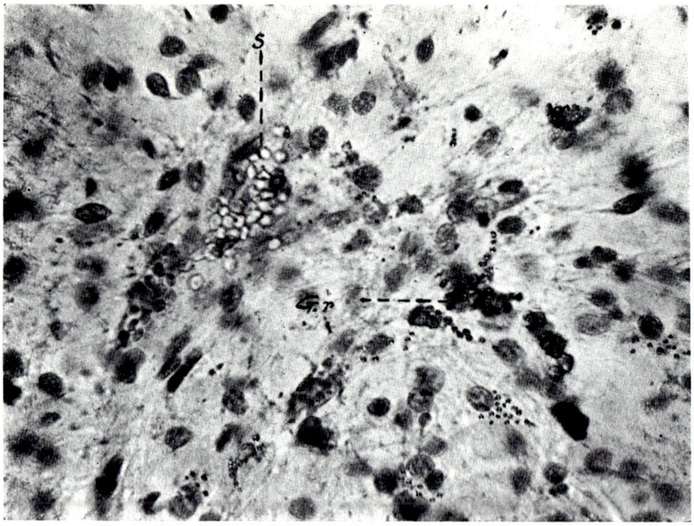

Fig. 18.
Meninges from a chronically cocainized animal. S = haemorrhage in the *pia*. Gr = fibroblasts filled with fatty droplets (From Bravetta and Invernizzi, 1923).

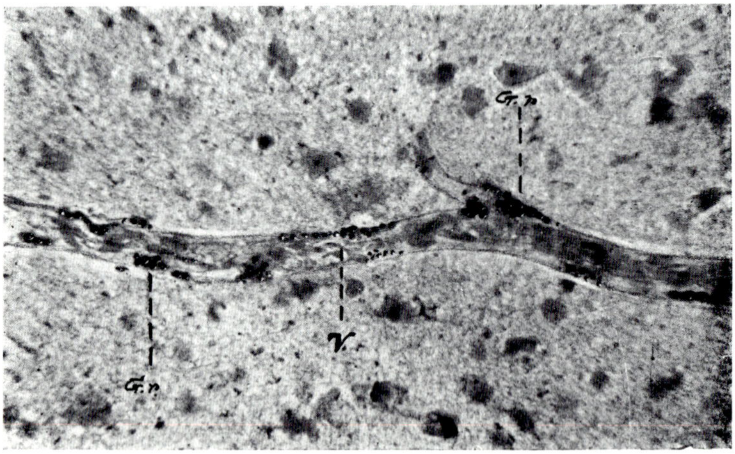

Fig. 19.
Section of brain. V = endocerebral blood vessel. Gr = adventitial cells with fatty infiltration (From Bravetta and Invernizzi, 1923).

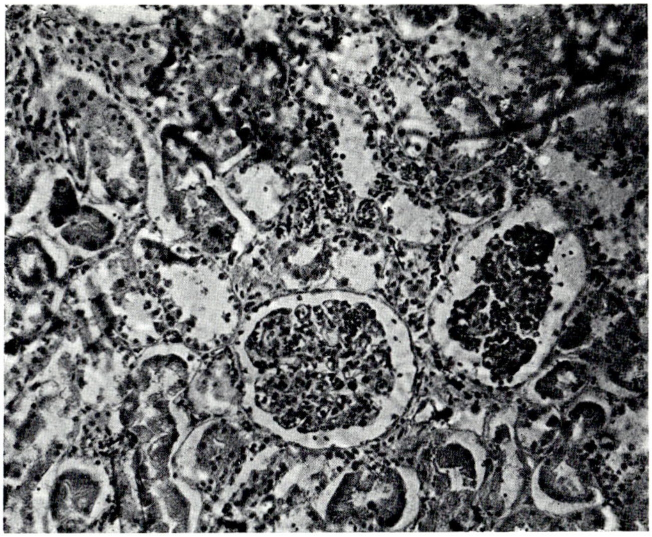

Fig. 20.
Kidney of a chronically cocainized animal. Note red blood cells in Bowman's capsule (Bravetta and Invernizzi, 1923).

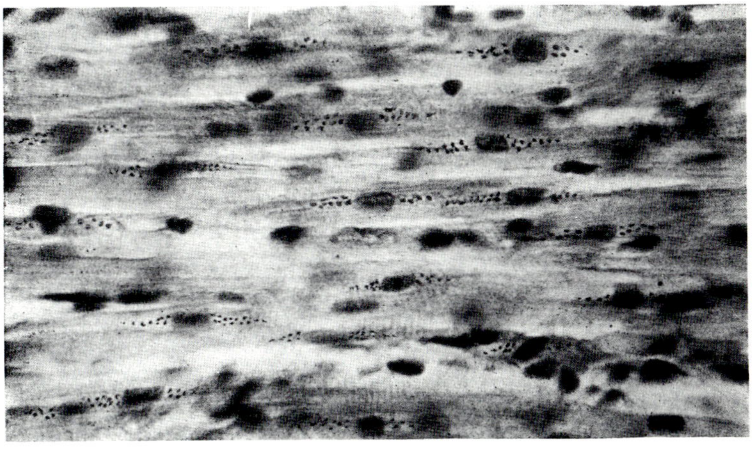

Fig. 21.
Section of myocardium, showing oedematous swelling, segmentation, fragmentation and fatty degeneration of the muscle fibers (Bravetta and Invernizzi, 1923).

mixed hallucinations just described. But sometimes the people that the patient sees in his visual hallucinations begin to talk and to answer his questions. While the "voices" in schizophrenia most frequently announce or articulate unpleasant things, this is not the case in the auditory hallucinations induced by cocaine, except when the patient is experiencing a strong anxiety state. One of my patients, for example, woke up the room maid of the hotel where he was staying in the middle of the night to request that she find out why the marvelous orchestra never stopped playing, while in fact it had ceased to do so several hours earlier. Another patient could hear all sorts of things related to his most private problems through the stethoscope. The voices are often uttering commands: "You must put an end [to it]!" or "Run away, or you'll be committed to an asylum!" At other times the voices utter insults at the patient whom they address by name, just as often happens frequently among schizophrenics. Not infrequently, the patients claim to hear voices of people whom they know to be several hundred kilometers away.

g) Gustatory and Olfactory Hallucinations

These hallucinations are significantly less frequent than the others and are primarily seen in cases of cocaine insanity. The patients taste and sniff and then claim that their food has been poisoned, or that foul-smelling substances have been added to their cocaine to annoy and torment them. One patient sounded the fire alarm because the whole house smelled full of smoke to him. Another sent back all his drinking water because he claimed it tasted like manure.

2. Disturbances of Cognition

a) General

There is no evidence at present of characteristic alterations of thought related to cocaine use. The most that can be said is that in manic states of intoxication the thoughts and ideas, including those with concrete meaning, are not clearly delineated and tend to blend with each other imperceptibly. In less severe states of intoxication, on the other hand, where thought processes are speeded up, the only abnormality observed consists in some loss of quality, the thoughts and ideas assuming a more superficial character.

From the point of view of language, the patients show some tendency to use code words, a phenomenon seen, moreover, in all groups of psychopaths that live in more or less intimate contact. Furthermore, the purpose of these substitutive terms among cocaine addicts is to mislead the authorities and evade their pursuit. The terms used to refer to cocaine are very varied and evidently different from country to country. In Germany the most common terms are "koks," "white snow" and "tea," while in France it is "coco." During the war, I often heard French cocaine addicts talk of "dardo." I was unable to find the origin of the term until a patient explained that it derived from the expression "The taking of the Dardanelles" *("La prise des Dardanelles")*. The term "prise," which means both "capture" and "nasal inhalation," was omitted, keeping only the first half of the word "Dardanelles" to refer to cocaine meant for sniffing.

An analysis of the association of ideas in uncomplicated and mild states of intoxication shows that they occur with greater facility and have a tendency to be superficial, often based solely on tonal or phonetic factors. This always happens in manic states. In more severe states of intoxication there is flight of ideas, occasionally reaching the level of incoherence.

One of our patients was brought to the clinic at the height of cocaine intoxication with his clothes torn and his arms and legs tied up. He cried and begged to be let free, insisted he was not ill and demanded that he be allowed to go home. Once untied, he stood in front of the fireplace, coughed, and then closed one nostril and began to blow vigorously through the other, shouting: "The damned drug must, absolutely must come out. I shall never again sniff anything like it. It is harmful. A handkerchief, give me a handkerchief! I say, a handkerchief! I shall not rest until someone gives me an appropriate handkerchief! There are some idiots in here but you are not one of them. They have no business here, doctor, but there are some idiots. Shame, shame (he begins to spit in all directions and becomes so violent that six people are required to hold him). Olga, it is you I want to see! Olga, Clara, Anna, Martha, Olga, Elsa, mother, father, Olga. I want you all around me, all of you who wish me well. Doctor, I am ready to obey you, but free me from these idiots. Promise that you will free me soon. I am young, I have to work." Once he has been taken up to the ward, it resembles a church; no, it is more like a horrible nightclub, but he does not know what kind. He has been in this dreadful state since he went to the restaurant at the station, where he had two cups of coffee and two small buns. He does not know how this happened to him. All of a sudden he saw policemen appear, one after another. A voice had told him he must achieve something major. The voice told him he was a doctor by profession, either of philosophy or of medicine, but about all he was was a mechanic (which is what he was, in fact).

When patients at the height of the intoxication are made to perform mental association exercises, there is a clear and abrupt increase in reaction time compared to that of spontaneous association of ideas. This is not due to any alteration of the association process itself, but rather to the difficulty that the patient experiences in fixing his attention on the exercise. Consequently, this appears to be due to an inhibition secondary to a disturbance of attention. The experimental associations of ideas reported by Joël and Fränkel (1924) were also slower. In their case, however, this was due to a post- intoxication inhibition, as opposed to the inhibition seen in my experiments which were performed in patients who were in a state of manic excitation. Here are, for example, the association times (in one-fifth seconds) of one cocaine addict following the inhalation of 0.5 g of cocaine:

green - 41 - tree	friendly - 39 - heart	proud - 75 - someone
water - 31 - stream	table - 19 - walnut tree	cat - 12 - animal
singing - 43 - art	to ask - 50 - things	ink - 52 - color
death - 16 - fear	village - 31 - hamlet	evil - 113 - crafty
long - 92 - to live	cold - 20 - warm	trip - 40 - railway
boat - 22 - wood	to dance - 14 - leg	blue - 40 - eyes
to pay - no association	lake - 24 - stream	sin - 143 - reprisal
window - 13 - house	sick - 12 - sad	

A repetition of the experiment 24 hours later, this time following the inhalation of 0.6 g of cocaine, yielded almost exactly the same set of responses.

The influence of emotional factors on this increase in response time is clearly evident. This response is generally characteristic of cocaine-induced disturbances, while consciousness still retains a certain degree of coordination.

On the third day, I performed another experiment on speed of association of ideas without administering cocaine. At the beginning, while concentration was good, the results were nearly normal, the reaction time ranging from one to two seconds. But after 15 associations the patient began to show fatigue and the reaction time doubled or tripled. The fatigue was obviously related to the state of withdrawal because it never manifested itself, not even in the longest experiments, while the patient was under the effects of cocaine.

Figure 10 illustrates the fluctuations in volition that occur under the influence of cocaine. The figure shows two curves of reaction time in the same patient who was mentally normal before becoming a cocaine addict, during two experiments, each one consisting of 100 associations. One experiment was performed after taking 0.4 g of cocaine, and the other while the patient was not under the immediate effect of the drug. The increase in reaction time was almost exclusively in response to stimulus words with strong emotional content, so that the curves, especially the one corresponding to the cocaine experiment, suggest a severe case of hysteria. When the experiment was repeated after six weeks of abstinence and general improvement of health, the curve was quite normal. These results permit the conclusion that the abnormalities shown in the figure were due to the effects of cocaine. These abnormalities, although naturally less intense than during the period of acute cocaine action, persisted distinctly for some days after withdrawal.

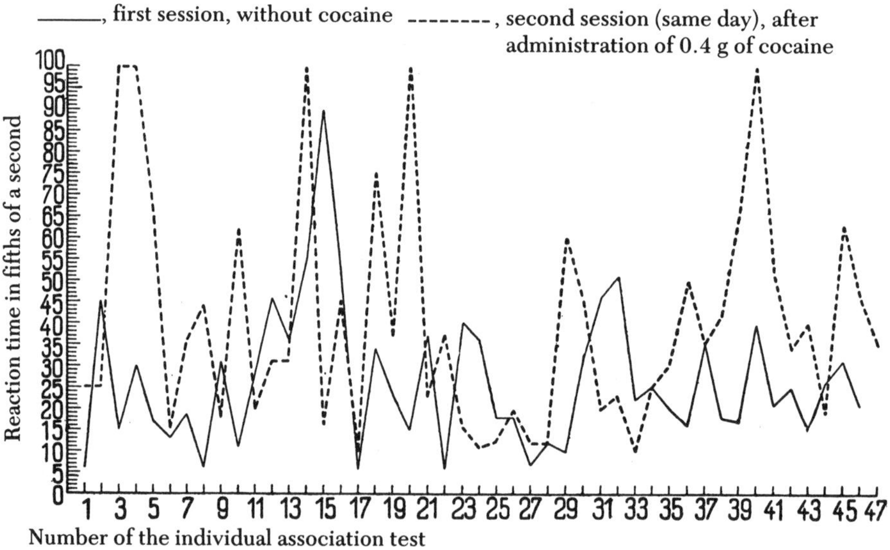

Fig. 10. Reaction times during two association test sessions.

The following associations come from a patient suffering from a subchronic paranoid and anxious delusional state. Time is expressed in one-fifth seconds. First the stimulus word is given. The + following the response word signifies that the patient gave only the correct response; the presence of a second word indicates that she gave more than one response, of which at least one was incorrect.

1. coal - 10 - coke/black
2. moderate - 11 - excess/excessive
3. song - 5 - singing/+
4. suspect - 13 - unsuspected/+
5. pain - 30 - yes, but. . .good deed/painful
6. lazy - 6 - industrious/+
7. moon - 7 - shy/sun
8. laugh - 8 - cry/distort
9. coffee - 5 - milk/+
10. wide - 8 - short/long
11. air - 15 - in the day light I was already. . ./light
12. frighten - 30 - no fright, no fear/fearful
13. plate - 10 - knife/porcelain
14. tired - 35 - restless/sleep
15. intention - 30 - it depends on which/unintentional
16. to fly - 16 - climb/air
17. eye - 48 - sight/timid
18. strong - 7 - weakness/weak
19. crop - 12 - fruit/+
20. to form - 9 - work/+
21. sail - 21 - ship/+
22. instruct - 20 - knowledge/ornament
23. floor - 8 - ground/+
24. to whistle - 23 - sing or laugh/+
25. goal - 11 - aims in life/+
26. hot - 11 - cold/through warmth
27. hand - 12 - foot/small
28. to wake - 20 - wake up/time
29. apple - 8 - apple tree/fruit
30. bad - 6 - excellent/+
31. mouth - 8 - teeth/chin
32. drink - 42 - dr. . .water/+
33. bed - 26 - B. how do you say it - pillow/bed-frame
34. pretty - 9 - ugly/ornament
35. danger - 28 - sure/escape
36. to visit - 14 - company/gladly
37. worker - 10 - helper/hard work
38. high - 7 - low/over
39. leg - 11 - arm/stone
40. notice - 12 - think/in mind
41. road - 9 - short/straight
42. round - 18 - course/+
43. blood - 15 - red/warm
44. claim - 63 - (strokes her hair) give/statement
45. foresight - 10 - insight/exert
46. joyful - 8 - sad/remain
47. market - 54 - sales booth/go
48. forget - 14 - unforgotten/forgive
49. drum - 8 - beat/+
50. free - 26 - through/+
51. wagon - 10 - wheel/+
52. eat - 15 - pleasure/drink
53. impudence - 11 - stupidity/against one's will
54. fast - 8 - slow/none
55. chimney - 8 - kindle/to sweep
56. to enjoy - 8 - pleasure - seeking/pleasure
57. parson - 9 - spiritual/black
58. easy - 8 - difficult/wing
59. throat - 10 - wide/necklace
60. to wish - 21 - memory/have
61. stone - 35 - again/be
62. aristocratic - 15 - politeness/mine
63. tube - 15 - rubber/smoke
64. to love - 12 - live/leave
65. brick - 10 - drive/+
66. mild - 10 - tepid/become
67. greed - 14 - throat/+
68. look for - 6 - find/show
69. cover - 12 - wool/lie
70. good - 9 - injustice/justice

71. leaf - 12 - four-cornered/book
72. dream - 21 - long for/plus
73. railway station - 11 - train/+
74. hard - 8 - soft/+
75. trust - 7 - find/have
76. buy - 9 - money/be able
77. cellar - 10 - room/be
78. useful - 10 - useless/become
79. forest - 13 - field/tree
80. understand - 8 - understanding/to decorate
81. duty - 12 - pleasure/be
82. give - 8 - have/alone
83. sofa - 17 - chair back/use
84. deaf - 10 - ears/to hear
85. honor - 8 - to the/+
86. to pay - 7 - ready/+
87. snake - 7 - poisonous/+
88. fine - 10 - thin/ornament
89. love - 10 - belief/+
90. to help - 6 - help/+
91. economy - 13 - country/economic
92. smooth - 31 -. . .oh. . . slippery/+
93. soldier - 19 - rifle/use
94. write - 5 - writing/+
95. mirror - 7 - picture/+
96. full - 13 - overfilled/+
97. intelligence - 17 - unintelligible/have
98. punish - 21 - punishment/through
99. bone - 7 - fracture/break
100. beautiful - 14 - ugly/hardly

Here again the associations are superficial in nature. During the first half of the experiment there is large variation in reaction time, which is on the whole shorter in the second half. In view of the marked dissociation of ideas characteristic of cases of this type, the increase in reaction time must be attributed to impaired concentration rather than to emotional factors. There was more than one response for 70% of the terms, and this was about equally distributed between the two halves of the experiment.

Because of their state of verbal excitation, cocaine addicts often show a tendency to versification. But generally the rhymes are quite superficial and seldom completed. I suggested to a female cocaine addict in a state of acute intoxication that she write down what she was experiencing. Here is what she wrote in a few minutes, being unable to concentrate on the task any longer: "Cocaine, this term which is so easy to pronounce, is not easy to define, not from a medical point of view, but from that of the creature (I say creature, because animals can take cocaine just the same as human beings even though the effects are not identical in both cases). Cocaine, in the medical sense of the term, or "coco" in my cocaine addict language, has produced the following effects on me:

My visions, from the first day that I began to sniff till today (the rest tomorrow).

After having spent three years in the midst of the most beautiful dreams I have recognized with my eyes open that my fate changed every day but my visions did not materialize.

To see and hear, to think of something and to then be able to see it and to determine its origin, to keep the cherished vision for as long as one wants, that is to say when this vision reminds you of an event in your life to be able to unroll it to the end like a cinematographic film.

But when the creature who uses cocaine no longer pursues any goal, or when she takes "coco" only to experience pleasant sensations or because her head is very dull, then the visions are mere fantasies, that is to say that the "coco" makes you believe when you are in a room, that you are in the middle of a park full of flowers, that everything around you is yours, in brief, one has delusions of grandeur."

In cases of organic brain damage produced by cocaine the associations of ideas show the same changes that are seen in other organic diseases. Their range becomes restricted due to the increasingly marked egocentricity of the patient, and there is generalized slowing down and marked perseveration. During the inhibitory stages that often occur in chronic cocainism, the subjects often experience periods of dreaming with their eyes open during which pleasant or frightening events unfold in front of their eyes. Their associations of ideas then reflect this dream-like state. These associations are characterized by a lack of purpose or goal, and they often assume bizarre features reminiscent of the thought disturbances of schizophrenia. In states of very marked excitation, there is true mental confusion, generally of an hallucinatory nature.

b) Delusional Ideas

As the associations slacken and become connected with the hallucinations and with the increased emotional tone of the thoughts and their corresponding complexes, delusional ideas make their appearance. These often reveal clearly both increased self-esteem and, at the same time, the simultaneous or alternating feelings of diminished efficiency and general inferiority with respect to the people around him. Feelings of euphoria, expressed as ideas of grandeur predominate at the beginning of the intoxication. But during withdrawal or when the level of intoxication increases, dysphoria assumes a predominant role and ideas of persecution replace the ideas of grandeur. At this stage, the connection between the distortions of reality due to sensory illusions and the disturbances of associative processes which the patient cannot correct becomes particularly close. However, due to the large individual variation in the ease with which hallucinations occur, there are cases, although very rare, of delusional syndromes without clearly delineated hallucinations. One of my patients, for example, was incontrovertibly convinced that his employer was bribing journalists so that they would print innuendos against him in the newspapers. Actors in the theater had been bribed to blow their noses in a special way while staring at him. This patient did not show any sensory illusions. These non-hallucinatory delusional symptoms, therefore, have something in common with those of paranoia. But the cases in which delusions and hallucinations co-exist are far more frequent. One of my female patients could see lighted signs on the ceiling and developed in this connection the theory that these signals were being used by the secret police to follow her in a very intricate fashion.

The everyday life of the patients is sometimes subjected to specific rules which they draw from their delusional ideas. One patient, convinced of his own inferiority, suddenly decided that from then on he would follow the "right" path. Though left-handed up to then, he began to use his right hand and to walk only on the right side of the street. But whenever he found himself in front of a church he would pass it on his left because he didn't want to have anything to do with the clergy. At the same time he noticed that with the aid of his ring he could attract the sun or order it to remain motionless. When he went inside a house, the sun also disappeared.

Symbolic connections are also frequent in the delusional ideas whose content stems from individual complexes and which, for this reason, are reminiscent of certain manifestations of schizophrenia. But the disturbances of association of ideas, the inhibitions, and the flight of ideas so characteristic of schizophrenia are absent in the delusional ideas.

Delusional ideas are present in states of acute delirium as well as in the chronic psychoses associated with cocaine addiction. One of my patients, for example, is convinced that he is a motion picture actor and that he must achieve extraordinary things in his profession in order to gain the respect of his beloved. But he finds nothing better to do than to climb up the front walls of houses. The delusions play a particularly important role in the chronic paranoid syndrome of cocaine insanity in which the euphoric stage is generally characterized by a mania for invention and discovery: the distortion exhibited by the succession of ideas is closely related to the corresponding hallucinations, the latter being then stimulated by the auto-suggestive influence of the delusions from which they derive their content. The same phenomenon occurs during the depressive phase of the paranoid psychosis which sometimes occurs simultaneously and in combination with the mania for invention in cocaine addicts.

Many authors consider that delusions of jealousy are characteristic of cocaine addiction. According to my own observations, though they undoubtedly can occur among cocaine sniffers they appear to be much rarer among sniffers than among cocaine addicts who inject the drug subcutaneously, and in whom the mental deterioration occurs much more rapidly. To the extent that I can judge (and on this point my conclusions are in agreement with those of other authors), they are much more frequent among men than among women. These phenomena show the greatest similarity to the equivalent symptoms of chronic alcoholism with respect to the manner in which they appear and with respect to their consequences, including violence against the persons accused of treachery and infidelity. They are seen, on the contrary, very rarely in cases of opiate intoxication. This is most likely due to the fact that these drugs quickly inhibit mental activity and that jealousy is incompatible with a purely passive attitude towards the outside world. In my opinion, the psychological genesis of this type of mania must be related to the impotence that cocaine soon produces in men. This impotence, which is the source of painful feelings for the patient, is attributed to causes projected by him onto the outside world. He must attribute the blame not to his passion for cocaine, but rather to the erotic frigidity of his lover who, since she scorns and neglects him, must necessarily be spending her affections and her libido on other men. This hypothesis explains, in turn, why this phenomenon occurs more rarely among female cocaine addicts, and why, when it does occur, it is provoked by their sexual insatiability: they interpret the failure of their man to satisfy all their desires as proof of his ill will and of his infidelity.

Since the personality of cocaine addicts remains reasonably intact during the chronic delusional state, it is quite understandable that their delusional patterns are most often related to their normal professional activities. The physician in a state of cocaine-induced mania makes astounding discoveries on the cause of cancer or of cataracts and of infectious and other diseases. While hallucinating, he finds the proof of his discoveries under the microscope or the magnifying glass, and even ends up following cell divisions and other infinitely small phenomena with the naked eye. The cocaine addict with technical knowledge invents extraordinary machines, solves the problem of perpetual motion and so on. The environment, in turn, frequently exerts an important influence on the content of the delusions. During the Great War of 1914-18, many cocaine addicts made military inventions during their delusional states. One invention, for example, was supposed to permit the destruction of the enemy army down to the last man by simply pressing on an electric button. I know, for example, that during the war the French Ministry of War received a large number of delusional projects from cocaine addicts.

The rationale for these discoveries can change very quickly because, in this respect, the patients are easily influenced by external suggestion. But the latter is incapable of eliminating the source of the psychosis itself. One of my patients connected the solution of the problem of cataracts to osmotic effects which had been recently discovered. But a few days after a colleague of his had said that this explanation was not convincing, he sought him out, told him that the first hypothesis was untenable, and proposed to him an equally unfounded hypothesis based on the influence of X-rays.

Affectivity is very marked and highly extroverted during the euphoric phase of the psychosis. This explains why many patients succeed in having their ideas accepted by mentally healthy persons in their environment. I have often seen the spouses or friends of cocaine addicts accept their delusional ideas and even allow themselves to be talked into accepting the related hallucinations.

From the point of view of content, Piouffle (1919) has classified the delusions of cocaine addicts into four groups. In the first place, the loss of self-insight leads the patient to exaggerate the importance of his personality and this results in ideas of grandeur, in a mania for discoveries and inventions, and in a delusional state during which the patient sees himself in possession of enormous wealth. In second place are the ideas of persecution and of jealousy, followed by the more rare ideas of guilt, penitence and self- recrimination. In the last place are the delusional ideas of a sexual character seen more frequently in the dreamy twilight states produced by cocaine intoxication.

The paranoid ideas of cocaine addicts often assume the form of delusional interpretations. This is not surprising considering that the hallucinations precede the disturbances of intellectual function, so that the patient, who still retains some lucidity, attempts to explain and subsequently to systematize the paresthesias as well as the sensory illusions, through these ideas. Thus Joël and Fränkel (1924) are correct when they say that a portion of the delusional ideas is so closely connected with the perception of primary sensations that it is impossible to describe them separately. Auditory illusions, in particular, are so often associated with feelings of anxiety that this symptom of cocainism was formerly considered as hallucinatory paranoia. "The anxiety, together with the corresponding delusional ideas, is the foremost symptom. This is so clearly the case that French authors speak of a panphobic seizure."

In the case reported by Mayer-Gross (1920) it was the patient himself who described his psychosis in terms of an anxious dread that his house would be broken into by burglars. This kind of fear is very common in these cases of cocainism. A soldier treated by Joël and Fränkel could hear, while suffering from this syndrome, and in accord with his circumstances (he was a border guard), the enemy soldiers approaching and firing their rifles. The patient would alert his comrades, even though in reality the most complete calm prevailed in the region.

Considering that cocaine addicts generally show a tendency to bursts of motor activity or other active psychic reactions, the delusions frequently give rise to hostile acts against people in their environment. The patient suffering from delusions of invention and discovery senselessly seeks legal action against his adversaries for refusing to believe or help him. Some cocaine addicts do not hesitate to resort to the use of firearms against their imaginary enemies or burglars during their attacks of anxiety. This is particularly dangerous because, as opposed to alcoholics, the cocaine addict is rarely ataxic and is quite capable of a good aim. Delusions of jealously can also impel the patient to serious acts of violence.

In states of organic dementia due to cocainism, delusional ideas similar to those already described can also occur. They are, however, less well integrated, lacking connection and systematization.

3. Disturbances of Memory

Memory is not affected in states of acute cocaine intoxication. While at the beginning of cocaine use other psychological functions are stimulated, memory does not appear to show any change. However, as opposed to what happens in alcoholic intoxication, the subjects can remember what happened during the states of cocaine intoxication and delirium. True amnesia occurs only in particularly serious states of mental confusion. Thus, cocaine addicts are capable of providing very precise descriptions of their delusional and hallucinatory states. These descriptions are in good agreement with independent observations of the patients.

When the chronic intoxication leads to lasting organic brain damage, loss of memory is one of the first symptoms to appear. Recent events are at first only vaguely recalled, and eventually not at all. These memory deficiencies are replaced by confabulation and thus the cocaine variety of Korsakoff's syndrome arises. Comparing earlier reports on this topic with contemporary observations, one gathers that these disturbances of memory of organic origin were more frequent when cocaine was used solely by subcutaneous injection, than among present-day sniffers. It is possible that this difference is due, at least in part, to the fact that the earlier users were also morphine addicts. I have, however, seen cases of Korsakoff's syndrome of rapid onset in cases of exclusive use of cocaine by injection.

Subconscious memory (cryptomnesia) is not rare among chronic cocaine users. Two of my patients would write down known poems while convinced that they had just finished composing these poems at that very moment.

Joël and Fränkel (1924) believe that the capacity for mnemonic storage decreases rapidly in cocaine addicts. That, for example, the capacity for experimental recall in a man with excellent memory can be cut in half following a dose of 0.5 g of cocaine by sniffing. This finding is not in agreement with the results of my own experiments on recall and association of ideas during the acute intoxication produced by comparable doses. They are, on the other hand, consistent with my own findings in sub-chronic delusional states. In my opinion, however, this is not so much a contradiction as a difference of interpretation, having to do with the effects of the drug on orientation and attention and, subsequently, on the ability to conceptualize. Thus, conclusions about disturbances of memory should not be drawn before eliminating this source of error, but this is not always possible.

4. Disturbances of Orientation

Orientation is generally unaffected in cocaine addicts. It is only in severe cases of delusional confusion or of serious organic dementia when the patient is unable to give coherent answers that disturbances of orientation can be at least suspected, if not proven. The judgments that the subject makes about himself in the normal state concerning details of his bodily performance as well as his attitude towards the external world, often undergo very serious distortions as a result of bodily and other hallucinations, or as a result of delusional ideas. For as long as the picture does not reach a state of mental confusion, some degree of insight co-exists with disorientation. This is one consequence of the dissociation of consciousness often seen in cocaine intoxication: the deluded part of the personality becomes disoriented while otherwise orientation remains unimpaired. While in similar schizophrenic states the patient usually has no insight into his illness, the cocaine addict, in most cases, has. In respect to questions, the delusional patient spontaneously recognizes that the drug is the cause of his state of excitation but, unable to draw from this recognition the implied practical conclusion, he immediately surrenders to the power of his delusions and behaves accordingly.

5. Disturbances of Personality and of Consciousness

Changes in personality are foremost in all the disturbances, whether mild or severe, caused by cocaine. When, after the first few doses of cocaine, the patient becomes accustomed to the somatic effects of the drug, he passes into an essentially euphoric phase which is most frequently of frankly manic character. He is subjectively and objectively extremely active. All his somatic and psychological processes occur with astounding ease. The inhibitions of the normal state increasingly disappear. He sees the world through rose-colored glasses. As the intoxication progresses, and depending on the individual predisposition, the subject begins to experience hallucinations and his personality undergoes even more profound and characteristic changes.

If we compare consciousness to a theater stage in which the events that unfold are always associated with the self, we can say that the hallucinations and delusional ideas that soon appear represent new characters on the scene. But what is characteristic in this case, contrary to what happens in *delirium tremens*, is that the attention of the spectator, instead of being fully preoccupied with these abnormal characters, is still usually aware of the normal environment and of the relationships of the normal self. He hears, for example, the voice of a person who is 200 kilometers away and who insistently pleads with him to come and join him forthwith. He knows perfectly well that this is impossible, that it is an effect of cocaine, but he still obeys the command of the voice and begins the trip even though realizing that the whole thing is absurd. These are not, furthermore, obsessional acts in the strict sense of the term, because they are accomplished without internal conflict. There is, on the one side, the morbid part of the personality and on the other the healthy side, and the patient perceives both as equally real, and as having the same right to exist. Which side prevails and determines the corresponding behavior depends on the intensity of the intoxication, on the individual predisposition and on the circumstances.

But despite this curious dissociation an internal bond of a fundamental nature persists. Both sides of the scene are related to each other by the psychological fact that the emotional reactions of the normal segment of the personality provide to the sensory illusions and to the delusional ideas their primary content. This results in an utterly peculiar entanglement of normal and abnormal content. While in the dissociation of the personality that occurs in hysteria there is a tendency, inherent to the disease itself, to push into the shadows, to obliterate from consciousness from time to time one aspect of the scene while the other succeeds in attracting all the attention of the subject, this is not the case in cocaine intoxication, where both aspects are equally illuminated and arouse the same interest.

This phenomenon provides the most striking resemblance to the disturbances of personality seen in schizophrenia. But there is no question that it can also occur in cases of cocaine addiction uncomplicated by schizophrenia and must, for this reason, be considered as a pure and simple effect of the drug. It is not very likely, however, that this is a specific effect of cocaine because comparable phenomena result from the action of opiates and of mescaline. If they are, generally speaking, less marked in morphine addicts, this is due to the decrease in overall activity of the personality produced under the influence of morphine and which results in a decrease or loss of interest in the outside world and in an increasing concentration on purely imaginary fantasies.

This specific disturbance of personality which accompanies toxic conditions as well as schizophrenic reactions, while it is absent in severe organic conditions such as general paresis or senile dementia, is at the same time of great theoretical interest. It lends support to the hypothesis that at least some of the symptoms of schizophrenia would be due, not to organic lesions, but to intoxications determined, in turn, not by exogenous toxins but by unknown substances of endogenous origin (endocrine?). In summary, schizophrenia would be a veritable auto-intoxication. This similarity has practical implications considering that it can easily give rise to the wrong diagnosis and a confusion of the symptoms of cocaine psychosis and schizophrenic reactions which happens quite frequently. But if this similarity is kept in mind and attention is paid to the somatic symptoms this error and confusion can be avoided.

Depersonalization, another symptom characteristic of schizophrenia, is also found in cocaine addicts. The patient has the firm conviction that he has undergone some radical change. He feels compelled to touch his body and to look at himself in the mirror to reassure himself that he is still the same. He has the feeling of acting automatically. During the apathetic phase of the intoxication which occurs most frequently shortly before or simultaneously with the symptoms of withdrawal, depersonalization is further complicated by an anomaly of volitional activity. Once a movement or an act begins the patients are unable to stop it and must persevere until a new stimulus from the outside or insurmountable fatigue redirects their behavior. A delirious cocaine addict in the oneiric phase is, for example, lying on his bed executing a movement consisting of stretching the arm towards the night table to pick up a handkerchief and bring it towards his nose. Despite having achieved his aim he continues to repeat the same movement, sometimes for one or two hours at a time, in such a way that anyone observing him would easily conclude he was a catatonic. But the fundamental difference is that the cocaine addict is perfectly aware of the absurdity of his actions, without however being able to alter them. There are, at the same time, psychic automatisms. One of my patients wanted to calculate how much he would have to pay for a stay of three days at his hotel at the rate of six francs per day. He said to himself that 6 x 3 = 18, and could not get rid of this idea. For more than an hour he did nothing but repeat in a low voice "three times six equals eighteen," until a friend walked into his room and finally succeeded in distracting him from this obsession by diverting his attention to something else.

This catatonic-like automatism can be observed in cases of extreme fatigue in healthy individuals, and in certain organic conditions, as well as in schizophrenia. It appears, therefore, to be a disturbance of volition for which there is a predisposition in the normal state and which can be activated by toxic as well as by autotoxic and organic factors.

During dream-like delusional states, cocaine addicts often come to identify their own personality with that of other people, particularly with those with whom they are emotionally involved. The patient identifies with his beloved, he turns into a woman and has the illusion of performing the sexual act, and of then experiencing the sensations characteristic of a woman.

Certain real or imaginary homosexual deviations, which, as already stated, can occur during cocaine intoxication can be explained on the basis of this type of identification with a person of the opposite sex. This identification is determined by certain deviations in the instincts and drives. Here again there are striking analogies with the disturbances of personality that occur in schizophrenia.

Among the qualitative disturbances of consciousness seen in cocaine addicts, the delirium, composed essentially of the hallucinations and delusional ideas, plays a primary role. Contrary to what happens in similar states caused by factors other than cocaine, the patients are able to recall quite well what happened during the delusional state, except when the latter is accompanied by severe mental confusion. Twilight states are more rare, and the narrowing of the field of possible associations can then occur to different degrees. These states occur particularly in men who for as yet unknown reasons, are refractory to the hallucinations of cocaine intoxication. Orientation in these subjects presents the same partial dissociation seen in disturbances of the personality, but even in severe cases of intoxication it may be absent. When dissociation is present the clearness of consciousness is much more impaired than in other twilight states. In order to show a concrete example of the action of cocaine on consciousness I shall quote a section of a self-report by a physician who was both a cocaine and a morphine addict (*Münch. Med. Wschr.* 72, 346, 1925).

> "....The physical effects of excessive use of cocaine are well known. Constipation is the most distressing symptom for the patient himself. Another remarkable effect is the complete loss of sexual libido, accompanied by marked physical impotence manifested as a decrease in erection power, but particularly by a very marked prolongation of the time it takes to ejaculate during coitus. This happens from the first few days of the establishment of the habit. A striking objective sign is the marked pallor of the subject, often in contrast with the redness of the nose. The pallor is due more to local vasoconstriction than to anemia proper. The aged appearance of the subjects, their malnutrition, the loss of hair and of teeth are other consequences of prolonged intoxication, but are also due, at least in part, to the inordinate squandering of energy that accompanies excessive pathological activity and gastrointestinal disturbances.
>
> But the most important symptoms of cocaine addiction are psychological, and they explain the persistence of the affliction, its almost unbelievable obstinacy. This is the very aspect that objective observers have failed to investigate as it deserves. The schizothymic manifestations reaching the level of schizophrenia have struck me the most (I have a cycloid predisposition). The emotional life undergoes a very rapid impoverishment. At the same time that one becomes insensitive to hunger, to cold (!) and generally to unfavorable environmental conditions, one loses all the emotional elements of the personality. There comes a time when one is unable to experience happiness, sadness, hatred, love or ambition, when one even loses the sense of duty. The same applies to the attitude of the patient towards himself. He does not close his mind to intellectual insight, but is incapable of sensing the danger that he faces. All other feelings, except the hunger and thirst for the narcotic, vanish. The addicted physician reacts to his

own forgeries in his prescriptions or to the deceptions of his orderlies with an indifference that bears witness to a state of true moral insanity with a marked schizothymic character. In addition, there is, of course, unscrupulous egotism which leads to neglect of all his everyday affairs, but especially of his professional obligations, and to the exclusive and intense pursuit of his petty and shabby love affairs. Another characteristic feature of his affective blunting is that he becomes sentimental. He assumes poses, catch words and tearful scenes which cannot and must not be taken seriously because these exteriorizations of feeling are totally lacking in sincerity."

6. Disturbances of Affect and of Attention

The disturbances of affect are most commonly of a primary nature. Emotions are labile, but often qualitatively unaltered. At other times they occur in an autistic setting and are quantitatively exaggerated but their duration is diminished in all cases. The only exceptions to this rule are the oneiric states (see below), and the idiosyncratic reactions of some individuals (see the self-report by the physician above). Most phases of the mild intoxication are primarily characterized by exaltation. In more severe or prolonged cases of intoxication, or during the withdrawal reaction, this state is abruptly replaced by depression which, however, is not always accompanied by impairment of intellectual performance. While the mental state remains stimulated, severe manifestations of anxiety develop. The most clear examples are the pathological fear of burglars and the delusions of persecution. We should recall in this connection the case of the cocaine addict who, seized by the most intense anxiety and covered in cold sweat, bursts into a police station demanding protection from the persecutors that he sees in his hallucinated imagination. Many other similar examples which have, furthermore, their counterpart in alcoholic psychosis, could be cited. At the same time the patients suffer from a very clear sensation of oppression and pre-cordial distress which may be attributed to disturbances of the circulation.

In some phases of cocaine intoxication there is, furthermore, a marked increase in irritability which can in some cases reach the level of true attacks of rage. In most cases these intense feelings, which are at the same time very labile, can be easily directed away from their objects. The patient himself is not always capable of checking the changes in his emotions and this results in a loss of self-control which often leads to violent explosions.

With respect to specific emotional disturbances, it should be noted that moral attitudes are the first to be altered by cocaine.

These changes occur much more rapidly and are more marked than in other types of intoxication. The subjects become more egocentric and show a clear and increasing tendency to prevaricate in general, but particularly with respect to their craving for cocaine. The cocaine addict will resort to any lie, a fact that can be demonstrated from the beginning of the addiction. Some patients begin to give away everything they own, not for altruistic reasons but because of their increasing indifference to everything around them and to the established order. During the withdrawal reaction the need to secure new supplies of the drug overrides and stifles all moral inhibitions and often forces the patient to lie or to commit robbery, housebreaking or acts of violence. This complication is much more marked among cocaine than among morphine addicts because they are much more enterprising and energetic in the pursuit of their aims. We have already referred to sexual perversions among cocaine addicts. We may add that they lose very rapidly their sense of propriety and the most basic esthetic feelings. They become indifferent to their own appearance and to that of the people and objects in their surroundings.

In connection with the general disturbances of affectivity and of the capacity for association of ideas, there is generally a marked decrease in the ability to concentrate leading to a combination of exaggerated vigilance and diminished perseverance. The tendency to fatigue is difficult to examine, precisely because it is impossible to have the patient sustain his attention on a particular object for any length of time. It is certain, however, that the threshold of attention fatigue is lowered substantially, and that this can persist for weeks and even months following withdrawal.

For as long as the personality of cocaine addicts remains more or less intact, they are extremely suggestible to the influence of the environment, especially of other cocaine addicts, and also show marked auto-suggestibility. When not engaged in apathetic daydreaming, cocaine addicts experience a pressing need to turn this suggestibility into action. This explains, at least in part, the passion with which they seek company in general and the company of other cocaine addicts in particular. This is why all these patients strive to make converts. This tendency is so strong that the patients often sacrifice their most cherished possession, cocaine itself. They will share it with others without thinking that sooner or later they may run out of the drug themselves. This trait clearly distinguishes cocaine from opium and morphine addicts, who do not experience any need for company and who are as thrifty as possible in the use of their drug.

Considering this harmony between the patient and his environment, the emotional life of cocaine addicts appears quite normal from a qualitative point of view. It is only during the states of apathetic daydreaming, which occur at the beginning of the withdrawal reaction, that this harmony becomes impaired. The patients barely react to external stimuli and show a certain autistic tendency reflected in their facial expression which appears directed inwardly, and is sometimes almost hostile. In such circumstances one has the false impression in some cases of being in the presence of affective disturbances of a schizophrenic nature.

7. Disturbances of Volition

The disturbances of volition caused by cocaine vary according to the manner in which the disturbances of affect and of the capacity for association of ideas arise, as we have just described. In most euphoric states there is, simultaneously with intense but unstable affect, a failure to sustain direction and to achieve the desired goals. This expresses itself in rapid changes of decisions, none of which is, however, carried out.

The marked suggestibility present simultaneously further contributes to the picture of weak will reminiscent of that seen in manic states. As the state of excitation becomes more intense, the patient is rendered incapable, despite the strong volitional impulses that he experiences, of a more or less coherent performance and one witnesses incoordinated, confused reactions. The withdrawal reaction, in turn, often provokes dysphoric symptoms, including anxiety as well as stupor. The latter also occurs periodically during the apathetic daydreaming states seen in chronic cocaine users. Besides these inhibitions which are, furthermore, comparatively rare, there is generally an intensification of the ability for decision-making and a marked desire for activity, sometimes reaching the level of true hyperkinesia, during which the patient indulges in more or less ridiculous pranks. For as long as the normal personality remains comparatively intact the patients themselves attempt to explain their state by invoking trivial reasons such as the mad desire for theatrics, comedy or motion picture acting. In the apathetic states during which the patients become incapable of interrupting a behavior already started, the volitional impulses soon acquire a stereotyped character. Thus, for example, motor behaviors of toxic nature such as chewing and swallowing provoked by disturbances of the corresponding reflexes persist even when their organic cause has disappeared. This is similar to the psychogenic *sequelae* of athymic nature (Maier, 1923) seen as the aftermath of epidemic encephalitis. But all these signs can be eliminated by suggestion, while the incoordinated and ludicrous hyperkinesia of cocaine addicts referred to above, cannot.

In comparatively severe states of intoxication in which the ability to reason is lost, the patient performs only impulsive actions which often lead him to criminal acts. It is known, in fact, that this is the main reason that criminal cocaine addicts are particularly dangerous. According to information given to me by many magistrates, cocaine addicts resort to the use of firearms not only against others but also against themselves at the slightest resistance and without any further thought.

8. Disturbances of Intellectual Function

We have already noted that even in mild cases of cocaine intoxication there is an increase in the sensitivity of some sensory nerves, especially the optic and auditory nerves. But cocaine addicts also tell us that, in such circumstances, their thoughts are quicker and more logical, their feelings are more intense and their physical performance is enhanced. Alcoholics make similar claims, but they are based principally on subjective impressions and on a loss of inhibitions, because objective examination often reveals impairment of performance efficiency. However, a simple conversation with an individual in a state of cocaine intoxication is sufficient to convince one that the phenomena of cocaine addiction are not at all comparable with those of alcoholism, and that the problem requires new and more thorough research. The inherent difficulty in such investigation relates to the fact that experiments on the effects of cocaine intoxication in the normal man are very dangerous because of the somatic effects of the drug and because of the risk of producing a rapid and disastrous habituation. Personally, I have never wanted to assume responsibility for exposing normal subjects to repeated experiments of this type, which require sizeable doses of cocaine. But here is what can be stated on the question of the disturbances of intellectual performance in cocaine addicts.

Taking into account only the positive effects on intellectual performance, and considering the enthusiastic accounts of South American coca chewers, there is a certain similarity between the psychological effects of cocaine and those of coffee. From this point of view I thought it would be interesting to perform a series of experiments on the effects of strong and decaffeinated coffee on intellectual performance. I have used for this purpose the addition test of Kraepelin (1910). Thirteen subjects performed additions of one-digit numbers during three one-hour sessions. The first was conducted after the ingestion of strong coffee, the second after decaffeinated coffee, and the third in the absence of any drug intake. There was a considerable increase in efficiency of performance in all subjects, amounting to 100% in some, a general decrease in errors, and elimination of the pathological causes of very rapid mental fatigue. Most subjects performed best after ingestion of coffee, while some did so after ingestion of decaffeinated coffee, i.e. coffee with a low caffeine concentration. These results warrant the conclusion that coffee produces a real and objective stimulation of intellectual performance due not only to the action of caffeine, but also to that of other substances, probably aromatic products of roasting, of the so-called caffeone group.

It would be most interesting to perform similar experiments with cocaine if, as stated above, such experiments did not involve a serious risk. For this reason these experiments must, in my opinion, be carried out on cocaine addicts under treatment, some of whom are willing to volunteer for a few days before complete withdrawal. It should be remembered, however, that in such patients the results are complicated by the possible influence of a state of chronic intoxication. For example, an increase in efficiency of intellectual performance could be attributed to the effects of chronic rather than of acute intoxication. But my experiments with coffee show, on the other hand, that the chronic effects of a substance which is a component of an edible plant must be distinguished from those of the whole plant. Just as roasted coffee beans and opium sap contain other substances besides caffeine and opium, whose nature and mode of action are not well known at present, it is possible that the body reacts to the constituents of dried coca leaves in a manner that is somewhat different from and more complex than that in which it reacts to pure cocaine. Thus it would be worthwhile for South American physicians to initiate research on experimental psychology in coca chewers at different stages of their habit, in addition to experiments on cocaine addicts.

I have had the opportunity of conducting an abbreviated addition experiment on a 21-year-old female cocaine addict (Case Report 27) at the beginning of treatment. The results are shown in Fig. 11, in which the ordinate shows the total number of additions of one-digit numbers per minute and the abscissa the successive minutes in which the calculations were performed. The lower graph corresponds to the results obtained in the tests without cocaine, in which the average number of additions per minute was 35.5. This

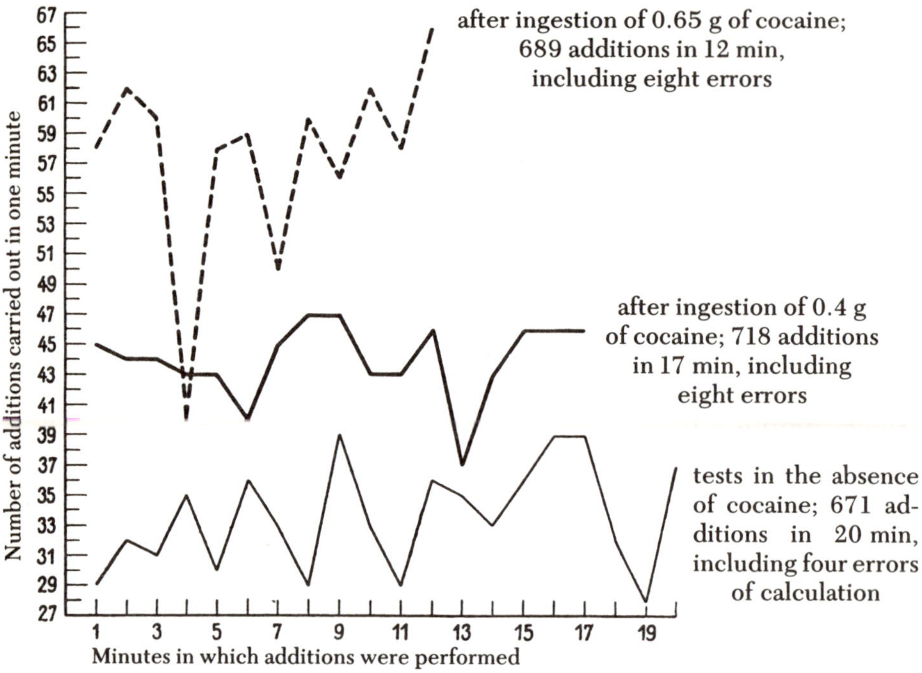

Fig. 11. Effect of cocaine on ability to perform successive additions of one-digit numbers.

figure was comparable to that obtained in a normal woman not particularly endowed with talent for arithmetic. The variation in performance from minute to minute, which persists in cocaine addicts for a long time after withdrawal, is striking. This is due to the marked lability of attention and motivation in such subjects. The middle and upper curves correspond to the performance after 0.40 and 0.65 g of cocaine respectively. The experimental sessions were performed two days apart in the order shown in the figure. It is improbable that learning played an appreciable role in the improvement of performance, which is proportional to the dose of cocaine. The number of additions per minute was almost twice as large after 0.65 g of cocaine than after 0.4 g. The figure of 66 additions per minute is very high and rarely obtained in normal subjects of comparable intelligence. The average performance was 33.5 additions per minute without cocaine, and 42.2 and 57.4 following 0.40 and 0.65 g cocaine respectively. The number of errors was small, i.e., four under control conditions, and eight under the effect of either dose of cocaine. Another characteristic finding is that the endurance for work diminished in proportion to the dose, being 20, 17 and 12 minutes respectively.

Joël and Fränkel (1924) have reported the results of three experiments on the verbal performance of cocaine addicts, which should be mentioned here. Although their results are not conclusive, they show, together with the results described above, the need for further research in this area. The results described above clearly do not justify drawing general conclusions about the action of cocaine. Solid and valid conclusions would require a larger number of comparable experiments. But the interesting point is that, in the experiment described above, intellectual performance, which was not initially below normal, increased 100% without any qualitative detriment. These results are generally in agreement with those that I have obtained during my investigations on the effects of cocaine, except that the absolute increase in intellectual performance is much higher. From this fact it is warranted to conclude that we have in cocaine a substance which acts not only indirectly by removing inhibitions but which actively stimulates mental associations. This conclusion is furthermore consistent with what can be observed in mildly intoxicated individuals.

We have already referred to the increase in physical performance when we reviewed the earlier literature.

The first thorough laboratory studies designed to obtain an experimental explanation of the psychological action of cocaine were carried out by Johannes Lange (1922). These experiments were performed in 1920 in Kraepelin's laboratory on six subjects to whom cocaine, morphine and scopolamine were administered in order to study the actions of these alkaloids on the ability to conceptualize, efficiency of intellectual performance, selective reactions, free association, and speed and accuracy of addition. He found that administration of cocaine was followed by a perceptible increase in the ability to perform additions, an intensification of muscular activity, and a decrease in complex reaction time. But he found, on the other hand, both a qualitative and quantitative decrease in the ability to conceptualize and a general narrowing of the range of associations which became more superficial and based primarily on phonetic similarities. But the predominant effect of cocaine, the one that overwhelmed all others, was an extremely marked degree of motor excitation. The associations of ideas, less rich and more superficial, occurred with greater ease. This may be explained in part by the fact that the central motor excitation greatly facilitated all voluntary responses and produced a decrease in feelings of fatigue. Most subjects showed very marked feelings of euphoria.

Lange noted that the intensification of motor excitability seen in cocaine intoxication is reminiscent of that produced by alcohol intoxication, except that the inhibition of all other functions, so characteristic of alcoholism, is absent in cocaine addicts. The author also believes that the appeal of cocaine lies in the euphoria that it produces, rather than in any real stimulation of performance. Taking into account that even a partial stimulation of performance results in a loss of accuracy, it is difficult to see of what practical utility cocaine could be, considered solely as a source of euphoria. Lange also found that the administration of small doses of scopolamine resulted in an inhibition of all motor and intellectual functions, the former being affected sooner than the latter. As opposed to cocaine, morphine produced a decrease in central motor excitability. On the other hand, the administration of small doses of morphine increases the speed and accuracy of perception of external stimuli; under the influence of the same substance conceptual processes also become more superficial, but in addition, slower, and volition is impaired.

Lange himself warns that his experiments do not permit many conclusions about the characteristics of chronic cocaine intoxication. He administered to his experimental subjects very small doses of cocaine (20 mg) apparently by mouth, on only two occasions, so that the effects must have been very mild and somewhat unreliable because the drug was given in all cases on the day following the administration of 10 mg of morphine. The subjective stimulating effect lasted approximately one hour, while the subjects were under observation for only three-quarters of an hour. This does not permit any valid conclusion about the duration of action of cocaine, and does not provide any information about inhibitory phenomena which may have occurred subsequently.

The results of this author provide interesting analogies to my own, particularly with respect to the enhancement of addition performance, the increase in speed and regularity of association of ideas, and the increase in motor excitation and euphoria. On the other hand, Lange found a lower degree of stimulation of performance while the number of errors was much increased. This discrepancy may perhaps have been due to the very small doses which he used, but also to the fact that individuals habituated to cocaine respond differently from naive subjects because in the former the subjective disturbances are much less marked. Lange has shown that the programming of this test, as used in earlier experiments by Kraepelin, is quite suitable for these investigations.

Jacob Mensch, who had assisted me with the experiments on the psychological action of coffee, undertook at my suggestion, in the laboratory of the psychiatric clinic at Zürich, some new experiments of this type. I shall describe them here because of their intrinsic interest and also because they provide information that can serve as the basis for further research.

They dealt, among others, with three in-patients at the clinic who were detoxified cocaine sniffers, and who were made to perform the addition test of one-digit numbers. Each subject worked for one hour after the administration of each of the following substances on an empty stomach: 20 mg cocaine, a strong dose of coffee rich in caffeine, nearly completely decaffeinated coffee, malt coffee and cocoa.

The most characteristic results were obtained in a 26-year-old bank clerk. The subject achieved a very impressive output while under the effect of cocaine. He was very excited and made the calculations in such a loud voice that the nurse in the adjacent laboratory, even though the doors were firmly closed, wondered what was going on. During the whole experiment the subject was very pale, and once the experiment was finished he had an absent look which lasted for some time. After taking coffee, the subject also made his calculations quickly and in a loud voice, but not to the same degree as under the influence of cocaine. During the experiment with decaffeinated coffee, he worked quietly and with ease, while committing the smallest number of errors. Malt coffee and cocoa had no favorable effect on the intellectual efficiency of the subject. It appears, rather, that they exerted an inhibitory action. He did not want to drink the malt coffee after tasting it and did so only at our insistence. At one point during the experiment with cocoa, the subject stated that he felt dull and heavy, as if he had eaten too much, and that he was experiencing much difficulty continuing his calculations.

The next two experiments show how variable the effects of these drugs are from individual to individual. In these experiments, the ability to calculate was so much decreased by the drastic impairment of attention following the administration of cocaine, that the overall result was lower than that obtained after the administration of the other drugs. The decrease in efficiency of intellectual performance became particularly clear during the last third of the hour. It should be noted that these two subjects were confirmed psychopaths. The commitment to perform the same task for a whole hour created a situation which became the source of very complex problems under the influence of cocaine. At any rate, these experiments show that the results can vary considerably and that very close attention must be paid not only to the effect of cocaine, but also to the general psychological state of the patient, and to his mood at the time of the experiment.

TABLE I
SUBJECT S: 26-YEAR-OLD CLERK WITH CHARACTER DISORDER AND COCAINE DEPENDENCE

Pre-Treatment	*Number of additions in* 1st-20th min.	21st-40th min.	41st-60th min.	*Totals in 60 min.* additions	errors	*Minute in which efficiency was* highest	lowest
None	900	906	833	2639	7	42nd	56th
Cocaine, 20 mg sniffed in 3 min.	973	1183	1167	3323	16	14th	32nd
Brazilian coffee	1006	1046	923	2975	9	33rd	60th
Decaffeinated coffee	1022	925	1021	2968	4	16th	23rd
Malt coffee	857	865	788	2510	8	11th	53rd
Cocoa	763	918	706	2387	9	36th	58th

TABLE II
SUBJECT SCH: 22-YEAR-OLD PERFORMING ARTIST WITH CHARACTER DISORDER AND COCAINE DEPENDENCE

Pre-Treatment	*Number of additions in* 1st-20th min.	21st-40th min.	41st-60th min.	*Totals in 60 min.* additions	errors	*Minute in which efficiency was* highest	lowest
None	485	602	447	1534	15	28th	12th
Cocaine, 20 mg sniffed in 3 min.	842	869	810	2521	33	13th	35th
Brazilian coffee	1003	1038	821	2862	11	31st	57th
Decaffeinated coffee	982	913	862	2757	8	16th	20th
Malt coffee	497	675	507	1679	5	35th	14th
Cocoa	469	406	580	1455	6	26th	10th

What is striking in the second patient is the large number of errors committed under the effects of cocaine while the total number of additions is not the largest. During both the cocaine and the coffee experiments, the subject worked in a hasty and hectic fashion. He was excited, his face was red and his hands trembled. After both experiments he fell into a state of profound depression. The most important and consistent results were obtained with the decaffeinated coffee when the ratio of errors to additions was lowest. During the experiment with malt coffee the subject complained of heartburn which he claimed impaired his performance. Between the 20th and 40th minutes of the experiment with cocoa, the patient complained of fatigue: "I feel lazy."

The highest speed of calculations in the third subject occurred after sniffing cocaine. But he was inattentive and fell behind at times. The same took place during the coffee experiment, but less markedly. During the cocaine experiment the subject had palpitations, with very obvious increased pulsations of the carotid artery. During the coffee experiment he complained of anxiety- provoking precordial discomfort. The best performance with the smallest number of errors and no subjective discomfort took place during the decaffeinated coffee experiment.

I shall report three other unpublished experiments made by Jacob Mensch on the action of cocaine and of caffeine on pulse rate, blood pressure and respiratory function. The examination of circulatory responses was carried out with Sahli's sphygmobolometer. The detailed protocol of one of these experiments and a summary of the results of all three experiments are shown in the accompanying table. I end by making some remarks about the psychological action of cocaine and of caffeine.

Specific Phenomena

The three patients were not aware that the powder that they took with milk was caffeine. But all three stated that it "stimulated" them like cocaine but to a lesser degree. Some euphoria, but less marked than with cocaine, was confirmed objectively.

B. Specific Symptomatology

1. Psychic Ill Effects Due to Cocaine Addiction

In the chapter on this topic in Kraepelin's textbook (8th edition, 1910), reference is made only to subcutaneous administra-

TABLE III
SUBJECT W: 18-YEAR-OLD DENTAL TECHNICIAN WITH CHARACTER DISORDER AND COCAINE DEPENDENCE

Pre-Treatment	*Number of additions in* 1st-20th min.	21st-40th min.	41st-60th min.	*Totals in 60 min.* additions	errors	*Minute in which efficiency was* highest	lowest
None	509	593	701	1803	10	50th	14th
Cocaine, 20 mg sniffed in 3 min.	814	710	689	2313	9	9th	33rd
Brazilian coffee	1000	922	839	2761	6	22nd	30th
Decaffeinated coffee	995	977	953	2925	4	27th	39th
Malt coffee	642	690	746	2078	7	34th	13th
Cocoa	636	639	659	1934	9	17th	10th

TABLE IV

A. COMPLETE RESULTS OF PHYSIOLOGICAL STUDY ON SUBJECT S.W.

	Pulse	Respirations	Blood pressure in mm Hg		Pulse volume		Pulse work	
	per min.	per min.	Systolic	Diastolic	Single	Per min.	Single	Per min.
(i) *Cocaine, 20 mg sniffed in 3 min.*								
Baseline	80	21	165	90	0.09	7.20	11.016	888.28
15 min. after sniffing	95	19	180	110	0.14	13.30	20.944	1989.68
30 min. after sniffing	90	19	180	110	0.14	12.60	20.944	1884.96
45 min. after sniffing	90	19	180	110	0.14	12.60	20.944	1884.96
(ii) *Caffeine sodium salicylate 280 mg in 150 g warm milk*								
Baseline	70	22	160	90	0.09	6.30	11.016	771.121
15 min. after drinking	80	22	175	120	0.10	8.0	16.32	1305.60
30 min. after drinking	78	20	175	120	0.12	9.36	19.584	1527.553
45 min. after drinking	78	20	170	120	0.12	9.36	19.584	1527.553

B. COMPARISON OF DRUG-INDUCED CHANGES IN PHYSIOLOGICAL FINDINGS IN THE THREE SUBJECTS

F.S.								
Cocaine	−2	−3	+15	+10	0	−0.14	+0.952	+66.640
Caffeine	+6	−3	+20	+10	+0.03	+2.52	+5.848	+472.192
S.W.								
Cocaine	+15	−2	+15	+20	+0.05	+6.10	+9.928	+1009.400
Caffeine	+10	−2	+15	+30	+0.03	+3.06	+8.568	+756.431
K.Sch.								
Cocaine	+32	+7	+20	+10	+0.01	+2.38	+1.632	+578.46
Caffeine	+10	−3	−15	−10	−0.02	−0.70	−3.264	−252.04

tion of cocaine, and the author emphasizes the simultaneous use of cocaine and morphine which was then common. He distinguishes first the cocaine intoxication state, characterized by a pleasant feeling of warmth and marked well-being, and probably with increased central motor excitation followed by inhibition, and its transition to delirious states of excitation which frequently end in fatal collapse. He then describes chronic cocaine intoxication with nervous excitation, marked sensitivity to sounds, mild flight of ideas, loss of will, impairment of memory and mood swings ranging from feelings of well-being to anxiety. This state is also characterized by loss of weight, an appearance of premature aging, physical weakness, exaggeration of reflexes and muscular activity, muscular spasms, rapid pulse, palpitations, increased sweating, impotence and insomnia. Kraepelin describes a third picture, designated cocaine insanity, which differs from alcoholic psychosis in many respects and is characterized by: rapid onset, changes in mood consisting of a mixture of anxiety and irritability, auditory hallucinations during which the patient hears voices addressed to him personally, visual micro-hallucinations, agitation, delusions of persecution often based on jealousy and a tendency to violent behavior. Consciousness is, for the most part, clear and the patient only occasionally experiences a transitory state of mental confusion which prevents him from recognizing people or having insight into his illness. From a symptomatic point of view, cocaine insanity can be placed somewhere between *delirium tremens* and alcoholic psychosis. When cocaine is discontinued the delirious states disappear in a few days and the delusional ideas in a few weeks or even months. In cases of combined cocaine and morphine addiction, cocaine should be discontinued first and morphine later.

Schroder's description (*Handbuch der Psychiatrie*, 1912) is almost identical to Kraepelin's (1910), while Bumke (*Handbuch der Neurologie*, 1912) already calls attention to the rapid propagation of cocaine addiction by sniffing in America and India. Based on data gathered at the Zürich clinic, Bleuler (*Lehrbuch*, 1923) emphasizes the spread of cocaine addiction by sniffing in Switzerland and calls attention, in addition, to a condition reminiscent of Korsakoff's syndrome. Bumke, in his *Lehrbuch der Geisteskrankheiten* (1924), recognized that cocaine addiction, especially by sniffing, had increased in Europe, but believed that its treatment should be the same as that used for addiction to morphine and that satisfactory results are rarely obtained in less than two or three weeks. Most other authors, on the other hand, recommend abrupt withdrawal since it is accompanied by comparatively mild symptoms.

Among French authors, Vallon and Bessiére (1914) proposed the following classification: 1) cocaine intoxication, characterized by a state of excitation, followed by a daydreaming phase; 2) chronic cocainism characterized by a decrease in intellectual performance and loss of memory; 3) acute, sub-acute and chronic hallucinosis, the latter giving rise to chronic and systematized cocaine delusions.

In 1918, Courtois-Suffit and Giroux distinguished two main groups, i.e., acute and chronic cocainism, while Piouffle (1919) differentiated between: cocaine intoxication with an excitation state, a delirious and a comatose phase; acute cocaine psychosis characterized mainly by the presence of hallucinations; chronic cocaine psychosis, subdivided into two subtypes characterized by mental confusion and by dream-like delirium; chronic systematized cocaine psychosis (cocaine delusions); cocaine paresis; and periodic cocaine addiction ("cocaine dipsomania"). Rogues de Fursac describes acute cocainism in his *Manuel de Psychiatrie* (1923) as a state characterized by pure and simple excitation evolving into a kind of intoxication with partial mental confusion, often of a delirious nature and ending in a comatose sleep. Sometimes the picture is complicated by convulsions, constituting a true cocaine epilepsis. Next to chronic cocainism, he distinguishes cocaine delirium with a tendency to interpretations and to hallucinations, but without loss of the sense of self. Legrain, in his *Traité de Pathologie Médicale* (1922), refers to a hallucinatory delirium of cocaine origin that he considers equivalent to *delirium tremens* and which sometimes becomes chronic and complicated by delusions of persecution and delusional hypochondriac ideas. His work makes no mention of the systematized cocaine insanity.

At the Zürich clinic we have had the opportunity to examine, sometimes very closely, about 100 cases of both in- and out-patients suffering from cocaine psychosis. Furthermore, I have been able to make use of detailed case histories provided to me by my colleagues in other Swiss clinics. Selected and characteristic case histories which give an adequate idea of the variety of clinical pictures are given below.

The following classification emerges, in my judgment, from my own observations as well as from those of other authors, which have already been described in the preceding chapters.

a) Acute Cocaine Intoxication

It is important to distinguish between the effects of a single dose of cocaine taken for the first time and those exerted by repeated doses on subjects more or less habituated to cocaine even if not on a continuous basis. The administration of the first dose of cocaine to a naive subject is followed by symptoms of physical stimulation and eventual inhibition which, for the most part, mask psychic excitation and euphoria. Thus the subjects, instead of experiencing a feeling of well-being, have a sense of severe malaise similar to precordial distress, with palpitations, dizziness, occasional muscle spasms and a marked state of psychomotor agitation. If a somewhat larger dose is administered to a sensitive individual, inhibitory phenomena accompanied by fainting occur rapidly and lead to paralysis of the respiratory center and death. The picture, rarer today than formerly, is seen in certain unfortunate cases of cocaine application in surgery.

In other individuals, on the contrary, psychomotor and physical symptoms following a first dose of cocaine are secondary and, a few seconds after an intravenous injection, or a few minutes after subcutaneous or nasal administration of cocaine, they experience a very marked feeling of euphoria. In women this euphoria may adopt a clearly sexual character accompanied by an active and irresistible desire for satisfaction, oblivious to all restrictions despite a very clear preservation of the sense of self. The effects last for approximately 20 to 40 minutes.

The causes of these individual variations in response are unknown. It is possible that they are due to psychological and physical individual constitutional differences. But it is also possible that they are related to the mood of the individual at the time or to the influence of the setting. It is known, for example, that alcohol may exert different effects on the same individual depending on the prevailing circumstances.

If, during the first intoxication, the subject exhibits a marked state of euphoria lasting one or two hours, one can be certain that he has taken several strong doses. This is most often followed by insomnia of one or two days duration, but occasionally the subject may fall abruptly into a comatose sleep followed in some cases by retrograde amnesia. This is an untoward complication which makes the investigation in cases in which the drug has been used for criminal purposes difficult if not impossible. In the case of a young girl whom I had the opportunity to examine, defloration and pregnancy were the only objective signs that permitted the reconstruction of the events that occurred while she was under the effects of cocaine.

Typical and severe cases of cocaine intoxication are seen in men who have made previous use of small doses of cocaine. This is probably due to the fact that, in cocaine-addict circles, naive subjects at first receive only small doses of cocaine in order to test their individual susceptibility and to get an idea of their pattern of response. Once reassurance has been obtained in this respect, the doses are increased rapidly. Euphoric reactions are then very marked. Psychic activity, even from an objective point of view, appears to be markedly stimulated, and inhibitions seem to disappear. Ideas are fleeting and the patient exhibits marked motor excitation simultaneously with very good motor coordination and increase in muscular strength. If no further doses are administered the patient calms down in 20 to 30 minutes and shows only a slight depression. When these euphoric states occur at close intervals or when the patient receives rapidly increasing doses, there is slight mental confusion accompanied by some degree of anxiety, despite the euphoria. Generally, hallucinations occur at this point. Most frequently, visual hallucinations appear first and they are related to the wish fulfillment of the subject. Sometimes they assume a cinematographic appearance, become frightening, and are complicated by tactile and auditory hallucinations which are unpleasant from the beginning. If further doses of cocaine are administered, irrational and frenzied motor outbursts can occur which are often accompanied by ideas of jealousy related to the people around. Finally, there may be inhibitory phenomena, with difficulty in respiration, cardiac insufficiency, ataxia and, eventually, more or less prolonged coma. In milder repeated intoxications, on the contrary, insomnia prevails during the periods of abstinence.

Piouffle (1919) is right when he says that the different types of acute intoxication already show all the symptoms seen in complicated cocaine psychoses, although in the latter they are grouped in characteristic patterns and are of longer duration. In this respect, as in many others, cocaine exerts a psychotic action much more profound than, and qualitatively different from, that produced by alcohol. The character of the hallucinations is quite different from that seen in alcoholism or alcoholic psychosis. As we have already stated, states of severe dissociative intoxication usually occur in patients who have already experienced cocaine intoxication rather frequently. Is the cause of this the repetition of the intoxication itself, or is it that some subjects have, generally speaking, specific psychopathological predispositions? The answer to this question must await a thorough and accurate study of a large number of reactions of this type. In the meantime we suggest that the underlying reason for the latter type of reaction is the individual premorbid psychopathological predisposition, because it is precisely such individuals who mainly, if not exclusively, become victims of addiction. It is possible that we shall eventually be able to differentiate between a normal and a pathological cocaine intoxication, as is the case in acute alcohol intoxication.

b) Chronic Cocaine Intoxication

As we have said in the preceding chapter, it is necessary to distinguish both sympatomatologically and prognostically, between those cases in which cocaine is used sporadically and those in which there is evidence of organic and mental disturbance even in the absence of acute intoxication or immediate withdrawal. This distinction would be comparable to that proposed by Bleuler (1917, 1923) in the case of alcoholism, except that, in the latter case, the habit is usually continuous, while in the case of cocaine addiction the need for the drug is often occasional and sporadic.

α) COCAINE ADDICTION

A considerable number of individuals have acquired the habit of using cocaine on certain occasions in order to experience euphoria or to surmount internal inhibitions that impair their work, as in the case of creative people, public speakers and others. Withdrawal phenomena or psychogenic factors provoke or enhance the need for cocaine in these individuals, but they are not compulsive users so that they have the opportunity to return to the normal state. Such individuals rarely allow themselves to fall into the fatal trap of steadily increasing doses. They retain their capacity to work even though this may be transitorily impaired after each intoxication. Experience shows that these people can easily become dependent on both cocaine and alcohol. It is very important, in my opinion, to recognize this comparatively benign morbid picture in order to avoid making a serious prognosis and subjecting the patient and his family to overly rigorous procedures. A cure often occurs following the patient's spontaneous decision to stop using the drug or as a result of a change in circumstances. Medical intervention is often unnecessary, and the patient can often be helped just as well or better by close friends or associates of the patient who have been informed of the critical situation.

Sometimes the need for cocaine is experienced periodically. This may be due either to a periodic return of the same psychogenic causes or to endogenous psychogenic causes. In the latter case, we would be dealing with the equivalent of dipsomania or, in other words, with epileptiform, psychopathological or, in some cases, perhaps even schizophrenic or manic-depressive fluctuations of mood. Piouffle (1919) has coined the rather unfortunate term "cocaine dipsomania" to refer to such cases. Such a term would be justified only in the presence of a simultaneous excessive use of alcohol. We shall use here the term *periodic endogenous cocainomania*, which describes the condition more aptly. The treatment should be directed towards the basic disturbance and adjusted to each case. In cases of this type it is always important to emphasize the need for a concomitant abstention from alcohol. This is, furthermore, a requirement for the treatment of cocaine addiction in general. The former method of treatment, which was based on substituting a drug believed to be less dangerous than the one to which the patient was addicted, has proven to be absurd and completely misguided. The best proof of this error was the outcome of the introduction of subcutaneous administration of cocaine for the treatment of morphine addiction. Anyone with a dangerous tendency in this respect must avoid all drugs and this must be the basis for the training of the patient's self-control. It is misguided to make people believe that they have shown proof of self-control when, instead of completely giving up the use of drugs, they have managed to use them in moderation. The general therapeutic principle that we follow, regardless of the illness, is an effort aimed at putting the individual totally beyond reach of noxious influences, rather than to achieve a quantitative decrease in such influences.

Cocaine addiction as described above is analogous to morphine addiction in individuals who, despite the use of the drug, are able now and then to abstain for more or less prolonged periods and thus avoid serious and lasting damage. However, this is less frequent in morphine than in cocaine addiction, partly because it has less attractive properties and social components and partly because morphine gives rise much more rapidly to tolerance, with a need for increasing dosage, and to withdrawal reactions. There are also very mild cases of morphine addiction. But the physicians who invoke them as proof that this addiction is not really very dangerous are wrong because they forget that 99% of morphine addicts are destroyed by their addiction.

β) TRUE CHRONIC COCAINISM

In chronic cocainism the withdrawal symptoms including feelings of oppression, depression, irregular sleep and palpitations are much more frequent and pronounced, and the intervals during which the subject abstains from the drug become briefer and increasingly rarer. The patients present not only a marked and lasting state of nervous excitation with motor agitation, but also inhibitory phenomena which soon assume a predominant role in the overall clinical picture. The initial stimulation of intellectual performance decreases. Associations of ideas become more superficial and conceptualization increasingly difficult. The will is weakened so that the patient ends up by being psychologically and physically incapable of performing a job that requires perseverance. Superficially, this handicap is concealed for some time under the guise of meaningless and empty activity, while the intellectual deficit is sometimes hidden behind an often intolerable loquaciousness. A characteristic trait of these patients is their mania for scribbling. The moral standards of the individual soon decrease, and this, in turn, soon becomes complicated by disturbances of memory. At first there is a decrease in the ability to recall accurately newly learned material. Then the patient becomes gradually incapable of recalling older engrams. The patient increasingly neglects his appearance and seeks the company of other cocaine addicts more and more exclusively. He develops ideas of reference towards people he knew before becoming a cocaine addict, in whose presence he feels inferior. This is, furthermore, somewhat justified by his overall social behavior. At first, while under the influence of cocaine he appears gay and full of self-assurance and it is only during periods of abstinence that he experiences depression that is often tinged with anxiety. As the drug use progresses this type of depression is experienced with increasing frequency, even during periods of acute intoxication, and may develop into an anxious delirium with which we shall deal later. Clear-cut physical signs and symptoms also appear. Cocaine addicts who administer the drug subcutaneously are often covered with abscesses produced by their increasing disregard of clean technique. Cocaine sniffers present a chronic dry rhinitis with reddening of the nostrils. In some cases, there is ulceration of the nasal mucosa, which may progress to perforation of the nasal septum, already described. Symptoms in the trigeminal region are also frequent. Disturbances of the autonomic nervous system manifest themselves principally by an increase in pulse rate which alternates with attacks of angina and dizziness. Gastrointestinal symptoms include diarrhea which later alternates with constipation. Gastric function also becomes irregular. Loss of weight which, it is claimed, is the rule in addicts to both cocaine and morphine, is rarely seen in sniffers. This is no doubt due to the abundant nourishment that they take between periods of intoxication. Some sniffers exhibit frankly pathological obesity. But whether he is thin or fat the cocaine addict always has a sickly appearance and gives the impression of physical deterioration. Men soon show lasting impotence, while among women there is at first diffuse menstruation with intense sexual excitation, while in the later stages they sometimes show amenorrhea. Pregnancy generally results in miscarriages during the first few months. Episodes of tremors and intense perspiration occur in both men and women. Motor control is at first intact, but this later gives way to ataxic phenomena. The skin often shows erythematous patches or transitory bluish spots due to localized vasoconstriction. For the same reason, the extremities are more or less livid and cold so that the patient is always seeking warmth, and there is a marked reduction in sensitivity to high ambient temperatures. In advanced stages of the illness the instinct of self-preservation is considerably weakened and energetic and often successful attempts at suicide are made for the most trivial reasons. In other cases the intensified emotional irritability and the loss of inhibitions lead the patients to dangerous impulsive acts. Although delusions of jealousy are frequent, they are, in my opinion, less typical of cocaine sniffers than of the earlier addicts to both cocaine and morphine. Due to a constant feeling of thirst, many patients become alcoholics as well.

c) Sub-Acute Cocaine Deliria

Long-standing cases of chronic intoxication often lead, especially in the presence of predisposing factors of an as yet unknown nature, to delusional states, which may last from several hours to days but which rarely last for more than two or three weeks. They are characterized by hallucinatory distortions of the environment and by some clouding of consciousness. Three modes of evolution may be distinguished: a euphoric state in which pleasant visual hallucinations predominate and which are associated with tactile illusions and very clear ideas of grandeur; a state of paranoid anxiety with frightening visual and auditory hallucinations and numerous tactile illusions which affect the feeling of physical well-being; a twilight oneiric state primarily characterized by cinematographic visual hallucinations most often accompanied by other types of sensory hallucinations, and especially by a somewhat anxious, indifferent mood. In the euphoric and paranoid states the patient exhibits marked motor activity leading sometimes to aggressive acts. In the oneiric state cocaine addicts generally exhibit marked motor passivity. A patient in this state stays indefinitely in his room completely motionless and only the need to secure new supplies of cocaine will stir him from his apathy. Clearness of consciousness remains in all of these states but the patient's perception of his relationship to his environment becomes seriously distorted. These conditions can last as long as the patient continues to take cocaine. Recovery usually takes place when the patient, because of the seriousness of his condition, is unable to procure more drug. This may also happen when the people around him, fearing discovery, cease to provide him with the drug, or when, through the initiative of the authorities or of his family, he is committed to a hospital. Under such conditions, the hallucinations disappear in a matter of hours or days. The patient, who up to this point has gone without sleep, falls asleep for 24 hours or longer, and when he wakes up the recollection of his delirious state is not totally lacking but is often quite vague. Usually the patient's awareness of the duration of the condition is particularly affected, and he tends to underestimate it. During the acute state the patient, as opposed to what happens in *delirium tremens*, is aware, to a certain extent, of the true cause of his condition, but is nevertheless incapable of drawing the relevant conclusion—that is, that he must give up the drug. Even if he were able to do this, he would totally lack the energy to implement his conclusion. Thus we have succeeded in distinguishing three types of delirium: a euphoric-hallucinatory state with a lesser or greater admixture of mania, an anxious paranoid state and an oneiric state. The anxious paranoid state is the most dangerous because it can often lead the patient to violent acts or to suicide.

d) Cocaine Psychosis

Most frequently, this is seen in patients who have already experienced delirious states of variable duration. After a preliminary phase characterized mainly by anxiety, the patient becomes extremely restless and agitated, and hallucinations and coherent and systematized delusional ideas develop in a few days. The hallucinations and the delusions most frequently show a psychological connection with real events in the life of the patient and assume the form of either ideas of grandeur with a mania for invention and discovery based on the patient's occupation or special personal interests, or ideas of persecution which are anxiety-provoking. Most often, the ideas of persecution appear first and are only subsequently combined with megalomania. In some cases, however, both appear simultaneously. In general, sleep is seriously disturbed, the patient eats poorly, loses weight, and becomes so weak that eventually he has to spend most of the day in bed. Generally, tactile hallucinations are at the forefront while visual hallucinations are next and auditory hallucinations are the least frequent. In terms of content, both the hallucinations and the delusions are very amenable to suggestion, but the latter does not eliminate them. The patient's consciousness is well-coordinated and the coherence of his associations is better maintained than in the sub-acute delirious states. The most characteristic feature of cocaine psychosis is the systematization of the psychopathological symptoms which exhibit such internal logic and emotional content that healthy people around the patient are often subject to his suggestions, leading to instances of induced insanity affecting, for example, the wife of the patient. Strictly speaking, the patients lack insight into their condition. The mood often fluctuates rapidly between a state of excited euphoria and a state of anxious suspicion accompanied by depression. The patients show an irresistible tendency to talk and to write, and a strong need for emotional and intellectual relationships with their environment, which is absent in the sub-acute deliria. If the subject continues to take the drug the illness may last for weeks or months. Withdrawal is followed, after several days or weeks, by a disappearance of the symptoms or by the development of a picture resembling the so-called Korsakoff syndrome. In some cases, organic brain lesions of a generalized character are the *sequelae* of cocaine psychosis. If a paranoid psychosis persists once the cocaine use has stopped, the condition is likely due to a combination of cocaine psychosis with pre-existing schizophrenic disturbances.

e) Cocaine Psychosis of Korsakoff Type

It is characterized by severe disturbances of memory with marked confabulation, while the ability for association of ideas remains comparatively intact. It may develop progressively during chronic cocainism or it may be associated with cocaine psychosis. I have not been able to observe, during the course of this psychosis, peripheral neuritis of the type associated with the alcoholic psychosis described by Korsakoff. The prognosis is favorable if strict abstinence is observed, but the danger of relapse is greater in this condition than in the equivalent alcoholic psychosis.

f) Cocaine Paresis

This syndrome includes the most severe types of organic and generalized cerebral lesions associated with prolonged and heavy intoxication. It is often impossible to make a clear-cut distinction between this condition and the preceding one. It can be stated, however, that the disturbances of memory are not prominent and that the main feature of cocaine paresis is a type of imbecility accompanied by absurd and incoherent ideas of grandeur. These symptoms, which were apparently quite frequent when subcutaneous administration of cocaine was common, are very rare among sniffers. This can probably be explained by the fact that, even when the sniffers increase their dosage rapidly, they can give up the drug more easily when the circumstances demand it, as for example when they develop a state of subacute delirium. I strongly believe, however, that the explanation for the higher frequency of paralytic-like states in former days was due to the combined use of morphine and cocaine. This result may be due either to the fact that morphine, by weakening the organism and frequently leading to general marasmus, renders it less resistant to the action of cocaine, or to the fact that the combination of these two drugs exerts a particularly disastrous action on the central nervous system. I have been able to observe personally former morphine addicts who had become cocaine addicts (by subcutaneous injection) and who, during the first few days, presented symptoms that could be mistaken for those of advanced syphilitic general paresis, except for a negative reaction in serum and spinal fluid. If lethal complications do not supervene, the diagnosis is usually established after the event by the fact that withdrawal of cocaine leads to rapid improvement of the paresis. But even after recovery, the patients often exhibit a lasting emotional and intellectual deficit.

The above considerations allow us to adopt the following *Systematic Classification of the Psychoses Associated with Cocainism*:

1. *Acute Reactions*. When the drug is taken for the first time the most frequent reaction is a mild state of intoxication with little or no euphoria, strong anxiety, marked motor excitation and inhibitory phenomena.

Alternatively, there may be marked euphoria with psychomotor excitation, mild hallucinations, but particularly vivid visual hallucinations whose content is in harmony with the personality of the subject. Consciousness is clear.

The third possibility is an acute delirious state with euphoria, excitation, anxiety, intense motor stimulation without ataxia and partial mental confusion.

2. *Chronic Reactions*. A cocaine habit without lasting consequences.

Chronic cocainism accompanied by lasting disturbances.

Periodic cocainism, or cocainomania, i.e., periodic need for narcotics in epileptic-like individuals and others with personality disorders (corresponding to the picture in dipsomania).

3. *Sub-Acute Cocaine Deliria*. A euphoric-hallucinatory syndrome with vivid hallucinations, especially visual.

An anxious paranoid syndrome with numerous visual, auditory and tactile hallucinations and marked motor excitation.

An oneiric syndrome with feelings of anxiety, visual hallucinations (cinematographic or otherwise) and auditory hallucinations. Motor passivity.

4. *Chronic and Systematized Cocaine Psychosis or Cocaine Delirium*.

5. *Cocaine Psychosis Corresponding to Korsakoff's Syndrome*.

6. *Cocaine General Paresis*.

2. Clinical Histories

I have personally seen nearly 100 cocaine users, but I shall describe here only those who most aptly illustrate the features already described. Several case histories made available to me by other psychiatric hospitals in Switzerland will also be included. The case histories include 28 men and seven women. This supports my observation that in Switzerland, as well as in Italy (see above), cocaine use is more prevalent among men than among women. The histories are presented according to the most important clinical features.

Six of the men were overtly homosexual and one was bisexual prior to use of cocaine. The illness began at age 14 to 20 in 14 patients, at age 21 to 30 in 15, at age 31 to 40 in two, and at age 41 to 47 in four (all of them physicians). The women included one physician, two wives of military officers, three business employees and one prostitute. The men included four physicians, one chemist, one jurist, two university students, one high-school student, one apprentice, seven business employees, four artists, one dental technician, one mechanic, two waiters, one pharmacist, one dancer and one decorator. Of the 33 patients who presented essentially with a toxic psychosis, 18 can be considered cured in the sense that they have abstained from cocaine use for a considerable time, judging from the information available. Five have relapsed, four committed suicide and information on the rest is unavailable.

a) Acute Cocaine Intoxication

Psychiatrists rarely have the opportunity to observe cases of acute cocaine intoxication. I have only one case available.

Case 1: E.B., domestic servant, born in 1901. Markedly neurotic mother, maternal grandfather with personality disorder. One paternal uncle committed suicide. The patient's behavior has always been strange and unpredictable and she has suffered much from headaches. For a year, following a bout of influenza in the spring of 1919, the patient remained in a state of intense physical weakness and of mild mental excitation. In Zürich in 1921, she met a drugstore employee with whom she often visited a coffee house frequented by cocaine users. One day she learned that her lover had a mistress who was pregnant. She had found the two of them together as they were about to leave Zürich to go abroad. She experienced a crying spell followed by depression, and her lover, to help her overcome this mood, gave her a substantial dose of cocaine. It is probable that during the preceding few weeks she had already sniffed some cocaine. Once at home she took a sedative (Dial) and was found in a dazed state, her face slightly reddish. The pupils were completely dilated and barely responsive to light. In this state, she was admitted to the clinic on December 1st, 1921, complaining principally of dryness of the mouth and of a feeling of constriction of the throat. The following morning she was lucid but the pupils remained markedly dilated. Chemical analysis of the stomach contents confirmed the presence of cocaine. On December 3rd, she was transferred to the Burghölzli Institute. She was in a peculiar dreamy state and the pupils were still widely dilated. Some days later, when she had fully returned to her normal state, she stated that after sniffing cocaine she could see pleasant things, such as theater scenes which gave her a great deal of pleasure. It is not possible to give much credence to these statements because it was established that the patient was a confirmed prevaricator. She was discharged cured on January 3, 1922. Diagnosis: acute cocaine intoxication in an individual with psychopathic predisposition.

b) Chronic Cocaine Intoxication

α) COCAINE ADDICTION

Five of my cases can be included in this category. They include a decorator, two university students, a physician who was a longstanding morphine addict and a woman physician. They all presented the characteristic phenomena of cocaine addiction and to the extent that accurate information is available, all can be considered as cured.

Case 2: E.B., decorator, aged 25. "In May of last year, in a men's club, I heard about cocaine for the first time. It was offered to me and curiosity made me try it. The first sniff failed to produce any pleasure. Therefore, after keeping the rest of the drug in my pocket for four weeks, I gave it to someone else. Ten months later, cocaine was offered to me again and it was only then that I found out what cocaine was really like. I immediately experienced a pleasant feeling in my teeth and a cigarette produced an extraordinary pleasure. Before taking cocaine, the cigarette smoke felt tasteless and strong, but after cocaine it was aromatic and sweet. This was enough to arouse my interest but I was not ready to fully appreciate the effects of cocaine until I found out that it prevented fatigue. It is an excellent drug for anyone who wants to dance all night, for example, without getting tired. I consulted books and found in the excellent work by Dr. Marta, of Milan, that some of the symptoms that I experienced under cocaine were the same as described by him. The action of cocaine, however, presents such individual variation that it is impossible to establish a general symptomatology applicable to all cases. Only at the beginning I experienced an abnormal tremor of the hands which disappeared after the first stage, and was replaced by a pleasant feeling of superiority and freedom from all cares. I never felt I was being persecuted, even when rumors about the police were circulating. My head was always full of ideas and I was able to talk about every conceivable subject for hours on end. It was a remarkable fact that I was always interested in the most beautiful and idealistic ideas, those designed to bring us all close together. The only trouble was that I couldn't concentrate my thoughts on one and the same subject for any length of time and I jumped with great ease from one idea to another. There was great openness among my associates as soon as we got to know each other a little. I trusted everybody. From a moral point of view I had nothing to reproach myself for, except the day when I gave cocaine to S., who was known to be a bit crazy. But I could not do otherwise because he kept on begging for it and later began to threaten me. I spent a great deal of money during the period that I snorted cocaine. The most important thing that cooled my enthusiasm for cocaine was that in the evenings after work, I felt too tired unless I took cocaine again. Therefore, I decided to snort only during my days off. With the exception of this drawback I did not experience any other untoward effects during the period of cocaine use. On the other hand, friends like C. and S., who used it chronically, showed obviously abnormal behavior. To be honest, I was happy the day that the police put an end to all this story and freed me once and for all of the self-reproach that I used to feel every time I lacked cocaine or the money to buy it. It was also fortunate for my friends, some of whom were beginning to behave peculiarly. Today I feel cured of this illness. I can think calmly about this period, and I have escaped from mental and physical deterioration. It is from understanding rather than from rules and regulations that I got the necessary will power.

Case 3: M.R., law student, born in 1898. He was brought to the psychiatric clinic by the police in December, 1917. His mother ran a boarding house and had, among her tenants, a few cocaine addicts who induced the young man to try cocaine, and occasionally morphine, following his university entrance examinations in September, 1917. He states that the effects of cocaine became evident almost immediately, within minutes after sniffing, and consisted of a pleasurable feeling and mental stimulation. Following this he would experience an unbelievable feeling of happiness and a sense of being distant from everything happening around him. When he walked in the streets under the influence of cocaine, it seemed to him that all the passersby were far away from him and that everything was pleasantly unreal. Visual impressions were more vivid than usual, the sense of hearing was abnormally acute and everything happening around him gave him the impression of a motion picture film. His visual hallucinations included seeing numerous cats moving over the wallpaper and then turning into winged wheels. His room seemed much larger than it really was. The effects of cocaine became milder after each inhalation, so that he had to constantly increase the dosage in order to obtain the same sensations. He experienced intense thirst and perspired profusely. However, sexual excitation disappeared quickly.

We felt that the young man was in great danger, but he left the clinic in mid-treatment after 14 days. We contacted his mother but we had the impression that she herself was not entirely drug-free. She did not appear to appreciate the seriousness of her son's condition and begged us strongly not to refer him to the police. According to subsequent information from the young man himself, he had given up cocaine use completely.

Case 4: M.W., student of Germanic languages, born in 1898. He was brought to the psychiatric clinic in Zürich by the police, who had learned that he was a cocaine user. He was a nervous intelligent man, with a gift for poetry. Under the influence of cocaine-using friends he injected cocaine several times in order to study introspectively the mental effects on himself. He experienced a marked stimulation of fantasy, but was unable to perfect the images that unrolled in front of him like a cinematographic film because of internal and motor agitation. During the weeks preceding the consultation, he had used cocaine sparingly, and a severe reprimand from the physician was sufficient to make him decide to give up further experiments of this type.

Case 5: A 30-year-old physician who was a perceptive observer and who had been hospitalized for excessive drinking, gave the following description of a period during which, while working as an intern, he had used cocaine.

"I had been tempted to try cocaine from the moment I heard about it. The same had been the case with respect to all other drugs. Generally, I was in the habit of testing on myself the pharmacological actions of most therapeutic drugs. In most instances, the effects were quite trivial because I am basically quite healthy and resistant, and also because most of the symptoms attributed to drugs exist only in the imagination of physicians who write paid articles about them.

Two years before I began sniffing I had been able to objectively study the effects of cocaine in friends and 'demimondaines' at G's.

My first dose was about 200 to 300 mg. The effect was mild. There was slight flight of ideas, a feeling of physical well-being and tunes followed each other quickly in my head. I even think that I heard melodies that I did not know. These were not true hallucinations, but rather a pleasant exaggeration of my normal tendency to experience musical fantasies.

The picture changed completely after a dose of 600 mg. I began by taking 200 mg. I lay naked on the bed and looked at myself in the mirror. I should mention in this respect that at age 17 I had experienced a transitory period of narcissism. But since then, generally speaking, the sight of my body is rather unpleasant. In the spring, during the swimming season I always had to force myself, particularly during the first few days, to get undressed and expose my body to the view of other bathers. I spent two hours wondering whether or not to take another dose of cocaine. I felt fine, completely occupied with the flight of my ideas, and lying motionless. Finally, I took the remaining 400 mg. I went back to my bed and waited. After five minutes I noticed two flies which obstinately kept flying around the lamp, but which I knew to be unreal and nonexistent. As I looked at the walls of the room, they became covered with a blue vapor, a moving mist. All the pictures in the room were in movement. I knew from my friend P.P. that one is able to give orders to one's fantasies. That is why, when the picture *Maternal Bliss* appeared in front of my eyes, I ordered the mother to lift up and kiss the infant, which she did immediately. I ordered the room to turn around its axis, and I truly had the physical sensation of being suspended from the floor, following a rotation of 180°. Soon the room also began to oscillate. I could see the couch rising and hovering over the table. I was even able to touch the ceiling. At will, I could turn the room into a forest in which I walked without having to get up. Most of the time I was either lying down or standing still. I was transported out the window on a flying machine, I dipped into the ocean, I could see all the surroundings. Later, I let the door open and allowed a remarkably beautiful woman to come in. I talked to her (though I had no auditory hallucinations, only physical and visual ones), undressed her, and, sure enough, had sexual intercourse with her.

I should at this point mention the objective physical symptoms, as I was able to observe them: there was dilatation of the pupils, slight perspiration, marked pallor, weakness, penile retraction, polyuria (1.5 liters of urine in six hours). During the imaginary coitus I could clearly feel the penis entering the vagina, and there was a voluptuous sensation in the loins and penis, although of course without ejaculation. This happened up to 30 times during the first night. Although there was always pre-cordial discomfort after the intoxication but never during it, the pulse rate after the imaginary coitus was markedly accelerated, reaching a level of 140 per minute, the same as after real coitus. I then looked at all sorts of pictures and postcards, I was able to enlarge the size of the persons in them at will and to make them assume the appearance of people I knew, to speak to them, have intercourse with them, and even to make them talk and make love to each other. This lasted approximately four hours. Perversions did not enter into my hallucinations at that time. Once the intoxication was over, the palpitations caused an unpleasant sensation. I was not able to provoke hallucinations except when I concentrated on one and the same object for a long time, and the visions were then less clear than before. On the other hand, all the pictures in the room continued to move on their own, especially a *Salambo* which I found very unpleasant. The hallucinations, consisting essentially of outlines, were much smaller than before. I could see, for example, a parade of horsemen, all very similar to each other. I was in a state of strong sexual arousal and I masturbated twice. During this, the penis remained very small, and the ejaculation time was very prolonged, about half an hour. This further increased the pre-cordial distress. This state lasted four more hours. I then spent an equally long time without being able to fall asleep, until finally I decided to go out and have dinner. Once in the street it seemed that everybody was looking at me and I felt embarrassed.

A second intoxication with the same dose produced practically the same effects. The hallucinations tended to become increasingly focused in the sexual area. After getting all I could from normal coitus, I began to imagine sexual perversions. This was stimulated by reading Krafft-Ebing's *Psychopathia Sexualis*, which I did at various times when I was under the influence of cocaine. The sensual feelings were less and less intense and the fantasies followed each other with increasing rapidity, though still under the control of my will during the state of intoxication. From that time on, the stage immediately following the intoxication was associated with progressively greater feelings of oppression. I could see large black shadows of men or of unrecognizable animals that came towards my bed and wanted to lie down on top of me. I was always aware that these were effects of the cocaine intoxication and I was not unduly concerned. The diminutive hallucinations of the third phase were always present and I could even provoke them artificially throughout the day by concentrating on a particular image, while attending to my ordinary duties as a country doctor. Quite frequently the hallucinations would lose their intensity and clarity for about a quarter of an hour, and then regain their intensity even in the absence of another inhalation. I explained this fact as follows: the anesthesia of the nasal mucosa by cocaine resulted in a decrease of the circulation in this region, interfering with the absorption of the drug. When the circulation returned to normal, the remaining amount of drug was readily dissolved and carried quickly into the general circulation. I have also noticed that the best effects are obtained by applying cocaine to the nasal septum. When the drug applied to this region was completely dissolved, substantial amounts still remained on the inside of the alae of the nose, especially towards the apex, and I removed them and placed them on the septum. The cocaine powder that adhered to the fingers, I would apply to my lips and this often led to complete anesthesia of the mouth. Furthermore, I would carefully gather in a piece of paper the last traces of cocaine spread over my bed so that I could use it afterwards. With two or three exceptions I have always sniffed every bit of cocaine at my disposal on any given occasion. The day following the intoxication, I would have such a distaste for the drug that I could discontinue its use for a time. I have taken cocaine in the street only very rarely and I was never able to surrender fully to my hallucinations for fear of being found out. On the other hand, I have often looked out into the street through my window and arranged the trees and bushes into images and scenes always of obscene nature.

The perversions finally progressed to the point where I could see myself as a woman, most often as a prostitute having relations simultaneously with several men and in all possible ways. I made for them whole fantasies involving sodomy, masochism and sadism. In this context I had strong olfactory hallucinations. Whenever I had hallucinations of incestuous relations with my relatives I always cut them off. Also, the homosexual fantasies never gave me any pleasure. At the beginning of the intoxication, I always had narcissistic preoccupations. I would stand in front of the mirror and indulge in all sorts of contortions in order to practise fellatio on myself, or I would stretch the penis until it would reach my mouth. I would also perceive the image in the mirror alternatively as a woman and as a man so that I could have intercourse. Afterwards I would spend the whole night looking at pictures, illustrated magazines, rugs and the landscape. I cannot tell how many times I would turn the light on and off, but it always required some effort to switch from one activity to another. And I was always in fear of being found out at the hospital by the night duty nurse who did, in fact, need me a few times. I simply gave her instructions through the closed door and, as I was able to check later, they were always appropriate. On the other hand, my voice was always hoarser and my speech rougher than in my normal state. Concerning physical symptoms, I should add that on numerous occasions I had sudden diarrhea shortly after sniffing. But during the night, there were no further bowel movements.

The next day I would feel a strong revulsion against all drugs, at first even including alcohol. I never resorted to using morphine and cocaine together, but at a certain point in time I got into the habit of taking alcohol before sniffing cocaine. I was thus able to experience the drug effects more rapidly, and with smaller doses of cocaine than usual. Altogether I took in the space of four years between 30 and 50 g of cocaine. I never took doses of more than 1.5 g and I never took the drug on two consecutive days. I should add that my actual sexuality, as well as that reflected in my fantasies, is exactly the opposite of that reflected in the hallucinations that I have described."

Case 6: A woman physician, aged 30 years and without hereditary stigmata of any note. She is obliged to live with her parents, with whom she is often in conflict. Three months earlier, while overworked and suffering from a severe head cold, she remembered that the running nose could be quickly alleviated by cocaine. For a period of three days she repeatedly sniffed doses of 0.1 g, which promptly decreased the nasal secretions and opened the air passages. But whenever the effect of cocaine subsided, a copious nasal secretion would begin again. The patient, therefore, continued to take new doses of cocaine, and after about a week she became clearly aware of euphoria and a subjective finding that her work was much easier. Once the coryza was over, she could not give up the use of cocaine. After four weeks she was using it at the rate of 1 g per day, and reached a dose of 4 to 5 g daily in three months. This resulted in total insomnia, loss of appetite and a loss of weight of about 10 kg. Her parents were baffled by the changes in personality experienced by the patient, who would be either extremely alert or anxious and dreamy. She was, however, able to continue her work well. Eventually, a large number of empty cocaine containers, as well as some drug, were found in her room and were confiscated. After psychiatric consultation, she was able to abstain from cocaine use completely over the course of a few days, through an effort of the will, and without interrupting her work. Since then she has remained well.

β) CHRONIC COCAINISM PROPER.

We include in this category 12 patients, four of whom were women. They were all hospitalized for various lengths of time. Four patients, including two women, later returned to the use of cocaine. One woman ended by committing suicide with *Somnifen®* sometime after discharge. Four patients, including one woman, have been definitely cured. We have reason to believe that the remaining patients have not returned to the use of the drug.

Case 7: G. *v.* K., the wife of a Russian officer, born in 1869. Many members of her family suffered from tuberculosis but there is no evidence of mental illness. Of frail constitution, and very well brought up, she married an officer whom she did not love, while she felt for many years strongly attracted to a colleague of her husband. She has had four children, and her successive pregnancies have left as a *sequelae* very painful hemorrhoids. A cocaine ointment was prescribed to alleviate the pain. As a result, she acquired such a habit that even after the pain had disappeared and her condition had improved, she continued to apply ointments with a higher and higher concentration of cocaine. Eventually she replaced the ointment with intranasal spraying of cocaine solutions. In this way she took several grams daily. Between 1894, when she began using cocaine, and 1900, her dependence on the drug had reached such proportions that she underwent hypnotic treatment in Kiev, though without any positive results. The same applied to several drug treatments to which she was submitted. The intelligent and formerly plump woman became markedly emaciated and suffered from insomnia and constant excitation.

On July 27, 1901, her family decided to refer her to a Swiss psychiatric clinic. On arrival she claimed she had no drug in her possession, but large amounts of cocaine were found in her personal effects. Despite rigorous surveillance she succeeded in smuggling in a certain amount of cocaine, probably in a pillow, at least during the early part of her treatment. She weighed 45 kg on admission, but at the end of three months she had gained 8 kg. Several 50 mg doses of cocaine were made available to the patient during the first few days. These had the effect of turning the feeble, emaciated, old-looking woman suddenly into an animated person with a lively expression. Six days after admission the only withdrawal symptom was a nocturnal bout of tachycardia, with faint pulse, coldness of the extremities and cardiac pain radiating to the left shoulder. Intellectual function appeared intact. Subsequent treatment was very well tolerated. She left the clinic on March 4, 1902, with the intention of giving up cocaine definitively. We have not heard from her since. We should add that the patient had never experienced delirious states, but that cocaine always produced in her marked excitation with speeding up of mental activity; depression occurred when she was deprived of the drug.

Case 8: G.T. officer's wife, born in 1878. No family history of mental illness. Normal mental development. Successful in her examinations to become a secondary school teacher. She has a strong physical constitution and is a tireless mountaineer.

In 1913 she underwent resection of a piece of bone from the nose. A physician gave her 1% cocaine injections post-operatively. She became dependent on the drug to such a degree that she could not do without it and constantly introduced cocaine solutions into her nose. She soon showed a marked change in personality, including irritability, fits of violence, ceaseless logorrhea, insomnia and total neglect of her appearance. In the early summer of 1918, after five years of cocaine abuse, her fits of violence assumed extraordinary proportions. Among her own friends she felt watched and insecure and began to seek only the company of washing women and seamstresses. The swings from depression to excitation became more frequent. According to the patient her daily dose during the last few months had not surpassed 1 g of cocaine. After the pharmacists of her own town refused to provide her with cocaine, she managed to have it brought in from elsewhere. A physician at the residential clinic which she attended brought her to the Institute on August 10, 1918, after failing to withdraw the drug by gradual diminution of the concentration of cocaine. During the trip and the first few hours at the clinic she disappeared several times to go to the washroom in order to sniff her cocaine solution.

The pulse was normal and there were no signs of poor nutrition. There was complete insomnia during the first night at the clinic but no other withdrawal symptoms. There was marked constipation and the sense of smell was nearly abolished. There was fine tremor of the hands, weak reflexes, great muscle strength and no other somatic or neurological pathological symptoms.

During the following few days, the patient could not understand the reason for her being at the Institute. She threatened her husband with divorce if he failed to take her out. She talked freely and her mood was labile. At the end of three weeks, there was onset of mild depression with anxiety. The patient would contradict herself frequently and would become angry when this was brought to her attention. Her affective responses were obviously shallow. She made friends with other patients indiscriminately and, among others, she became madly involved with a young mentally retarded girl. Towards mid-September she became calmer and her mood was more even. Her sleep also became more regular. She recognized that she was very excitable, and she distinguished between a "red rage" during which she could attack everyone randomly and a "white rage" which she could control, but during which she was more untrustworthy and craftier.

On September 28, 1918, the husband was allowed to take the patient out of the clinic, with the promise that he put her in a private sanitarium. In December of 1921, the husband let us know that his wife was again showing all the signs of cocaine use. Considering the psychological make-up of the patient, this did not surprise us at all.

Case 9: J.P., businessman from the south, aged 23 years, brought to us in March, 1917 by the legal authorities because of a charge of swindling.

No information available on hereditary background. The patient was brought up in the Far East where his father was a senior official. He had a good education, had never been ill, had travelled much with his mother and had, from time to time, worked *ad honorem* at a bank. In 1915, he came to Switzerland to undergo treatment for chronic gonorrhea. He had shown homosexual tendencies since puberty. In 1916, he lived in a French-speaking Swiss town where he had a quarrel with one of his best friends. On the advice of women of his acquaintance, he began to use cocaine in order to forget his cares and claimed to have taken up to 10 g of cocaine daily for some months. The drug made him feel more cheerful and alert. Under the influence of cocaine, he could play the piano more easily and talk more freely. During the daytime, he stayed in bed in a darkened room because he could not stand the bright light, and listened to music or read, waiting impatiently for night to arrive. At night he would go dancing, talking and carousing, or else he would amuse himself with acting, going to the cemetery in search of gruesome thrills, imagining himself to be Chopin. All his friends ended up using cocaine, suggesting illusory visions to each other, such as bears walking over the furniture. Once a young girl succeeded to such a degree in convincing him that she was covered with fleas that he ended up seeing the fleas himself. On another occasion a member of the group suggested that the house was full of mice and everybody spent the whole night chasing mice even though they knew perfectly well that there were really none there. At night he would also often have pleasant auditory hallucinations. Once, for example, the patient called the maid of the hotel where he was staying in the middle of the night to ask her to find out why the orchestra was still playing, while in fact it had stopped long before.

In order to reinforce the effects of cocaine this group would resort occasionally to ether inhalations, but this was of only secondary importance. The patient would incur debt after debt with complete indifference towards his financial situation. One day, while in this state, he forged two cheques using the name of one of his friends. This act resulted in three weeks of detention pending investigation, until he was judged not legally responsible (December, 1916) and released. He regarded this whole judicial matter as a very funny episode. Shortly afterwards he was placed in an open sanitarium in Zürich through the intervention of a friend of his father. In January, 1917, while still at this hospital, he made a very theatrical suicide attempt with sleeping pills after learning of the death of one of his friends. He took advantage of his leaves to get cocaine to such an extent that it was necessary to expel him from the institution for disciplinary reasons. He moved to a hotel and again started to take cocaine in doses of 3 to 5 g per day. Unable to pay his hotel bill, he was sued and brought to us for expert opinion.

On arrival he removed a supply of cocaine from his silk stockings. His nostrils were slightly reddish. There was atrophic inflammation of the nasal mucosa and marked exaggeration of the tendon reflexes. The intelligence was normal but the moral sense was highly impaired. He recovered physically quite quickly and gained 5 kg in four weeks. But the mood remained unstable for a long time, fluctuating between gaiety and spontaneous depression.

We concluded that the swindle which had led to the last charge had been committed while he was under the effects of cocaine and incapable of understanding the legal consequences of his acts.

Careful recording of his body temperature revealed that it would reach 38°C during periods of mental excitation. He was incapable of sustained work. He had the exaggerated mannerisms of homosexuals, being extremely concerned with his appearance, and using face powder. In October, 1917, he was sent under guardianship to Ticino where he was soon approached by cocaine traffickers offering their services. After resisting for some time, he again gave in to the temptation and it was again necessary to confine him to a mental hospital.

Case 10: S.B., a 19-year-old high school student, admitted to the clinic with severe cocaine addiction. The mother is of nervous temperament but the other members of the family are healthy. The patient was not very strong as a child, and masturbated from the age of three. From age 10 to 17 he was educated in a boarding school, and subsequently in a secondary school in Zürich. At age 18, he began to live in an undisciplined fashion, freed himself from his mother's authority and started to frequent nightclubs. In the autumn of 1916, he began to behave most peculiarly and had an affair with a dancer. By day he was obviously sleepy. Since his father was dead, his mother requested and got the assistance of the orphan's service. He had shown neurotic symptoms and stammering for quite some time. He stated that in March of 1917 his girlfriend had had the idea of leaving him, and he had obtained some cocaine from an acquaintance in order to relieve his misery. The effects were quick. He forgot his worries and his thoughts became less oppressive. He sniffed 4 to 5 g of cocaine daily. After a brief reconciliation, he and his girlfriend parted again, following which he acquired the habit of smoking several pipes of opium per day in addition to the cocaine. He joined a club of cocaine addicts in Zürich which had approximately 100 members. When the members of this club used cocaine, they carried out certain rituals, the nature of which they were bound to keep secret. Each member had the duty of recruiting new adherents for whose discretion they were responsible, and whom they then introduced to the use of cocaine. Our patient had committed robberies under the influence of cocaine in order to get money for purchasing the drug. Thus, he had succeeded in selling behind his mother's back most of the library of scientific books which his brother-in-law had left in her custody before going to war. On admission to the clinic the young man presented with a marked state of physical and mental deterioration. He would fall asleep in school, in the middle of a class, when he did not have cocaine to stimulate him. But he recovered quickly after admission and withdrawal of all drugs. From August of

1917, and while still at the clinic, he began to prepare for his university entrance examinations, which he successfully passed in October.

In April, 1919, he was admitted for a second time. While still a student he had contracted debts amounting to 5,000 francs and, unable to pay them, he decided to join the army. He was rejected because of an acute case of gonorrhea. He denied using cocaine again. Ten days after admission, he was transferred to the dermatology clinic. Here is what he wrote in his autobiography about the origins of his addiction to cocaine (1917): "That spring, following very violent scenes, I wanted to commit suicide when an acquaintance recommended cocaine to make me feel better. I followed his advice and found such relief that I continued to use the drug. All my mental faculties becamc impaired, while my nervousness increased. I came here voluntarily in the hope of becoming totally cured."[15]

In connection with this case, I discovered that this patient was by no means the only high-school student using cocaine at that time. In cooperation with general practitioners, and after orientation of the parents, I did everything in my power to get these young people away from the drug. I succeeded in some cases. I learned subsequently that others, while still students, were again showing signs of illness, but I lost track of them completely.

Our patient, who was an intelligent young man, described his symptoms of cocaine addiction as follows, after several weeks of abstinence:

"During the first two or three days I began with 1 g of cocaine per day. This would last me through the day and night. The effect of this dose was to make me feel very happy and indifferent to everything. I became very egotistical, thinking and acting exclusively for myself and believing that was the way it should be. At first I had the feeling of being drunk. This would begin with a feeling of sadness which would last only 10 minutes, after which I would suddenly feel gay and happy without any particular external reason. At the same time, my mind became very lucid. In July we had the written mathematics test. I had not prepared myself at all for it. The test began at 7 o'clock and by 9 o'clock I had not done a thing. Around 9 o'clock, I took approximately 0.5 g of cocaine. My mind became immediately clear. I solved four problems in a short time and I passed the test successfully. Much the same thing happened with several other examinations. To be deprived of cocaine causes dreadful suffering. It

[15] Ed. note: This quotation is in French in the original text.

is truly a torture. One is capable of doing almost anything to obtain it. I knew that I was even capable of killing someone in cold blood in order to secure it. I was indifferent to everything, even to whether or not I would pass my examinations. The reaction to cocaine is very variable. The effects at night are different from those during the daytime. Moreover, one takes a lot more then. Towards the end I was taking 1 or 1.5 g in one dose. I would take this dose lying on my bed, and I would feel my whole body become tired and weak. This was followed by a kind of seizure, and I would start trembling. I felt it as a very pleasant state. I felt somewhat like a man with a double personality. I knew I was lying on my bed under the influence of cocaine, and that my feelings were unnatural, but I was living in pure spirit. It is like a sort of split consciousness. Everything is clearer than in dreams, and one thinks logically. The mind is lucid. One is capable of solving the most difficult problems. You know you are capable of doing this, but you lack the strength, you don't want to do it, you couldn't care less. This stage lasts approximately 20 minutes. The seizure subsides. You feel a very pleasant sensation, you are not conscious of your body and you believe you are suspended in mid-air even though you know that you are lying in your bed under the effects of cocaine. Then you become restless. You feel an unpleasant sensation on the back of the neck, as if worms were crawling over it. You know they are not there but you cannot stop bringing your hand to the neck, scratching the skin for hours and feeling the worms running while you chase them with your hands. These movements are totally involuntary. Hearing becomes exquisitely sensitive. If you rub your fingers together, you can hear the noise. I could hear all the bells of the town. In order to get rid of the worms you take more cocaine. Sometimes the worms also crawl over the front of your body, but they usually start behind the ears. If you have no more cocaine left, the worms become stronger and stronger. You start to run around the room, and you lick with the tongue every spot where you find a few specks of cocaine. You look for remnants of cocaine on the bed. During this, you feel strong palpitations of the heart. After a dose of 3 g you are seized by a cramp, the heart slows down but its beating becomes more perceptible, and you feel cold. I would have very pleasant fantasies about what it would be like if I were found dead. I would think that each slow beat of my heart was going to be the last. My body was immobile, in opisthotonus.

I never wanted to take cocaine in the presence of other people. When you start to speak you never know where to stop and you reveal all your secrets. Whatever you start doing you are never able to stop. If, for example, when you are reading you move your finger up and down just once, you keep doing it for hours on end. Once I sat up in my bed and I remained still like that for hours, until I fell down from exhaustion. All this is due to cocaine. At the same time, you keep on thinking, unable to stop. For example, you say to yourself: 'Now I am an emperor.' At that moment you are convinced you are an emperor but, at the same time, you know quite well that you are not.

The mouth is always open and you do not feel your tongue. The eyes are wide open and it is impossible to close them. When you stop thinking, you explore the void with your eyes. One then sees clouds, for example, in which one can suddenly observe the bodies of women. I knew that it was spirits who were talking to me. I always said to myself that there wasn't a woman on earth as beautiful as the most ugly one in my visions. But on these occasions I did not experience any sexual feelings. When you take cocaine and experience the seizure, you feel absolutely impotent sexually, yet this is not an unpleasant sensation. You do not think about sex. You cannot and you do not want to experience it. It seems unnecessary. Women get all worked up under the influence of cocaine and they masturbate.

Everything is sheer fantasy and one knows it. If I concentrated on a particular point in the dark, this point would come nearer and nearer to me. I could distinguish in it marvellous shapes. Suddenly the point would become very luminous and it would light up everything. If I was dazzled by the very strong light and looked away for just a moment, everything would disappear. I have seen a great many things in such a point. These things were usually very small, and constantly changing. The skin was completely insensitive, even to the touch. Everything depends on the personality of the individual. One woman addicted to cocaine, for example, experienced an extraordinary feeling of well-being after each inhalation, but nothing else. Another woman, who took cocaine only five times, always saw only spiders and other animals wanting to climb over her. During the first few times, one simply feels well, without experiencing anything else. The more anxious the individual, the sharper are his experiences. I have personally never heard voices. Moreover, you always know that the whole thing is artificial. Cocaine addicts know each other well. Many homosexuals are cocaine addicts. Women experience such a level of sexual excitation that they become homosexual for lack of something better. One becomes extremely thirsty and unable to eat, but one has to drink in order to alleviate the unpleasant sensations in the throat. One tolerates alcohol very well. Once you start talking you cannot stop. The same applies to writing and to everything else. My letters were disorganized because I would write everything that came to my head without bothering about proper sentences. At first one experiences very intense feelings, but eventually you become indifferent. One's main preoccupation is to find ways of getting money to buy cocaine. I knew perfectly well that this obsession could be disastrous, but I did not care. I could think only of the present.

One hates the light and likes the dark. You're reluctant to go out during the daytime. In general, you don't like walking. You prefer to remain lying down or sitting. You have to get up four or five times during the night to urinate, but micturition is not painful. Bowel movements occur only every two or three days. When you manage to sleep, there are no dreams and the slumber is heavy and unpleasant. You do not hear anything and it is very difficult to be aroused. One lies and steals without qualm. You are only concerned with yourself and the present. You don't care what will happen tomorrow or the day after. I ended up by taking 5 to 6 g daily. This is the habitual dose of most cocaine addicts.

During the cocaine intoxication colors are more brilliant and beautiful. During withdrawal everything is unpleasant. During the intoxication sounds are also very intense and very beautiful. I am very musical. When the bells were really sounding I could hear whole symphonies, the most beautiful that I have ever heard. Occasionally, I also believed I was composing. You feel the need to smoke if for no other reason than to see many things in the smoke. You lose interest in the news and the newspapers. You hold the newspaper without reading it. In general you lose all interest in the world around you."

Case 11: W.M., actor, born in 1899, single. Admitted to the Zürich psychiatric clinic in December, 1917. Alcoholic father, deceased. After spending a few months in a high school, he enrolled, at the age of 17 years, in a trade school. He became acquainted with shady characters and engaged in both hetero- and homosexual activities. In June, 1917, he met a homosexual cocaine addict who introduced him to the drug. Though the patient got no real pleasure from the homosexual relationship with this person, he allowed him to do whatever he wanted of an erotic nature. At the end of a few weeks, he had become enslaved to the drug, which produced in him pleasant states of intoxication with visual illusions. He became totally unable to work and in five months spent all his mother's savings (4,000 francs), which he had extorted from her under false pretenses to buy cocaine for himself and his friend. When this source of funds became exhausted, his friend persuaded him to earn money for the purchase of cocaine by acting as a homosexual prostitute. Shortly afterwards his friend committed suicide. Pressed by financial difficulties, highly disturbed by all these events, and influenced by our treatment, he decided to give up cocaine. His most troublesome abstinence symptoms included very intense itching, marked instability of the pulse rate, exaggerated tendon reflexes, and very marked dermographism. During the first 14 days of treatment, he suffered, in addition, from insomnia and constant restlessness, and large doses of Veronal were only partially effective in calming him down. He had enough stamina to abstain from cocaine at least until January, 1919. From that date on, I lost track of him. In the last letter that I received from him he gave me, at my request, some details related to his period of cocaine use: "Today, for the first time during the past year, I have remembered the word 'cocaine' and it has evoked in me memories which are both sad and bizarre. I have never since experienced any desire to use cocaine and it is only rarely that I think about that period, but what I see in my soul when I do evokes in me a feeling of cold horror. I see myself lying on a bench, furtive, struggling against death, mumbling prayers, my eyes wide open into the surrounding darkness of the night, and this picture of my past still makes me tremble with fright. At first cocaine seduces you with the wonderful joys that it provides but, once you yield, you are lost. You don't truly enjoy cocaine until you have used it daily for three or four months. Otherwise, you are not a cocaine addict strictly speaking. But once you are hooked, you cannot give it up except through the intervention of the police authorities. In my opinion, and according to my own experience, an unintelligent man can never assert that he is a cocaine addict, because he doesn't know how to take advantage of the number and richness of the thoughts that go through his mind. In such a man, cocaine, on the contrary, produces confusion and intellectual impoverishment. The very clear awareness that one is on the way to physical destruction soon changes into the opposite idea that you are spiritually much superior to people who do not use cocaine. This happens even though you recognize the lies you resort to all the time, as one of the principal characteristics of the cocaine addict. But you feel that every lie is a white lie, because it is the greatest sin, which one must not admit, to know that one is lying to oneself, denying oneself. However, today I am cured and my health is fine."

In this case the treatment at the outpatient department was at least made more effective by the fact that, at the request of the physician, the public guardian took an interest in the patient and supervised him actively. This young man can be considered cured.

Case 12: C.W., dental technician, born in 1904, single. Alcoholic father. The paternal grandmother had a character disorder. The mother and a brother had personality disorders. As a child, the patient had been very ill-treated by his alcoholic father. In school he had received attention because of his restlessness and stubbornness. Later he became an apprentice dental technician, liked his trade very much, but did not get along with his colleagues. In 1921, he found work as a dental technician. In February, 1922, he met a musician who was a cocaine addict and at the same time he established a relationship with a girl who was closely associated with cocaine-using circles. As he had expressed the desire to find out what cocaine was all about, she brought some one day and they started to sniff it together. The first time, cocaine made him dizzy. He was unable to eat anything, had a feeling of tightness in his whole body and cried and laughed for no apparent reason. He was unable to sleep for the whole night and was sexually impotent with his lover. He tried cocaine again one month later and was delighted to see that his pupils had become beautifully big and brilliant. He experienced a very pleasant feeling, and believed, through some sort of delusion of grandeur, that he was in some way quite special and others, who did not take cocaine, were stupid. He gradually grew into the habit of taking 250 mg of cocaine daily. Eventually he lost interest in everything, including his work. He increased the dosage continually. After one of his friends, committed for cocaine addiction, had informed on him, he was put under surveillance by the police and committed to a psychiatric clinic on July 6, 1922.

On admission he gave the impression of being blasé, apathetic and somewhat anxious. Since the patient had not taken cocaine for several days, his pupils were normal. He had fine tremor of the hands. The patellar reflex was quite weak. Both the inside and the outside of the nostrils were reddened. The association of ideas was quick and random. A perception test, performed early on, showed mild impairment. On August 2, 1922, he was transferred to a hospital in his native city for the purpose of prolonged treatment and no further information is available.

Case 13: H.S., clerk, born in 1897, single. Member of a family of seven children. His father, a severe alcoholic, was subject to sudden fits of anger. One brother was known for his rashness and one sister was rude and aggressive. The patient apparently had a normal childhood development, and went through public school without much difficulty. After two years in high school he enrolled in an institute for the study of foreign languages. From 16 to 19 years of age he took commercial training. Then he found a job as a clerk, but having inherited 10,000 francs, he worked irregularly. It was not long before he squandered his inheritance, associated with bad company and began to sniff cocaine. Partly under the influence of the drug, he misappropriated funds from the firm and lost his job. Unable to find employment, he lived for a year and a half from the considerable profits derived from illicit cocaine traffic. He lived extravagantly making, for example, unnecessary car trips, costing 150 francs each.

In the spring of 1922, his health became seriously affected by his abuse of cocaine. He had lost a great deal of weight, became pale and had much difficulty getting up in the morning. He would sign bills and then be unable to recall the amounts.

He traced the beginnings of his cocaine addiction to the spring of 1921. After spending a night drinking, he had gone for a car drive during which he became ill. His driver gave him a little cocaine to sniff. He followed this advice and, approximately 15 minutes later, he felt like another man, completely relieved, fresh and fit, and at the same time highly aroused sexually. Three hours later he had a sudden crying spell. From this time on he sniffed cocaine regularly in order to dispel his gloom. He spent a few months in comparative abstinence, using cocaine only on Saturdays in amounts of 1 g each time. During this time he felt relatively well and felt hyperexcited sexually, mainly because cocaine made him less inhibited than in the normal state. From February, 1922, when his worries and concerns increased, he started to sniff about 1 g of cocaine every day. He once took 4 g in a single night. He now began to experience withdrawal symptoms, which always led him to take more drug. In the spring of 1922 he had often felt that people stared at him in the streets in a peculiar fashion and that detectives were observing him in the cafés. He felt without energy, had become indifferent to everything around him and often, during periods of abstinence, he experienced profound depression and self-reproach. Sexual arousal had diminished considerably and he rarely felt any desire for intercourse. Finally, he began to experience bizarre cutaneous sensations. Several times he had the feeling that a spider was crawling over his left shoulder and the back of the neck and he would reach out with his hand to brush it away. Furthermore, cocaine made him very contemplative. He would spend hours on end involved in obscure philosphical exercises or sitting on a bench admiring nature, a thing he had never done before. The sexual excitation produced by cocaine was psychological rather than physical. He had also become more perverted than normally and experienced a special delight in half-dressed young girls. After very large amounts of cocaine, he felt an overwhelming need to drink and smoke.

Because of his extravagance and his refusal to work, the police referred him to the public trustee's office which put him under its surveillance. However, despite this he continued to sniff cocaine. His guardian therefore had him committed to the Burghölzli Clinic on the strength of a medical certificate, on July 13, 1922. The physician who signed the certificate reported that the young man was excitable, lacking in energy, very emotional and lacking in insight.

At the clinic, cocaine was withdrawn immediately, a procedure that the patient withstood well. The tendon reflexes were markedly exaggerated, but there was no other physical symptom worthy of note. The patient gained weight rapidly, but he proved to be a superficial young man, somewhat impertinent, and incapable of sustained steady work. At the initiative of his guardian he left the clinic on a trial basis on October 1, 1922 to take a job that had been found for him.

Our prognosis was utterly unfavorable. His work was irregular and, towards the end of 1923, he again began to mix with the company with whom he had started to use cocaine. In February of 1924, he was seen several times by a physician who found him in a very depressed dream-like state, which was easily traced back to cocaine use. Committed for the second time to the clinic on February 11, 1924, he claimed that, since his relapse, he had not used more than 2 g daily. Abrupt withdrawal of the drug did not produce even the slightest abstinence symptom. The patient showed rapid physical improvement and, as no one was willing to pay the expenses for the appropriate longer treatment at the clinic, he was discharged as "improved" on the 26 of May, 1924.

Case 14: W.S., building technician, trafficker in cocaine, aged 26, married. The father, an architect, had died young. The widowed mother started to live off the avails of prostitution. A maternal uncle was an alcoholic. The patient has a brother and five sisters, all of whom appear to behave quite normally. The patient himself had suffered from nocturnal enuresis until age 14, but otherwise had developed quite normally. From childhood on he had been morally very weak and at the age of 23 he had been condemned to three months in the workhouse at L. After that he worked as an architectural draughtsman but never stayed at the same job for very long. He served in the army for a while but was then discharged. Around 1920, he met a prostitute who taught him to use cocaine. He states that the first time, cocaine, far from inducing pleasant sensations, threw him into a "stupid state." However, the drug soon made him very loquacious and this allowed him to shine socially. Three months later, during Mardi Gras of 1921, he met a number of other cocaine addicts including a chemist who held a licence to obtain cocaine legally. This enabled them always to have enough drug and they sniffed as much as they wanted. Some time later, the patient began to buy comparatively large amounts of cocaine and resell it by the gram at a profit of about two francs per gram. In this way, he made a good deal of money. It was especially during weekend parties that he and his friends used cocaine heavily, up to 1.5 g in 24 hours. They would become very excited and did not have the slightest need to sleep. The patient himself always felt very thirsty after taking cocaine. The drug induced in him a rather pleasant, partially stuporous, state during which he could hear the slightest sounds much more sharply than normally. He got married at this time and, obsessed by his need for cocaine, he did not have the slightest qualm about pushing his wife into prostitution in order to secure enough money to finance his pleasures. During the time he used cocaine, he had no sexual urges of his own. His wife stated that she never took cocaine herself but that when her husband was under the influence of the drug, he would stay away from home for up to 14 days at a time. He would then suddenly reappear, suffering from severe withdrawal symptoms and go to bed for three days while he perspired profusely. He became totally incapable of any work at all. Since his marriage in October of 1921, he has practically not had sexual intercourse with his wife, claiming that he didn't feel up to it. When trafficking in cocaine did not provide enough funds, he resorted to fortune-telling for his mother's clients.

During his stay at our clinic, the patient improved considerably. Cocaine was withdrawn from the very beginning. His appearance became more orderly and he no longer gave the impression of moral deterioration. But because of his unstable tendencies, he was declared legally incompetent. In order to continue the treatment he was referred to a mental hospital in his native city on February 15, 1923. The information available from there suggests that he has not gone back to using cocaine.

Case 15: N.H., businessman, cocaine trafficker, aged 20 years, single. Irresponsible father. Mother a psychopathic liar. As a young boy, the patient was, or appeared to be, docile and intelligent. At the age of 16 he fell in with bad company, began to run around with girls and had to drop out of high school. At age 18 he was found guilty of an attempt at swindling and was sentenced to three days in jail. He attended private schools in Zürich and in French- speaking Switzerland until, having begun to sniff cocaine, he stopped working altogether. He became so obsessed by his habit that he needed more and more money to satisfy it. He experienced hallucinatory states of considerable duration and primarily of a visual type. As a result of selling cocaine, mainly to secure funds to finance his own needs, he came to the attention of the police.

Medical examination was physically negative. But it was soon established that the patient was a constitutional psychopath with a character defect that three years of cocaine addiction had made even worse. The patient was put under guardianship and placed in a strictly-run training school in the country.

Case 16: M.L., hotel waiter, single, aged 26 years. No information concerning hereditary defects. The patient claims to have always been healthy. He was a reasonably good student in a modern high school and then enrolled in a hotel management school. He states that he has had strong homosexual tendencies from childhood on and that he has never been interested in girls. He has worked a great deal in hotels in foreign countries where, in 1920, he learned to sniff cocaine. The drug always produced in him pleasurable sensations and stimulation of his homosexual relations with his friends. For the last year he had worked as a waiter in a hotel located in a building which also housed a drugstore. He succeeded in stealing from the pharmacist several wholesale packages of cocaine, though he later reimbursed him for them, at least in part. He increased the dose gradually, reaching a level of 1 to 2 g per day. This amount made him feel weak and unable to perform his duties adequately. He was, therefore, very happy to find a job as a domestic and lover of a homosexual aristocrat who spoiled him thoroughly and even gave him a car as a present. However, he finally decided, on the advice of a physician, to undergo a withdrawal cure, and on April 19, 1922, he entered the Burghölzli Clinic.

He was very thin and had the dandified dressed-up appearance that is common among homosexuals. Cocaine was withdrawn immediately without giving rise to abstinence symptoms. But he showed marked emotional instability and was not inclined to undergo intensive psychotherapy. He stated that in various large hotels in which he had worked during the previous two years, cocaine use was rampant not only among the guests, but also among the staff, particularly among those who worked at night. On May 15, 1922, his detoxification was complete and he expressed the desire to leave the clinic, even though he was not yet very strong. According to his own description, his states of intoxication were accompanied by visual hallucinations, at first pleasant, and later painful, but he never had delusions of persecution. According to information available to us, the patient did not relapse.

Case 17: O.K., chambermaid, prostitute, born in 1897, aged 25 years. On her father's side she came from a healthy and honorable family of civil servants. On the other side of the family, however, the maternal grandparents, an uncle and an aunt were alcoholics. Three of the patient's sisters are office workers, all of whom have a crafty and complicated temperament. As a child the patient was healthy, happy and moderately endowed. She did well in public school. She did not show emotional disturbances until the war when, working as a chambermaid and as a munitions factory employee, she came into bad company. According to information provided by her father, she became acquainted with people who taught her to sniff cocaine. From this time on she did not work properly and underwent marked emotional deterioration. For this reason she was deported in 1920 to her native town. There, however, she was allowed total freedom, and she led a vagrant life, became a prostitute and as such was arrested several times by the Zürich police during the past few years. Since 1921, she was known to the police as a dangerous cocaine trafficker who, at the same time, used the drug heavily herself. But for a long time she could not be caught. On February 22, 1922, during an inspection of a boarding house the police found her in a locked room where, according to her dossier, she was attempting to jump out the window. With great effort she was prevented from carrying out her intention. She then resisted arrest, raged as if possessed and tried to swallow an open safety pin. In order to protect her from new attempts at suicide, and because of her senseless unruly behavior, she was committed to the Burghölzli Clinic.

She was in an extremely excitable state, physically and mentally deteriorated. She refused to answer any questions or to respond to any encouragement. During the weeks that she was under observation she told us that she had learned to take cocaine in Geneva, three years earlier. She said that the drug gave her a pleasant sensation and that when she was depressed, a moderate dose was enough to put her in wonderful spirits. Stronger doses made her feel persecuted everywhere. In the streets she always felt that a black man was following her. Later she described her hallucinatory states in greater detail. In the sky she could see comets of the most varied colors travelling harmoniously along the Milky Way and on many other paths. She then felt very light, as if she herself were gliding in the air.

I had, by chance, the opportunity of meeting a young man who had been one of the numerous victims of this cocaine addict. He told me that one night at about eleven-thirty she had approached him in the street asking him to go with her to a café because she was terribly thirsty but did not dare to go in alone because it was so late. He agreed, and half an hour later he offered to take her home. She said that it was still too early and that she had something she wanted to show him. She then knocked on the window of a warehouse where the night watchman, who was in league with her, opened the door. She sat in a secluded corner with the young man and started to sniff cocaine and to push some into his nose. He had hallucinations, which amused the woman very much. They kept on sniffing all night at the instigation of the woman. The young man lost all control of himself and did not manifest the slightest sexual desire towards his friend. He gave her most of the money he had on him, and when morning came they went out and went their separate ways. Soon afterwards, he caught the attention of the police because he was wandering in the streets in a peculiar dream-like state. After being taken to the police station, he made the statement that we have just summarized. He was referred to a physician who succeeded in convincing him about the dangers implicit in his adventure and in not following through with the promise he had made to meet the patient the next night for another cocaine spree. O.K. had promised him that she would then bring along a large amount of cocaine.

At the clinic the patient proved to be unamenable to psychotherapy. She could not see any advantage in changing her lifestyle. Therefore, the police took her out of the clinic, and on May 17, 1922 the municipal authorities of her birthplace placed her in a convalescent home in the country. Shortly after leaving this institution she went back to her ways and probably to using cocaine again. She committed suicide, probably by an overdose of sleeping pills, in the spring of 1925.

Case 18: R.H., cashier, born in 1891, married. She belongs to a well-educated family. Both parents were musicians and were said to be rather headstrong. The patient had been born out of wedlock. A maternal uncle was an alcoholic. While working as an office clerk when she was 21 years old, the patient was convicted of embezzlement and sentenced to four weeks in jail. A short time later she was sentenced to two days in jail for stealing a pair of shoes. Subsequently she often lived a dissolute life. In 1914, she met the man whom she later married. For a time she was his mistress and did not marry him until 1917. The man was unreliable and treated her badly.

At about this time, she was hospitalized in the medical clinic as a result of a theatrical attempt at suicide. She stated that, in 1918, a dentist, to whom she had weepingly confided her troubles, gave her a little cocaine to relieve her depression. It was not long before she became habituated to the drug and began to sniff it regularly. For the first few days she only experienced discomfort after the drug, but this was later replaced by pleasurable sensations. She no longer took anything to heart and she became totally indifferent. At first it was the dentist who provided her with cocaine, but when he died of influenza she was able to get the drug through two dancers who were known to be confirmed cocaine addicts. In the spring of 1922 the patient was arrested for embezzlement in the firm where she worked as a cashier. A package of cocaine was found in her cash-drawer and she was directed to the psychiatric clinic for examination. We were immediately struck by the typical redness of the nostrils and the pronounced atrophic rhinitis, clear signs of cocaine addiction. At the same time it was possible to shut off her source of the drug, and in addition she was short of funds. Therefore it seems probable that she did stop sniffing cocaine at that time. Her defence lawyer in the pending embezzlement trial claimed that, as a cocaine addict, she was not responsible for her acts. We did not share this opinion, first because the examination of the patient did not reveal any serious mental disturbance which could be attributed to the action of cocaine and, secondly, because the patient had already been convicted several times for embezzlement and robbery before becoming a cocaine addict. At the same time, she was involved in divorce proceedings and a suit for damages against her, as a result of a relationship she had with a married man, through which she exploited him and harmed other persons.

From July 29 to October 14 she was confined to the Burghölzli Clinic, to which she had been referred by the court for expert assessment. No mental illness, in the legal sense of the term, was diagnosed, but she was considered to have a character defect with confusion of thought. Considering the objectionable lifestyle of the patient, we recommended that she be put under guardianship and possibly committed to a correctional institution. The patient has apparently not returned to the use of cocaine but continues to behave in conformity with her constitutionally unstable character.

c) Sub-Acute Cocaine Deliria

Sub-acute cocaine deliria occur only in those chronic cocaine users in whom expansive euphoric syndromes alternate rather frequently with anxious paranoid oroneiric delirious states. The 10 cases to be described, including one woman, illustrate this type of syndrome. One patient ended by committing suicide through an overdose of cocaine. Four men and one woman can be considered cured, and we have no accurate information with respect to the remaining patients. All of them required prolonged, and some repeated, hospitalization.

Case 19: O.W., doctor of philosophy, chemist, born in 1870. In his professional capacity he had to work with alkaloids frequently. His brother is said to have had a personality disorder, but otherwise the patient had no demonstrable hereditary defect. Because of physical illness he had been obliged in the past to use morphine but had not become a morphine addict. He had acquired the cocaine habit three years earlier. Once he experienced a state of cocaine-induced mental confusion sufficiently serious to require hospitalization but he did not stay in the clinic long enough to recover completely. In April and May of 1921, he again sniffed progressively larger doses of cocaine, compounding the problem by resorting to injections of morphine. This behavior was facilitated by the enforced absence of his wife, who was ill. When she returned, he was strikingly apathetic, indifferent to his professional responsibilities and almost totally unable to work. His thoughts were often confused and he would quickly forget everything. His appetite had been impaired for several weeks. He ate little and irregularly and he had lost a great deal of weight.

One night his wife, who had a separate bedroom, heard a noise in the house. She got up to find out what had happened and found our patient sitting confusedly on the floor in the corridor, unable to get up and trembling all over. He stated that he had fallen down. His whole face was covered with cocaine powder. When his wife tried to help him to his bed he struggled against her to such a degree that she had to call a physician who succeeded with difficulty in putting him to bed and giving him a morphine injection. When I was called as a consultant the next morning I found the patient in a sleepy intoxicated state, his face still covered with white powder, the pupils constricted and barely reacting. When we succeeded in waking him up by shaking him, he was very angry and tried to push me out of the room and lock himself in. In taking his history we learned that the patient had already had several delusional episodes following prolonged intake of cocaine, during which he wanted to attack his imaginary persecutors with all sorts of weapons. During the previous 14 days the patient had sniffed approximately 60 g of cocaine. His speech was slurred, resembling that of patients with paralysis. He showed an uncontrollable need to talk, while at the same time being unable to sustain a conversation. When the health inspectors came to pick him up he offered such a strenuous resistance that he had to be half carried to the automobile. After arriving at the hospital he fell asleep and when he woke up two hours later he started to insult everybody around him in his slurred speech. The following night he slept little. The next day he denied that he had ever taken any drug whatsoever but, when confronted with the absurdity of his allegations, he stopped arguing. He pleaded like a child to be set free right away. The pulse rate and pupils were normal and there were no withdrawal symptoms. After several days at the clinic the patient regained his calm but he slept little and poorly. Despite this no sedatives were administered. He became completely rational within a week. Since neither the mental status nor the personality of the patient had been seriously or significantly affected, it was decided to discharge him on a trial basis after four weeks, under the close supervision of his regular doctor and on condition that he abstain from drinking, because alcohol was particularly likely to facilitate his relapse into the use of cocaine. He has totally abstained from cocaine use for four and a half years. His physical state is excellent, he is again the reliable family head he used to be and is working successfully in his profession.

Case 20: D.G., businessman, born in 1899. The patient's father has a severe personality disorder and shows a pathological intolerance for alcohol. The mother is given to violent outbursts. An emotionally disturbed brother with a character defect had been in a mental hospital and later in prison. Another brother suffers from fits of anger despite being otherwise a reasonable man. His four sisters are very nervous. The patient was brought up in a disturbed family environment rampant with arguments and fights. As a child, he was physically healthy but suffered from sleepwalking spells. He was only a mediocre student, and from the age of 14 on he showed a tendency to silly pranks and began to associate with increasingly disreputable people. At 17 he had become a sort of pet of a number of homosexuals. At 19 he was found guilty of stealing some clothes in a school and was put on probation. Following this he stopped working altogether and nine months later he was again accused of stealing and taken to court. He was even stealing from his own father. During the hearing, he did not show the slightest sign of remorse. After his release from jail he eloped with a prostitute. In 1920, he did three months of military service during which his behavior was unreproachable. Soon afterwards he began to sniff cocaine and after 14 days presented with his first episode of mental confusion. After taking a very large dose of cocaine he started to pace his room feverishly, carrying a gun, and with a strange expression in his eyes. After further doses of cocaine, he believed that people sitting in the automobiles driving by on the street were following him on his father's orders.He threatened his persecutors with a knife and it was difficult to stop him from jumping out the window. The next day he did not remember anything about this. His family gave him money so that he could move to another city, but he used it to buy cocaine and started to sniff again. Several days later he again had visual hallucinations. In the middle of the night he thought he suddenly saw a theater, and all of a sudden he discovered a crack on the wall which had been there for a long time. He was very depressed and on the verge of tears when brought by his family to Burghölzli for the first time on October 6, 1920. Here he stated that he was getting his cocaine from a homosexual pharmacist who tried to use this means to enter into an intimate relationship with him. He had begun to use cocaine two years earlier at the insistence of one of his friends who was also a user. Having had only an unpleasant reaction the first time, he did not try it again until five months ago when he wanted to forget the miserable life he was leading.

The clinical examination showed unquestionable moral defect, but appropriate affect, and an I.Q. just a little below average. Experimental association tests and particularly the word associations, revealed superficiality. We made the diagnosis of moral idiocy and cocaine addiction. The patient was sent to the mental hospital of his native canton. Having been released from this hospital after a few weeks, he relapsed, became involved with another prostitute whom he followed to Zürich, and started to use large amounts of cocaine again.

Shortly before midnight on May 18, 1921, and while under the influence of cocaine, he left a café and climbed, with the agility of a monkey, up the lightning rod of the telephone exchange building located on the busiest street in town. He reached the third floor and climbed through an open window into the lighted offices of the night service. The operators who were working there, scared by the wild appearance of the man, thought he was a burglar and rang the alarm. He put up a desperate resistance against the men who came to apprehend him and it was with the greatest difficulty that he was overcome and taken to the police station. There he admitted he had taken 1.5 g of cocaine during the preceding few hours, following which he could see all sorts of scenes and believed that he was working in a motion picture. He thought that his role called for scaling the wall of a house to burglarize it. He could not understand how he had performed this acrobatic feat since he was not at all athletic. He was handcuffed and brought to the clinic. When asked what day of the month it was, he was off by only one day. He was in a whining mood, but became violently angry, with marked motor excitation, at the slightest provocation. During the following days, he stated that during the past few weeks he had sniffed a great deal of cocaine, always in the company of large groups of people. He also expressed great pleasure in the fact that cocaine use was spreading into increasingly larger and more respectable circles. He related that while he was climbing up the building he kept on asking himself whether he was truly working in a film or was again doing something very silly and was perhaps becoming ill. When, after four days he had completely calmed down, he was removed from the clinic by the police who sent him back to his native town.

But he was admitted again at our clinic on June 25, 1921. He said that he had spent the last few weeks in B. where he had been able to get several grams of cocaine. While under the influence of the drug he had come back to Zürich to look for his beloved, knowing perfectly well that he had been prohibited from coming to this city and that if he were apprehended he would be punished. However, in his intoxicated state this knowledge had no particular significance for him. Once in Zürich he went to a restaurant where he sniffed 2 g of cocaine and again experienced the need to perform physical feats. He abruptly went out through a window, climbed to the roof, fell down, but started again to climb up the front of the building. Once again he resisted with superhuman strength the attempts to seize him and, once subdued, he declared, as before, that he was working in a motion picture. He also said that at one point during the climbing he had become anxious, but that he had then seen clearly a large mattress lying on the ground below him (this was not true) and had therefore continued climbing. The police brought the patient to Burghölzli. He was violently angry, struck out around himself with arms and legs, and bit at everybody who came near him. Despite the fact that he was handcuffed, four strong attendants were barely able to get him to the ward. As a result of the fall he had experienced during the climbing, his face was covered with blood and his nose was badly swollen. Encouraged by the doctors, whom he soon recognized, he eventually calmed down sufficiently and he was untied. He understood very quickly what was said to him and spoke quite accurately about his previous stays at the clinic, but, suddenly and without any apparent reason, began to make dreadful grimaces, to roll his eyes, or to move his lower jaw from side to side. The pupils were extremely dilated, reacting quickly but not fully. His speech was sluggish. Flight of ideas was clearly evident in his later speech. He perspired profusely. The pulse was small and at a rate of 100 beats per minute. On the ward, he suddenly became extremely excited again and six men were needed to restrain him. Then, quite abruptly, he calmed down again, and explained that he had to go into such a rage to show his talent as a movie actor. Then he suddenly asked whether all this was now real or film-acting. He passed quickly and repeatedly from a mood of great gaiety to tearfulness, without any evident external cause. After half an hour, he tried to write his autobiography but, unable to concentrate and to control the tremor of his hands, he soon had to give up. He stated that he needed cocaine to write better and more fluently. That night he slept reasonably well and afterwards he was completely lucid but he appeared depressed and unhappy. He could remember every detail about his state of excitation of the previous day and continued to toy with the idea of becoming a movie actor and of achieving brilliant success. Experimental association tests performed on that day showed large variations in reaction time. Most of the reaction time figures were very short, under two seconds, but some were as long as nine seconds regardless of the affective content of the words. The reaction time curve was very similar to that produced by hysterical patients, except for the fact that some of the prolonged reaction times could not be explained on psychological grounds. The patient was able to perform 100 associations without showing the slightest fatigue. From the point of view of content the word associations were utterly superficial and, as in manic states, included many compound words. In the recall tests, only 61 of 100 reactions were correctly reproduced, indicating some impairment of attention.

When, on June 28, 1921, the patient was presented at medical rounds, he behaved very properly, described every detail of his states of cocaine intoxication and promised, though superficially and unconvincingly, to reform himself. On that very day the police removed him from the clinic and sent him to a reformatory in his home town.

On the day following his last cocaine intoxication his writing still clearly showed features of manic agitation. The size of the characters was variable, many words were underlined and, here and there, there were signs of indecision, suggestive of an organic disturbance. This is what he wrote:

"Here I am again at Burghölzli, despite the warnings and the threats. I can hardly understand—will I be able to make you understand the reason why I have not paid attention to the warnings?? No—!

Last week I completed the punishment to which I had been

sentenced for having returned to the canton which I had been forbidden to enter, and I had been freed on condition that I get a passport within 10 days and go to Australia. Otherwise I would be locked up in a mental hospital. I came to Zürich and right away went to see my parole officer to straighten out my affairs. We agreed that I could go to Argentina. I worked as hard as I could, to put as many of my affairs in order as could possibly be done in one afternoon, because I very much wanted to show that I was really trying.

On Friday evening I left for Basel to pick up clothes that I had left there, and the first person I met was a cocaine addict. He approached me, kept on talking to me, and, even though I made it clear to him that I wanted him to go, he refused to leave me alone. 'He knows me,' he knows that I am all too familiar with the drug, he is counting on the fact that my desire, which I was able to control in Zürich, will be reawakened and won't go away here. And yet I only came here to put my things in order, and then go away again, when everything was taken care of. That's what a cocaine addict's friends are like.

I could not resist the temptation, and I know that others wouldn't have either. At the moment when I introduced the first dose into my nose I did not quite know what would happen to me. However, I reproached myself for yielding to the temptation and, in order to prevent this inner pain from getting worse, I could find nothing better to do than to sniff more and more. What happened then, when I came back to Zürich on Saturday following a sleepless night, is so self-evident to me. But you, although you are psychiatrists, will not understand this moment, and even less explain it. You will barely be able to follow the sequence of my thoughts. You will say: 'The fellow was set free too soon,' and God knows what other faults, based on your science, you will attribute to me, just as you did the first time when you wrote in your history: 'Public danger, moral flaws, tendency to steal, has shown a distaste for work since his youth.' I am supposed to be all of those things—and today you are incapable of understanding me when I write that the defects that your science attributes to me are the cause of the things that I have done under the influence of cocaine, and of what I do generally.

How and why should you understand that I am upset and repelled to the core of my soul by what you call your expertise, because it has destroyed me instead of helping, as I used to believe.

You know me well. Perhaps you will not believe me, but I tell you that the defects and vices that you have attributed to me have made me suffer deeply because I am absolutely convinced that my state is not what you believe it to be, what your psychiatry claims it to be.

I can see you, 'shaking your head in disbelief,' and you think: 'this young man is not being serious,' but to that I answer: 'You can think what you want, but I am expressing my innermost thoughts, knowing quite well that it will be of no use, although it won't hurt me any longer, either.'

The business about the movie-acting and its relation to the young girl whom I love—I know that it is useless to explain to you the reasons and the feelings because you will not understand. Besides, why should I confide in you? In order to have every word I utter misinterpreted, as it happened the first time?

And now I would like to beg you that, if you are interested in my acrobatics, you should have Mr. B.M. come here and he will give you useful information."

After leaving the clinic the patient disappeared and we have reason to believe he is abroad.

Case 21: N.A., druggist, single, born in 1898. No known hereditary problems. Normal physical and mental development. After school he worked in a drugstore as a packer. His employer was so pleased with his work that he found him a job in a pharmaceutical firm where he was able to become trained as a pharmacist. The patient has always been normal, without any sign of emotional disturbance. Impressed by an article on cocaine addiction that he had come across by chance in the summer of 1920, he began to steal cocaine from the company where he worked and to sniff it. At that time, he had problems at work and felt dissatified about the study of social and religious questions. He was engaged and got along very well with the young girl. From time to time, he sniffed 0.5 g of cocaine. The first few times cocaine produced only a pleasant feeling, but later he began to hear frightening noises and to see everywhere all sorts of small objects in motion. Sometimes the noises sounded like human footsteps or like a cat walking over dry leaves. At this time, he was quite indifferent to the dangers of the drugs which were entrusted to him and one day he gave some morphine to an acquaintance who had requested it. The acquaintance used the morphine to try to poison himself and his fiancée and, because of this, the patient became involved in a criminal investigation. Despite the exhortations and pleas of his fiancée and of his friends, the patient could not give up the use of cocaine. While intoxicated, he was sometimes happy and sometimes depressed. Every two weeks or so he had severe episodes of mental confusion during which he would not go to work and would come back home at night with a strangely anxious, tense expression, suffering from hallucinations. He avoided his friends and, when unable to secure cocaine, would threaten to commit suicide. He did not dare any longer to look at anybody, because he believed that people could tell from his face that he was a cocaine addict.

On October 16, 1920, he was again intoxicated with cocaine and did not go to work at all. That evening he came home disoriented, obsessed by ideas of persecution. He placed his loaded gun by the side of his bed either to protect himself from his hallucinations or with the intention of committing suicide. He told the physician who had been called to see him that he had to be ready to defend himself against his attackers whose arrival was imminent. On October 18,1920, he was therefore hospitalized at the psychiatric clinic. He was in a state of anxious and slightly rigid depression.

The pupils were dilated but reacted quickly to light. There was no hand tremor and the patellar reflex was very weak. There were no significant neurological or somatic findings. It was not surprising that there were no acute symptoms since the patient had not taken any cocaine during the previous two days. All further use of cocaine was completely proscribed immediately after hospitalization and the patient fell into an apathetic state with considerable inhibition of the ability for word associations. A fact of considerable significance was that the patient remembered only vaguely or not at all what he had experienced during his states of intoxication. He clearly recognized the need for treatment. After some weeks he was emotionally and mentally more alert but never troublesome. Sleep was disturbed only during the first few days at the clinic. The patient kept actively busy and, as his hospitalization continued, the improvement in his emotional strength became evident. On May 21, 1921, he was judged sufficiently improved to be discharged and allowed to join his friends in the country. He has been apparently well since then. It should be remarked that the patient had used cocaine in comparatively mild doses for only three months.

Case 22: W.S., musician, born in 1900. No significant hereditary flaw. As a child, the patient had been somewhat unruly but bright and had shown an aptitude for drawing and music quite early. He had always been very generous and often had to be reprimanded for his extravagant tendency to give away his belongings to others. At the age of 16, he fell in with bad company. At 18 he was found guilty of robbing a grocery store of 348 francs and was condemned to serve eight months in a reformatory. After this, he worked as a laborer and made some extra money by playing in orchestras on Sundays.

Around Christmas of 1921, following the example of his musical colleagues, he began to sniff cocaine. From then on he lost all control, began to borrow money everywhere and even pawned his musical instruments, to which he was very attached, in order to buy cocaine which he could procure easily from various middlemen. One day, one of his friends robbed a drugstore in order to get hold of a large cocaine stock. Generally, our patient took several grams of cocaine on Sundays, leading to states of intense excitation, and then stayed in bed for several days. He stated that every time he sniffed cocaine he felt very happy and very eager to work. But this never amounted to anything because his attention was always diverted toward other things. According to the statement of his girlfriend, he became sexually impotent shortly after beginning to use cocaine. Cocaine acted upon him in two ways. Either he would become excessively gay and excited, tackling every conceivable job, which usually ended in a great conflict, or, following continued use for several days in a row, he would become depressed and inhibited, even without withdrawal. At such times, in the streets he believed himself followed by strangers and he would lock himself up in a cellar where he would spend hours looking through the key-hole to see if anyone was following him in. He would then feel utterly miserable and would constantly sniff more. In the spring of 1922, he lost a great deal of weight and became totally indifferent to his own appearance. He said that when he was deprived of cocaine he felt extreme repugnance for everything and his body would twitch all over. When this happened he had to go to bed, where he would spend several days in a miserable state and incapable of the slightest effort. Towards the middle of May 1922, some blood-covered pieces of cartilage suddenly came out of his nose. On May 25, 1922, the patient experienced an intense state of cocaine intoxication during which he became so violent that his family had to call the police, who committed him to Burghölzli.

The physician who signed the admission certificate found traces of cocaine still present on the alae of the patient's nose. The nostrils were slightly red. In the upper part of the septum, approximately 3 cm from the nostrils there was a round perforation of about 0.5 cm in diameter. The mucosa showed atrophic inflammation. Flight of ideas was very marked. The patient would answer questions very quickly but in fragmentary phrases rather than complete sentences.

"(Why were you brought in precisely today?) well, my uncle. . . . Yes, you know. . . the bicycles. . . isn't that so?. . . ah, yes. I am lost (how were you brought here?) well, yes. . . I sniffed for three days and three nights. . . isn't that so?. . . do I have any other illness?

Do I have syphilis as well?...Yes, my uncle...I didn't want to sniff anymore, I'd sniffed for two days already, and there I was sitting on a bench trying not to sniff...it began to tear at my legs, down below...by the toe...oh!...then I sniffed for more....(But why were you brought in today?)...My uncle...he said: now you are going to go to bed, you are not going to take anymore...and in fact I did not take again...I pulled myself together...ah, yes...I had to make music...but not me....Are you finished with me, doctor?" His whole manner of speaking gave a superficial, cinematographic impression. His mood was a mixture of indifference and of mild despair, but this did not prevent him from joking about his miserable state. The pupils were markedly dilated but slightly reactive to light. The next day, although sleepy, he answered questions correctly. His indifferent mood persisted and was somewhat reminiscent of hebephrenia. The skin over the whole body was slightly hyperesthetic. There was no patellar reflex. The serum Wasserman reaction was negative and the urine was normal. A few days later the cutaneous hyperesthesia had disappeared and the patellar reflex had returned to normal.

The patient remained under treatment in hospital for 10 months. The apathy disappeared in time, but a psychopathic instability, probably constitutional, as well as some degree of moral indifference, came to the fore. Nevertheless, the treatment was successful in bolstering the patient's resolution to give up the drug definitively. Allowed to go out on Sundays, he always returned properly and on time. Fearing, however, that he was in serious danger of relapse if he came into contact with the wrong kind of people, he was entrusted to a guardian who, on March 7, 1923, found him a job as assistant to a gardener in a place far away from the city. Since then his behavior has been irreproachable.

Case 23: V.E., sculptor, single, born in 1895. The father, in his old age, had suffered from arteriosclerosis. The paternal grandfather and one paternal uncle were alcoholics. The patient's mother is emotionally ill and somewhat hysterical. As a child, the patient was healthy and very intelligent but his performance in school lacked dedication and perseverance. Later he specialized as a sculptor, a profession for which he had a good deal of talent. He has always been spoiled by those around him. Furthermore, he is charming and a little extravagant.

In 1914 he began to sniff cocaine in the absence of any medical reason. His personality soon began to show some profound changes. He began to lie and became impatient and irritable. His family had him treated several times in open sanatoria, but no reduction in his cocaine dosage was achieved because he succeeded in securing the drug through the staff of the institutions where he was being treated. Starting in October of 1918, he became very agitated at night. He would get up in a state of total restlessness, move the furniture around constantly, and insult and mistreat his mother who would try to calm him down. It was discovered at this time that he had squandered the best part of his father's inheritance, nearly 50,000 francs, on cocaine. It was therefore decided to put him under official guardianship. Shortly afterwards he began to have states of anxiety and to scream loudly at night. It became necessary to call a physician, who recognized the presence of anxiety, visual hallucinations and nocturnal mental confusion. According to information provided by his mother, the patient had already had the same symptoms, including mental confusion and anxiety-provoking hallucinations about women, during several nights in June of 1917. Now he complained that he was being persecuted by means of suggestions and that his fingers were releasing electricity. The physician prescribed a hypnotic. But around midnight he started to shout again, called his mother, pointed out to her hallucinatory electric signals on the ceiling, and talked about his frightening visions. The next morning he could not remember anything about the previous night. He was hospitalized in a psychiatric clinic on January 23, 1919. There he stated that he had obtained the first dose of cocaine for sniffing from a girl in a public promenade and that this had produced a very pleasant insensitivity of the buccal mucosa. From that moment on he could not give up the habit because during the three or four hours following each inhalation, he could work extremely well at his art, and felt full of strength and vigor. To prevent a large increase in dosage, he mixed the cocaine with equal parts of lactose. It was, however, during his stays at the open sanatoria that he used the largest amounts of cocaine because it was there that it was most easily obtainable. Under the influence of cocaine he began a homosexual relationship, whereas prior to that he had been sexually attracted only to women. At the same time, however, both he and his male friend continued to have heterosexual relations as well. In 1918, he came to Zürich and the police referred him to the psychiatric clinic for the treatment of his cocaine addiction. However, the attempt to have him committed to the hospital with the agreement of his legal guardian failed because he was warned by his mother, who helped him to run away.

He was confined to the mental hospital in his native city, where cocaine was withdrawn immediately. This led to a rapid disappearance of his hallucinations and of his anxiety states. A diagnosis of "cocaine psychosis on a background of psychopathy" was made. The patient did not present with marked neurological symptoms, but showed some degree of moral turpitude which could reasonably be attributed partially to the drug. After spending some time at the hospital he was discharged on condition that he abstain from cocaine. We have not heard from him since.

Case 24: G.G., clerk, born in 1895. Later became a homosexual prostitute.The paternal grandfather and the father were alcoholics. The latter later developed general paresis. One of the patient's brothers was a heavy drinker and two of his sisters presented marked sexual instability. The physical and mental development of the patient had been quite normal. He completed a course in commercial school. At age 19, he contracted a painful case of gonorrhea, which was treated by a physician with swabs soaked in a cocaine solution, inserted into the urethra. In this way he became habituated to the stimulant action of the drug and, once the gonorrhea had been cured, he resorted to the goodwill of some friends to obtain cocaine for sniffing. He had shown homosexual tendencies since puberty. Having become a cocaine addict in 1914, he became unable to work any longer and established a relationship with a homosexual aristocrat who provided him with an easy and luxurious living. In these circumstances it was easy for him to secure and use larger and larger amounts of cocaine until he ended up sniffing 8 to 10 g daily. When his dose of cocaine became very large he would not only sniff it but, to obtain a more rapid effect, he would rub the drug into the buccal mucosa. To counteract the insomnia and excitation produced by cocaine he resorted now and then to morphine. In the spring of 1917, his patron was arrested on a charge of espionage. As a result, he found himself temporarily in financial trouble and therefore began to have relations with other homosexuals who, in turn, attracted the attention of the police to him. He spent some time in Zürich, where he recruited a number of potential cocaine addicts. Once when he was arrested, six prescriptions signed by one physician and amounting to a total of 90 g of cocaine were found on his person. He had had these prescriptions refilled several times. In addition to this, he frequently drank heavily. In May, 1917, he was again arrested. He admitted his homosexuality to the physician and stated that he only once tried, unsuccessfully, to have heterosexual intercourse. It was established that the patient had intercourse with many young men at his home, often as many as six in one night, and that they gave him large sums of money and sniffed cocaine with him.

On August 21, 1917, in a state of marked excitation and extreme thinness, he was taken to a physician. The latter was struck by the miserable appearance of the patient and by his loquaciousness and tachycardia, and soon learned that another physician had recently submitted him to a withdrawal cure at home, by means of a mixture of cocaine and antipyrine. This treatment had failed completely. While the physician tried to get him to a hospital, the patient managed to escape but he was recaptured the same day and admitted to the clinic. He had the typical grooming and facial make-up of a homosexual. He was still very anxious, the pulse rate was 120 per minute, his face was pale and his cheeks hollow, and his thinness was striking. He spoke of all sorts of visions which he had had recently. His memory was slightly impaired. He could not remember a fit of anxiety which he had had the day before during which, in some unexplained manner, he had suffered a blackened eye. He struggled vigorously when being taken to the special ward. Despite all precautions he succeeded in smuggling in some cocaine. The next day when his pressing demand to be discharged immediately was rejected, he threatened to take cocaine that very evening. One of his fellow patients indeed saw him swallowing a powder. A quarter of an hour later, he was stretched on his bed, the eyeballs rolled upwards, the respiration irregular and the pulse rapid and irregular. He moaned and did not respond when spoken to. Every two or three minutes he had violent extensor spasms, with thrashing about of the whole body, twitching, and often with complete loss of consciousness and foaming at the mouth. He calmed down towards morning and fell into a deep sleep. It is probable that this time he tried to poison himself with a particularly strong dose. But this question could not be clearly answered because only traces of a white powder were found. During the following days his condition began to improve rapidly. His appetite was voracious. The delirious ideas, the hallucinations and the attacks of anxiety disappeared completely. However, there remained a clear moral defect and homosexuality. He did not obtain any more cocaine. On August 30, he managed to escape from the hospital's courtyard and telephoned from the city that he would return of his own accord. But naturally he did not and he took advantage of his freedom to get more cocaine. He was arrested again on September 9, 1917, and the authorities decided this time to confine him to hard labor for one year. But the morning following his arrest he was found in his cell suffering from severe withdrawal symptoms including profuse sweating. The police surgeon therefore returned him to his family for transfer to a private mental hospital. But while the admission formalities were being carried out, he managed to escape and, with suicidal intent, took an extremely large dose of poison. He was found dead a short time later.

Here is a 1918 court report concerning the case just described:

"A physician was brought before a police magistrate for prescription of very large doses of cocaine. It had to do with doses of 10 to 20 g which this physician had prescribed for a young man, amounting to the considerable total of 75 g in one month. The physician stated that the patient was a severe cocaine addict and that he had prescribed cocaine not for internal use but as a powder for sniffing. It is clear from the evidence that this young man represented a serious social danger, not only as a result of the secondary effects of his addiction, but also because he tried to convert everyone he came in touch with to cocaine use. When he was about to be transferred to a correctional institution, he committed suicide either with cocaine or with morphine, both of which he always carried with him. The Department of Health judged the behavior of the physician to be grossly negligent, more serious than the offence committed by the pharmacist who filled the prescriptions. It was considered more than a mere formality that the physician had from time to time omitted the exclamation mark, as required by law on prescriptions for toxic substances. The magistrate sentenced the convicted physician to a fine of 150 francs for gross violation of duty.

Case 25: R.C., aged 29 years, office worker, single. Born out of wedlock.The father and the paternal grandfather were alcoholics. The mother had tuberculosis. One of his sisters had died very young of tuberculous meningitis, and one paternal uncle had been hospitalized as a schizophrenic.

The patient has been sniffing cocaine since November, 1919. It makes him feel stimulated and self-confident but it has also driven him to alcohol abuse. He increased the dosage gradually, reaching a level of 2 to 3 g per day. Under the influence of such doses, he could see his bed surrounded by butterflies, flames, Liliputian figures and snakes. He could hear noises, the sound of steps, and often, also, insulting voices reproaching him for his addiction and denouncing him as a homosexual. Furthermore, he had unpleasant cutaneous sensations. When deprived of cocaine he experienced anxiety states, was suspicious and irritable, perceived allusions to himself everywhere, and believed himself followed by the police in the streets. After some months the ideas of persecution became systematized and outlasted the states of intoxication. He believed that his employer was paying journalists to write allusions to him in the papers and bribing actors to blow their noses in a peculiar fashion while staring at him. To take revenge on his boss, he stole from him

50- to 100-franc banknotes, most of which he burned. On January 23, 1921, while at home, he had a fit of frenzy during which he broke some furniture. On January 28 of the same year, he tried to asphyxiate himself with coal gas and was taken to the medical service of the hospital, where his cocaine addiction was not recognized, and he was given a diagnosis of *dementia praecox*, and transferred to the psychiatric clinic.

There he immediately became completely lucid. A tendency to obesity was observed but no neurological abnormalities. The cartilaginous part of the nasal septum had a large perforation and the nasal mucosa was markedly congested (rhinitis). The patient complained of insomnia and anxiety. He had the typical appearance of the consitutional homosexual, with very effeminate bearing. He admitted that he had frequently practised mutual masturbation with other young men. Ever since adolescence he had derived pleasure from his friendship with a homosexual and he had lived since then in a homosexual milieu. The passive role in anal intercourse gave him very strong sexual satisfaction. Although not impotent with women, he experienced a much weaker orgasm with them.

Cocaine was withdrawn immediately on his hospitalization, and the hallucinations disappeared. His delusions of persecution disappeared gradually over a period of several months.

He stated that, when he sniffed cocaine, his libido was particularly intense, but only in homosexual relations. He said that, according to his observations, cocaine was a stronger sexual stimulant for women than for men. Some of them lose control to such a degree that they simply take their clothes off and seek sexual satisfaction by any means available. In men, the psychological sexual drive is markedly stimulated but it is impaired by complete physical impotence. It was as though the penis were actually being held back. Furthermore, according to the patient, cocaine has the property of driving people towards sexual perversions. Sexually normal men sometimes become actively and passively homosexual for several hours, following inhalation of cocaine. Once the state of intoxication is over, they realize perfectly well what they have done but are unable to understand why they have yielded to perverted tendencies which are alien to them in the normal state. Among women even mild states of cocaine intoxication produce an irresistible degree of sexual stimulation. This is nearly impossible to satisfy and it also evokes perverted desires which sometimes last several hours. In clubs of cocaine addicts these erotic orgies often take place in large gatherings. The next day, once the intoxication is over, the participants are so ashamed of what they have done that they avoid looking at each other. But the next time they take cocaine, the same thing starts anew.

At the time of admission, the patient showed numerous bite marks over the chest, which had been inflicted upon him by a cocaine-using woman in a state of great sexual excitation. Withdrawal of cocaine led to a considerable decrease of erotic excitation in the patient. Insomnia disappeared quickly but he slept without dreaming and had occasional nocturnal emissions. The impairment of memory and of the ability to concentrate, which at first was very marked, disappeared after some weeks, and the patient worked quite satisfactorily in the administrative office of the clinic. We have reason to believe that the patient remains well. No schizophrenic symptoms were ever found.

Case 26: M.X., born in 1895, office worker. On July 11, 1916, I was consulted by the father of a student whose personality had inexplicably changed the last few months and who had stopped working altogether. The questioning finally revealed that the young man had recently been frequenting a hotel where a great deal of cocaine-sniffing goes on, that he was sniffing cocaine himself, and that the beginning of his present condition was correlated with cocaine use. A subsequent investigation showed that the clientele of this hotel consisted mostly of artists, but that many other people also gathered there after the cafés and pubs had closed for the night. We also learned that recently a colleague of ours had been called to the same place to see a female cocaine addict (M.X.) who was close to asphyxia but that the doctor was unsuccessful in his efforts to have the patient enter hospital. I personally went to this hotel and at noon found this woman in an unlocked room, in a deep, nearly comatose sleep from which she could be aroused only with great difficulty. She woke up in half an hour and immediately stretched her hand towards the cocaine lying on the night table, with the intention of sniffing some more. Further investigation showed that many other cocaine addicts lived there, that they gave cocaine to all the visitors, and that they all would meet in the sitting room to sniff together. Cocaine was provided, in unlimited amounts, by an unscrupulous pharmacist. He would deliver even at night on the strength of a telephone call. He was referred to the police and fined. The supplies of cocaine in this place were so plentiful that it was regularly given to the dog which, after sniffing it, would have visual hallucinations that made him bark madly, to the great amusement of all those present.

The patient, M.X., to whom we have just referred, was finally able to get up. She had some difficulty getting dressed because she had practically nothing to put on: a few weeks earlier she had owned a substantial wardrobe but she had, by now, sold much of it to buy cocaine and had given away the rest of it while she was intoxicated. She was taken to the psychiatric clinic right away where she had a mild episode of cocaine psychosis during the night. She listened anxiously to the voices that pursued her but refused to disclose what the voices were telling her. She would shift her gaze very frequently because, as she put it, the frightening visions became stronger if she looked in the same direction for a long time. The pupils were very dilated and barely reacting. Her eyes gleamed with a peculiar anxious tension. The conjunctivae and the nostrils were reddened. The nasal mucosa presented a dry atrophic rhinitis. It was established that during the last few days preceding her hospitalization she had been sniffing an average of 8 g a day. Because the pulse was somewhat irregular and weak and the patient was sweating profusely, she was given a total of 1 g of cocaine in multiple small doses which she sniffed avidly until 4 a.m. Four hours later she fell into a deep sleep, reminiscent of narcosis, and it was extremely difficult to wake her in time for lunch. She fell asleep again after lunch but woke up suffering from terrifying auditory and visual hallucinations which did not disappear, but became less unpleasant, following new small doses of cocaine.

July 14: The patient was sleepless until 1 a.m. and constantly had visions which, strictly speaking, were illusions, the content of which was mostly determined by the desires and apprehensions of the patient. After small doses of cocaine the visions were generally pleasant, but at other times they were unpleasant. She could see, for example, her mother or one of her lovers or else she would suddenly see menacing men coming towards her or a skeleton sitting on her arm. According to the patient, these sensory illusions were always very small, ranging from 10 to 15 cm in height.

July 15: The patient slept for seven hours after being given 1 g of Veronal. Since the patient continued to experience illusions during the day, she was given 250 mg of cocaine in multiple small doses. While her nurse was giving her a German lesson, she was able to concentrate for half an hour after which she became tired and inattentive.

July 16: In the morning she was given only 200 mg of cocaine. After lunch she showed withdrawal symptoms including weak pulse and a strong desire for cocaine. She now stares straight ahead of her, is irritable and hardly talks at all. She displays marked motor excitation, is unable to stay in one place and is so uncoordinated in her movements that she inadvertently breaks a windowpane. In contrast to her high spirits of the previous few days she is now tearful and her mood is unstable. Despite this she is not given cocaine in the evening, but an injection of scopolamine is administered instead. She grabs the cotton swab impregnated with ether, which the physician had used to disinfect her skin, and sucks the ether eagerly.

July 17: The patient is calmer. After receiving 100 mg of cocaine she is able to concentrate her attention. We succeed in obtaining a history which is subsequently completed with information obtained through outside enquiries or provided by her mother. This permits the reconstruction of the following history:

The patient belongs to a family of minor officials. There is nothing worthy of note from a hereditary point of view. As a child, she enjoyed good health and performed very well in school, specializing later in office work. She was very temperamental and rather devoted to her own pleasure and, as a result, she had had numerous quarrels with her mother. She began to work in an office at age 17. At this time, she began to suffer rather frequent attacks of nausea against which a physician recommended ether inhalations. As a result of the use of ether, she became so irritable that one day (she was 18 then), following an argument with her mother, she left home and went to a nearby town to look for a job. She was brought back home four days later by her family. Some time later, she confided her domestic problems, as well as her first and allegedly platonic love affair with her dentist. The latter advised her to take cocaine instead of ether and gave her a supply of the drug. She began to sniff cocaine right away and soon fell into a state of moral indifference, got involved in sexual relations, became incapable of carrying on her professional work and broke with her family. In 1913, she and her boyfriend went to Paris where both of them continued to sniff cocaine and began to frequent the cocaine-addict circles. From the beginning of 1914, she had sniffed cocaine every single day. After quarreling with her lover, and unable to return to her usual kind of work, she became a dancer. Her dances, partly obscene and partly sentimental, and which she always performed in a state of cocaine intoxication, brought her a certain amount of success. She spent all the money she made, or that was given to her, for the purchase of cocaine. She paid an average of five Swiss francs per gram during the day but at night she had to pay a great deal more. Once, she gave her bicycle to a pharmacist in exchange for 2 g of cocaine, and at another time a valuable piece of jewellery, because her craving for the drug was so overwhelming. She calculated that during a period of two and a half years, she had spent on cocaine the equivalent of about 35,000 Swiss francs in the form of jewels, clothes and money. During 1915 and 1916 she had had several episodes of cocaine delusions. During one period she heard voices that persecuted her for weeks and, although aware that they were sensory illusions, she nevertheless experienced intense anxiety. She had gone to the police for help on several occasions but they already knew her and sent her away without taking her seriously. Once while walking by the sea at midnight, she suddenly saw frightening shadows and heard persecutors talking about her. In despair, she jumped into the sea but was saved only with great difficulty, by some passersby, who took her home. One day at the railway station in Zürich she heard the voice of a girlfriend asking her to come to Geneva. She knew perfectly well that it was an illusion but this did not prevent her from getting onto a train which was about to leave for Geneva. Since she had nothing to do there, she returned to Zürich on the following day. A few months later, while living in Geneva she heard a voice calling her to Zürich. She was in her room, almost nude, and under the influence of cocaine. She pulled on an overcoat, rushed to the station, and arrived stockingless in a bizarre state in Zürich on the night train. There, as if in a dream, she began to wander through the station where an acquaintance, who was there by chance, recognized her and took her to a hotel.

Concerning the hallucinations that she had at the clinic while undergoing withdrawal treatment, we recorded the following observations:

July 14: The patient saw a man with a revolver in his hand, crawling on the floor. He aimed at her. He was a rejected lover. He said that she must remain forever where she is, because she had made him lose his reason.

July 15: She saw Kaiser Wilhelm on a tree, and took him for a cow. Then the vision bowed to her in gratitude. Still on the tree, she saw a shoe, similar to those she had been given at the clinic, but gigantic. And, next to them, she saw a woman watching the objects in astonishment, as if she had never seen shoes before. At the bottom of the tree she saw a beautiful white Saint Bernard dog.

July 16: She often sees her mother's head, but she always turns away in great sadness. She also saw two Geneva policemen in dress uniforms. One day, before coming to the clinic, she had seen a French nurse who had betrayed her country by setting up in the ruins of a bombarded house an apparatus through which she was sending signals to her German lover. She saw a raven which was dismembering an emperor moth. She saw her mother's head in her hand. It looked like a miniature, and she heard her mother tell her not to turn her eyes away, that she was indeed in a clinic and everything must go well.

July 17: Smoke was seen rising near Zollikon. The patient

claimed she could distinctly see a cannon and that the smoke was coming from it. In a dark cloud, next to a small light one, she saw Mount Vesuvius in full activity.

July 18: A little sediment settled on the bottom of a cup of camomile tea. She believed it was fly legs and that if she swallowed them they would eliminate the effects of cocaine. The previous evening she was to receive a scopolamine injection. She had resisted strongly, shouting and crying because she believed that someone had been paid to turn her mad and that the injection would have that effect. After the injection, she experienced strong anxiety, the effect of scopolamine expressing itself as fear. As she was falling asleep, she was still saying that she did not want to sleep.

July 19: The previous evening she could not sit on the chamber pot because there were a lot of people there to watch her. The day before she had seen many students around her. She did not want to go to bed before seeing an airplane, and she succeeded in seeing one. Why? She said she didn't know. She dreamed that she was in Lausanne, that she had 1.5 francs and that she had gone to a fruit store to buy some fruits. There were white apples and black apples, but really black. She asked what the price of these was. She was told it was 50 cents for half a pound. She picked three white apples and three black apples and asked how much that cost. It was 90 cents. She calculated she would have 60 cents left. The apples were good and easy to peel.

Because, at the time, our experience in the treatment of cocaine addiction was limited, and also because the weakness of the patient's heart and her crises of anxiety and agitation were becoming alarming, we adopted the following regimen. Before admission the patient's daily cocaine dose was 8 g. After admission she received:

On July 12 - 0.50 g
On July 13 - 1.50 g
On July 14 - 1.25 g plus 1 g Veronal
On July 15 - 0.90 g plus 0.5 g Veronal
On July 16 - 0.95 g plus 1 mg scopolamine
On July 17 - 0.10 g

After the 17th the administration of narcotics was discontinued.

During the first days after taking cocaine, she had shown a tendency towards flight of ideas and tonal associations and had written some short poems. Her writing was then very irregular and full of crossed out words, whereas in the normal state her writing was very regular and even.

During a clinical presentation of the patient on July 19, 1916, she showed an odd mixture of euphoria and mistrust. She took some of the listeners to task because she claimed they were going to talk scornfully about her in their own conversations. She related that after taking cocaine she had often seen small animals, tigers, cats and snakes, though she was quite aware that they were only visions. When she ran out of cocaine she would often lie on the floor to gather the remaining white powder which, more often than not, was non-existent. Also after taking cocaine, she often had the sensation that her skin was swollen and she could see purple spots appearing on it. She tried to convert everybody she met to cocaine use, because the pleasure it produces is much greater if it is taken in the company of others. She could see her father's head and a heart on a blank sheet of paper held up in front of her. During the clinical presentation she took a little cocaine. A quarter of an hour later she could see her mother's head in her hand. Her appetite had diminished considerably and she could spend whole days without eating. She added that, on the other hand, cocaine produces exaggerated thirst, so that it is very easy to become a heavy drinker.

The patient further relates that she has sniffed a great deal of cocaine while in larger social groups. Lately many of these groups in various Swiss cities have become veritable cocaine clubs. They always meet at night and these gatherings are very animated. When enough cocaine is taken in a social setting the visions appear very easily and quickly, while the solitary user requires longer use and considerably larger doses to achieve the same effects. In such a gathering of cocaine users, for example, if one of them says that there are beautifully colored butterflies flying around in the room, all the others will see them as well and run around trying to catch them. There then develops, especially after prolonged intake of cocaine, a remarkable sexual excitation which expresses itself in a different manner in women from that in which it expresses itself in men. Women undergo very intense sexual desire which is satisfied more easily than without cocaine; a woman might achieve satisfaction from four to six times in the same length of time that it would normally take her to do it only once without cocaine. The sexual excitation in men is limited to fantasies, while physical sexual impotence develops very rapidly. Homosexuals, in whom cocaine stimulates physical excitation, are an exception to this rule. But, in any case it is always a question of perverted practices among the latter. It must be extremely rare for a female cocaine addict in such a state of sexual arousal to become pregnant. The patient knows at most one case in which pregnancy occurred under such conditions.

The neologisms invented among these circles are equally

interesting. The patient, who during the war period had been moving exclusively in French cocaine-using circles, related that among them cocaine had been known for some months as "Dardo." The origin of this term was finally traced as follows: In order not to give themselves away the patients are always looking for new names to refer to cocaine. The origin of the phrase "la prise"[16] is quite obvious. At that time the allies had the Dardanelles under siege and their capture (prise) was imminent. Abbreviating the term "Dardanelles" from the expression "la prise des Dardanelles" led to the coining of the term "Dardo."

During the 14 days following the complete withdrawal of cocaine, the patient showed marked emotional instability. When, for whatever reason, her wishes were not satisfied, she would become violently angry. Once she even threw some cups and saucers on the floor. Sometimes she experienced states of discomfort with unstable pulse and the appearance of illness for hours on end. Sleep improved within 10 days and became almost normal. Sometimes, when she was feeling well, she slipped into strange states, during which she was lost in daydreams, claiming to have sensory illusions including either pleasant visions parading in front of her eyes or the sound of her favorite love songs. But, on close questioning, it was possible to establish that these were not, strictly speaking, sensory illusions but fantasies, products of her imagination, which, as a result of a certain instability of her sense of reality, easily gave her the illusion of reality. The suspicion that these might be schizophrenic disturbances was not confirmed. Her relationships with the various physicians who looked after her at the clinic were always cordial.

At the end of August, the patient once again presented with mild withdrawal symptoms, including discomfort as well as fantasies of an unpleasant nature, which at times resembled true sensory illusions.

In the afternoon of August 28, for example, she saw a large number of frightening heads. In the evening she seemed to be immersed in her dreams and her facial features were distorted by anxiety, as they had been while under the influence of cocaine. In the clouds she could see heads with red eyes, and she refused to go to the bathroom because she felt that she was being observed. While sitting on a sofa she would suddenly feel acutely anxious and would pull her legs up high while refusing to say what she was afraid of. On September 11, while shopping at a store she suddenly became totally

[16] Ed. note: Sniffing, taking.

absent-minded, stuck her fingers into her mouth and let the nurse who was accompanying her look after everything, without paying the slightest attention. When she was later questioned about this episode she declared that at that moment she was so entranced by a tune that she had heard a short while earlier at a café, that she had lost all interest in everything that was happening around her.

Her temperature was normal throughout her stay at the clinic. Her urine, as well as all other bodily functions, was normal. Her appetite improved consistently. Her outward appearance improved, her pupils became normally reactive, and her face lost the expression of anxiety and tension.

On September 14, 1916, the patient left the clinic nearly cured and went to live in the south with the family of a physician. After some weeks there she started to take cocaine again, soon reaching large doses and again experiencing vivid hallucinations. Therefore she was hospitalized at the psychiatric clinic of her home town, where she remained for several months. Her behavior was often so trying and hysterical that she frequently had to be kept in the security observation room. She never presented with schizophrenic symptoms. After leaving the hospital she took a job as a salesclerk and lived with her family. After some months, she again began to associate with cocaine users, left her family and her job and returned to her previous dissolute life. Toward the end of 1917, she met an artist to whom she became deeply attached. He succeeded in separating her from the cocaine-using group and took her into his home as his housekeeper. He did not shy away from using quite drastic measures to make her give up cocaine definitively. According to reliable information available to us, the patient has remained with this man for six years and she has taken no more cocaine. She is said to work with great zeal and her mental equilibrium has been restored to such a degree that, if our information is truly correct, she can be considered completely cured.

Case 27: T.S., hotel waiter, born in 1895. His mother was schizophrenic and had been committed to a mental hospital. All his six sisters are somewhat unstable in character and his two younger brothers are morally deviant.

The patient had a normal birth and a normal physical and mental development, but suffered from nocturnal enuresis until the age of 12. He had begun his apprenticeship as a bricklayer but was dismissed at the end of six months for dishonesty. He also failed as a farm worker and finally ended as a barman and hotel waiter. During his military service, his behavior was very bad. He contracted a venereal disease and was sentenced to 20 days of imprisonment for breach of discipline. Following his military service, he led a slothful life, worked only occasionally as a waiter, and was suspected of also acting as a pimp. He related that as a soldier in 1916 he had received for the first time some cocaine from a comrade but that, after sniffing it, he had not experienced any recognizable effect. Some time later, in 1917, a dancer in Geneva had paid him 50 francs on condition that he spend the night with her sniffing cocaine and entertaining her. He agreed and for the first time experienced the pleasurable effects of cocaine. Subsequently, he had often sniffed cocaine in the company of young women and he was always pleased that cocaine completely eliminated his sexual desires but made him feel very spirited so that he enjoyed himself talking all night long. To experience this type of effect, however, it was necessary to take the drug in small doses repeated every half hour, instead of in single large doses. If used in this way, cocaine acts as a stimulant rather than as a hypnotic, so that it is possible to talk and go out walking all night long and enjoy it. Sometimes it is difficult to achieve this pleasant mental stimulation in a social setting. It is then best to sit very relaxed beside the girl, with both fastening their gaze on some fixed point, giving free rein to their thoughts. In this way you end up by having identical thoughts and this is what is so beautiful. After spending one night with friends, he went to the railway station restaurant at 6 a.m. where he was provoked by a drunk. He then sniffed a little cocaine and felt a wave of anger rising in him. He became dizzy and while trying to sit down he fell to the floor. He was picked up by some passersby and taken to the lounge in the station. There he felt that everybody was staring and making fun of him. Finally two police officers, called by the spectators, took him to the police station. He was released at once, and went to a café where he suddenly had a fit of agitation. A psychiatrist who was called to attend him thought the man was hysterical and sent him to the psychiatric hospital immediately (November 27, 1921).

Once there, the patient had a violent fit of excitation with shouting, struggling and flailing about with his arms and legs. It was with difficulty that he was held down in a chair. After responding to the physician's greeting he started to shout again, got loose from those who were restraining him, went to the fireplace and, after clearing his throat loudly, he closed one nostril and started to blow strongly through the other in order to expel the damned drug which he was never going to take again because it does no good. "A handkerchief, give me a handkerchief, I shall not calm down until I have a decent handkerchief. They are idiots, not you madam doctor, but all of those there are idiots. Shame! Shame! Once more, shame!" He spits in all directions, again lashes out while six people hold him in order to take his shoes off. He starts to call: "Olgi, I want to see you Olgi, Klärli, Anni, Marthi, Olgi, Elsi, Mama, Papa, Olgi, I want to see everybody around me, all those who wish me well. Madam doctor, I do want to obey you, but to hell with these idiots. Promise me that I will leave soon, I am young, I have to work."[17] It was impossible to make a physical examination. He was given an injection of morphine and scopolamine and taken to the special ward by six attendants.

There, it was extremely difficult to undress him and to put him in the bathtub. Once out of the bathtub he refuses to put on his bedshirt. He makes all sorts of grimaces, constantly changes his position, looks pathetic most of the time, begs to be set free and promises that he will never again take the drug. Again he starts to call: "Olgi, Anni, Elsi, etc." and finally lets the physician take him to his bed. At first, he does not respond to the questions that are put to him but accedes, after some time, on condition that the idiots leave because he doesn't want them in front of his eyes. Above all he wants to leave this house, it doesn't suit him. Questioned on this point he replies that this building resembles a church, no, it is a repulsive tavern, but he is not sure what kind. Presumably he had been brought here by automobile. He had been sitting in the third class restaurant at the station where he had drunk two cups of coffee and eaten two small rolls. It was then that he had fallen into this terrifying state. He didn't know how this had happened. Many police officers had appeared, one after the other, and had seized him. He had driven past Dr. S. and then was in a waiting room, but didn't know whose. He no longer knew anything about anything. When he is asked what day it is or other similar questions, he does not answer at all, but in spite of this is well oriented. It is not possible to confirm the presence of visual or auditory hallucinations. The patient only claims to have heard all sorts of things, and hears the voices of people he cares about such as Olgi, whom he wanted to marry and with whom he expected to live a beautiful life. Everything shimmered before his eyes. He has been told and instructed that he must accomplish something very important. Professionally, he is a doctor of philosophy. . .or of medicine. But, above all, he is a mechanic, he doesn't know where but he has worked in every place

[17] Ed. note: *Sic*; though this is clearly the same case as that cited on p. 169, the patient's comments are not quoted identically by Maier in the two places.

where there was something to do. He has lived alone at 23 Mühlestrasse. He becomes impatient, sticks his tongue out now and then, complains of thirst but refuses to drink. He closes his eyes and complains of fatigue. The pulse, at 107 per minute, is regular and small. The pupils are equal, moderately dilated, and reacting well to light and accommodation. The tongue is dry and clean. The skin of the face, neck and front of the chest is red and dry with nothing else worthy of note. It is impossible to continue the examination of the patient.

Some hours later, he fell asleep in the observation ward. The next morning he was still sleepy, but showed no other mental disturbances. A diagnosis of "cocaine delirium with slight debility" was made. On February 11, 1922, he was transferred to the dermatology ward because of bladder distress, without positive smear for gonococcus. There his behavior was poor and he tried to establish relationships with prostitutes. On May 9, 1922, having recovered from his physical troubles, he was transferred back to the psychiatric ward. During the second stay there his behavior was irreproachable. On July 5 of the same year he found a job and was discharged. Apparently he has not used cocaine since then. His record disclosed that the young girl with whom he had sniffed cocaine was O.K., a well-known cocaine addict who is also described here as *Case 17*. Besides numerous normal sexual relationships, he has had occasional homosexual relationships.

Case 28: B.J., apprentice, male, single, born in 1898. A paternal aunt suffered from schizophrenia. The patient had given evidence of instability since his youth. At the age of 11 years, he had been operated on for tubercular lymph nodes. In the summer of 1915, enticed by his friends, he began to sniff cocaine. After using cocaine for about a year he developed delusions of persecution and refused treatment of venereal disease because he claimed that the physician was trying to poison him with his gaze, and had paid 10 francs to a police officer to do the same thing. He felt he was being followed in the streets and for this reason he did not want to go to sleep at his mother's home any more. He preferred to sleep at a night hostel or at a friend's place and would tell everybody that his mother was persecuting him and throwing him out of the house. On July 19, 1916, under the influence of strong doses of cocaine, and talking to himself, he started to roam through the municipal offices of the city and finally went to the police station where he declared that someone wanted to poison him. There he showed marked incoherence of thought and it soon became apparent that he was having visual hallucinations. In the car on the way to the mental hospital, he absolutely refused to sit down because he was convinced that the police officers who were escorting him wanted to give him injections from behind. The next morning, his pupils were still very dilated and reacted poorly to light, while his patellar reflexes were markedly exaggerated. On the following day he was still obsessed by ideas of persecution but his mother, who partially believed his statements, came for him at the hospital and took him to her home. But the police brought him back about10 days later, on August 4, 1916. In the meantime, he had again taken large amounts of cocaine and was more convinced than ever that everybody wanted to poison him. On admission, a large amount of cocaine was found on his person. The pupils were again very dilated, reacting poorly to light. He calmed down and lost his delusions quickly, appeared rather indifferent to his surroundings and, after a stay of four weeks, was again removed from the hospital by his mother. We have not heard from him since.

d) Cocaine Psychosis

The four patients belonging in this category include one woman and two physicians. The latter were morphine addicts at the time they began to use cocaine, but gradually they became cocaine addicts almost exclusively. From time to time, both had shown symptoms resembling those of Korsakoff's syndrome and of general paresis, in addition to their cocaine delusions. Their condition improved considerably during their hospitalization but they were discharged too soon and both relapsed and ended up committing suicide.

Case 29: G.J., business woman, born in 1878. No hereditary defects. Normal physical and mental development. She had worked in a commercial firm until her marriage. In 1914, her husband went to the war. Shortly afterwards she met some rather frivolous people and began to sniff cocaine with them. She increased the dosage to at least 3 g per day. Taking advantage of the fact that her husband was away, she broke into his storehouse and sold automobile tires that he had there to a cocaine trafficker at the rate of 20, 30 or 50 g of cocaine per tire. In 1915, she became involved in a love affair. The following year her husband heard about this and put her under surveillance. In October of 1916, under the influence of increasing doses of cocaine, she began to attach a delusional interpretation to this surveillance. She believed that every man she met in the streets was a detective. In the evening of October 18, 1916, while she was in bed sniffing cocaine, she suddenly saw light signals on the ceiling and became immediately convinced that they were evidence of the secret police. Despite the fact that it was raining very heavily, she fled her apartment wearing only a nightgown and a robe. She backed away from everybody she met on the quay. She threw away the keys to her house and wanted to jump into the lake to avoid her persecutors. But at the last minute she changed her mind and, still feeling that she was being hotly pursued, started to run along the bank and finally took refuge in an isolated area where she was picked up by the police. At 4 o'clock in the morning, she was brought to the psychiatric clinic in a state of marked excitation and suffering from anxiety-provoking delusions of persecution. She admitted she had taken 3 g of cocaine during the night. The next morning she was in a heavy toxic sleep, resembling that of an alcoholic following an episode of *delirium tremens*. On admission, she was thoroughly wet and covered with dirt. She had an anxious expression on her face, her eyes were wide open and the conjunctivae red. Her glance kept shifting all the time. Her general nutritional condition was good. There were no noticeable neurological signs. On October 21, following 24 hours of sleep, she was remarkably well-oriented and making efforts to get rid of her ideas of persecution, while claiming that they were not due to cocaine. Her mood was good, she had no abstinence symptoms and she left the hospital on October 28, cured of her cocaine psychosis. It is not known whether or not she relapsed.

Case 30: P.C., single, born in 1892, formerly a dental assistant, later a dancer. Before the war he had lived in France where, as a dental technician, he had acquired the habit of sniffing cocaine. As an Austrian citizen he was able to go to Switzerland after the declaration of war, was subsequently exempted from military service because of a hernia, and became a dancer. He lived with a woman dancer who was also a cocaine addict. They performed together in public and enjoyed great success as a result of their bizarre and eccentric dances, generally executed while under the effects of cocaine.

A friend of the patient provided us with the following information. When he had met him in August of 1916, the patient was already using large amounts of cocaine. Although this led to states of marked hyper-excitation, he did not yet appear ill. In October of the same year, his hyper-excitation had become worse. He was incapable of remaining quiet, of sitting still or of staying at home. In November and December, mild ideas of reference appeared. He believed that everybody who knew him was mocking and making fun of him. Although his economic situation was poor, he began to squander the little money he had. For example, one day at a café he paid the bills of all the customers who looked to him comparatively poor. Under the influence of cocaine his intellectual performance became increasingly obtuse and slow, while his motor performance became quicker and smoother. His sexual drive was clearly diminished. At the end of 1916, his whole body began to twitch every time an automobile or street car passed by, and he became obsessed with the idea of passing on the left everybody he met in the street. He also began to suffer from loss of memory. He would, for example, forget his most familiar dance routines, and he would have lapses of attention lasting from 10 to 15 minutes. On December 31, 1916, he went to Basel with his friend and, at the hotel he started to run up and down the stairs non-stop, like a madman. In his room, he began to look about for something under the beds, along the walls, in the bookshelves and in every corner, but was unable to say what he was looking for. He even searched the mattress and his hair, which he combed endlessly. During the night, he suddenly came to his friend's room half-dressed, took out the money he had in his pockets and counted it over and over. Finally he searched through his friend's room also, without saying a word, and then went to bed with his hat on. On January 6, 1917, at night, he suddenly declared that he could see a star which he could direct with his eyes; it had told him that something was going to happen, but he did not know what. This star had also told him that his friend was related to him and that the Rhinegold belonged to him, to the patient and to his mistress. He referred to a Viennese woman artist as his cousin. He listened to her conversation in rapture, while at the same time claiming that she had betrayed Austria, and that he wanted to take revenge on her. Then he began to talk politics and to repeat endlessly that he was going to achieve peace. He then stated that Rome was black and Germany green, and that this had to change. Blue-white must be victorious. Then he began to establish relationships between numbers and colors. The number '7', for example, was green. Then he started to shove into his pockets everything in sight. In the evening, while dancing in public, he suddenly stopped as if in an absent-minded spell. The audience, believing this was part of a new routine, began to applaud most enthusiastically. Next day, he suddenly decided he would go and light up all the gas lamps, then went to the station and held the main gate shut. Eventually his employers obtained a medical certificate that allowed them to cancel his contract. The patient then went to Zürich where he spent the night running around outside in the bitter cold. On the morning of January 10, he went to the station, stood against a wall, began to clown around and tried to stare at the sun through his ring. He believed he had the power to steer passing cars by turning his body, and he claimed to have the power to make the hair grow on people's heads. He also believed that it was a result of his power that the trees would stretch towards the sky or shrink back. He beat his girlfriend almost every night. On January 18, 1917, he had to be taken to a physician. He was then in a state of marked motor excitation, appeared happy and gave the impression of being intoxicated. The pupils were dilated and reacted poorly to light. He was well-oriented in time and space and his speech was animated but somewhat incoherent. He said he felt extremely well, and that he knew the contents of all the newspapers even before they were printed. The diagnosis of "cocaine psychosis" was made and the patient, considered dangerous, was committed to a mental hospital on the afternoon of January 21, 1917. It was not possible to obtain any reliable information concerning the amounts of cocaine he had taken. He said that he could see many beautiful yellow and green lights where no one else could see anything. He then fell into a toxic sleep from which he could not be aroused despite pinching his skin and shaking his limbs. He slept for nearly 36 hours and it was barely possible to feed him during this time.

On January 29, he was euphoric and demanded his freedom, but it was not very difficult to convince him to stay quite contentedly in the clinic. He still held firmly to his delusions, however.

An examination conducted on January 25 gave the following results: for some time already he had felt ill at ease among his friends and tended to withdraw. From the day he had seen the star in Basel, his ideas had changed markedly. He could see this star even during the day, against a blue sky. From this day on, he was able to tackle anything he wanted and said he had succeeded in making trees, animals and men grow rapidly. This is no longer the case, but he doesn't know whether this was real or not then. Once, while he was half asleep, he heard someone telling him: "After all, we are only electrical people." After this he only had to stick his finger into his left ear to be able to hear the most distant telephone conversations. The latter were very funny, but he cannot remember their content. If he stood in front of an orchestra and began to move his feet, the musicians would be compelled to play everything that passed through his head. Was this really so or was it only his imagination? He was not sure today. When other people talked, it always seemed to him they were saying funny things and he had the feeling that everything they said referred to him. Since he saw the star, he has been able to look directly at the sun without blinking. He has seen the sun come out from behind the clouds and another sun suddenly emerge behind it. He could see a wire in contact with the sun and had developed a connection with it; since then, all silver objects are repelled by him and all iron objects attracted to him. He used to be left-handed, but after making this observation about the sun he has become right-handed. It was also after making this discovery that he became able to stop breathing for several minutes, to understand all languages and to speak English, something he had not been able to do before. He has felt himself to be dreadfully strong, and this is still the case. Then some phenomena occurred but he couldn't tell whether they were real or due to mental clouding. With the help of his ring he had acquired the power of attracting the sun or of ordering it to remain immobile. When he went into a café the sun disappeared. All the characters in the letters that he received were surrounded by minute printed signs which totally altered the meaning of these letters in a way that was absolutely clear to him. However, today he thinks that this was just an illusion. He could see before his eyes some microscopic vesicles which had a black spot in the center and which moved about in all directions. When he looked hard at the people he knew, they would become very small. The head would decrease in size first and then the body. Even today, he confirms that birds do not fly away from him. He could read funny things in the sign-boards along the streets. Then he decided he had to follow the right path. This is why he suddenly became right-handed and why he adopted the habit of always walking on the right side of the street. He would take the left side only when passing through Church Street, because he didn't want to have anything to do with the clergy.

The patient succeeded in getting rid of these delusional ideas after three days, but he remained exceedingly conceited. During the following days he drafted a very lucid presentation in which he begged the government to order his liberation. He succeeded and, on February 2, 1917, left the clinic cured of his delusions and cocaine psychosis but still suffering from an excessive self confidence. He did not receive any narcotics during his stay at the clinic.

A year later, on February 13, 1918, he was again committed to the Institute. We then learned that he had started to sniff cocaine again shortly after his first discharge. At the end of January of 1918, he again presented with states of excitation. He was very irritable, beat his mistress, threw hot milk in her face and so on. On the night of February 12, he couldn't stay in bed even for a moment, unscrewed the lock on the door, let the bathtub overflow, put the whole house in a state of turmoil and urinated and defecated without realizing it. For some time he had been sniffing cocaine again, together with his mistress, in doses of at least 3 to 4 g a day. He purchased the drug in large amounts (once he spent 75 francs on one purchase) from a pharmacist who would even have it delivered to the hotel by a messenger boy. During recent weeks, sometimes he would not eat at all, or he would eat immoderately, like an animal, even dispensing with knife and fork. In addition, he was in continuous agitated motion, tearing and destroying anything that wasn't nailed down. Between him and his mistress, also intoxicated with cocaine, there were constant arguments and jealous quarrels. The physician who came to look after him found him submerged in a deep sleep. When he woke up he seemed to find the visit from the doctor quite natural. It was impossible to follow his train of thought. Attention was markedly impaired and he could not say what year or day it was. He did not know whether it was morning or evening. He didn't remember at all his fits of rage of the night before and claimed that he had slept peacefully. His movements were so uncoordinated that he had to be dressed like a child and was unable to put on his jacket and overcoat properly. He passively let us take him to the clinic by car, limiting his motor activity to fussing around senselessly with all the handles and screws, which he tried to remove; all during this he said nothing. Taken to his room he immediately turned the electric light on and started to handle all the objects lying on the table as though he were at home. In the administrative office of the hospital, he sat in front of a typewriter, began to play with the keys like a child, rearranged all the papers lying on the table and pulled a curtain retainer from the wall. Then he started to grimace, appearing to fix his sight on a particular point in space which was not visible to others. He kept on silently looking around him, as if in search of something, and even tried to climb up on the chairs. His movements were somewhat uncoordinated and his fingers were bent like claws, giving the impression that he had to overcome the hindrance of muscle spasms. Then he picked up a stethoscope which was lying on the table, put it against his ear and appeared to be listening to things which he refused to communicate to anyone else. It was extremely difficult to divert his attention from all these movements and gestures which he performed without saying a word. Repeated examinations showed that the patient was totally disoriented with respect to time. His attention kept on switching from one object to another. While he was being escorted to his room, he made a pointless escape to the courtyard. When he was caught he kept on repeating in a tearful and stereotyped manner: "My word of honor to my father and my mother, to papa and mama." He then alternated between laughter and tears, with such vivid and quickly changing facial expressions that often the upper half of the face still showed a sad expression while the lower half was already laughing. He referred to one of his guards as "papa," while a woman doctor was his "mama" and he tried to kiss her hands. His pupils were moderately dilated but they could not be examined properly because of the continued restlessness of the patient. It was very difficult to undress him and to give him an injection of scopolamine, which was unsuccessful in making him sleep. Another one, given later, was equally ineffective. The next day, as during the previous night, it was impossible to keep him in bed. His orientation with respect to time and space, however, had returned to normal. He kept on seeing small spots, similar to those on the signs painted on the streetcars but infinitely smaller and multi-colored. He could again see the flowers growing and could detect on the sun three spots of different colors. He itched intensely all over the body, scratched himself continuously and had numerous scars produced by scratching himself. His mistress was forbidden to come to see him because she had tried to smuggle in cocaine for him. On February 14, he was still unable to stay in bed. When attempts were made to put him to bed he suddenly became impulsively aggressive, could hardly be controlled and had to be isolated in a cell. During this he kept on repeating that he felt extremely well and that he wanted to travel at once to begin a new engagement. His agitation persisted despite another scopolamine injection. He paced his cell endlessly, and feverishly leafed through the papers without, however, reading a word. With his face taut, he stared out into the night and raised his fingers spasmodically and in slightly uncoordinated fashion, as if menacing someone. His hands showed marked coarse tremor. On the night of the 15th, he calmed down and slept until morning. However, when the staff came to see him in the morning, they found that he had torn up his trousers, vest, shirt, underwear and the bed sheets into small pieces. He was calmer but did not speak at all. On February 16, he claimed he had been in the clinic for three weeks when in fact he had been there for three days. He had torn his clothes apart on impulse, and could no longer remember the state of excitation in which he had been since entering the clinic. His movements were no longer spastic. During the following days his delusional ideas disappeared under our very eyes. He rationalized that if he had used cocaine it had been against his will. He claimed that it had been given to him while he was half asleep, but this was, of course, not true. From March 10 onwards, his condition became completely normal and he had succeeded in getting rid of the mental symptoms, as far as he could remember them.

On March 29, 1918, following a new request, he was again discharged, recovered from his cocaine psychosis. We subsequently learned, however, from confidential sources that soon after his discharge he had started to sniff cocaine again, usually with his mistress, and that he had left the country shortly afterwards. No further information about him is available.

Case 31: Dr. P.L., born in 1874, physician, married, normal childhood development. He married in 1903, but the marriage was unhappy, allegedly because his wife was unbearably jealous. He got divorced in 1905 and remarried in 1908. Shortly after his second marriage, he began to take morphine by injection, allegedly to treat his headaches. It was not long before his wife began to do the same. Both underwent a withdrawal cure, but relapsed shortly afterwards. In 1911, in order to counteract the pain caused by the injections the couple decided to add cocaine to the morphine. They soon experienced states of excitation, with shortness of breath and a sense of oppression. In order to counteract the insomnia caused by cocaine, which sometimes lasted for several nights in a row, they resorted to hyoscine in doses of 1 mg. Further increase in cocaine dosage soon brought on sensory illusions. The patient claimed that the walls of his room were thin and hollow, so that one could hear everything through them. He could hear scratching, loud noises and sometimes also voices. He stated that the water had a smell of poison and the food had a peculiar taste. His wife also suffered vivid hallucinations. She could hear insults coming from the next room and exhortations to give up cocaine. She could see blood in the area of her husband's heart, while he declared that he was suffocating. At night the physician had his wife promise under oath that she would commit suicide two to three hours before he himself was buried. After taking strong doses of cocaine continually for several days in a row, the couple developed marked ideas of persecution. Finally, in a state of intense excitation, the wife swallowed a large dose of hyoscine solution and died, while the husband ran around the apartment dressed only in his shirt, and carrying a gun in one hand and a syringe in the other. He impressed those who saw him at this time as a madman. He declared that it was his duty to follow his wife to the grave. He had very vivid hallucinations and felt currents run through his body. He was taken to a clinic in a state of great excitation. There he again declared that it was his duty to die, that his heart had already burst and that he was happy to die. He complained that the few moments he had left to live were being spoiled with electric currents. He claimed that his whole bed was charged with the currents, so that he could hear very well the schemes that were being wrought against him.

According to the available medical information, he had been taking 2 g of morphine and 1 g of cocaine daily for the last while. Cocaine was discontinued immediately, but the morphine dosage was reduced gradually. For some days the patient continued to have unpleasant olfactory sensations and expressed strong feelings of jealousy against his dead wife. At the same time, he presented some good-natured dullness and showed not the slightest remorse or feelings of guilt. His memory was poor, full of gaps. Within a few days morphine was completely discontinued, although this gave rise to strong withdrawal symptoms. He was accused of complicity in the death of his wife, but the proceedings were discontinued following a psychiatric report which concluded he was not legally responsible for his acts. After a few weeks he was discharged from the hospital and he then went to Zürich where, on November 28, 1911, he was found unconscious in his hotel room. A farewell letter addressed to his family was found next to him and it was possible to determine that he once again had taken a large amount of morphine and hyoscine. He was revived and taken to Burghölzli where he arrived in a state of violent excitation and vomiting strenuously.

The legs were covered with injection scars and a large abscess was present. During the following days, he suffered from marked difficulty in swallowing and from insomnia. At night, there was clouding of consciousness and anxiety, and he wanted to jump out the window at any cost. The difficulties in swallowing and the insomnia disappeared within a week. He showed a certain degree of insight and appeared very busy, but did not have a real desire to work. He was discharged, comparatively well, at the end of six months.

Here is how he himself described the effects of cocaine:

"Little by little, I had fallen so low that I had the appearance of a confirmed morphine addict and I felt almost ashamed of meeting people who knew me. I became so sensitive and hyperesthetic that I hesitated to stick the needle under my skin, because just touching it with the point of the needle caused an unbearable pain. To prevent this and to be able to continue my injections without pain or difficulty, I decided, for the first time at the end of May, 1891, to add a certain amount of a 1:50 cocaine solution to the morphine. At first I used only a little, but gradually I added more and more cocaine. This was my undoing because soon morphine, even in large doses, did not produce any effects, unless I added cocaine. As I continued to use large amounts of cocaine I soon became aware that my senses of taste and smell were changing in a peculiar way. At first I did not suspect that this was due to cocaine. I couldn't eat anything anymore, because everything I put in my mouth had a frightful smell and taste, as though I were eating everything in an anatomy dissection room. Only then did I realize that these were gustatory and olfactory hallucinations due to cocaine. It was comparatively late, as opposed to the usual course of events, that I began to be tormented by visual and auditory hallucinations. The latter appeared first and were not complicated by visual hallucinations, which made my life unbearable, until two or three weeks later. It goes without saying that I could no longer practise my profession. Gathering all my strength I went to a hospital near F. to undergo a withdrawal cure. I did not, however, find there what I was looking for. The physician in charge of the institution was not nearly energetic enough to help a patient as seriously ill as I was, who took such large doses and could no longer contribute to his own detoxification and recovery. Furthermore, it was easy to obtain morphine and cocaine while still in hospital. Therefore, I decided to leave this clinic and go to another where the supervision was stricter. I believe that at the time I had the best of intentions, but, much too uncertain and weak, I decided at the last minute to go home. Being already mentally very ill, I then began to decrease the morphine dosage gradually while increasing the cocaine dosage until I was taking only cocaine, and a great deal of it indeed. I then had the most dreadful hallucinations and sensory illusions of a sexual nature, quite similar to those of alcoholics. These were complicated by the most dreadful feelings of jealousy. Finally, came the tactile hallucinations that literally drove me crazy. When I was in bed I believed that I was being influenced by electric currents. I could feel the electric wires directly under me and I had sensations of tickling and burning, and such strong pain sensations that I had to jump out of bed to protect myself. But naturally I would find the wires again on the floor, on the chairs, everywhere, so that I could not find respite anywhere."

Case 32: B.C., physician, born in Italy in 1868. Rather bad hereditary background. The father was a constitutional psychopath. One of his brothers had died young from complications due to alcoholism. The patient's development had been normal. In high school he was an intelligent student, but he showed early traits of presumptuousness, marked vanity and a peculiar instability. His medical studies were successful, he worked hard as an intern, and later also became very interested in social problems related to his profession. He married early and had three children, the youngest of whom had epileptic attacks on two occasions. He had a very successful practice, but lived beyond his means. In his forties he became addicted to morphine and underwent treatment for this on several occasions, unsuccessfully. At first, he hid his illness from his wife. In 1912, he became unable to work as a result of his increasing abuse of morphine and again entered a private sanatorium. Morphine was withdrawn only partially, and he was advised to take injections of 20 to 40% cocaine solutions in order to recover his energy. From September 1913 on, he began to use principally cocaine, in rather large doses, but he still used a fair amount of morphine and occasionally atropine. Earlier, when he took morphine alone, it always made him sleepy and listless. But now cocaine made him very animated and busy in a peculiar way. He tackled nonsensical research projects, even though his previous scientific publications had been sound and serious. Above all he wanted to solve the problems of astigmatism and cataracts. Every time that he had an idea concerning these problems he would send a telegram to his colleague saying: "Eureka!," or "Cataract problem progressing." His latest theory about cataracts was aimed at making surgery unnecessary, basing everything on diosmotic actions. But a friend of his told him that, although not convinced of the validity of his theory, he did not want to say that it was totally absurd when he recalled the discovery of X-rays. Ten days later, the patient told him that, he had given up the diosmosis explanation and decided instead that he could explain his observations on the basis of X-rays. He thus demonstrated a certain degree of suggestibility in relation to his odd ideas. He claimed to have discovered some new invisible rays which, in myopic people, were concentrated to such a degree by the glasses that they made the adipose tissue surrounding the eyes disappear. While under the influence of cocaine he could see radiating lines in the lenses of his patients' eyes, and with the naked eye he believed he could see cells undergoing division as well. At the beginning of 1914, he telegraphed a specialist colleague to come and look after his practice for him because his discoveries were of such importance that he had decided that from now on he must dedicate himself entirely to this work. When his colleague came to see him on the first day, he described his new explanation of the cataract problem. The next day he explained to his friend the origin and treatment of astigmatism and on the third day he gave him a lecture during which he tried to demonstrate that the current theory of accommodation was totally absurd and that only the one he had discovered the previous night was in accordance with the facts. During the afternoon of the same day, he had solved the problem of cancer and had formulated a new theory of colors. Scientific discussions with him on these topics were impossible. The slightest contradiction made him furious. At night, he examined his own eyes in the mirror and found the pupils to be very dilated under the influence of atropine and cocaine. He could see the radiating lines in the lens and the cellular divisions. His colleagues, whom he called as witnesses, could not see anything. His wife, on the other hand, was under the influence of his suggestion to such a degree that she confirmed everything he claimed to see. He always stayed in bed all morning and ate very little. He totally neglected his appearance and went around the house wearing only his nightshirt. One night at the end of January, 1914, he alarmed everybody in the house, asserting that there were burglars. At the beginning of February he had hallucinations of hearing his patients screaming at night. At this time, he was taking 5 to 6 g of cocaine and 0.3 g of morphine daily by injection, in addition to "Migränine" and atropine. At about the same time, he also began to carelessly prescribe toxic substances for his patients, such as a 10% cocaine solution to take home, or inunctions with an ointment containing 5% atropine. At the same time, he said that the proof of his theory was important enough that even if it cost the loss of a patient's eye, it would be worth it. He got in touch with a large manufacturer of chemical products, in order to exploit his method for the treatment of cataracts, and sent extremely long telegrams to a famous institute of optics to persuade it to manufacture glasses for myopics, made of albumin because the ordinary glasses, which concentrate the invisible noxious rays, would ruin their eyes. He sent a telegram to another chemical institute to announce that he had discovered a new medicine which could bring in millions. In the meantime, he became increasingly erratic in his practice, made errors in treatment, and on many occasions, when highly intoxicated, he had fallen in the operating room. His friends, who feared that he could harm his patients in this condition, brought him to the psychiatric clinic on February 21, 1914. They were not precise about the diagnosis, suggesting that it could be incipient general paresis, paranoia or a toxic psychosis.

On admission the patient was mildly euphoric and showed a constant drive to keep moving. The pupils were moderately dilated and reacted weakly. There were a few slightly inflamed injection marks on the skin of the abdomen. The neurological examination was essentially negative. Urinalysis, performed on February 22, revealed traces of albumin which disappeared quickly. A bottle containing a 40% cocaine solution, 11 empty vials, and four vials each containing 30 mg of morphine, were found in his clothes.

On the ward, he showed clear flight of ideas. After an injection of 10 mg morphine and 10 mg cocaine he calmed down, but he asked for the doctor again after two hours. He seemed near collapse, sweating profusely and complaining of nausea. He was given another injection and an hour later he was loquacious, there was flight of ideas again and his speech was slightly slurred. He continued to believe firmly in his discoveries but did not want to speak about them because he noticed that they were considered insane. On the basis that before admission, the patient was using daily doses of at least 2 g of cocaine and 0.25 g of morphine, the detoxification schedule was set up as follows:

	Morphine	Cocaine
February 21	0.16 g	0.35 g
February 22	0.13 g	0.13 g
February 23	0.11 g	0.08 g
February 24	0.13 g	0.015 g
February 25	0.13 g	0
February 26	0.11 g	0
February 27	0.105 g	0
February 28	0.09 g	0
March 1	0.08 g	0
March 2	0.065 g	0
March 3	0.06 g	0
March 4	0.05 g	0
March 5	0.042 g	0

During the first few days, the rather slurred speech of the patient, the flaccid and rather anxious expression of his face, and his inability to sustain any conversation made us think of a diagnosis of general paresis. However, the latter became increasingly unlikely as the process of detoxification progressed. Eventually it became obvious that it was a case of cocaine psychosis complicated by morphine addiction. The diagnosis of general paresis was totally discarded when negative results were obtained on the Wasserman test and on the examination of the cerebro-spinal fluid obtained by lumbar puncture.The diagnosis of paranoia was inconsistent with the nature of the onset of the morbid state, the organic character of the picture and the predominant role of the profuse microscopic visual illusions. The withdrawal reaction differed from that of ordinary morphine addicts in the marked loquacity of the patient, the persistence with which he defended his delusional discoveries, and his tendency to write lengthy documents, covering many sheets of paper with a loose but not ataxic writing, adorned with numerous high-flown terms. The patient continued to follow in the mirror the cellular divisions in his eyes and to sketch drawings of them which were in fact all illustrations, drawn from memory, of earlier microscopic observations. He also showed some degree of sexual excitation which manifested itself by desires and erotic fantasies rather than by erections. This is not seen in pure morphine addicts. After discontinuation of cocaine and reduction of the morphine dosage, it became more and more difficult to restrain the patient. He started to complain, protested constantly against his confinement and even brought in a lawyer. He overwhelmed his wife with his demands and finally persuaded her to have him transferred to a private sanatorium (March 15, 1914) where he had been promised more freedom.

There he remained firmly convinced about the soundness of his discoveries and found a large number of articles in the medical literature that he claimed had been inspired by his ideas. The withdrawal cure continued at an extremely slow pace. The patient could be considered demorphinized by April 15, 1914. He was then allowed to go out, first accompanied by an attendant and later alone. He immediately took advantage of these outings to obtain new supplies of cocaine and of morphine. As a result, his condition got worse towards the middle of May. The insomnia returned, he started to examine his eyes in the mirror again and even succeeded in burning his cornea. His gait, which until then had been steady, became wavering. He became extremely irritable and would not tolerate anyone telling him anything. A physician brought him a collection of histological sections of brain to study. After examining them the patient declared that he had seen in his eye, without the aid of the microscope, most of the cell types (plasma cells, glia and neurons) found in these preparations.

The patient disappeared suddenly from the sanatorium on June 9, 1914. He must have taken rapidly increasing amounts of cocaine during the following weeks. On July 22 of the same year, he dropped dead as he was entering a large building in X. Unfortunately the pathologist who performed the autopsy was not aware of the patient's history and did not make a microscopic examination of the organs. The post-mortem report stated: "Atherosclerosis of the coronary arteries with almost total obstruction of the anterior descending branch of the left coronary artery. Acute passive congestion of the lungs and kidneys. Small hemorrhage in the upper lobe of the left lung. Acute tracheo-bronchitis. Small hemorrhage in the jejunum. Hyperostosis of the roof of the cranium. Adhesions of the *pia mater*. Paronychia of the nail-bed of the right middle finger. Ecchymoses of both forearms. Subcutaneous injection marks in both groins."

Death was probably due to a particularly large dose of cocaine and to atherosclerosis of the coronary vessels.

Case 33: K.W., born in 1861, in Germany, physician. No accurate information concerning hereditary history. The patient was a specialist in skin and venereal diseases. He was single and had practised in Zürich since 1890. Some time between 1895 and 1900 he became a morphine addict. Several attempts at detoxification had been unsuccessful. In 1905, he had acquired the habit of adding cocaine to morphine, probably in order to facilitate withdrawal of morphine. Since 1908, he had become visibly less able to work. In 1910, he had delusional ideas under the influence of increasing doses of cocaine, the exact magnitude of which could not be determined. He complained a great deal about a sensation of crawling under the skin and claimed this was due to swarms of insect larvae to be found there. He cut out small pieces of skin, embedded them in Canada balsam, put them under the microscope and claimed to see the larvae and insects coming out. The larvae, he stated, would poison his body and make him suffer horribly. He discovered the same disease in a large number of patients and reached the conclusion that these larvae, rather than gonococci, were the cause of gonorrhea. He therefore began to treat gonorrhea among his patients by excising these insects (which he saw, in his hallucinations, in every case) from the skin of the trunk and legs, instead of treating the disease locally. It is interesting that this new treatment was well received by the public and gained a large clientele for our patient for some weeks. In connection with this, he came to believe that these insects were very infectious and lethal. This was probably what caused him to go into a state of profound depression, together with violent excitation which was particularly serious at night. He would complain incessantly and strike out at his imaginary enemies with his cane, greatly disturbing the other residents of the building, until it became necessary to take him to the psychiatric clinic on September 8,1910.

On admission, his speech was indistinct, faint and unintelligible. His body was covered with injection marks and the scars caused by the skin excisions. The pupils were moderately dilated and reacted well. The right facial nerve was somewhat weaker than the left. The patient's whole personality gave the impression of profound neglect. The fingers of both hands were strongly flexed and it was not possible to straighten them. The physical strength was markedly decreased. There were fine tremors of the hands and the gait was somewhat unsteady. There were no other neurological signs. From the mental point of view the patient presented with a state of obtundation and apathy, with mild dementia. He complained of itching and scratched himself constantly. Furthermore he showed clear-cut morphine withdrawal symptoms including yawning, sweating, diarrhea and unstable pulse. A course of morphine detoxification, during which he showed very marked insomnia, was carried out until September 18. Cocaine was withdrawn completely and immediately. During the following weeks the patient felt very tired when spoken to. Because the prognosis concerning his toxic psychosis was considered poor, and because the patient remained obsessed by delusions about insects, although to a lesser degree, the authorities decided to revoke his licence to practise medicine. On October 20, 1910, he was transferred to a closed institution in his native country. He was fully detoxified, but mentally and physically very weak.

At the time that he left our psychiatric clinic he had the appearance of a patient suffering from general paresis in remission, even though, strictly speaking, he actually showed none of the signs of general paresis proper. His speech was still somewhat indistinct and a certain degree of dementia was evident. He was released from the hospital in his native country after some weeks. He was unable to work, however, and had no other means of subsistence. In March of 1911, he committed suicide with cyanide.

APPENDIX: COCAINE ADDICTION IN SCHIZOPHRENICS

We have seen among cocaine addicts a large number of individuals with psychopathological predispositions and of marked prior emotional ability. It is therefore not surprising that cocaine addiction can be associated with a large number of other mental disturbances. Like alcoholism, cocaine addiction can often develop in a schizophrenic background. We have already noted, in our review of the literature, cases of this type reported by Heilbronner (1913) and Marx (1923), which gave rise to an erroneous diagnosis and a mistaken evaluation of the consequences of intoxication. Here we shall add two cases of our own.

Case 34: A.H., single, born in 1893. Belongs to a very well-educated family. No accurate information concerning hereditary stigmata. The father was 54 years old at the time of the patient's birth. The patient had a normal mental development but from early on showed a lack of perseverance and a tendency to be lazy. He did not finish high school, where he had already shown signs of moral deviance. He had entered a school for the training of hotel employees but was expelled at the end of two months for bad behavior.

Being musically gifted, he wanted to follow a career in this area, but he did not accomplish much in this field either. When he came of age at 20, he received a modest capital which he squandered in a few months, engaging in cocaine orgies with people of dubious reputation. Cocaine abuse in his case gave rise to vivid hallucinations. As the drug made him sexually impotent, he became homosexual, this being facilitated by his mental predisposition in this respect. After spending 5,000 francs in this fashion, and becoming a serious nuisance in his native city as a result of his nearly constant states of cocaine intoxication, he was committed to the psychiatric hospital there on January 15, 1916. He stayed there for nine months and was then transferred to an open sanatorium in the country. However, the authorities had neglected to put him under guardianship. Therefore, when he inherited another few thousand francs, he managed to run away and rejoin his former cocaine-using friends. His family would have nothing more to do with him and two years later he found himself penniless. He made some weak and unsuccessful attempts at suicide and, after defaulting on the payment of a hotel bill, he ran into trouble with the police and was committed to a psychiatric clinic in July, 1919. The diagnosis was "cocaine addiction in a constitutional psychopath." After admission his friend,who had used cocaine with him and who was also destitute, committed suicide by shooting himself. The patient was transferred to our Institute in August, 1919.

It was soon established that the patient was a psychopath with schizophrenic symptoms, that he was weak-willed and that his moral sense was extremely poorly developed. In July, 1921, we tried to let him out of the clinic and put him in the care of a family. At the same time, he was to try a simple office job. But within three weeks he had spent a great deal of money on useless things, was neglecting his work, lied brazenly to us and had engaged again in homosexual relationships. It was therefore necessary to hospitalize him again. During the short time he had spent outside the clinic he had not had much opportunity to use cocaine again. He is still in our clinic and we intend soon to try sending him to the country once more.

The patient relates that when he was 21 years old his mistress first introduced him to cocaine. He had experienced a feeling of well-being from the beginning, and what he appreciated most was the ability to spend the whole night pleasantly chatting with his mistress. He began using only 0.5 g daily but ended up purchasing 50 g bottles from the druggist of a neighboring town. This amount lasted him four to five days. He sniffed pure cocaine and the largest dose he ever took was 19 g in one night. High doses produced restlessness, insomnia and loss of appetite. They also allowed him to move about barely clad in an unheated room in the middle of the winter, without feeling at all cold. He had the impression that his sensory acuity was enhanced, while his sexual potency decreased strikingly. The sensation of hunger had disappeared completely but he suffered from extreme thirst. He experienced hallucinations and illusions. He could hear people whispering and the sound of a dripping tap. He never suffered from headaches. Unpleasant withdrawal symptoms included a strong feeling of weariness and a sensation of hunger while being unable to eat at all. In this state, he was capable of anything in order to secure some cocaine. He often awakened physicians in the middle of the night to try to get cocaine from them. He finally reached a persistent state of depression and disgust with life, even while under the effects of cocaine. Indeed, during his first hospitalization he was always in an apathetic and depressed state.

Case 35: R.N., jurist, born in 1880. No accurate information regarding his hereditary history. Since puberty he had suffered from periodic episodes of bad mood. During one of these periods, at the age of 12 or 13 years he ran away from home and went to stay overnight with a friend and it was necessary to resort to the police to find him. Later these episodes, reminiscent of ambulatory automatism, would last up to two days. The intervals between these states were variable, ranging from one to several months. These episodes were heralded by several days of general irritability. Attempts at controlling them were generally unsuccessful because, even in the best of cases, there still was a marked discharge of physical activity. As he grew older, he became increasingly attracted to narcotic drugs during these episodes. First it was alcohol, and from the age of 22 on, it was cocaine, which he took exclusively by mouth. He eventually became habituated to this drug, taking 0.5 g daily regularly. He married in 1907, but this aggravated his condition because marriage made him feel restricted and watched. He made a trip to the East during which he reached a daily dose of 1 g, which he took mostly at night. He ended up having nocturnal fantasies and hallucinations. He could hear knocking on the door and could see people in his room. He was aware that they were simply hallucinations but he always went back to believing they were real. The sensory illusions disappeared during the day and he could then sleep better than at night. He gave toothaches as an excuse to justify his use of cocaine. In fact, it was probably only gingivitis. Because of his cocaine use, he was confined to a closed mental hospital in 1911. After admission, he fell into a state of anxiety and agitation which lasted two days. Following this, he was transferred to the open ward where he behaved very well. At the end of four weeks, on February 10, 1911, he experienced another episode of hyper- excitement. On March 12, he left for his native city where he had to deal with urgent professional matters, promising that he would return in two or three weeks. He did not come back.

Second admission. On November 25, 1912, the patient again arrived at the sanatorium and declared that he had been using cocaine again for more than a year in doses of 0.5 to 1 g daily. He had unsuccessfully tried to get rid of his habit by having Dr. B., a psychiatrist in his native city, hypnotize him. The nocturnal hallucinations reappeared after his relapse into cocaine use. He could not look after his professional duties any longer and had to give up his law office. Since he has been under the influence of cocaine constantly he has ceased to notice his former periodic attacks of bad temper. In the sanatorium the hallucinations continued, despite withdrawal of cocaine. He has often heard voices before falling asleep and when, as is his custom in the evening, he has wanted to play the piano in the dark, he has had the feeling that he is not alone in the room, that someone is stirring near him. He has to turn the lights on. The voices speak in his mother tongue and generally come from a corner. Sometimes they are unintelligible blurred whispers but at other times they are perfectly clear and distinct. They always say the same thing: "You are threatened by a misfortune, you should not have come here. Your wife has already given orders to put you back in the closed ward. You shall stay here forever."

The patient had no hallucinations during the day. On December 9, 1912, after being well for several days, he heard voices, even before dinner time, in relation to some bad news he had received from his wife. The voices said: "You must put an end to it." During dinner he appeared distracted, did not pay any attention to the conversation, and asked the doctor to give him something to calm his very upset nerves. In this connection, he told him about his obsession with feelings of jealousy. He was struggling in vain against the feeling that his wife was unfaithful, even though he knew perfectly well that he did not have the slightest evidence of this. It is only since he started to use cocaine that these feelings have become so strong. The voices also talk to him about his jealousy and tell him that only an evil fellow can have such unjustified suspicions, and that the only thing left for him to do is to shoot himself. To the question of what he would do if his wife were truly guilty, his terse and obvious answer was that he would kill her, the other man and himself. If she were innocent, he must kill only himself. On December 11, 1912, he had peculiar, almost theatrical, hallucinations in the dining room, during which he plugged his ears. None of this prevented him from looking after some business affairs quite reasonably. On December 14, 1912, he had hallucinations in the middle of the day. This time the voices spoke not only in his mother tongue, but also in German. Once he expressed fear that the psychiatrist (Dr. B.) in his native city would hypnotize him at a distance, and asked whether this was possible. Despite being reassured to the contrary by the doctor, he claimed that he was becoming completely mad. On December 20, he had strong hallucinations and fell into a strange state of complete indifference. He stayed in his room and refused to speak at all about what he was feeling. He explained that he must atone for his abuse of cocaine, that he was already mad, or was about to become so. On December 21, 1912, he announced that he was going to join the army. This, he said, might still save him, because the quietness of the sanatorium made him feel oppressed, and his throat felt choked. While he was saying this his appearance was listless and anxious. While at first the voices were impersonal, he could now clearly distinguish the voice of his wife, of his mother-in-law and of other people.

He begged his family to take him home and, even though they did not agree, he left the hospital in a somewhat better mood, because the staff refused to assume further responsibility for him in the absence of constant supervision, something that he absolutely refused.

We made a diagnosis of alcoholism and cocaine addiction in a schizophrenic presenting with episodes of depression of endogenous origin. We have no further information about this patient.

3. Differential Diagnosis

Recognition of the physical and mental signs of cocaine intoxication is naturally easiest if the presence of the alkaloid itself can be confirmed. But the analysis must be done promptly because this substance undergoes rapid changes in the body so that its identification becomes impossible within a very short time. Zangger (1922, 1924), for example, has called attention to the fact that, after fatal poisoning with morphine and cocaine together, traces of morphine can still be found in the cadaver after quite some time, while no traces of cocaine can be identified even when much larger doses of the latter drug have been taken.

It is a fact that the variety of intoxications resorted to either for pleasure or for criminal purposes have increased markedly in number and complexity during the last few decades. Therefore, when confronted with an illness or death of dubious origin it is advisable to consider the possibility of drug intoxication. Cocaine intoxication should be especially suspected when the victim is known to have been associated with certain groups in the big cities or to have dealings with the underworld. Cases of cocaine intoxication, however, can also be observed occasionally in small towns and in the country. I have personally been able to confirm the presence of a veritable epidemic of cocaine use in a very small community where a woman, for whom a cocaine rectal ointment had been prescribed, ill-advisedly recommended it to all her friends.

It is therefore highly desirable that physicians, and to some degree police and health officials, should familiarize themselves with the clinical manifestations of these intoxications, in order that they should at least be aware of the possibility of drug poisoning in the cases which they encounter.

As is the case with morphine addicts, cocaine addicts who resort to subcutaneous injections show clear injection marks or scars over the extensor surfaces of the body. A characteristic sign of cocaine sniffers is the redness of the nostrils where one also often finds remnants of white powder. In most cases, when the acute effects of cocaine on the nasal mucosa have subsided, the subjects have a running nose. Examination of handkerchiefs sometimes provides valuable clues, including small cocaine crystals or traces of diluents such as boric and salicylic acids, singly or in combination. Furthermore, it is advisable to search thoroughly the clothes and the surroundings of suspected users, because one can often find there small stocks of cocaine, empty cocaine bags, prescriptions or other drug containers. It should also be kept in mind that fruit drinks and various other fluids are often used to dissolve cocaine for oral use, and that the drug can also be added to ointments and sprays. A rapid and simple method of identification of remnants of white powder, or of relatively concentrated solutions, consists of placing a little of the material on the tongue. If it produces a localized sensation of numbness and of cold lasting for a few minutes, the substance is probably cocaine. Information provided by the subjects themselves should be suspect because they generally resort to every ruse at hand in order to prevent the physician from discovering their addiction. Some reach a veritable level of virtuosity in the art of lying. We have already described in a special chapter the chemical procedures for the identification of cocaine. These tests, however, are so complicated that they can usually be carried out only in specialized laboratories.

Chemical analysis of the body fluids performed as quickly as possible is of very great importance. But it should be remembered that the traces of cocaine or of its derivatives disappear rapidly. Therefore, if one wants to identify cocaine in the urine, for example, and this cannot be done immediately, it is advisable to add chloroform to the urine in a ratio of 1:3, to shake the mixture, and to close the container firmly. In some cases in which the urine gives a negative result, cocaine can be found in the gastric juice. In critical cases, immediate stomach lavage is indicated.

It goes without saying that the confirmation of the physical symptoms characteristic of cocaine addiction is of the greatest importance. Examination of the pupils should be performed first because this symptom disappears quickly in most cases. Perforation of the nasal septum is strongly suggestive of cocaine addiction, if industrial poisoning or syphilis can be excluded. Sympathomimetic symptoms and itching should also be taken fully into account.

In his most recent monograph on poisoning, Zangger (1924) emphasizes the fact that most cases of cocaine intoxication, either acute or chronic, go unrecognized. He says that cocaine addicts use all the means and ruses at their disposal to resist these investigations and to mislead the physician. My own experience is in complete agreement with Zangger's. In cases of fatal cocaine intoxication, the victim's friends try their best to cover up the cause of death, and the physicians are generally willing to make a posthumous diagnosis of a heart attack to the astonishment as well as the satisfaction of the people concerned. The diagnosis is often complicated by the fact that other drugs, including opiates, yohimbine, mescaline, hypnotics and alcohol, are also involved. According to Zangger (1922, 1924), cocaine is often used at present out of bravado or for purposes of seduction or crime. For this reason the objective demonstration of cocaine use may be the major if not the only decisive means of establishing proof of serious crimes such as rape of unconscious victims or attempted blackmail.

In subjects who are not habituated to the drug, cocaine intoxication often produces few characteristic symptoms. Very often the subjects themselves are unaware that they have been given a toxic substance, for example in a drink, and are therefore unable to produce any information. When they find out about it, they prefer to keep silent for fear of the police or to avoid problems with their friends. Such subjects often present with angina, cold extremities and small rapid pulse. If these symptoms are accompanied by fever, the misdiagnosis of an infectious disease is readily made. It is important to remember that in non-habituated individuals the typical cocaine euphoria is often absent, or even replaced by states of anxiety, or by delirious confused states which may end in collapse and respiratory arrest. Whenever young people without known cardiac disease present such pictures, particularly after being in company at parties or if they belong to suspect groups, it is advisable to consider the possibility of cocaine intoxication. The most disastrous medical error that can be made in cases of this type is the unthinking administration of morphine to calm the patient down, because this greatly increases the tendency to collapse and respiratory arrest, and may thus bring about death.

In euphoric states, the mild manic excitation resembles alcoholic intoxication to some degree. But an important point in the differential diagnosis is that, in cocaine intoxication, the blood vessels are constricted rather than dilated, the pulse is hard and small, and the psychomotor excitation is more marked, more theatrical in character, and reflects the emotional make-up of the individual. On the other hand, the characteristic dissociation of the personality, which allows cocaine users to be partially aware of their state, is generally not present in alcohol intoxication. Furthermore, despite his more daring activity, the behavior of the cocaine addict is more reasonable and there is usually no motor or speech ataxia as seen in the alcoholic. The differential diagnosis between cocaine and alcohol intoxication becomes much easier in cases which present with paresthesias and sensory illusions. But, on the other hand, this picture can then be mistaken for *delirium tremens*. Careful clinical examination, however, can easily distinguish between the two conditions: the tremors seen in alcoholics are much coarser, their hallucinations are of a totally different type, and general disorientation constitutes one of their dominant traits. In alcoholic delirium the sensory illusions vary rapidly, they are black, grey or colorless, and their content bears no relationship to the emotional make-up of the individual in the normal state. In cocaine delirium, on the contrary, almost the direct opposite is true: the hallucinations are characterized by their vivid colors and by their often artistic level of elaboration. Only the cinematographic hallucinations of cocaine addicts present an overall shadowy grey tone. In this case, the patients themselves say that they have the feeling of being in the theater, while the alcoholic experiences anxiety about his imaginary visions, which he mistakes for reality. Auditory hallucinations, which are frequent among cocaine addicts, are, on the contrary, very rare in alcoholics who have no schizophrenic predisposition.

Acute cocaine deliria, particularly in patients experiencing some degree of confusion which precludes communication with them, are easily mistaken for schizophrenic states of excitation.

Somatic hallucinations, some degree of dissociation of consciousness and a strong influence of emotional complexes on the content of the symptoms, are observed in both morbid pictures and sometimes make the differential diagnosis difficult. But, as opposed to what happens in catatonic states, good affective rapport can generally be detected in states of cocaine excitation if the patient is observed for a sufficiently long time, and if the observer behaves as though he were sharing the pathological sequence of the patient's thoughts. In this case it is soon realized that incomprehensible emotional outbursts and interruptions in intellectual and volitional activity are lacking, and that in cocaine intoxication everything, or nearly everything,can be explained by the reaction of the patient to his paresthesias, his illusions and the delusional interpretation of his surroundings. Confronted with a patient with an anxious tense facial expression, with the corners of the mouth turned downwards, whose haggard eyes are fixed on a faraway point in space and whose neck muscles are most often rigid, the inexperienced physician can easily make the diagnosis of catatonia, especially since the latter often also shows some degree of dilatation of the pupils and weak reaction to light. In my own experience, however, the distinction is not difficult because the markedly anxious facial expression of the cocaine addict, possibly even approaching *risus sardonicus*, is in no sense autistic but reflects, instead, a very vivid affective relationship to the environment and presents, as the patient is studied and observed, the most subtle modulations. The anxious and expectant expression of the patient in a state of cocaine intoxication has nothing in common with the rigidly strained and unapproachable expression of the schizophrenic. The most consistent sign in the latter is the rigid immobility of the part of the face surrounding the eyeballs which plays such an essential role in the character of the facial expression. The cocaine addict shows nothing of the sort. In my opinion, incidentally, this is the most important sign on which to base the distinction between the face of a catatonic and that of a parkinsonian.

The examination of the other mental symptoms of cocaine addiction and of the concomitant somatic phenomena eventually makes it possible to establish the differential diagnosis with certainty.

On cursory examination, cocaine psychosis can occasionally be mistaken for the phenomena of paranoid schizophrenia. But, in my experience, the characteristic nature of the paresthesias and of the hallucinations, particularly those of vision and touch, as well as the blend of a certain tendency to delirium, excellent affective rapport, and occasional partial lucidity, contribute considerably to facilitate the distinction. This is further reinforced by the fact that one generally has the opportunity of observing these cases for a sufficiently long time. Careful observation of cocaine addicts soon provides evidence of withdrawal symptoms and this immediately removes any doubt about the nature of the diagnosis.

When cocaine intoxication is accompanied by epileptic-like crises, the possibility of a false diagnosis of epilepsy arises. The epileptic-like attacks of cocaine addicts do not, of course, necessarily differ from true epilepsy. On the other hand, the speed of the mental and emotional reactions of cocaine addicts, their exaggerated suggestibility, the frequent signs of flight of ideas, as well as many other comparable and equally characteristic symptoms, are sufficiently different to put the observant physician on the right diagnostic track. Cocaine intoxication can occasionally be mistaken for uremia because it is accompanied in many cases by kidney complications, including albuminuria or anuria, headaches, muscle spasms and disturbances of consciousness. Zangger (1922, 1924) correctly points out that one should always think of cocaine poisoning when epileptiform states, or other conditions reminiscent of uremia, occur in young people under unclear conditions in a questionable drug-using milieu. Suspicion of it should be especially aroused when the patient's associates provide information about him grudgingly and incompletely. In these circumstances, the explanation will be provided by observation of the clinical condition, chemical examination of the stomach content and urine, inspection of the nose and the skin (especially the scratch marks which are so common in cocaine users), and the whole milieu.

If long-term cocaine intoxication leads to significant organic damage of the brain, the clinical picture may resemble that of a progressive syphilitic general paresis. Organic dementia, with vague incoherent delusions of grandeur, often of a rather silly type, is found in both conditions. In cocaine paresis, however, visual or tactile hallucinations are generally more prominent; a certain ataxia of speech can also occur in this condition, but the characteristic jumbling of syllables is absent. Hypalgesia and partial loss of pupillary light reflex are of no differential diagnostic value, and the pupils can also be variably dilated and somewhat distorted in the most severe cases of cocaine poisoning. If by chance the cocaine user is also syphilitic, the differentiation becomes even more difficult. However, examination of the cerebrospinal fluid can generally provide valuable clues. Above all, however, the anamnesis and the clinical course are best able to clear up the question rapidly, because removal of the alkaloid results promptly in the appearance of withdrawal phenomena, followed by gradual general recovery which goes parallel with detoxification. This course can thereby be differentiated from that of a spontaneous remission in luetic paresis.

To my knowledge, the differentiation of these two diseases has never yet presented major difficulties if careful clinical observations are made. Often, however, it is more complicated to distinguish between cocaine intoxication and other types of intoxication of the nervous system, if the toxic material itself cannot be obtained for study.

Chronic intoxication with opium or morphine gives rise to a type of euphoria similar to that produced by cocaine, but never to the tendency to manic states, the typical hallucinoses and the systematization of growing delusions seen in cocaine addicts. In addition, rapid onset of severe physical symptoms and often of anxious delirium is prominent in opiate withdrawal reactions, but not at all in cocaine withdrawal. The latter is characterized by only rather mildly unpleasant subjective symptoms of quite short duration. The same points of differentiation also apply with respect to abuse of codeine and heroin, which at the present time is widespread mainly in America, and also to Eucodal[18] addiction, which is now encountered more frequently in our own country. In the last few years, a proprietary mixture known as Chlorodine has been particularly widely used in England and its colonies. It produces quite vivid intoxication states which stand some chance of being confused with cocaine delirium. This is based on the fact that this preparation contains, in addition to morphine and Indian hemp, both chloroform and ether.

Mescaline, an alkaloid with actions which are in many respects similar to those of cocaine, deserves more detailed consideration. This drug has been the object of considerable interest in recent years, both in experimental psychology and as a dangerous drug of abuse. This toxic substance is formed in a plant of the *Anhalonium* family, which grows mainly in Mexico. Credit must be given to the Berlin pharmacologist Lewin for having studied this plant since 1886. It has been named, after him, *Anhalonium Lewini*. He succeeded in obtaining, from ripe seeds, the first samples of this plant to grow in Europe. It contains four alkaloids, including mescaline which produces sensory illusions. The inhabitants of the north of

[18] Ed. note: A proprietary mixture of dihydro-oxycodeinone plus chloral hydrate, used as a morphine substitute.

Mexico call this variety of cactus peyote and ingest it in characteristic rituals. According to Lewin, mescaline is not the only alkaloid in this plant capable of producing mental effects. Rather, the effects of the plant are a composite of the effects of all these alkaloids. These effects are very complex and vary markedly from individual to individual. The subject under the action of mescaline has a sensation of being isolated from the world, and this is soon followed by the appearance of very pleasant visual hallucinations. The sensory illusions turn ordinary things into marvellous objects which acquire a veritable symphony of colorations. Auditory, gustatory and olfactory hallucinations are rarer. The subjects may experience a sensation of weightlessness, capable of reaching the level of depersonalization. In the midst of all these symptoms, the subjects remain lucid and capable of concentrating their thoughts. Beringer (1923), who has experimented with mescaline on himself, speaks of the unique feeling of space that it induces and of the ongoing state of wonderment that he has experienced. He lost all feelings of physical being and became convinced that the answers to all the problems of the future of the world had been revealed to him. He saw himself surrounded by imaginary pictures, marvellous ever-changing architectural patterns, and cosmic systems following each other according to a certain rhythm. Later this was followed by the appearance of some unpleasant symptoms including trismus, grinding of teeth, profuse sweating and painful muscular sensations. At the same time he could again hear glorious music.

I have described in some detail the effects of peyote and mescaline, its active principle, because they bear a remarkable resemblance to those which have been reported by subjects in a state of cocaine intoxication. There is, however, a marked difference between the effects of these two alkaloids. Outwardly directed mental and motor excitation is absent in mescaline intoxication, and the sensory illusions are more systematized, richer in imaginary details and associated with a higher esthetic pleasure than the agitated, jerky, irregular cocaine hallucinations. Studies on the action of mescaline are, however, just beginning and we lack information with respect to chronic peyote intoxications in Mexico. I know, however, that at the present time, in some places of amusement, attempts are being made to spread the use of mescaline for purposes of economic gain. It is therefore quite possible that some people have experienced mescaline intoxication without knowing what drug they have actually taken. In such circles it would be quite easy for mescaline to be mistaken for cocaine. If that were the case, the above information taken from Lewin's writings could be useful to identify the drug responsible for the intoxication. Our knowledge of mescaline shows precisely the ease with which unscrupulous profit-seeking succeeds in exchanging toxic substances whose use is already broadly spread, for other drugs which are even more dangerous. It is gratifying, therefore, that the creation of the international convention for the fight against narcotics makes it possible to include toxic substances such as mescaline, which are as dangerous as cocaine or morphine, under the legal restrictions already in force.

The smoking of Indian hemp *(Cannabis indica)* is widespread at present in Asia and Africa, and is also found occasionally in our ports and large cities. Cannabis smokers describe pleasant dreams, accompanied by strong sexual excitation and by hallucinations of vision, hearing and general sensation. Auditory acuity in particular becomes extraordinarily exaggerated, to the point that the slightest sound acquires the strength of a cannon shot. As opposed to what happens in the case of opium smokers, cannabis smokers become very animated, laugh without cause, and those who have not become sufficiently habituated present states of odd motor excitation comparable to those seen in cocaine delirium. Cannabis abuse often produces serious psychoses which can be graded according to their severity as follows: a) delirious states without ataxia, but accompanied by numerous optic hallucinations; they subside in a few days; b) sub-chronic states with delusions of persecution, frightening hallucinations and manic excitation; they may persist for several months;(c) states of organic dementia with manic excitation appearing after each new dose of the drug. This intoxication produces physical and mental impairment, particularly in the offspring of the users. These toxic effects are not difficult to distinguish from those seen in cocaine addiction because in cannabis abuse the disturbances of the personality are much more marked, while the hallucinations show nothing specific, and there is an absence of systematized delusional ideas. The manner of intake of the drug is a particularly important clue in establishing the differential diagnosis because cocaine is only rarely smoked.

The use of fly agaric and its alkaloid, muscarine, which is widespread in northern Asia, quickly produces a very marked state of stupor accompanied by sensory illusions. This intoxication is extremely rare in this part of the world and it is unlikely to be confused with cocaine intoxication because of the much more serious disturbances of consciousness that it produces.

The intoxications produced by the nightshade plants, particularly atropine contained in belladonna, and scopolamine, are much more important. Morgenstern (1923) has recently reported two cases of delirium due to belladonna which he observed in our clinic and has, in this connection, compiled and reviewed all the literature on this subject. This substance produces very marked physical signs of intoxication of which vertigo, dryness of the throat, constriction of the pupils[19] and ataxia are particularly prominent. For this reason confusion with the disturbances produced by cocaine is very difficult. Despite the close chemical resemblance between the two substances, their pharmacological actions are in many respects markedly different. The psychological effects of atropine consist of marked disturbances of memory for recent events, generally reaching the level of complete amnesia, anxiety-provoking hallucinations, and characteristic deliria which are accompanied by pronounced alterations of the personality. These symptoms differ markedly from those produced by cocaine. In scopolamine intoxications, the initial state of excitation is outweighed by the drug's hypnotic effects.

Ether intoxication, a practice which has become rather common in many parts of Europe, is characterized by marked ataxia, inebriation, hallucinations of a dreamy nature and not the slightest need for motor activity. Therefore the differentiation from cocaine intoxication does not present any difficulties. This is further facilitated by the characteristic odor on the breath of ether users.

It is known that the hypnotics (barbital, dial, chloral) can also provoke delirious states. But in this case the hallucinations play a totally secondary role. Motor activity is inhibited and the subjects present clear-cut ataxic phenomena. On the other hand, in these, as well as in cocaine intoxication, there are disturbances of bladder function. The distinction between intoxications due to hypnotics and to cocaine can be made easily because of the general tendency to somnolent twilight states, which even occur between the more or less intense delirious episodes in the case of the former drugs. Chloroform intoxication is characterized by severe disturbances of consciousness, impulsive states of excitation and absence of delirium.

Intoxication by carbon monoxide can also manifest itself by transitory excitation, accompanied by aggressivity and irritability. The hallucinations, however, are rudimentary in nature, provoke anxiety and are infinitely less rich and mobile than the hallucinations of cocaine intoxication. During more prolonged observation of the course of the intoxication, comatose manifestations can be seen which could be mistaken mainly for the acute effects of nearly fatal

[19] Ed. note: *Sic*; atropine actually dilates the pupil.

doses of cocaine. In such cases, it is not always possible to make the differential diagnosis on the basis of the symptoms exclusively.

Among industrial intoxications only those produced by benzene and by carbon disulfide present symptoms similar to those of cocaine. Zangger (1922, 1924) points out that these cases are rarely acute. Generally the intoxication appears only after many days of inhalation of the toxic substance, and this greatly facilitates the diagnosis. These intoxications produce an irresistible need to talk, marked irritability, as well as a type of torpor resembling inebriety, which is clearly different from the well-preserved personality seen in cocaine intoxication.

In practice, the most common differential diagnosis required is that between cocaine and alcohol intoxication. This is all the more so since alcoholism and cocaine addiction are often associated in a large number of individuals. My own experience leads me to the general impression that cocaine inhibits or neutralizes the effects of alcohol on the brain. We already know that caffeine, the effects of which although weaker, are comparable to those of cocaine in a number of respects, counteracts to a considerable degree the symptoms of alcohol intoxication. If, however, cocaine is taken in doses which impair the sympathetic nervous system, or mental activity, its combination with alcohol can easily be fatal. This picture is distinguished from that of pure alcohol intoxication by the fact that the latter causes much more profound disturbances of the personality, and motor and speech ataxia. On the other hand, the tendency to hallucinations, particularly those of touch with their concomitant itching, and to visual hallucinations, is absent in uncomplicated alcoholism. In general, *delirium tremens* can be clearly distinguished from acute cocaine delirium by the strong coarse tremors, the different nature of the hallucinations (see above), the absence of activity and of the connection between the behavior and the pupillary symptoms, which exists in cocaine users. In alcoholic psychosis, the hallucinations are almost exclusively auditory, whereas in the paranoid psychosis of cocaine addicts, tactile and visual hallucinations are almost always present. Furthermore, the facial expression and other physical symptoms of alcoholics differ to such a degree from those of cocaine addicts that the distinction rarely presents any difficulty, except when the two intoxications coexist in the same individual. In the delirious alcoholic the tactile hallucinations are simple and limited to the surface of the body. The patient feels water drops, feathers or single animals on his body. In the cocaine addict, these phenomena are much more complex. The sensations are experienced sometimes within and sometimes under the skin, and the patient makes systematized connections among his hallucinations. He follows with his eyes the movements, transformation and even procreation of the imaginary animals. He tries to scratch or cut them out of the skin, or other such procedures.

4. Prognosis

a) Acute Cocaine Intoxication

The prognosis in cases of acute cocaine intoxication does not rest on the dose taken, as much as it does on the individual predisposition at the time, on the level of tolerance to the drug, and on its distribution throughout the body. The most dangerous effects are not the peripheral ones, but those in the central nervous system. Thus when cocaine is injected into a limb either just before or after a tourniquet is applied the prognosis is good because cocaine undergoes rapid destruction in the body and loses its toxic properties before it has a chance to act in the central nervous system. But when absorption takes place through the nasal or other mucosae, or when the drug is swallowed, the central effects appear rapidly, usually within three to five minutes. Following an intravenous injection administered, for example, by accident during dental surgery, one can witness within seconds the most severe state of intoxication with paralysis of the respiratory center and cardiac arrest, sometimes preceded by convulsions. The longer the respiration is maintained in these cases, the greater the chances that cocaine will be destroyed in the body and thus lose its toxicity. But even then, it is best to be very cautious about the prognosis. Zangger (1922, 1924) has reported a case in which artificial respiration was successfully maintained for six hours, with the result that the patient died suddenly at the end of that time.

Such acute intoxications can be seen following the therapeutic administration of cocaine. In particularly sensitive individuals, even doses below the maximum therapeutic dose of 30 mg are sometimes sufficient to provoke severe accidents. Many physicians, particularly otorhinolaryngologists, have found themselves in the terrible situation of seeing a robust individual apparently dying a few minutes after an application of cocaine for a trivial surgical intervention. Fatalities of this type were unfortunately quite frequent in earlier days. Even leaving aside the danger of dependence, the possibility of accidents of this type is sufficient to justify total elimination of cocaine from the medical and therapeutic arsenal and its replacement by an equally effective derivative which is free of this danger, such as psicaine.

Among cocaine addicts, acute intoxications are often seen

when a very large dose is taken with suicidal intent or by error. The latter generally occurs when individuals who have been using highly adulterated cocaine find themselves suddenly in possession of pure cocaine, without being aware that they are now using a much stronger drug. This type of acute intoxication has a worse prognosis than that following therapeutic application because the physician is not on the spot to assist the patient immediately, and also because the patient's friends often avoid calling a physician or do so too late, for fear of giving themselves away. In such cases, a state of motor and mental excitation manifests itself immediately. The initial euphoria turns into anxiety as the respiratory disturbances become more serious and eventually there is coma. This may last several hours or even several days, and then disappear, being followed by complete recovery. Alternatively, it may end up in arrest of the respiratory center, often accompanied by convulsions leading to death. In practice, such bizarre cases of death are seldom diagnosed correctly as poisoning because of insufficient probing of the people surrounding the patient. The autopsy itself, if it is limited to macroscopic examinations and omits chemical analyses, only rarely provides positive results. I have been able to confirm that three of my former patients died in the circumstances just described, while their death certificates merely gave a diagnosis of "cardiac arrest." Autopsies were performed in two of them but the poisoning was not discovered.

b) Chronic Cocaine Intoxication

It is necessary to consider separately those individuals who take small doses of cocaine periodically, or during periods of physical or mental strain. They abstain from the drug in the intervals which may sometimes be very long, and thus avoid the need to increase the doses and the corresponding consequences. Such users are referred to as "cocaine devotees." As is the case with morphine, there are, among cocaine users, exceptional individuals who can take the drug for years without experiencing the slightest difficulties. But such individuals are very rare, amounting, according to my experience, to less than 10% of the total number of those who try using cocaine for non-medical purposes. Generally, sooner or later, sometimes after some years, the resistance dwindles and a state of chronic intoxication occurs.

In such cases the prognosis is somber, particularly if detoxification is not attempted successfully during the first year. Generally this cure must be compulsory even though there are some strong individuals capable, through their own willpower, of pulling themselves back from the path to deterioration. I know two patients who, despite a daily intake of 2 to 3 g of cocaine, were able on the advice of their physicians to make this effort and achieve detoxification. Aschaffenburg (1923, 1925) has reported a similar case. But these are only the exceptions.

In the absence of medical intervention, the continued increase of the daily dosage often leads to a parallel increase in the severity of intoxication, loss of the ability to work and deterioration of the personality. This is followed by increasingly serious symptoms of chronic cocainism, which may lead eventually to anxious deliria of rather long duration, cocaine psychosis or cocaine dementia. It is certain that all these symptoms are much less frequent among sniffers than among the older subjects who used to take cocaine by subcutaneous injection. The syringe seems to make it much more difficult to break the vicious circle. When the physical condition of the sniffer becomes seriously compromised, so that he begins to show signs of impairment or of chronic psychosis, he easily loses social contact with his comrades who, for fear of being themselves found out, avoid him as much as possible and stop providing him with cocaine. Because the abstinence symptoms of cocaine addiction are comparatively mild, the cocaine addict thus banished from society and deprived of his drug, remains in his room for a couple of days until he has recovered to some degree. Then, sobered by his experience, he avoids his former company and enters a period of remission. In most cases this does not last very long, but is sufficient to prevent the onset of Korsakoff's syndrome or of pseudo-paretic symptoms. Some sniffers succeed in freeing themselves from their dependence when they are placed in a totally different environment and are subjected to strong beneficial influences which can often be as effective as hospitalization. But the majority, unless hospitalized, fall victim to intercurrent illnesses such as tuberculosis or other infectious diseases. A considerable proportion end in suicide. Most often this is committed by means of large amounts of mixtures of drugs, but men sometimes resort to firearms.

Despite successful detoxification, whether it is enforced or voluntary, the danger of relapse is always very great. Almost all authors are in agreement that the prognosis is perhaps even worse than in morphine addiction. The longer the habit the worse the prognosis. The picture is more optimistic in the case of sniffers whose habit has not lasted more than a year, provided, of course, that the pre-morbid personality of the patient does not present compromising features. I have, however, seen patients who have remained well for several years despite having suffered previously from cocaine addiction that had lasted for four or five years. Naturally the prognosis also depends to a considerable extent on external circumstances, on the possibility of completely removing the addict from his previous cocaine-related environment, and on the psychotherapeutic skills of the physician.

In cocaine addicts presenting with severe psychotic symptoms, the prognosis will depend on the chances of administering rational and appropriate treatment. The only approach capable of preventing the patients from committing potentially fatal acts during their delirious states, of assuring the total and complete suppression of cocaine and other drugs, and of providing immediate medical attention for the emergencies which may arise, is forced commitment to a psychiatric institution which can provide constant supervision. If this is not done, such seriously ill patients, precisely during psychotic reactions, often increase their doses of cocaine to the point of causing a fatal acute intoxication; in such cases the state of mental confusion may be prolonged until it ends catastrophically. But when, on the contrary, these patients are supervised and the drug is withdrawn in time, they usually recover rapidly. Even the symptoms due to chronic use of cocaine effectively disappear in the space of a few weeks or months. Even then, however, the subjects' moral equilibrium and will power remain impaired, often for years, so that the danger of relapse persists. This is particularly so if there are any serious external or internal problems still to be overcome, or if the apparently recovered patient is confronted by enticements coming from the former drug-related surroundings. Close examination of morphine addicts who have undergone difficult detoxification cures has shown that, even in favorable cases, their psychic and somatic reactions show marked instability even a year later. In this connection, it is worth noting that morphine addicts continue to show an abnormal erythrocyte sedimentation rate for many months after completion of withdrawal. Even though the withdrawal symptoms of cocaine addicts are clearly less marked and disappear faster, my personal experience indicates that the more subtle mental reactions take some time to become normal, particularly in cases in which the addiction had lasted more than six months and the symptoms were comparatively severe.

5. Anatomical Alterations

We have very little information based on autopsies of cocaine addicts. This is due to the fact that, in most cases of death due to acute intoxication, the existence of the intoxication is unrecognized. Therefore either the autopsy is considered unnecessary or it is not carried out in such a way as to uncover the specific alterations caused by cocaine intoxication. Chronic cocaine users most often die of suicide or of intercurrent diseases.

Joël and Fränkel (1924) cite a case reported by Fagerlund in Finland, of marked *rigor mortis* which appeared quickly in an individual who died after a large dose of cocaine, and which persisted for two days despite the hot weather at the time. In experimental cocaine intoxication in dogs, however, *rigor mortis* tends to be delayed. These observations are not sufficient to permit generalizations because it is known that cases in which *rigor mortis* persists for two days are not rare.

What autopsy does reveal most often, following acute intoxication, is marked hyperemia of the internal organs, especially of the liver, spleen and lungs. Maurel (1892) claims that cocaine produces swelling and deformation of the leucocytes. As a result of the vasoconstriction due to sympathetic stimulation, the capillary circulation is slowed down, contributing to the formation of very small thrombi, which may break loose and cause embolism, particularly in the lungs. In fact, infarcts of the lungs, mostly of very small dimensions, have often been found in autopsies performed in Paris in subjects who had died of cocaine intoxication.

According to Erlich, the phenomena characteristic of cocaine intoxication include fatty degeneration of the hepatic parenchyma, of the walls of the biliary ducts and of the hepatic blood vessels, as well as formation of vacuoles in the hepatic cells. Since similar phenomena also occur in other types of intoxication, it seems quite questionable whether they can be considered pathognomonic of cocaine intoxication. There is also supposed to be hyperemia of the brain and the meninges. Guinard claims to have observed chronic thickening of the *pia mater*, but this phenomenon has also been found at autopsy of individuals who have died of severe alcoholism.

Piouffle's monograph (1919) does not deal at all with autopsy findings.

In view of the sparseness of these data, the partial report of an autopsy performed by Eugenio Bravetta (1922) should be considered particularly important. It concerned a chronic cocaine user who died in 1922 following the intake of an overdose of cocaine. Enticed by a prostitute, the subject, aged 28 years, had sniffed cocaine regularly during the year preceding his death. According to information provided by his wife, he had never been intoxicated with alcohol or any other drug. In a diary found on his person at the time of his death, the subject had described in great detail the phases of euphoria, anxiety and hallucinations which he had experienced and they are totally consistent with pure cocaine addiction. The autopsy revealed the following:

Rigor of the lower jaw and lower limbs. Large ulceration of the mucosae of the right side of the nasal septum. Hyperemia and marked edema of the brain. Inflated, cyanosed and hyperemic lungs. The right lung weighed 765 g and the left 640 g. The cut surface, particularly of the lower lobe, was covered with a bloody foam. There were, in addition, pulmonary infarcts and sub-pleural ecchymoses. The heart was flaccid, engorged with blood, and the myocardium was pale. The spleen was hypertrophied, soft and hyperemic, and the liver was slightly enlarged and hard. The renal parenchyma and the adrenal glands were also hyperemic, and the latter were enlarged.

Macroscopic examination: edema and stasis in the brain, liver, spleen, kidneys and adrenal glands. Edema and infarcts in the lungs, and sub-pleural ecchymoses.

Unfortunately, the microscopic examination was performed only in the brain, one section of which was fixed in 95% alcohol and the other in formaldehyde.

The ganglion cells showed diffuse chromolysis and vacuoles. The nuclei were diminished in size and misshapen. Other cells were atrophic and sclerosed. A Bielchowsky's stain showed the fibrillary reticulum missing in a large number of cells. The neurofibrils were shrunken in the periphery. Sometimes the cells gave the appearance of a granular mass, and at other times only a pale and colorless remnant could be seen. But the Daddi-Herxheimer fat stain permitted the demonstration of the most characteristic alteration, i.e., the presence of marked and widespread fatty infiltration in nearly all the nerve cells. The fatty droplets were gathered in large numbers around the nucleus, or distributed in other places or in the protoplasmatic processes. The glial cells showed only some shrinkage, but no proliferation. Fatty degeneration was present here also. The nerve fibers showed dilatations, often arranged in rosettes. The *pia mater* appeared edematous and slightly hyperemic. Here and there there were clusters of lymphocytes. Some fibroblasts showed fatty degeneration. The blood vessels of the brain were dilated and full of blood, and the same could be observed in the perivascular lymphatic spaces which also showed mast cells. The blood vessel walls were also affected by fatty degeneration. There were numerous thrombi in the smallest vessels. Most of the cells of the adventicia showed a large vacuole with fatty degeneration. The degeneration of the blood vessels was as marked in the white as in the grey matter.

Summary of the results of the microscopic examination of the brain: edema of the *pia mater* and of the brain substance; moderate lymphocytic infiltration of the *pia* and blood vessels, more intense in some places, occasionally accompanied by mast cells; widespread fatty infiltration and degeneration of the ganglion and glial cells; degeneration of the nerve fibers; marked fatty degeneration of the blood vessel walls; red thrombi in the smallest blood vessels.

Bravetta illustrates these observations with the figures which are reproduced with his permission.

Pathological investigations performed in animals intoxicated with cocaine have provided the following results:

According to Nissl, the ganglion cells of rabbits which had received large doses of cocaine for a few days showed slight coloration of their normally colorless cytoplasm, while the borders of the nuclei appeared blurred. There was infiltration of lymphocytes in the *pia mater* and in the blood vessels. In 1899, Daddi performed two series of experiments. In the first, dogs which had been fasted received a lethal dose of cocaine. In the second series, a slow and gradual intoxication was produced in well-fed dogs. Daddi found that in the well-fed dogs the spinal ganglion cells showed clear-cut chromatolysis, particularly in the periphery. In the fasted animals, the cellular alterations were more widespread; even the achromatic substance appeared altered and full of vacuoles both in the center and on the edges. The ganglion cells [*sic*]of the medulla presented very clear fragmentation of the chromatic substance and chromatolysis in the periphery. These phenomena were all more marked in the fasted animals. In the cerebellum, many Purkinje cells were enlarged and bloated and some of them presented very marked chromatolysis. The same changes occur in the cerebrum. In many cells, the achromatic substance was rarified and spotted with vacuoles. The most marked chromatolysis was found in the area of Ammon's horn. Some cells also presented alterations of the nuclei. On the other hand, nothing of note was found in the glial cells. Daddi concluded that these results were not characteristic of cocaine intoxication because they are also observed in morphine, arsenic and lead poisonings, as well as in some infectious diseases. Camia examined the nervous system in dogs that had been poisoned with different narcotics. He confirmed Daddi's observations but found nothing that could be considered as pathognomonic of cocaine intoxication.

In 1922 and 1923, Eugenio Bravetta and Giuseppe Invernizzi published the results of investigations performed in a much larger number of animals subjected to cocaine intoxication. Three rabbits and a dog, under the influence of chronic cocaine intoxication, presented with the characteristic phenomena of excitation, with tonic-clonic convulsions, and alterations of the pupils and pulse. One of the rabbits had been given cocaine injections for 31 days, another for eight days, and the dog for 77 days. The three animals were then killed by administration of much larger cocaine doses than normal. The third rabbit had been given cocaine orally for 43 days but since the effects of the drug under these conditions were negligible it was given increasing doses of cocaine by injection for 108 days, until death occurred. During the experiment it first appeared that the toxic reactions were increasingly smaller, that is to say, the animals were gradually becoming tolerant to the drug. But with more prolonged and severe intoxication, the sensitivity of the animal increased so that the effects of a given dose became more marked and long-lasting as the drug effect accumulated.

The authors summarized their microscopic observations in these four experimental animals as follows: fatty infiltration of the adventicial cells of the blood vessels; numerous small hemorrhages in the brain, the liver and the kidneys; erythrocytes inside Bowman's capsule. The authors considered that these hemorrhages were due to alterations of the endothelium. There was, in addition, fatty infiltration of the liver and kidney parenchyma and of the epithelial cells of the biliary ducts. These alterations were not present in a rabbit that received cocaine for only a short time. The alteration of the cerebral cells of this rabbit, however, were very marked, suggesting that cocaine affects the nerve cells first. In all these animals, the myocardial cells were broken into segments. This was probably due to the toxic agonal disturbance. But what was characteristic was that the intensity of fatty infiltration of the myocardial cells was proportional to the length of time the animals had been exposed to the drug. The ectodermal nerve elements presented remarkable alterations, the most important of which were chromatolysis of both the center and periphery of the cells, and atrophic sclerosis. There was also marked fatty infiltration of the ganglion cells, particularly in the area of Ammon's horn. Some nerve fibers showed atrophic protoplasmatic processes, agglutination of the endofibrillar reticulum, and signs of general degeneration. Numerous fat droplets were also visible around the nuclei of the glial cells.

The authors believe that the tendency to formation of petechial hemorrhages and thrombi of various sizes can be considered characteristic of cocaine intoxication. The other phenomena, particularly those occurring in the cells, are not pathognomonic because they can be found at autopsy in animals fatally poisoned with other drugs such as morphine. Spielmeyer has also recently called attention to the fact that the fatty degeneration of the ganglion cells, which the Italian authors have emphasized so much, is also found in a large number of drug intoxications, infectious diseases and cachectic states in mentally healthy individuals. It can develop very quickly and Spielmeyer once found it in quite severe form in a case of acute morphine intoxication only 12 hours after the absorption of the drug. The same applies to the fatty degeneration of the glial cells.

Even if the results obtained by Bravetta and Invernizzi (1922, 1923) cannot be considered characteristic of cocaine intoxication, they offer a valuable basis for further studies on the pathological alterations produced by intoxication due to alkaloids. Such studies, furthermore, could take the form of animal experiments and also of very thorough detailed autopsies of cocaine users because, in the large cities, deaths due to cocaine poisoning are much more frequent than pathologists generally realize. Through the courtesy of Bravetta and Invernizzi, their figures illustrating the lesions found in their experimental animals are reproduced here as Figures 16-21.

We can say, in summary, that individuals who have died following cocaine intoxication are rather certain to show edema and hyperemia of the internal organs and of the brain, and usually small but occasionally larger thromboses and hemorrhages, especially in the lungs and in the vessels of the brain. These hemorrhages and thromboses appear to be rather characteristic of cocaine addiction and are the physiological consequences of vascular constriction and of alterations of the leucocytes. The fatty infiltration of the adventicial vessels, as well as the other degenerative lesions of the ganglion and glial cells, nerve fibers, hepatic and kidney cells, can be found in cocaine intoxication with the same frequency as in other intoxications and, to some degree, in degenerative lesions due to infections and other debilitating conditions. Considering that the body is capable of recovering quickly from cocaine poisoning, it would be of great interest to study systematically the process of rapid recovery of severely damaged ganglion cells in parallel series of experimental animals.

6. Treatment

a) Acute Cocaine Intoxication[20]

From a therapeutic point of view, there is practically no difference between accidental acute intoxications, whether of medical or other origin, and those which occur in cocaine addicts follow-

[20] Ed. note: The drugs recommended by the author are no longer used for this purpose.

ing the intake of a very large dose. It goes without saying that, in the latter case, the doses involved are far greater and very variable depending on the severity of the addiction. One point that must always be emphasized is that in both types of case, the total dose taken does not give any indication of the severity of the condition. It is well known that there is large individual variation in the sensitivity to the drug, even with respect to lethal doses.

First, it is important to obtain detailed information concerning the route of administration, in order to eliminate as much of the drug as possible before it has an opportunity to be absorbed and, more importantly, before it can act centrally. Unfortunately, we should not pin too high hope on the success of this type of intervention, because the drug is generally absorbed and distributed to the tissues within minutes of its application to a mucosal surface or its parenteral injection. In any case, if the physician is called in time, he is well advised to irrigate the nasal mucosa or other location (tongue, rectum, throat, surgical site) to which the drug was applied, or to carry out gastric lavage. Considering the high solubility of cocaine, pure water is the preferred lavage fluid. Animal charcoal, which is a powerful adsorbant, may be added in the proportion of one tablespoon per 0.5 liter, according to the suggestion of Joël and Fränkel (1924). When cocaine has been injected by error into an extremity, e.g., when it is mistaken for another drug, the most efficient means to prevent it from reaching the central nervous system is to apply a tourniquet. This arrests the circulation and allows for rapid local detoxification of the drug.

When central nervous system symptoms are already evident, attention should be paid first of all to the dangers of respiratory arrest, circulatory disturbances and epileptiform convulsions. Therefore, the patient should be placed in such a position that he cannot hurt himself by a sudden fall and all dangerous objects around him should be removed to prevent him from using them against himself or others during the confusional states that may arise. In our experience, some physicians have an almost automatic tendency to administer a morphine injection every time that they have to deal with a state of excitation. Nothing could be more dangerous when the state of excitation is due to cocaine. The physician who considers the administration of morphine in such cases becomes guilty of a serious professional mistake because morphine can only contribute further to respiratory arrest. The same can be said of all the other opiates, which, for this reason, are absolutely contraindicated. The same considerations apply to the administration of amyl nitrite, ether and chloroform, all of which were very popular in earlier days. Some authors recommend chloral hydrate in rather large doses. It is true that this drug exerts a favorable effect by facilitating the circulation and diminishing the state of excitation of the central nervous system. But because it can only be administered orally or by rectum, its action is too slow in cases where prompt action is of the essence. Of course, chloral hydrate can always be tried when nothing better is available. The best treatment, however, is the intravenous administration of a hypnotic, which contributes to lowering the blood pressure somewhat. According to the experiments of Hofvendahl (1920, 1921) mentioned above, barbital and similar compounds are the most suitable for this purpose, as well as *Somnifen*, an injectable member of the same group produced by Hoffmann-LaRoche. Physicians who often have occasion to administer cocaine for professional purposes or who practise in environments where cocaine poisonings are frequent, such as in emergency services or in posts attached to the police, are well advised to always have at their disposal injectable barbiturates. It is important, however, to remember that intravenous injection of *Somnifen* carries its risks because it may suddenly and markedly lower the blood pressure. Therefore, this procedure should be avoided, even in the presence of the usual indications when the circulation is already impaired, as is generally the case in the paralytic stage following massive cocaine injections. In any case, *Somnifen* should never be administered in doses larger than one ampoule (2 ml) in the space of two to three hours.

If, during the course of intoxication, the pulse is tense, and there is marked pallor followed by cyanosis and sweating, increased muscular excitability and a tendency to contractures and spasms, i.e., when there is evidence of particularly strong sympathetic overstimulation, administration of calcium may be tried because it generally alleviates these symptoms very quickly. Here again, intravenous administration of *Afenil* is required because orally administered calcium is too slow in acting. The injection should be administered very slowly, over 10 minutes or so, to avoid collapse. This is easy when the patient is unconscious, but often impossible in patients in a state of excitation.

If this method of treatment in turn fails, an alternative approach is to produce central inhibition of the sympathetic system. This is most easily and quickly obtained with ergotamine. A preparation of this type, manufactured by Sandoz, has been available for some time under the name of *Gynergen*. It can be injected intravenously in amounts ranging from half to one ampoule. I have used this medication in other states of sympathetic hypertonia with very good results, and other authors have made similar observations in severe cases of hyperthyroidism. Even though I have not yet had the opportunity of using *Gynergen* in cases of acute cocaine poisoning, I still recommend trying it, with the proviso that it would obviously be contraindicated when symptoms of circulatory collapse are already evident. When the respiration is severely slowed down, or is of the Cheyne-Stokes type, artificial respiration, applied sometimes for several hours, should be resorted to. External cardiac massage should also be applied if the circulation fails. Strong doses (e.g., 10 g of a 10% solution) of camphor oil can also be tried. Coramine (pyridine-β-carboxylicacid diethylamide), manufactured by Ciba at Basel, has become available recently. This preparation has the combined effects of camphor and of a nicotine residue, thus acting as a respiratory stimulant. In cases of *delirium tremens* with circulatory disturbances and impaired respiration, especially when there is danger of pulmonary congestion, *Coramine* has given me results which are clearly superior to those of camphor alone. For this reason, I would recommend that it be tried in cocaine poisoning, in doses of 1 to 3 ampoules (1-3 ml). Its advantage is that it can be administered intravenously in cases of immediate danger, as well as intramuscularly or subcutaneously. The observations by K. Guth (1925) at the Heidelberg Surgical Clinic should also be remembered in this connection. He obtained better results with *Coramine* than with pure camphor in cases of narcotic overdose, circulatory and respiratory disturbances, excessively long narcosis, or other states of collapse. When there is danger of respiratory paralysis, Zangger (1922, 1924) recommends trying an injection of atropine (1 mg), possibly mixed with adrenaline in the same dose. He does not make great promises for the effectiveness of this treatment, however, because the disturbances in question are usually long-lasting, while these drugs have a short duration of action and cannot be repeated frequently. Injectable *Bellafollin Sandoz* (in ampoules) which is less dangerous and of more reliable action, may also be tried.

I have already said that the prognosis of acute cocaine poisoning is always doubtful because collapse or states of severe excitation may recur suddenly, even after hours of comparative improvement. It is therefore advisable, even when everything appears to be progressing favorably, to keep the patient under observation for two or three days, preferably in a hospital. When the poisoning occurs in a cocaine addict, rather than accidentally in a patient receiving the drug for therapeutic purposes, by far the best approach is to send the patient at once to a psychiatric institution during the most serious stage of the intoxication. During this stage, the patient's friends are least likely to oppose having the patient admitted, and only if this is done can the absolutely necessary detoxification procedure be carried out. This is why, in some cases, an acute intoxication with favorable outcome provides the cocaine addict, as *delirium tremens* does for many alcoholics, with a valuable opportunity. He may, on this account, come under the care of a psychiatrist who may be able to rid him of his addiction.

b) Cocaine Addiction

We include under this heading individuals who, from time to time, or more or less regularly, are unable to resist the craving to use cocaine for its euphoriant effects, but who do not develop the phenomena of chronic cocainism. This is observed probably more often with cocaine than with morphine.

It is, moreover, important to remember that the ability of the human body to develop tolerance to cocaine, though generally present, differs from that concerning the opiates, and is certainly less marked. With respect to alcohol, we know, for example, that its action during the course of chronic intoxication does not diminish, but simply has less obvious external manifestations. In fact, drinkers in the final stages of alcoholism generally become intolerant to alcohol.

Two patients of Joël and Fränkel (1924) who were chronic cocaine users reacted to a cocaine dose of 500 mg, administered over several hours, in exactly the same way as a control subject who was not at all habituated to cocaine. On the suggestion of these authors, Frantz (1923) gave injections of only 50 mg of cocaine and found that they produced the same effects in individuals who had been habituated to cocaine for many years as in healthy control subjects. Most of my own patients have told me that the effect produced by one inhalation does not diminish in intensity with continued use, but that they feel an ever greater desire to shorten the intervals between inhalations, so that the total daily dose increases more and more to 10 or even 20 times the initial daily dose. This is quite understandable if one considers the inability to work produced by cocaine, the feeling of mental void which the subjects experience, and their desire to get rid as quickly as possible of their withdrawal symptoms. The experiments in animals referred to above, the findings of which cannot be applied directly to humans, have not provided up to now decisive proof of either an increase or a decrease in the sensitivity to cocaine after chronic administration. I am in complete agreement with Joël and Fränkel (1924), who have studied this problem in depth, when they conclude that neither tolerance nor increased sensitivity to cocaine upon chronic use has been proven as yet. Nevertheless, the investigations of these authors are not sufficient to resolve the problem. At least, one must point out that large single doses of 0.5 to 1 g do not produce alarming somatic toxic symptoms in chronic users. Whether rightly or wrongly (this remains to be established), no one would dare to administer such single doses to a naive subject.

Some evidence that tolerance to cocaine is not very marked is provided by the fact that, in chronic cocainism, just as in chronic alcoholism[21], abrupt withdrawal does not give rise to severe withdrawal symptoms such as those seen in morphine addicts. There is no evidence that the abrupt withdrawal of the drug can lead to the development of psychotic states. We should equally emphasize that the so-called abstinence deliria seen in alcoholics following the abrupt withdrawal of alcohol are also far from being proven. The conclusion to be drawn from all this is that cocaine can and should always be withdrawn immediately every time that a patient requests medical help. This is completely different from the situation, riddled with moral conflicts, that arises with respect to morphine addicts. If, for whatever reasons, clinical treatment of morphine addicts cannot be instituted immediately, the only course to take in order to avoid potentially fatal dangers, is to continue to prescribe morphine.The fact, furthermore, that it is often necessary to withdraw morphine gradually, reinforces in the patient a counter-productive mental attitude towards a drug that he considers of vital importance, particularly because he receives it from the physician. Nothing of the sort need occur among cocaine addicts because it is possible to withdraw the drug abruptly. On the basis of our present state of knowledge, the physician does not have the right to prescribe cocaine even to the most confirmed addicts, even when the latter claim, as they always do, that they experience unbearable abstinence symptoms. The physician who yields to such demands makes a professional mistake for which he can and should be accountable.

The only attitude that the physician must adopt when confronted with chronic cocaine use of any type, is to absolutely forbid the patient to use the drug. One often finds that cocaine addicts themselves are the last to understand adequately the dangers of cocaine use, and consider it as middle-class narrow-mindedness to

[21] Ed. note: The modern view is the opposite of Maier's because abrupt withdrawal of alcohol and other general depressants can, in severe cases, be fatal, whereas pure morphine withdrawal is rarely, if ever, fatal.

refuse to use a drug that produces such pleasant effects, helps one to cope with frustrations and increases pleasure. The physician who is reasonably familiar with the problem and who has enough psychological acumen should not find it too difficult to enlighten the patient and convince him of the opposite point of view. Considering the seriousness of the problem, the physician who feels that he is not sufficiently knowledgeable in this respect should refer the patient to a properly qualified specialist, rather than content himself with a few inconsequential remarks which will have no impact at all on the patient.

The treatment of this type of chronic cocaine user should be highly individualized. Each case has its own characteristics and, in many instances, the insurmountable need to resort to drugs is only a sign of some other type of disturbance. Furthermore, the choice of cocaine in preference to other drugs is very often a matter of sheer chance. Therefore, if the objective is to get to the root of the problem, it is necessary to make a psychological examination in depth, without, of course, neglecting the physical examination.

Many of these cocaine users are psycho-neurotics with feelings of inferiority, situational anxiety and other symptoms of inhibition. I know of a university where it became customary among the students to resort to cocaine to cope with the anxiety of examinations; many then continued the habit, to cope with other difficult situations in life. Perfectly healthy individuals did not resort to this practice, but the proportion of individuals with neurotic predisposition is high in all intellectual circles. The same often happens among artists; if it becomes public knowledge that a particularly admired or envied one takes cocaine as a stimulant from time to time, this is enough to make the habit become nearly epidemic among the rest of the group.

Once the habit takes root in groups of this type, drastic measures are required to get rid of it. These include the threat and actual practice of immediate discharge, with or without severance pay, of anyone guilty of providing cocaine to others, compulsory commitment of particularly severely affected individuals and, of course, a wide-reaching campaign of information and education.

For individuals with particularly marked neurotic traits intensive psychotherapy is often as important and significant as a direct attack against the addiction itself, if not more so. The type of psychotherapy should vary according to the individual characteristics of the patient and of the physician, as well as the environmental circumstances. In general, preference should be given to an approach that will ensure prolonged contact between the physician and the patient, and the supervision of the latter for many years in order to rehabilitate the patient and bring about an important re-education of his personality. For these reasons, rational therapy based on education and intellectual analysis, rather than purely suggestive therapy such as hypnosis, seems to me much more appropriate. It is important for the physician to have objective proof that the patient is not lying to him concerning any kind of excess; for example, the physician might obtain the cooperation of understanding relatives, friends, superiors or colleagues. Even when psychotherapy has been apparently successful, it is still necessary for a long time, if not permanently, to prevent the patient from re-establishing contact with groups where cocaine is found frequently, such as bohemian circles of any sort, some health spas, the large cities and ports. I have myself been able to confirm that cocaine traffickers always keep themselves informed about the fate of their affluent customers and approach them with new offers when the clients reappear in any of the places they used to frequent during their addiction. But in the case of cocaine, relapses are particularly easy because its administration does not require any preparation, not even the use of a syringe or any other apparatus.

There is a group of intermittent cocaine users who periodically use the drug heavily in response to endogenous emotional disturbances (periodic cocainism, cocaino-dipsomania of Piouffle, 1919). These may be epileptics, psychopaths, or schizophrenics in a depressive stage of their illness. The same tendency is of course also seen in manic-depressives, in which case the best approach is to deal with the underlying illness from the very beginning.

These prophylactic and therapeutic efforts have often been attacked on the grounds that, since drug addicts of any kind have prior abnormal personalities, it does not much matter how they end up. The same skepticism has often been expressed with respect to efforts designed to combat alcoholism. But the statistics available concerning the results of these efforts from a social hygiene point of view are sufficient to rebut these arguments.

In the case of cocaine addicts it is certain that a large proportion of them (precise statistics are not available) suffered from psychological abnormalities prior to the onset of addiction. It would be erroneous, however, to use this as a reason for slackening one's therapeutic efforts, because experience has shown that most of these patients are capable of achieving a reasonable level of mental equilibrium if the drug is withdrawn. It is important to recognize, furthermore, that these mentally unstable people include many richly-endowed personalities. It has been my personal experience, however, that healthy and strong individuals, particularly among the young, can be affected by the contagion of cocaine use if, during a period of temporary emotional stress, they come into contact with groups who use this drug. Glaserfeld (1920) has also found among his patients in Berlin many worthy individuals who, prior to their cocaine addiction, were completely normal. Even healthy people undoubtedly have a tendency to use one intoxicant or another to forget the pain of distressing experiences or to increase the pleasure of happy occasions. If this tendency is activated at a time when the individual finds himself either accidentally or more or less deliberately in contact with drug users, the danger of trying cocaine becomes very real. Whoever has tasted cocaine once can no more be sure of being able to stop than the physician who injects himself with morphine for the relief of some physical illness.

All attempts at temporarily substituting other narcotic or psychoactive drugs for cocaine in cases of cocaine dependence are ineffective from a practical point of view and erroneous from a theoretical one because the main therapeutic aim is to strengthen the will of the patient against escape into the use of any drug. Even if a dangerous drug is replaced by a less dangerous one, misuse of the latter is likely to become harmful in time and the greatest likelihood, in any case, is that, when the physician stops seeing him regularly, the patient will go back to using a more harmful drug. The first era of cocaine addiction arose as a result of substituting cocaine for morphine, giving rise to the more disastrous simultaneous addiction to cocaine and morphine. In the same way, attempts have been made to make the withdrawal of cocaine less painful and more bearable by administering small doses of morphine. We have already shown the irrationality of this approach, even from a physiological point of view, since the two drugs potentiate each other's physical and mental dangers. Some authors have suggested the administration of rather large doses of bromide for a limited time during the course of cocaine withdrawal, and the administration of barbiturates to combat the insomnia which is, incidentally, transitory. In my opinion it is best to abstain from such measures. When for subjective reasons it is impossible to avoid administering some sort of medication to an individual patient, one can be sure that the addiction was much more advanced than originally believed. In such cases, detoxification must be carried out in hospital. E. Meyer (1924, 1925), of Königsberg, is right when he says that patients of this type must be withdrawn from all psychoactive drugs, even from tobacco. Even in these cases, however, individual circumstances must be taken into consideration.

In principle, hospitalization must be considered the best

therapeutic approach in all cases of advanced cocaine addiction. We recognize, however, without contradicting this principle, that in very mild cases or in the case of individuals with relatively well-preserved and well-directed will power and basically good psychic structure, the cure can be achieved without hospitalization. In all cases, the physician should, from the beginning, impress upon the patient, and particularly upon his relatives, the advantages of hospitalization. Only if this cannot be carried out should he try out-patient treatment. The latter approach will stand at least some chance of success only if the patient is put under the supervision of a trustworthy attendant with experience in this field, and if he is removed from the drug-associated milieu. If, despite all these measures, the patient relapses, the physician should refuse all further responsibility unless hospitalization is made an absolute condition of treatment. Where the law applies, the physician should report the patient to the authorities.

The choice of institutions should be governed by the same principles as in the case of morphine addicts. Those private clinics that claim to be able to treat drug addicts "without deprivation of liberty" should be especially avoided. Most often, these are profit-seeking sanatoria whose organization and personnel are so untrustworthy that the patient can do as he pleases and secure, behind the physician's back, all the drugs he wants. When he is discharged, he may be not only uncured but actually in considerably worse mental condition. Well-run mental hospitals under government control offer the best guarantee of rigorous detoxification and subsequent work therapy. It is often impossible to persuade the patient's parents, particularly if they are affluent, of the need for such an approach until the patient has had many relapses. In such circumstances, there are, however, very well-organized private institutions available in most districts. For withdrawal treatment, the physician should consider only those which have closed as well as open wards so that the patient can, at least at the beginning, be submitted to rigorous control. As a matter of principle, patients should not be accepted by voluntary admission because it often happens that as soon as their hospitalization and surveillance become most essential, i.e., when unpleasant withdrawal symptoms appear, they can demand to be released and evade any effective supervision. Also the physician in charge should complete, either alone, or according to the local circumstances and regulations, with the cooperation of a colleague or an authorized physician, a certificate documenting the need for commitment, the impossibility of effective treatment outside an institution and the dangers that the patient constitutes for himself and others. One can assume that the patient, even in the absence of clear-cut suicide attempts, is a danger to himself in most cases. When the candidate for commitment can, in addition, be considered dangerous to others, the point should be particularly emphasized. He may have already committed dangerous acts against others while under the influence of cocaine, or threatened to commit such acts, or provided cocaine to others, with or without payment.

Immediately after hospitalization, cocaine should be withdrawn and simultaneously psychotherapy and rehabilitative work therapy should be initiated. Following this, special care should be taken that the patient, once cured, does not re-establish contact with other drug addicts. If his type of work makes such contacts inevitable, he should be retrained for another occupation. Care should be taken, furthermore, that the relatives or friends with whom the patient will be living when he leaves the hospital are made familiar with the disease and the signs of relapse, so that they will be able to maintain supervision of the patient if there is no physician available for this purpose.

It is impossible to set down rigid rules with respect to the length of stay in an institution. This will depend on the severity of the illness in each individual case and on the characteristics of the pre-morbid personality. When the addiction is long-standing, and particularly when the signs of chronic cocainism are present, the patient will probably need to be hospitalized for a year, as is the case with alcoholics and morphine addicts. In milder cases, in cases in which the patient has a strong character, and when the environmental circumstances are favorable, shorter stays are often sufficient.

It is particularly important that, during hospitalization, the patient should not only learn to avoid cocaine but also to accept the necessity of doing without any other drugs to the degree that this is possible, in order to avoid the danger of relapse. Based on my personal experience, I consider it important that these patients abstain from even moderate use of alcohol because the danger of relapse into cocaine use is particularly marked during states of mild alcohol intoxication.

When the patient presents epileptiform disturbances these should naturally be treated in the hospital simultaneously with the addiction. Care must be taken to ensure that the appropriate treatment is continued after discharge. The same approach should be used with respect to all other complications. With cocaine addicts, one always has to consider also the question of whether or not they should be placed under legal guardianship. This will be discussed later.

c) Chronic Cocainism

In chronic cocainism the phenomena of cocaine dependence are complicated by mental and often somatic disturbances which may persist even during the intervals between periods of acute intoxication. The condition is therefore more serious. The picture is complicated by the more prominent withdrawal symptoms and is primarily characterized by loss of will power and moral sense. This is why, as opposed to what happens in cases of uncomplicated cocaine dependence, in a large number of these cases one cannot count on the cooperation of the patient to achieve a cure. Lying and unreliability are particularly common and the patient's promises must be taken with great caution. No positive results can be obtained unless the patient is hospitalized in a closed institution and submitted to rigorous supervision. Private open institutions are even more contraindicated in cases of chronic cocainism than in milder forms of cocaine abuse. Home care is impractical even with the assistance of two competent attendants and the enlightened cooperation of the family. Patients of this type always find the means to procure cocaine by mail or through the complicity of intermediaries. Even in these cases, the first measure to be taken after hospitalization is the immediate and total discontinuation of the drug. The patient should be allowed to withstand the withdrawal symptoms without the aid of other drugs. Bed rest should be ordered during the first few days. If the patient suffers from insomnia, a calming and favorable effect can be obtained by the use of hot baths, especially at night. Marked vascular disturbances can often be treated successfully by hydrotherapy, such as alternating hot and cold baths. This can alter vascular reactions by a virtual gymnastic effect. After the first few days, particular emphasis should be put on the nutrition of the patient. Visits should be allowed only under the strictest surveillance of the staff to prevent the patient from obtaining any smuggled drugs. His correspondence should also be inspected. In jurisdictions where the law permits it, it is often advisable to put the patient under guardianship. Sometimes the patient can be persuaded to accept this arrangement voluntarily. But if this is not possible, an effort should be made to obtain legal authority for such measures.

It would be a mistake to conclude that the need for hospitalization is ended after a few weeks or months, when the signs of damage associated with chronic cocainism have disappeared, as they usually do. It is precisely then that the most important stage of the treatment begins. This includes the reshaping of the patient's personality, his readaptation to regular work and the systematic reinforcement of his resistance against future relapses. This task requires not only the special personality of the physician but also the participation of everyone concerned with the patient. Therefore, it is important to choose for patients of this type an institution which can provide the right ambience for detoxification cures. In my experience, abstinence from alcohol, not only by the patient but also by the staff (at least on the premises), is an essential condition for the success of the treatment. It is also advisable not to keep many patients of this kind together in the same ward because they have a tendency to influence each other, generally unfavorably.

An appropriate environment where the patient can be sent after discharge should be chosen from the beginning, in agreement with the patient's family or guardian. Once in this new environment, the patient should be subject to continued supervision. This, however, should be done so discreetly that he does not constantly perceive it as evidence of mistrust, and thus feel it as an injury to his own self-esteem. At the slightest sign of relapse, and before the addiction again assumes serious proportions, the patient should be brought back to hospital. This is necessary for medical and educational reasons. Only in this way can a significant number of cocaine addicts be cured and freed from all supervision after some years. The others will relapse repeatedly and, in various ways, eventually reach a bad end. At the beginning, it is difficult to make a differential prognosis in this respect. But the physician who wants to achieve any positive results must always tackle this rather thankless task in the spirit of therapeutic optimism.

As a rule, the somatic symptoms disappear rapidly following withdrawal of the drug. After some weeks the patient's appetite increases remarkably and there is a gain in weight, sleep becomes regular and of normal duration and depth. If there are marked lesions of the nasal mucosa, rhinologic treatment may hasten the healing. However, in most cases this is unnecessary. Small perforations of the septum and the ulcerations of the mucosae gradually heal, but large lesions of the cartilage generally do not fill in spontaneously and, if the patient has distressing difficulties as a result, plastic surgery is often necessary.

Incurable chronic cocaine users, that is, those who relapse repeatedly, should be hospitalized indefinitely whenever possible in a custodial institution where they can be protected from themselves and prevented from causing harm to others such as, above all, spreading their habit. But most often these patients, who recover quite quickly, succeed in obtaining their discharge and then have further relapses until they die from either an intercurrent illness or suicide.

d) Complicated Cocaine Psychoses

In all states of severe acute excitation following cocaine abuse, as well as in cases of sub-chronic anxious delirium and cocaine delusions, hospitalization in a closed institution is the only appropriate approach. On the one hand, this takes care of the immediate necessary security of the patient and of those around him and on, the other, it permits the strict enforcement of the detoxification cure which in such cases is always of long duration. The choice of an institution with enough well-trained staff is particularly important in acute cases because these patients are much more violent and dangerous than, for example, delirious alcoholics.

They are generally brought to our clinic well-escorted and physically restrained. Some of them, after being untied, have required as many as six strong orderlies to take them to the special ward. If this precaution is not taken, one runs the risk of unfortunate incidents because these patients make the most reckless use of their physical strength, which is highly increased under the influence of cocaine. The better the institution is equipped to deal with agitated patients, both architecturally and with respect to staff, the easier it is to avoid the administration of sedative drugs. This is very important, not only from an educational point of view, but also because it helps to prevent the danger of sudden collapse and central respiratory arrest.

If these agitated patients are left at liberty they always find the means of obtaining more cocaine. The result is a prolongation and worsening of their condition, suicidal attempts, dangerous acts against others and often death by unintentional overdose.

Cocaine addicts presenting with paresis or Korsakoff's symptoms are generally in very poor physical condition. This is one more reason why they should be hospitalized.

VII

COCAINE ADDICTION AS A SOCIAL DANGER. ITS LEGAL CONTROL

Spread of Cocaine Use and Accompanying Criminality

Formerly, when cocaine was used by subcutaneous injection, such use was a sporadic phenomenon which did not have a high risk of spreading. Most patients were also morphine addicts. Morphine, by inhibiting their general level of activity, also reduced their possibility of spreading the habit of using cocaine. But this situation changed abruptly when sniffing was introduced. The ease and simplicity of this mode of administration, together with the cocaine users' need to seek the company of other users, caused an immense wave of cocaine use to spread rapidly through all civilized countries, especially through the large urban centers. According to my personal experience, a single cocaine user is capable, in the space of several weeks, of recruiting to cocaine dozens of other individuals. Each new recruit can in turn become a new focus of contagion. Thus the French authors, as well as Zangger and others, are right when they say that each cocaine addict is a dangerously contagious patient against whom the most severe measures must be taken in the interests of society as a whole.

During a field trip, I have had the opportunity to observe the formation of a similar mass contagion in a small town. This is how it happened:

In a primarily middle-class district, a married couple who ran a tobacco store also started a profitable illicit traffic in cocaine. Soon the husband and wife became cocaine addicts themselves, to the point of being unable to tend to their store for more than a few hours a day. But in order to look after their large clientele, they persuaded the daughter of a small innkeeper, who lived in the same house, to take their place during the rest of the day for the sale of 1 g packets of cocaine. The results became evident very soon. The inn, which until then had not been doing much business, suddenly became crowded and the young girl, in turn, started to sniff cocaine herself in doses of several grams per day. As she was quite pretty she had many admirers whom she invited now and then, after closing hours, to sniff cocaine with her in a back room. Thus a sort of club of cocaine sniffers was soon formed. Since the police had heard about these goings on and had the place under surveillance, the cocaine traffic was transferred to three small restaurants in the same street, which I visited personally. The customers of these restaurants, that is, the cocaine sniffers who frequented them, included the higher status workers at a nearby machine factory and some employees of the railway station and the main post office. One mechanic had become so ill and socially deteriorated in the space of six weeks, that he had been forced to leave his employment and sell all his possessions, except what he was wearing, in order to buy cocaine. Thus a veritable center of cocaine addiction arose in the space of three months in this small middle-class district of a medium-size town. The victims were almost exclusively industrial workers and lower middle-class people.

This anecdote shows how wrong it would be to assume that cocaine use spreads only among those who are wealthy enough to squander their money indiscriminately. Indeed, the demimonde often serves as the starting point. In these circles, minor employees who have access to cocaine sources are bribed, and those who succeed in securing cocaine stocks share the drug freely with their associates. Cocaine addicts quickly lose the ability to work, while at the same time their need for the drug becomes increasingly compelling and their money to buy it increasingly scarce. But in the centers of nightlife that they prefer to visit because of their insomnia, there is always a prostitute or a pusher who can teach them how to solve their problem: the simplest solution is for them to become cocaine dealers themselves, since they have firsthand knowledge of the milieu and the customs of cocaine addicts. This course of action makes it possible for them, on the one hand, to earn enough money for their needs and, on the other, to reserve for their own use plentiful supplies of cocaine by adulterating that which they sell. At the level of street dealing, such adulteration is the rule. They get their supplies either directly or through an intermediary from large-scale dealers in chemical products who can always be found in the areas where cocaine addicts congregrate. These dealers are rarely cocaine addicts themselves because they are well aware of the risks of their trade. But they seek all means of expanding their market and they are very successful at this, thanks to the small dealers and intermediaries who are generally cocaine addicts themselves and are totally dependent on them. When the police learn of an organization of this type, it is the small street dealers who are caught first while their suppliers, who most often work under false names and have fictitious addresses, generally escape.

On the basis of information provided by patients, I have often had the opportunity to inform the police about areas of this sort and even to take part in investigations. In the course of these investigations I have realized how sophisticated these people are and how difficult it is to catch them. Occasionally, some have made experiments on themselves for which they have paid dearly. I would cite, for example, a police report from 1922 concerning some traffickers who had tried to produce a mixture of chocolate, opium and cocaine for sale abroad under some inoffensive name. They tasted the product themselves. One of them soon showed severe paralytic phenomena lasting several days. Another died on the way to the hospital. The forensic autopsy showed the presence of opium, but not of cocaine.

Many of these small dealers are hotel and bar waiters, washroom and cloakroom attendants, musicians in cafés, chauffeurs and prostitutes. It goes without saying that the pimps also take an active part in this business and, represent a link with a particularly dangerous criminal aspect of cocaine addiction. For example, the following declaration was made to the police about S., a degenerate individual who was a cocaine user at the time, and who had been previously hospitalized at our clinic:

> Lately I had had a lot of money and a steady relationship with an Italian woman whom S. had introduced to me. S. always had cocaine with him, and offered it to others at the appropriate times. I observed that those who sniffed his cocaine became stupefied for a while, so that it was easy to take money from their pockets without their noticing it. Sometimes the action of the drug did not go that far, but the people in question became so indifferent and incapable of putting up resistance after sniffing, that they let themselves be robbed of their money with astonishing passivity. By this method S. got me, against my will, to pay bills that had nothing to do with me.

During the past few years, in many places there have been very daring burglaries of drug stores and chemical warehouses, the only object of which was to secure cocaine and other similar substances for criminal purposes of the type just described or for personal use. An individual who took part in one of these ventures provided me with the following information on the relationship between cocaine and crime:

> He was a 25-year-old burglar and had been convicted for the first time at age 16. He had been convicted nine times subsequently and these convictions included some for complicity in stealing drugs. He had used cocaine frequently, either when he felt depressed or when facing a particularly difficult and daring robbery. In these circumstances cocaine made him feel confident and unself-conscious. It

eliminated all inhibitions and embarrassment. He knows that it is not only people of his kind who use cocaine. Painters and artists whom he knows by name resort to cocaine and hashish in order to work better. He says he can always find cocaine if he has the money. When a burglary is committed under the influence of cocaine, he says, it is dangerous to carry arms, particularly firearms, because of the risk of using them unnecessarily and unsteadily. He had become acquainted with cocaine four years earlier through a Dutchman who was a client of the firm where he was then working. He had made friends with this man very quickly. During the first night this man had given him two small snorts of cocaine approximately every half hour. This produced strong palpitations, headaches, heaviness in the limbs and an aged appearance. The next morning, he felt so bad that at noon his friend gave him another dose of cocaine and only then did he experience a pleasant feeling of inebriation. From then on, he always found that cocaine would take away his worst worries. He always carried a small amount of drug with him and used it to get a lift every time that he felt he was losing his energy, for example, when he was about to commit a crime. Since he knew about adulteration of the drug, he always carried a magnifying glass in order to identify the characteristic crystals. But the states of inebriation and the magnificent hallucinations that hashish produced in him gave him greater pleasure than the effects of cocaine. He said that cocaine makes men impotent but that it has the opposite effect on women and homosexuals. When he robbed drug stores and pharmaceutical factories his main goal was to get hold of cocaine and other drugs in order to sell them at high prices. This was very easy. But he and his accomplices generally would first administer to themselves large amounts of the drug, in some appropriate place. He is resolutely against any legal restriction of cocaine production because he believes that this would lead to the proliferation of many dangerous substitutes and would encourage the illegal manufacture and smuggling of cocaine. Although not very well-educated, he—as well as his accomplices—are very well-informed about other drugs, such as morphine, hyoscyamine and scopolamine. Among his acquaintances these substances are now encountered a great deal.

During the last few years this connection between cocaine and crime has become very frequent. Other narcotics have also acquired popularity, similar to that of cocaine, among professional criminals (see Aschaffenburg's book, *Crime*, 1923).

Most comparatively intelligent professional criminals are able to provide very detailed information about the ways of using cocaine for their purposes. In some cases, I have been able to establish that these individuals add small amounts of mescaline to cocaine in order to have their victims fall more rapidly into a state of euphoric hallucination, which thus makes them defenceless. At the same time the criminals always carry small amounts of cocaine which they take at the appropriate moment in order to increase their courage and energy before an important job. Experienced officers of the drug squad greatly fear this effect of cocaine because the criminals become very recklessly daring and make use of their weapons at the slightest provocation. When they are not under the influence of cocaine, under similar circumstances they would run away (personal communication from a police officer).

A new kind of offence connected with cocaine use is the sale, most often illegal, of cocaine heavily adulterated with salicylic or boric acid. Sometimes this misrepresentation is carried to an extreme degree, such as selling as cocaine and at its illicit price, totally inactive and worthless substances like flour. I know of a large number of trials where the accused had introduced into the market products of this type contained in counterfeit packages with forged labels of well-known firms, Merck for example. The label even had a typographical error.

We should therefore distinguish three types of crime-related cocaine users: a) criminals who resort to cocaine occasionally, before big ventures; b) the victims of one crime or another who have been intoxicated with cocaine to make them easier prey; c) cocaine users without past criminal records, who have become criminals only under the influence of cocaine. Or, in other words, there is cocaine use in criminals, involuntary cocaine use in victims, and criminality among cocaine users. We have discussed the latter category in the chapter on the medico-legal implications of drug addiction[22] and we have said that these individuals can be considered as legally not responsible. On the other hand, we are in complete agreement with Leppmann (1921) when he says that, concerning criminals who resort to cocaine only to avoid last minute indecisions and scruples, one should think twice before declaring them partially or totally free of responsibility. In most cases, there are reasons to hold them completely responsible. There are mixed cases, however, in which these people have become so addicted that they present very marked psychotic symptoms. These must obviously be taken into account in the determination of the degree of responsibility. Individual circumstances should be strongly taken into consideration in this respect. Obviously, the prognosis for criminals who use cocaine is

[22] Ed. note: Not included in this translation.

much less favorable than that for cocaine dependence in people who have become criminals as a result of cocaine use, precisely because of the psychopathic traits of the former. These people present great danger to society and therefore swift and thorough security measures are indicated. There may be cases, for example, in which the assumption of diminished legal responsibility on these grounds should actually warrant sentencing to longer prison terms, or at least as long a period of internment as possible in a custodial institution. *Article 40* of the proposed Swiss penal code considers, for example, the indefinite detention of these habitual criminals regardless of the length of the sentence imposed. A special law in the canton of Zürich, effective since April, 1925, concerning the measures to be taken with respect to incorrigible individuals, confers the same powers on the authorities. It would be desirable for similar legal measures to be adopted and, most importantly, applied in all countries. This would be one way of preventing in the future this dangerous association between criminality and drug addictions.

VIII

SUMMARY AND CONCLUSIONS

The oldest form of cocaine addiction, which is still prevalent in Peru, Bolivia and eastern Brazil[23], consists of chewing the dried leaves of the coca bush, which undoubtedly contain, in addition to cocaine, a number of other alkaloids. The abuse or excessive use of these leaves causes hallucinatory delusional states and dementia, often accompanied by serious gastrointestinal problems and marasmus. The effects of moderate use of the leaves are said to include improvement of physical performance, alleviation of the symptoms of mountain sickness, inhibition of hunger and induction of strong euphoria. Efforts to introduce the habit of chewing coca leaves into Europe have fortunately failed.

Broader interest in the coca plant did not develop until the discovery of its active principle, cocaine, in 1859-60, and particularly following its introduction into medicine by Koller and others in 1884. Although this alkaloid can be synthesized, its extraction from coca leaves is much simpler and cheaper, and remains to this day its only method of preparation. Starting in 1886, cultivation of coca began in the Indies, and especially in Java and Madoera whose plantations provide the raw material for the chemical industries of Europe, North America and Japan, while the South American product has gradually diminished in importance in world markets. In 1922, Java alone exported 1,250,000 kg of the dried leaves, with an average content of 1.5% cocaine. Cocaine contains a methyl group, and benzoyl and ecgonine moieties. Cocaine has a dual physiological action: through the benzoyl residue it produces peripheral anesthesia and, through the nitrogen-containing ecgonine residue, it acts as a stimulant of the central nervous system.

As an anesthetic in surgery, the alkaloid acts either directly on the endings of the sensory nerves, or by blocking conduction through the nerve trunks (conduction anesthesia and spinal anesthesia). The central action of cocaine is exerted primarily on the cerebral cortex, some parts of the brain stem and especially on the sympathetic system. The stimulant action gives rise to enhancement of intellectual activity, euphoria, a tendency to increase motor

[23] Ed. note: This is probably a typographical error in the original. Though it says eastern Brazil, it should have said on the eastern slopes of the Andes in western Brazil.

activity and to induce epileptiform seizures, increased body temperature through stimulation of the thermo-regulatory center, dilatation of the pupils, widening of the palpebral fissure, vasoconstriction, tremors and sweating. This action may change rapidly, although with a high degree of individual variation, into inhibition of the same systems, leading to collapse, paralysis of the respiratory center, lowered body temperature, vasodilatation and death. When cocaine is used as a local anesthetic, these central stimulating effects are so serious and unpredictable that safer substitutes have been sought for this purpose. Novocaine, atoxicocaine and tutocaine have proven to be both practical and effective as local anesthetics. But in some types of surgery, especially in otorhinolaryngology where topical anesthesia of bone and cartilage is required, they act either too slowly or too weakly. For this reason, cocaine is still used in this specialty. But psicaine, discovered in 1924 by Willstätter, is free from all these drawbacks. If it turns out that this tartrate of *d*-pseudococaine does not exert any central stimulating effects, particularly psychic, we would have a drug which could totally replace cocaine in the medical armamentarium and thus the hopes expressed so often by Straub (1919) and others would be fulfilled.

The measurement of cocaine in body organs and fluids is a very cumbersome procedure which never gives fully reliable results because of the rapid breakdown of the alkaloid. The methods to measure cocaine have been described in Chapter I[24]. It is hoped that the development of spectroscopic techniques will increase the reliability of these procedures.

The physiological action of cocaine varies considerably in some particulars from species to species. It is therefore necessary to review the detailed description given earlier.

Cocaine exerts a very strong psychostimulant action, followed by inhibitory effects, and dependence to it develops very quickly. The development and propagation of cocaine addiction constitute a very interesting and instructive chapter in the history of medicine, and more particularly in the history of psychopathology. The anesthetic properties of cocaine produced an immediate impact, but it took the medical profession a quarter of a century to recognize some of the practical implications. The enormous interest at that time (1884) in the surgical application of cocaine coincided with a misinterpretation of, and a complete failure to appreciate, the central stimulating effects of the drug. The erroneous idea that cocaine was more effective than other methods in the treatment of drug addic-

[24] Ed. note: Not included in this translation.

tions, especially alcoholism and morphine dependence, spread in both the United States and Europe. And thus the iatrogenically-induced and particularly dangerous new pathological picture of combined morphine and cocaine addiction was born. Despite the fact that some serious investigators, most notably Erlenmeyer (1885), were prompt to argue against this ill-conceived notion, it was not entirely abandoned until many years later. In addition, the number of pure cocaine addicts was relatively small during the last decades of the 19th century, and in most of them the addiction was of iatrogenic origin. Most of them took the drug subcutaneously and this was certainly an impediment to both the widespread propagation of the habit and the exaggeration of its psychological ill effects. Around 1900, the incidence of cocaine addiction soared alarmingly in the United States, and above all in British India. The native population of that country has a particularly strong penchant for the use of narcotics, and they were the first to adopt, on a large scale, the oral rather than parenteral use of cocaine. It was not long before cocaine addiction became a serious public health problem. The first reports of cocaine sniffing by the blacks of North America appeared in 1902, and soon this practice was also reported in various European countries. The first observations of perforation of the nasal septum due to cocaine sniffing were made at the same time. However, the centers of cocaine addiction remained more or less isolated until a few years prior to the Great War. But then a true epidemic of cocaine addiction began in the Paris underworld (demimonde) and soon became very dangerous. The concern of public authorities was aroused and more or less stringent measures of control, rather ineffective at the beginning, were instituted.

These various types of cocaine addiction are of interest because they permit an assessment of the damage that this drug can cause. The toxic substances absorbed through the chewing of coca leaves amount to only 1% of their weight and cause harm only after very prolonged use. After the isolation of the pure alkaloid, the medical use of cocaine by injection gave rise to a form of abuse which spread rapidly through various countries, but which remained confined to small numbers. But from the moment that the custom of taking cocaine by mouth, and particularly through the nose, became known, the habit spread as a true epidemic through the urban centers of all civilized countries. This was further facilitated by the mood of psychological unrest caused by the war in some segments of the population in many countries. An internationally organized and highly profitable illegal traffic in the drug developed quickly.

The action of cocaine on the body consists of suppression of sensory perception as a result of localized inhibition of peripheral nerves. Centrally, the drug exerts a strong stimulatory effect followed by inhibition of the sympathetic nervous system. Consistent with this effect there is first an increase in pulse rate and frequently in the blood pressure, palpitations, increased respiratory rate, dilatation of the pupils which remain reactive to light, widening of the palpebral fissure, exaggerated brightness of the cornea, a tendency to diarrhea and tenesmus of the bladder, impairment of sexual potency in men and enhancement of libido in women. The mode of administration of the drug is clearly revealed by cutaneous scars in parenteral users and chronic rhinitis with nasal eczema in sniffers. In the latter group, ulceration of the nasal septum often leads to round punched-out perforation. In cases of severe acute intoxication, there is often elevation of body temperature of central origin and, less frequently, epileptiform seizures. Increasingly severe depressant effects can lead to coma and death during an epileptiform seizure or as a result of respiratory arrest. There is no need here to recapitulate the complete list of symptoms.

From a psychological point of view, the first doses of cocaine often lead to unpleasant symptoms such as retrosternal pressure, shortness of breath and a feeling of unbearable tension. This is quickly followed by a remarkable state of euphoria. The whole picture is reminiscent of a hypomanic state. Thought processes become quicker though more shallow, but under the influence of cocaine as opposed to that of alcohol, even complex mental tasks are performed quickly and with no increase in errors, to the degree that the impairment of concentration will allow. Since sensory acuity is at first enhanced by cocaine, perception of new stimuli remains quite good. The impairment of thought processes begins much later. In addition, there is pronounced psychomotor stimulation, and it is common for the subject to execute all types of motor functions with greater self-assurance. Ataxic phenomena occur only in severe states of intoxication or after very prolonged use. Moreover, mildly intoxicated individuals are often capable of performing balancing acts which are quite beyond their ability in the normal state. In terms of affect, cocaine addicts are very susceptible to suggestion, and for this reason they are quite pleasant socially. The initial euphoria is followed, particularly as the effect of the drug wanes, by anxious excitement which may develop into extreme anxiety accompanied by an overwhelming need for a new dose.

Stimulation of the sympathetic system gives these individuals a peculiar appearance, reminiscent of hyperthyroidism. The widely opened and slightly protruding eyes, shining and with dilated pupils, are in striking contrast to the facial expressions and other body movements which are abnormally animated and precise and of a uniform emotional tone. Despite the subject's rather dreamy appearance, his attention is fully concentrated on his surroundings. During this stage the patients, while dissipating their energy in verbal expression of their fantasies and in all sorts of psychomotor activity, become exceedingly sociable, are subject to each other's power of suggestion, and have a particular need to relate to other fellow addicts. Consequently, the danger arises that they proselytize in order to create around them their own society in which they feel at ease.

It is in this respect that they differ from morphine addicts, who are much less dangerous. In general the latter are quite happy and content for as long as they are able to obtain the drug for their own use. Their proselytizing occurs only under special circumstances, as for example when they attempt to conceal their own sexual impotence by making their sexual partners equally inadequate sexually through the use of morphine. Cocaine addicts, on the contrary, are prone to squander their drug by giving it away to others. Since the drug abolishes the need to sleep, the time of day is of little importance to them. Although the appetite is also inhibited, cocaine addicts are customarily extremely thirsty, and this often leads to alcohol excesses.

In man, the ejaculation time is markedly prolonged and later this is followed by the sudden development of impotence although, at the beginning at least, it is accompanied by increased mental libido. In contrast, the effect of cocaine on women consists of a stimulation of both the mental and physical manifestations of sexuality. Moreover, cocaine intoxication often leads to sexual orgies, including the manifest expression of all types of sexual perversions especially facilitated by the removal of moral inhibitions. There is no doubt that homosexuals have a particular predilection for this drug. But, despite the claims of certain authors, there is no conclusive evidence that the sexual potency of homosexuals is enhanced by cocaine. The most probable explanation is that cocaine eliminates the inhibitions which are normally present. The same explanation applies to ordinarily heterosexual individuals, who, under the influence of cocaine, engage in homosexual activity consistent with latent tendencies which in the normal state are relegated to the unconscious.

In more severe states of intoxication, due either to the intake of larger doses or to a higher susceptibility to the drug, there may be hallucinatory phenomena, associated with ideas of reference, true delusions of persecution and of grandeur, fear of burglars, etc. The most prominent types of hallucinations are visual ones, the content of which is determined by the make-up of the individual, and tactile hallucinations of foreign bodies, worms, etc., on or under the skin (Magnan's symptom). In some cases the patients also hear voices either directly addressed to them, or coming as though from the stage of a theater. As opposed to the optical hallucinations of alcoholics, those of cocaine addicts are vividly colored. They appear faded or devoid of color only when they assume a cinematographic quality. In these states, the subjects are mentally confused but memory and self-awareness remain comparatively intact.

These states of acute cocaine intoxication show most of the symptoms of the more complex cocaine psychoses in which they become characteristically organized. We have classified them thus: cocaine addiction (cocainomania) without permanent damage, chronic cocainism accompanied by permanent damage, and states of intermittent addiction which can be considered symptomatic of other, more or less serious, disturbances. There are, besides, subacute cocaine delusional states in chronic cocaine users, including euphoric-hallucinatory states, paranoid anxiety reactions and oneiric deliria. The most serious complications are cocaine psychosis, a state similar to Korsakoff's psychosis, and a picture resembling that of luetic paresis.

From a psychopathological and differential diagnostic point of view, the most significant symptoms are the frequently observed hysteria-like phenomena and a certain degree of autism with a tendency to stereotypy, and auditory and tactile hallucinations which, to a degree, reflect the subject's affectivity, and volitional disturbances with a marked schizophrenia-like character. These cocaine-induced syndromes must be differentially diagnosed from other toxic states, epilepsy, progressive general paresis and the psychoses of hyperthyroidism.

The prognosis of acute cocaine intoxication must be made very cautiously because there is a large individual variation in lethal dose. Treatment should be essentially symptomatic and the use of morphine and other opiates is contraindicated. Withdrawal phenomena in chronic cocaine users are quite trivial, and therefore the drug can be discontinued at any time without the slightest danger to the patient. Although in the treatment of morphine addiction one occasionally must continue the drug until an appropriate method of management is found, we can say that, according to the present state of knowledge, any physician who under the pretext of some emergency prescribes cocaine to an addict, commits a serious professional error. Only mild cases of cocaine addiction can be treated on an out-patient basis. In the vast majority of cases, confinement to a closed institution for six to 12 months under firm and rigorous surveillance is mandatory. Permanent cures of cocaine addiction which has lasted more than a year are not more frequent than those of morphine addiction, and perhaps less so. The symptoms of cocaine psychoses disappear quickly when the patients are submitted to rigorous treatment in an institution, but they tend to reappear in the same form with each new intoxication. Finally, the patients usually die of coma due to overdose, suicide or intercurrent infections facilitated by physical debility.

Criminal activity among cocaine addicts is a feature of particular importance. On the one hand, cocaine can drive them to very dangerous acts of violence. On the other, criminals often resort to cocaine to bolster their courage at critical moments or to deprive their victims of any means of defence, especially women in cases of rape. Burglaries and armed robbery for the purpose of securing cocaine or other drugs are at the present time not rare in large cities.

For these reasons, in most countries physicians, public health authorities and legal guardians, courts of law and the police are all equally eager to fight against this type of addiction, which is so dangerous from a social point of view. Moreover, there is need for coordinated action among all the interested groups, and the purpose of this study is to make accessible to everybody the knowledge needed to achieve these aims. A point that requires particular emphasis is that each cocaine addict is a dangerous source of contagion, and that the numerous traffickers, often themselves cocaine addicts, have a vested interest in increasing the size of their clientele by spreading this type of drug addiction. Therefore, it is important to adopt administrative and legal measures, including permanent confinement of recidivists, that will make possible the institutional treatment of these patients even against their will. Complete elimination of the illicit traffic will not be achieved until there is rigorous and full control of the amounts of cocaine produced or imported into each country, from the point of production to the point of use, so as to preclude completely any deviation of it to the illicit market.

The consequences of the illicit traffic are no less dangerous than severe bodily assault. Since the traffic is highly profitable, the punishment should consist of long imprisonment, and in the case of guilty medical personnel, of suspension of their licence to practise. The fight against cocaine addiction, to be effective, requires international agreements because, since the drug is manufactured in only a few countries, large-scale smuggling has developed. The League of

Nations deserves high credit for having adopted and implemented the resolutions of the 1912 International Opium Convention at the Hague. The recent Geneva Convention of 1925 is directed more particularly at the fight against addiction to cocaine and to other similar drugs. Despite the cooperation of the large pharmaceutical firms in this respect, it should be remembered that the extraction of cocaine from the coca leaves is a very simple operation which can be undertaken by small factories located in overseas countries and especially dedicated to this purpose. Even though the recent Opium Convention also includes the control of exportation of coca leaves, it should be noted that up to the present, it has not been possible to achieve either control or limitation in the cultivation of the coca plant, and it is doubtful that this will be feasible in the foreseeable future in some of the countries concerned.

Significant progress will be achieved when a substance possessing the anesthetic properties of cocaine, but none of its drawbacks, is developed. Such a discovery would automatically and completely eliminate cocaine from the medical armamentarium. Psicaine may prove to be such a substance, but it is too early to say because experience with it is too limited. Nevertheless coca leaves would still be a much cheaper source of starting material than synthetically produced precursors for the preparation of this new drug. Therefore, there would still be a danger of illict production of cocaine for non-medical purposes. However, cocaine would vanish from the drug stores, thus eliminating the main source of the drug for the population-at-large. It should be added, however, that we are far from reaching this ideal situation and that, for a long time to come, we shall have to rely on individual methods of prevention. It will be incumbent upon us to protect the youth of our large cities from the temptation of resorting to unhealthy sources of pleasure by training it to acquire healthy and natural recreational habits. But this will not be enough. It will be necessary, in addition, that the medical profession, the authorities, the pharmaceutical industry and the pharmacists, as well as the police forces and the courts of all countries, make a united and concerted effort not only to bring about legislation against the most dangerous drugs among which cocaine unquestionably belongs, but, above all, to ensure its implementation. Even today there are physicians, including some who practise in areas where cocaine addiction exists, who do not sufficiently recognize the dangers of the drug. This is because the patients, fearing discovery and confinement, successfully conceal their condition.

Although it is common to discuss the horrors of chemical

warfare, not enough attention has been paid to the much larger public danger posed by the threatening spread of the non-medical use of strong intoxicants, such as cocaine. It is still possible and probably not too late to eradicate this addiction if it is caught at an early stage of its development. Let us hope that we are so successful in these efforts that this account of the origins, development and characteristics of cocaine addiction will be of value only to the historian of medicine interested in the study of the mistakes and errors of judgment of our phase of civilization!

BIBLIOGRAPHY[25]

Abadie, C. [No title]. *Bull. Soc. Ophtalmol. Paris* 1: [No page], 1888.

Aducco, V. [No title]. *Ann. Freniat. Sci. affini.* [No vol., page], 1890/91.

Aducco, V. Sur l'existence et sur la nature du centre respiratoire bulbaire. *Arch. Ital. Biol.* 13: 89, 1890.

Albertoni, P. Wirkung des Cocains auf die Contractilität des Protoplasma. *Pflügers Arch. ges. Physiol. Mensch. Tiere* 48: 307, 1891.

Albertoni, P. Azione de la cocaina sulla contrattilità del protoplasma. *Mem. R. Accad. Sci. Ist. Bologna* 10: 607, 1890. See also *Arch. Ital. Biol.* 15: 1, 1891.

Anonymous. The cocaine habit in America. *Brit. Med. J.* 1: 834, 1902.

Anonymous. The abuse of cocaine in Kentucky. *Brit. Med. J.* 1: 1369, 1902.

Anonymous. Über Perforationen der Nasenscheidewand durch Kokain. *Int. Zentralbl. Laryngol. Rhinol.* 36: 248, 1920.

Anonymous. Les priseurs de cocaïne. *Prat. Méd. (Paris)* 18: 145, 1904.

Antheaume, A. La cocaïnomanie et son traitement. *Rev. Thérap. Méd. Chir. (Paris)* 79: 837, 1912.

Aschaffenburg, G. Zur Einwirkung des Kokains auf das Geschlechtsleben. *Dtsch. Med. Wochenschr.* 51: 55, 1925.

Aschaffenburg, G. *Das Verbrechen und seine Bekämpfung*. Third Edition. Heidelberg: Winter, p. 98, 1923.

[25] Ed. note: Insofar as possible, the references listed below have been verified by checking against the original journals or, when these were not available, the *Index Medicus* and other standard bibliographic works. However, many of the references could not be located in this way, and many others in Maier's list were found to contain errors. Therefore, the following procedures were adopted:

1. Where Maier's citation was incorrect, but the original was located, the correct reference is given in the Bibliography.
2. Where Maier's citation was incomplete, and it was not possible to locate the original, the missing information is noted in square brackets, e.g. [No author], [No year], etc.
3. Where the original journal was available, and no article by the cited author was found in the volume or year given by Maier, or in the volumes or years preceding or following it, the reference is reproduced as given by Maier and followed by the annotation "[Original error]".

Aschenbrandt, T. Die physiologische Wirkung und Bedeutung des Cocain. Muriat. auf den menschlichen Organismus. *Dtsch. Med. Wochenschr.* 9: 730, 1883.

Aschenbrandt, T. Der Cocawein, ein neues Verpflegungsmittel. *Allg. Militär.-Ztg.* [No vol., page], 1886.

Authenrieth, W. *Die Auffindung der Gifte.* Fifth edition. Tübingen: Mohr, p. 172, 1923.

Barbé, A. and Bénoist, E. Les troubles de la sensibilité dans la morphinomanie, la cocaïnomanie et l'héroïnomanie. *Anthropologie (Paris)* 1: 257, 1911.

Bauduy, J.K. Cocain in disorders of the nervous system. *Med. Times* [No vol., page], 1885.

Beaussart, P. Le cocaïnisme collectif. *Bull. Soc. Clin. Med. Ment.* [No vol.]: 279, 1912 (?).

Becker, [No initial]. Stuporlösung durch Kokain. *Psychiatr.-Neurol. Wochenschr.* 23: 219, 1921.

Bentley, W.H. [No title] *Ther. Gaz. (Detroit)* [No vol., page], 1878.

Bentley, W.H. Erythroxylon coca in the opium and alcohol habits. *Ther. Gaz. (Detroit)* 4: 253, 1880. See also Huse, E.C. Coca-Erythroxylon—A new cure for the opium habit. *ibid.* 256.

Berger, H. Zur Pathogenese des katatonischen Stupors. *Münch. med. Wochenschr.* 68: 448, 1921.

Beringer, K. Experimentelle Psychosen durch Meskalin. *Z. ges. Neurol. Psychiat.* 84: 426, 1923.

Beringer, K. and Wilmanns, K. Vergleichende Untersuchungen über die Wirkungen des Kokains und Psikains. *Münch. med. Wochenschr.* 71: 852, 1924.

Biberfeld, J. Cocain. In: Ergebnisse der experimentellen Toxikologie. Teil II. Organische Substanzen. A. Alkaloide. *Ergeb. Physiol.* 17: 215, 1919.

Bier, A. [No title] *Dtsch. Z. Chir.* 51: 361, 1899.

Bilancioni, G. I disturbi nervosi provocati dalla cocaina per anestesia locale.*Riv. Ospedale* 7: 600, 1907. See also *Med. Nuova (Roma)* 10: 14, 1919.

Billeter, [No initial]. [No title]. *Corr.-Bl. Schweiz. Aerzte* [No vol., page], 1886.

Binswanger, O. Die Haager internationale Opium-Konvention und Artikel 69 der Bundesverfassung. *Schweiz. med. Wochenschr. 54: 517, 1924.*

Bleuler, E. *Lehrbuch der Psychiatrie*. Fourth Edition. Berlin: Springer, 1923.

Bleuler, E. Diskussionsbemerkung über Kokainismus. *Schweiz. Arch. Neurol. Psychiatr.* 1: 243, 1917.

Bommer, M. *Eine neue, vollständige Synthese von Tropin und razemischem Kokain* (Thesis). Zürich: Eidg. techn. Hochschule, 1918.

Bonhoeffer, K. and Ilberg, G. Über Verbreitung und Bekämpfung des Morphinismus und Kokainismus. *Allg. Z. Psychiatrie* 83: 228, 1925-26.

Bonvicini, G. Die lokalen Erscheinungen bei den Kokainschnupfern. *Jb. Psychol. Psychother. Med. Anthropol.* 44: 1, 1925.

Bornemann, [No initial]. Zur Kokainsucht. *Dtsch. Med.-Ztg.* [No vol., page], 1886.

Bose, K.Ch. Cocaine intoxication and its demoralizing effects. *Brit. Med. J.* 1: 1020, 1902.

Bose, C. Cocaine poisoning. *Brit. Med. J.* 1: 16, 1913.

Botti, A. Il nuovissimo pericolo: la cocainomania. *Rass. intern. clin. terap. (Napoli)* 1:82, 1920.

Braun, H. Ueber den Einfluss der Vitalität der Gewebe auf die örtlichen und allgemeinen Giftwirkungen localanästhesirender Mittel und über die Bedeutung des Adrenalins fur die Localanasthesis. *Arch. Klin. Chir.* 69: 541, 1903.

Braun, H. Ueber die Bedeutung des Adrenalins für die Chirurgie, besonders für die Lokalanaesthesie. *Münch. med. Wochenschr.* 50: 352, 1903.

Braun, H. Experimentelle Untersuchungen und Erfahrungen über Infiltrationsanästhesie. *Arch. klin. Chir.* 57: 370, 1898.

Braun, H. *Die Lokalanästhesie,* [No city, publisher], p. 83, 1905.

Bravetta, E. Diaria e Autopsia di un Cocainomane. *Bull. Soc. Med.-Chir. Pavia* 35(6): [No page], 1922.

Bravetta, E. and Invernizzi, G. Il Cocainismo. *Note Riv. Psichiatr.* (Pesaro), Vol. X and XI, 1922/23.

Bravetta, E. and Invernizzi, G. Il Cocainismo. Osservazione cliniche. Ricerche sperimentali e anatomopatologiche. *Note Riv. Psichiatr.* 10: 543, 1922; 11: 179, 1923.

Brennan, E. A contribution to the treatment of cocain poisoning. *N.Y. Med. J.* 68: 733, 1898.

Briand, [No initial] Un singe cocaïnomane. *Bull. Soc. Clin. Med. Ment.* [No vol., page], 1913.

Briand, [No initial] and Vinchon, [No initial]. Les priseurs de cocaïne. *Bull. Soc. Clin. Med. Ment.* [No vol.]: 266, 1912.

Brodt, K. and Kümmel, W. Klinische Erfahrungen über Schleimhautanästhesie mit Psikain. *Münch. med. Wochenschr.* 71: 851, 1924.

Brouardel, P. *Opium, Morphine et Cocaïne-Intoxication. Intoxication Aiguë par l'Opium, Mangeurs et Fumeurs, etc.* Paris: Baillière, 1906. See also *Ann. d'Hyg. (Paris)* 4: 223, 1904.

Brower, D.R. Insanity from cocaine. *Med. Assoc.* [*sic*; J.A.M.A.?], 1886. [Original error].

Brower, D.R. The effects of cocaine on the central nervous system. *Philadelphia Med. Surg. Reporter,* 1886. See also *J.A.M.A.* 6: 59, 1886.

Bucelli, R. Cocainismo e delirio cocainico. *Riv. Sper. Freniat.* 20: 69, 1894.

Bühler, [No initial]. [No title]. *Corr.-Bl. Schweiz. Aerzte* [No vol.]: 608, 1886.

Bumke, O. *Handbuch der Neurologie* (Lewandowsky). Vol. I, Part 2, Berlin: Springer, p. 1044, 1912.

Bumke, O. *Lehrbuch der Geisteskrankheiten*. Second Edition. München: J.F. Bergmann, p. 666, 1924.

Bundesrat (Federal Government of Switzerland). Botschaft an die Bundesversammlung betr. die Ratifikation des internationaler Opiumabkommens vom 8. Feb. 1924. Bern: Bundesrat, 1924.

Bychowski, G. Zur Wirkung grosser Kokaingaben auf Schizophrene. *Monatschr. Psychiatr. Neurol.* 58: 329, 1925.

Charpentier, A. Quelques observations sur les effets physiologiques de la cocaïne. *Mém. Soc. Méd. Nancy* [No vol.]: 40, 1884/85.

Charpentier, A. Action de chlorhydrate de cocaïne sur la fermentation alcoolique et sur la germination. *Compt. rend. Soc. Biol. (Paris)* 2:17, 1885.

Chaslin, P.H. *Éléments de Sémiologie et Clinique Mentale.* Paris: Asselin & Houzeau, p. 328, 1912.

Cloetta, [No initial]. Die Vergiftungen durch Alkaloide und andere Pflanzenstoffe. *Handbuch d. Inn. Med.* 6: 696, 1919.

Collins, C.F. *The Drug Evil and the Drug Law.* Monogr. Ser. 20. New York: Dept. of Health, 1918.

Comanos Bey, [No initial]. Die Wirkung grosser Dosen von Cocain auf das centrale Nervensystem. *Berl. klin. Wochenschr.* 23: 631, 1886.

Copeland, S. The Narcotic Drug and the New York City Health Department. *Weekly Bull., Dept. Health, City of New York,* 21 Feb. 1920.

Corning, J.L. Prolonged local anaesthetization by incarceration of the anaesthetic fluid in the field of operation. *N.Y. Med. J.* 43: 12, 1886; see also *Med. Record* 291, 18. (Cited by Braun, H. *Lokalanästhesie*, p. 180, 1905, and Odier, R. [No title], Thesis, Geneva, p. 9, 1903).

Coronedi, G. L'attuale epidemia di cocainismo. *Giorn. Clin. Med.* 2: 321, 1921.

Courtois-Suffit, [No initial] and Giroux, R. *La Cocaïne*. Paris: Masson et Cie, 1918.

Courtois-Suffit, [No initial] and Giroux, R. Le trafic de la cocaïne d'après les documents judiciaires récents. *Ann. d'Hygiène Publ.* 35: 251, 1921. See also *Bull. Acad. Méd. Paris* 85: 720, 1921; *Presse Méd.* 30: 1253, 1922.

Courtois-Suffit, [No initial] and Giroux, R. Règlementation internationale des stupéfiants, notamment de la cocaïne. *Ann. Méd. Lég.* 3: 294 and 391, 1923.

Cramer, A. L'intoxication par la cocaïne et la cocaïnomanie. *Rev. Méd. Suisse Romande* 41: 806, 1921.

Crothers, T.D. Cocaine Inebriety. *Philadelphia Med. J.*, pp. 1002 and 1898, May, 1920. See also *Med. Rec. (N.Y.)* 77: 744, 1910.

Cyril, V. and Berger, [No initial]. *La "Coco," Poison Moderne*. Paris: Ernest Flammarion, 1924.

da Costa, J.C. Four cases of cocaine delirium. *J. Nerv. Ment. Dis.* 16: 188, 1889.

Daddi, L. Sulle alterazioni delle cellule nervose nell'avvelenamento cronico da cocaina. *Clin. Moderna (Pisa)* 4: 204, 1898.

Daddi, L. Sulle alterazioni del sistema nervoso centrale nell'avvelenamento lento da cloridrato di cocaina. *Lo Sperimentale* 53(1): [No page], 1899.

Danilewsky, B. Ueber die physiologische Wirkung des Cocaïns auf wirbellose Tiere. *Pflügers Arch. ges. Physiol. Mensch. Tiere* 51: 446, 1892.

de Fursac, J.R. *Manuel de Psychiatrie,* p. 266. Paris: Alcan, 1923.

Déjerine, J. Sur un cas d'empoisonnement par injection souscutanée de cocaïne, chez un cocainomane, terminé par la guérison. *Compt. Rend. Soc. Biol. (Paris)* 4: 772, 1887.

del Greco, F. La personalità del tossicomane. *Riv. Ital. Neuropat. Psich. Elettroterap.* 13: 359, 1920.

Demole, V. Commentary on paper by A. Cramer (q.v.) *Rev. Méd. Suisse Romande* 41: 820, 1921.

De Quincey, T. *Confessions of an English Opium Eater.* Macdonald, London, 1956. First published in 1822; revised in 1856.

Detlefsen, F. *Zur Casuistik der halluzinatorischen Cocain-Paranoia.* Berlin: Rower, 1890.

Dixon, W.E. The drug habit. *Brit. Med. J.* 2: 819, 1921.

Dragotti, G. Cocaina e cocainismo. *Policlinico* 28: 1099, 1921.

Dufournier, [No initial]. Des dangers de la cocaïne. *Arch. Gen. Méd.* 2: 432, 1889.

Emmert, [No initial]. Kokain. *Corr.-Bl. Schweiz. Aerzte* [No vol., page], 1885.

Erben, [No initial]. In Dietrich's *Handbuch der ärztliche Sachverständigentätigkeit*, Volume: "Vergiftungen," Clinical Section. [No city, publisher], [No page], 1910.

Erlenmeyer, A. Über die Wirkung des Kokains bei der Morphiumentziehung. *Zentralbl. f. Nervhk. Psych. u. gerichtl. Psychopath.* 8: 289, 1885.

Erlenmeyer, A. Die Kokainomanie. *Med.-Ztg.* [No vol.]Number 44: [No page], 1886.

Erlenmeyer, A. Über Kokainsucht. *Dtsch. Med.-Ztg.* 7: 483, 1886.

Erlenmeyer, A. *Die Morphiumsucht und ihre Behandlung.* Third Edition. Berlin: Heusser, p. 154, 1887.

Fabry, E. Chlorkalzium bei Kokainvergiftung. *Münch. med. Wochenschr.* 69: 969, 1922.

Falke, E. Nebenwirkungen von Intoxikationen bei der Anwendung neuerer Arzneimittel. *Therap. Monatsh.* [No vol., page], 1890.

Farrère, C. *Fumée d'Opium.* 58th Edition. Paris: Ollendorff, 1919. Translated as *Black Opium* by S. Putnam, New York: N.L. Brown, 1929.

Feinberg, J. Zur Cocainwirkung. *Berl. klin. Wochenschr.* 23: 52, 1886.

Feinberg, J. Weitere Mittheilungen zur physiologischen Cocainwirkung. *Berl. klin. Wochenschr. 24: 166, 1887.*

Féré, C. Note sur l'influence des injections préalables de solutions de chlorhydrate de cocaïne dans l'albumen de l'oeuf de poule, sur l'évolution de l'embryon. *Compt. rend. Soc. Biol. (Paris),* Sér. 10, 4: 597, 1897. Cited by M. Grüter, *Arch. exp. Path. Pharmakol.* 79: 337, 1916.

Fischer, C. [No title]. *Monath. Tierhlk.* 15: 145, 1904.

Fleck, Ü. Uber Kokainwirkung bei Stuporösen. *Z. ges. Neurol. Psychiat.* 92: 84, 1924.

François-Franck, Ch.-A. Action paralysante locale de la cocaïne sur les nerfs et les centres nerveux. *Arch. Physiol.* Sér. 5, 4: 562, 1892.

Fränkel, F. Bemerkungen zu Marx' Beitrag zur Psychologie der Cocainomanie. *Z. ges. Neurol. Psychiat.* 85: 61, 1923.

Fränkel, F. Studien über Kokainismus. *Zbl. Neurol.* 33: [No page], 1923.

Frantz, [No initial]. Über die individuelle Verschiedenheit im Wirkungsablauf mittlerer Kokaindosen beim Menschen (Dissertation). Berlin, 1923.

Freud, S. Über Coca. *Zentralbl. ges. Therap.* 2: 289, 1884. Reprinted and enlarged version published separately by Perles, Vienna, 1885.

Freud, S. Beitrag zur Kenntnis der Cocawirkung. *Wien. Med. Wochenschr.* 35: 129, 1885.

Friedländer, [No initial]. Entziehungskuren und Therapie einiger wichtiger Intoxikationen. *Handbuch Therap. Nervenkrankh.*, 1916.

Friedländer, A. Über Morphinismus und Kokainismus. *Med. Klin. (Berlin)* 9:1577, 1913.

Friedländer, [No initial]. Der Morphinismus und Kokainismus. *Z. Ärztl. Fortbild.* [No vol., page], 1913.

Gadamer, J. *Lehrbuch der chemischen Toxikologie,* Göttingen: [No publisher], p. 570, 1909.

Gaskell, W.H. *The Involuntary Nervous System. Monograph on Physiology*. New Edition, London: Longman, Green & Co., p. 38, 1920.

Gilbert, A. and Carnot, P. Sur une lésion exclusive des cellules endothéliales du foie par la cocaïne. *Compt. rend. Soc. Biol. (Paris)* 54: 1383, 1902. Cited in *J. Physiol. (Paris)* 5: 197, 1903.

Gilbert, D.D. The cocaine habit from snuff. *Boston Med. Surg. J.* 138: 119, 1898.

Giroux, R. Étude clinique de l'intoxication par la cocaïne. *Gaz. Hôp. Paris* 92: 245, 1919.

Giroux, R. Acute and chronic cocaine poisoning. *Med. Rev.* (London) 22: 225, 1919.

Glaserfeld, B. Über das gehäufte Auftreten des Kokainismus in Berlin. *Dtsch.med. Wochenschr.* 46: 185, 1920.

Goldscheider, A. Die Wirkungen des Kokains und andrer Anaesthetica auf die Sinnesnerven der Haut. *Monath. prakt. Dermatol.* 5(2): [No page], 1886.

Goldscheider, A. Zur Dualität des Temperatursinns. *Pflügers Arch. ges. Physiol. Mensch. Tiere* 39: 96, 1886.

Gompel, M. and Henri, V. Étude quantitative de l'absorption des rayons ultraviolets par les alcaloïdes du groupe de l'atropine. *Compt. rend. Acad. Sci. (Paris)* 156: 1541, 1913.

Gordon, A. Insanities caused by acute and chronic intoxications with opium and cocain. *J.A.M.A.* 51: 97, 1908.

Gosse, [No initial]. *Monographie de l'Erythroxylon Coca*. Brussels: Acad. Royale, 1861.

Gottlieb, R. Pharmakologische Untersuchungen über die Stereoisomerie der Kokaine. *Arch. exp. Pathol. Pharmakol.* 97: 113, 1923.

Gottlieb, R. Ueber die pharmakologische Bedeutung des Psikains als Lokalanästhetikum. *Münch. med. Wochenschr.* 71: 850, 1924.

Grasset, J. De l'action physiologique de la cocaïne. *Compt. Rend. Acad. Sci.(Paris)* 100: 364, 1885. See also *Semaine Méd.* 5: 272, 1885.

Greenfield, A.D. *Treatment of Drug Addiction.* Washington: USPHS, 1919.

Grode, [No initial]. Über die Wirkung längerer Cocaindarreichung bei Tieren. *Arch. exp. Pathol. Pharmacol. 67: 172, 1912.*

Gros, O. Über Narkotika und Lokalanästhetika. *Arch. Exp. Pathol. Pharmakol.* 62: 380, 1910.

Gros, O. Ueber eine Methode die anaesthesierende Wirkung der Localanästhetika zu steigern. *Münch. med. Wochenschr.* 57: 2042, 1910.

Gros, O. and Hartung, C. Ueber Narkotika und Lokalanästhetika (Pt. II). *Arch. Exp. Pathol. Pharmakol.* 64: 67, 1910-11.

Guiges, P. Cocaïne et essence d'anis. *Bull. Sci. Pharm.* 31: 258, 1924.

Guillain, G. *Études Neurologiques*. Paris: Masson & Cie., 1922.

Guillain, G. L'Intoxication par la cocaïne. *J. Med. Fr.* 7: 235, 1914.

Guth, K. Über Koramin. *Münch. med. Wochenschr.* p. 562, 1925. [Original error]

Hammond, [No initial]. Kokain und Kokainsucht. *Dtsch. Med. Wochenschr.*, 1886. [Original error]

Hammond, W.A. Cocaine and the so-called cocaine habit. *N.Y. Med. J.* 44: 637, 1886.

Hammond, W.A. Remarks on cocaine and the so-called cocaine habit. *J. Nerv. Ment. Dis.* 11: 754, 1886.

Haupt, [No initial]. Ein Fall von Kokainsucht bei einem Kinde. *Dtsch. Med.-Ztg.* [No vol., page], 1886.

Hautant, A. Über den chronischen Kokainismus mit nasaler Anwendung. *Int. Zentralbl. Laryngol. Rhinol.* 25: 138, 1909. See also *J. Inebriety (Boston)* 32: 28, 1910.

Heiberg, P. A quelle partie de la molécule de cocaine est due la psychose de la cocaïne? *Rev. Neurol.* 1: 676, 1901.

Heilbronner, K. Kokainpsychose? *Z. ges. Neurol. Psychiat.* 15: 415, 1913.

Heimann, C. Cocain in der Psychiatrie. *Berl. klin. Wochenschr.* 24: 278, 1887.

Heimann, C. Ueber Cocain-Epilepsie. *Dtsch. med. Wochenschr.* 15: 232, 1889.

Heinemann, V. *Medizinische und psychologische Erfahrungen und Überlegungen zur Schaffung einer Gesetzgebung gegen Kokain-Missbrauch.* Zürich: A. Oelschlager, 1923.

Henri, [No initial]. Notes sur un cas de cocainisme aigu. (With a Discussion by Leglas and Saury). *Ann. Méd. Psychol.* Sér. 7, 10: 275, 1889.

Hertwig, O. and Hertwig, R. *Untersuchungen zur Morphologie und Physiologie der Zell.* Vol. 5, p. 39. Jena: [No publisher], 1887.

Hess, W.R. Über die Wechselbeziehungen zwischen psychischen und vegetativen Funktionen. *Schweiz. Arch. Neurol. Psychiat.* 16: 285 and 289, 1925. Also published separately: Zurich: O. Füssli, 1925.

Heymann, [No initial]. Ueber Intoxikation durch Cocain. *Berl. klin. Wochenschr.* 22: 795, 1885.

Higier, H. Beitrag zur Klinik der psychischen Störungen bei chronischem Kokainismus. *Münch. med. Wochenschr.* 58: 503, 1911.

Hinsen, W. Cocainwirkung bei stuporösen Paralysen. *Z. ges. Neurol. Psychiat.* 74: 602, 1922.

Hirsch, C. Versammlung deutscher Naturforscher und Ärzte 1920. *Int. Zentralbl. Laryngol. Rhinol.* 36: 350, 1920.

Hofvendahl, A. Die Bekämpfung der Kokainvergiftung im Tierversuch. *Int. Zentralbl. Laryngol. Rhinol.* 36: 353, 1920. See also *Biochem. Z.* 117: 55, 1921.

Hofvendahl, A. Zur Bekämpfung der Kokainvergiftung. Praktische Ratschläge. *Monatsschr. Ohrenheilk. Laryng.-Rhinol.* 55: 887, 1921. See also *Acta Oto-Laryngol. (Stockholm)* 4: 238 (1922-23).

Hoijer, O. *Le Trafic de l'Opium et d'Autres Stupéfiants. Étude de Droit International et d'Histoire Diplomatique.* Paris: Spes, 1925.

Hubbard, S.D. The New York City narcotic clinic and differing points of view on narcotic addiction. *Monthly Bulletin of the Department of Health, City of New York.* [No vol., page], 1920.

Hunziker, H. Über Kokainismus und seine Bekämpfung. *Schweiz. Apoth.-Ztg.* 45, 1922.

Ihlow, W. Über Morphio-Cocainismus und hallucinatorische Cocain-Paranoia (Dissertation). Berlin: G. Schade, 1895.

Impens, E. *Pflügers Arch. ges. Physiol. Mensch. Tiere* 51: 446, 1892. [Original error]

Jaeckel, [No initial]. Zur Behandlung der Morphiumsucht mittelst Cocain. *Dtsch. Med.-Ztg.* 2: 913, 1885.

Joël, E. Studien über Kokainismus. *Ther. Gegenw.* 63: 247, 1922.

Joël, E. Kokainismus. *Med. Klin.* 19: 817, 1923.

Joël, E. and Fränkel, F. Der Kokainismus. Ein Beitrag zur Geschichte und Psychopathologie der Rauschgifte. *Ergeb. inn. Med. Kinderheilkd.* 25:988, 1924.

Joël, E. and Fränkel, F. Kokainismus und Homosexualität. *Dtsch. Med. Wochenschr.* 51: 1562, 1925.

Johnston, [No initial]. *Chemie des täglichen Lebens.* Translation by F. Dornbluth. 2nd edition. Stuttgart: Krabbe, 1887.

Kahn, [No initial]. A propos d'un cas de morphinomanie. *J. Psychol.* [No volume]: 150, 1908.

Kasparjantz, [No initial]. Zur Kasuistik der Perforationen der Nasenscheidewand. *Moscow Oto-Rhino-Laryngol. Soc., Meeting of Feb. 20, 1908,* Proceedings Vol. 2, 1911 (in Russian).

Kellert, E. Cocaine poisoning: report of a case with necropsy. *J. Lab. Clin.Med.* 4: 129, 1919.

Klug, I.A. *Die Kokshansl, das Kokainlaster in den Kreisen der "unteren Zehntausend".* Vienna: Eigenverlag, 1924.

Knopf, S.A. One million drug addicts in the United States. *Med. J. Rec. N.Y.* 119: 135, 1924.

Kochs, W. Ueber die Wirkung des Cocain auf freipreparirte gemischte Nervenstränge. *Centralbl. Klin. Med.* 7: 793, 1886.

Koebner, F.W. *Kokain, Skizzen.* Berlin: Grotilgo-Verlag, 1921.

Kohlhardt, H. [No title]. *Verh. Dtsch. Ges. Chir.* 30: 644, 1901.

Kohlhardt, H. Über Entgiftung des Kokains im Tierkörper. *Arch. klin. Chir.* 64: 927, 1901.

Kolb, L. and Du Mez, A.G. The prevalence and trend of drug addiction in the United States and factors influencing it. *Publ. Health Rep.* 39: 1179, 1924.

Koller, K. Über die Verwendung des Kokains zur Anästhesierung am Auge. *Wien.med. Wochenschr.* 34: 1276 and 1309, 1884.

Korentschewsky, W. Vergleichende pharmakologische Untersuchungen über die Wirkung von Giften auf einzellige Organismen. *Arch. exp. Pathol. Pharmakol.* 49: 7, 1903.

Kraepelin, E. *Psychiatrie. Ein Lehrbuch für Studierende und Ärzte*. EighthEdition, Vol. II, Part I. Leipzig: Barth, p. 228, 1910.

Krüger, H. [No title]. Dissertation. Berlin, 1885.

Laarss, R.H. *Dämon Rausch.* Leipzig: Talis-Verlag, 1925.

Laborde, J.V. *Compt. Rend. Soc. Biol. (Paris)* 1: 753, 1884; 2: 241, 1885;4: 560, 1887.

Laignel-Lavastine, M. *Pathologie du Sympathique*. Paris: Allan, 1924.

Lange, J. Psychologische Untersuchungen über die Wirkungen von Cocain, Scopolamin und Morphin. In: E. Kraepelin, Ed., *Psychologische Arbeiten*. Vol. 7, p. 354. Berlin: Springer, 1922.

Langlois, P. and Richet, C. Cited by C. Richet in: Les poisons convulsivants. *Arch. Int. Pharmacodyn.* 4: 293, 1897-98.

Laubi, [No initial]. Beitrag zur Kokainwirkung bei subgingivaler Anwendung. *Corr.-Bl. Schweiz. Aerzte* [No vol.]: 615, 1886.

League of Nations. *Report of Sessions 1-6 of the Consultative Commission on the Opium Traffic.* Geneva: General Secretariat, 1921-1924.

Legrain, [No initial]. Cocaïnomanie et Cocaïnisme. In: *Traité de Pathologie Médicale et de Thérapie Appliquée*. Volume XXII (Intoxications), p. 375, Paris: Maloine et Fils, 1922.

Leopold, [No initial]. Ein Fall von Cocain-Intoxication. *Berl. klin. Wochenschr.* 31: 838, 1894.

Leppman, F. Zur forensischen Beurteilung des Kokainmissbrauches. *Ärztl. Sachverst.-Ztg.* 27: 89, 1921.

Léquyer, [No initial]. Un cas de cocaïnisme chronique par la muqueuse nasale. *Gaz. Méd. Nantes* 23: 206, 1905.

Leudesdorf, [No initial]. Einige Erfahrungen über die Heilkraft der Coca. *Z.Prakt. Ärzte* [No vol.]Number 7: [No page], 1899.

Levinstein, [No initial]. *Die Morphiumsucht. Eine Monographie.* 3rd edition. Berlin: [No publisher], 1883.

Lichtenstein, [No initial]. Septumperforation bei habituellem Gebrauch von Narcoticis. *Med. J.* (New York) 2, 1915. Cited in *Int. Zentralbl. Laryngol. Rhinol.* 32: 274, 1916. See also Crookshank, F.G. *Brit. Med. J.* 2: 917, 1921.

Logoz, P. La Cocaïnomanie en Suisse. *Schweiz. Z. Strafrecht* 35: 150, 1922.

Lossen, [No initial]. Über das Kokain. *Ann. Chem. Pharm.* [No vol., page], 1865.

Love, [No initial]. The cocaine habit. *Med. Record* 28: 336, 1885.

Lubet-Barbon, F. [No title]. Société de Laryngologie, etc., de Paris, Meeting of February 18, 1908. Cited in *Int. Zentralbl. Laryngol. Rhinol.* 25:138, 1909.

Maass, [No initial]. Zur therapeutischen Verwendbarkeit des Trivalins. *Dtsch. med. Wochenschr.* 46: 884, 1920.

Magnan, V. *Über drei Fälle von chronischem Kokainismus*. Translated by J.P. Moebius in *Psychiatrische Vorlesungen von V. Magnan,* Vol. 6, p.40. Leipzig: Thieme, 1893.

Magnan, V. and Saury, [No initial] Trois cas de cocaïnisme chronique. *Compt. Rend. Soc. Biol. (Paris)* 1: 60, 1889.

Magnus, R. Pharmakologische Untersuchungen an Sipunculus nudus. *Arch. exp. Pathol. Pharmakol.* 50: 86, 1903.

Maier, H.W. Über Kokainismus und dessen Ausbreitung in der Schweiz. *Schweiz. Arch. Neurol. Psychiatr.* 1: 243, 1917.

Maier, H.W. Untersuchungen über die Wirkungen des Koffeins und des Kaffes auf den Menschen. *Schweiz. Arch. Neurol. Psychiat.* 9: 244, 1921, and 10:80, 1922.

Maier, H.W. Neue Beiträge zur Symptomatologie und Bekämpfung des Kokainismus. *Schweiz. Arch. Neurol. Psychiatr.* 11: 142, 1922.

Maier, H.W. Allgemeines zur zentralen Kokainwirkung auf den Menschen. *Schweiz. med. Wochenschr.* 55: 631, 1925.

Maier, H.W. Über katathyme Wahnbildung und Paranoia. *Z. ges. Neurol. Psychiat.* 13(5): [No page], 1912.

Maier, H.W. Über einige Arten der psychogenen Mechanismen (Katathymie, Athymie, Synthymie). *Z. ges. Neurol. Psychiat.* 82: 193, 1923.

Mannheim, P. Ueber einen Fall von heftiger Cocain-Intoxication. *Dtsch. med. Wochenschr.* 12: 489, 1886. See also *Berl. klin. Wochenschr.* 23: 583, 1886.

Mannheim, P. Über das Cocain und seine Gefahren in physiologischer, toxikologischer und therapeutischer Beziehung. *Z. klin. Med.* 18: 380, 1890-91.

Mantegazza, P. *Sulle virtù igieniche e medicinali delle cocaina (Autoosservazione).* Monograph, Milano: [No publisher], 1859. Also printed in *Ann. Univers. Med. Chir.* 167: 449, 1859.

Marta, F. *La Cocaina. Storia, Clinica, Remedi.* Milano: Sonzogno [No year].

Marx, N. Beiträge zur Psychologie der Cocainomanie. *Z. ges. Neurol. Psychiat.* 80: 550, 1922-23.

Mattison, J.B. Cocaine habit. *Amer. Med. News* [No vol., page], 1886. See also *Lancet* 1: 1024, 1887.

Mattison, J.B. Cocainism. *Med. Record (N.Y.)* 42: 474, 1892.

Maurel, E. Recherches sur les causes de la mort par la cocaïne. *Bull. Thérap. (Marseille)* [No vol., page], 1892.

Mayer, K. Zur Therapie der Cocainvergiftung. *Schweiz. med. Wochenschr.* 51: 767, 1921.

Mayer, K. Zur Bekämpfung der Kokainvergiftung. *Z. Ohrenhlk. Krankh. Luftw.* 82: 42, 1922.

Mayer-Gross, W. Selbstschilderung eines Cocainisten. *Z. ges. Neurol. Psychiat.* 62: 2, 1920.

McIver, J. and Price, G.E. Drug addiction. *J.A.M.A.* 66: 476, 1916.

Meister, W.B. Cocainism in the army. *Milit. Surg.* 34: 344, 1914.

Meyer, E. Über Morphinismus, Kokainismus und den Missbrauch anderer Narkotika. *Med. Klin. (Berlin)* 20: 403, 1924.

Meyer, E. Bemerkungen zur Behandlung des Morphinismus. *Münch. med. Wochenschr.* 72: 228, 1925.

Montiers, A. *Les Petites Visionaires.* Paris: [No publisher, year].

Moreno y Maiz, T. [No title]. *Thesis.* Paris, 1868.

Morgenstern, S. Beitrag zur Frage des Belladonna-Delirs. *Z. ges. Neurol. Psychiat.* 82: 231, 1923.

Morselli, E. Nota sulla psicosi cocainica e sue varietà nosografiche. *Riforma Med.* 12, Part 2: 554 and 566, 1896.

Morselli, E. and Buccola, G. Ricerche sperimentali sull'azione fisiologica e terapeutica della cocaina. *Rendiconti del R. Ist. Lombardo.* xiv: [no pages], 1882.

Mortimer, W.G. *History of Coca, "the Divine Plant of the Incas."* New York: J.H. Vaile & Co., 1901.

Mosler, [No initial]. Zur Frage der Beeinflussbarkeit katatonischer Stuporen durch subkutane Kokain-Injektionen. *Arch. Psychol.* 66: [No page], 1922.

Mosso, U. Über die physiologische Wirkung des Kokains. *Pflügers Arch. ges. Physiol. Mensch. Tiere* 47: 553, 1890; see also *Giorn. R. Accad. Med.* 38: 65 and 297, 1890; *Arch. Ital. Biol.* 14: 247, 1891 and 21: 234, 1894; *Arch. exp. Pathol. Pharmakol.* 23: 153, 1887.

Müller, F.H. Trivalinismus. *Dtsch. med. Wochenschr.* 44: 380, 1918.

Münzer, W. *Phantom.* Berlin: Borngräber, 1919.

Nagel, W. Versuche zur Sinnesphysiologie von Beroë ovata und Carmarina hastata. *Pflügers Arch. ges. Physiol. Mensch. Tiere* 54: 165, 1893.

Natansohn, L. and Lipskeroff, L. Über Perforation der knorpeligen Nasenscheidewand bei Kokainschnupfern. *Z. Hals-, Nasen-, Ohrenhlk.* 7: 409, 1924.

Neutra, W. Kokainismus und Morphinismus. *Wien. med. Wochenschr.* 69: 2443, 1919.

Niemann, A. Über eine neue Base in den Kokablättern (Dissertation). Gottingen, 1860.

Nordenskjöld, E. *Forschungen und Abenteuer in Südamerika.* Stuttgart: Strecker & Schröder, 1924.

Norman, C. A note on cocainism. *J. Ment. Sci.* 38: 195,1892.

Norris, G.W. A case of cocain habit of three months' duration, treated by complete and immediate withdrawal of the drug. *Philadelphia Med. J.* 1: 304, 1901.

Obersteiner, H. Über die Morphiumsucht und ihre Behandlung. *Zentralbl. Nervhlk. Psychiatr. gerichtl. Psychopath.* [No vol., page], 1884.

Obersteiner, H. Zur internen Anwendung des Kokains bei Neurosen und Psychosen. *Wien. med. Presse* 26: 1253, 1885.

Obersteiner, H. Über Intoxikationspsychosen. *Mitth. Wien. med. Doct.-Coll.* 12: 42, 1886. See also *Wien. Klin.* 12: 33, 1886.

Obersteiner, [No initial]. Kokain und Morphinismus. *Wien. med. Wochenschr.* [No vol., page], 1888. [Original error]

Opium Convention: *Soll die Schweiz die Haager Opiumkonvention ratifizieren?* A position paper by the Swiss pharmaceutical industry. Basel: Böhm, 1923.

Oppe, [No initial]. Kokainschnupfer. *Aerztl. Sachsverst. Ztg.* 29: 1, 1923.

Ostermann, G. [No title]. *Arch. Fisiol.* 1: 1, 1890.

Oswald, A. Über die Beziehungen zwischen chemischer Konstitution und Wirkung der Arzneikörper. *Schweiz. med. Wochenschr.* 52: 40, 1922.

Oswald, A. *Chemische Konstitution und pharmakologische Wirkung: ihre Beziehungen zueinander bei den Kohlenstoffverbindungen*. Berlin: Bornträger, 1924.

Palmer, [No initial]. Erythroxylon coca in the opium and alcohol habit. *Therap. Gaz. (Detroit)*, 1880. [Original error]

Palmer, H.B. Notes of a case of cocaine poisoning. *Lancet* 1: 718, 1898.

Pandy, [No initial]. Uber die Schnelldiagnose der Epilepsie mit besonderer Rücksicht auf die Kokainmethode. *Orvasi Hedlap.* [No volume] Number 50: [No page], 1917.

Pichon, G. Considérations sur la morphinomanie et sur son traitement. *Encéphale* 6: 307, 1886.

Piouffle, H. *Les Psychoses Cocaïniques*. Paris: A. Maloine et Fils, 1919.

Pisano, V. Esiste un antagonismo reciproco fra cocaina e strichnina? *Arch. Farmacol. Sper. Sci. Affin.* 34: 174, 1922.

Poeppig, E. *Reise in Chile, Peru und auf dem Amazonenstrome während der Jahre 1827-1832.* Leipzig: Fleischer, 1836.

Poporkoff, [No initial]. Cocainismus und Cocainomanie. *Korsakoffsches J. Psychiat. Neurol.* [No vol.] Number 5: [No page], 1904; and [No vol., page], 1905.

Popp, [No initial]. Über den Nachweis von Kokain und Novokain in Leichenteilen.*Chemikerztg.* [No vol.]: 1004, 1922.

Poulsson, E. Die Kokaingruppe. *Heffters Handbuch der experimentelle Pharmakologie.* Volume 2, Part 1, p. 105, Berlin: Springer, 1920.

Poulsson, E. *Lehrbuch der Pharmakologie*. Sixth Edition, p. 100. Leipzig: Hirzel, 1922.

Poulsson, E. Beiträge zur Kenntnis der pharmakologische Gruppe des Cocains. *Arch. exp. Pathol. Pharmakol.* 27: 301, 1890.

Provost, M. Un cas de cocainisme nasal. *Bull. Soc. Clin. Méd. Ment.* [No vol.]: 277, 1912.

Pulay, [No initial]. Beobachtungen über Kokainmissbrauch. *Med. Klin.* 18: 399, 1922.

Reiche, K. Die Erythroxylaceen. In: Engler and Prantl, Eds., *Natürliche Pflanzenfamilien,* Part I, Section 4, p. 37. Leipzig: Engelmann, 1897.

Rican, [No initial]. Morphinism and alcoholism treated with cocain. *Gaillard's Med. J. (N.Y.)* [No vol., page], 1885.

Ricci, A. Eine Cocainvergiftung. *Dtsch. med. Wochenschr.* 13: 894, 1887.

Richard, [No initial]. Action de la cocaïne sur les invertébrés. *C.R. Acad. Sci. (Paris)* 100: 1409, 1885.

Richter, [No initia]). Über Cannabinon und Kokain. *Dtsch. Med.-Ztg.* [No vol., page], 1885.

Rifatwachdani, S. Das Schicksal des Cocains und Ekgonins im Organismus. *Biochem. Z.* 54: 83, 1913.

Rigal, H. *Les Stupéfiants.* Paris: Attinger Frères, 1916.

Ring, F.W. Cocaine and its fascinations, from a personal experience. *Med. Record* 32: 274-276, 1887.

Romanese, R. Osservazioni medico-legali sopra un avvelenamento acuto da cocaina. *Riv. Med. Legale (Pisa)* 10: 39, 1920.

Rossier, [No initial]. Sur l'action physiologique des feuilles de coca. *Echo Méd.* [No vol., page], 1861.

Sabatucci, F. Sindromi neuropsichiche nei fiutatori di cocaina. *Policlinico (Roma)* (Sez. Med.) 29: 235, 1922.

Saurian, A. *Morfinismo e Cocainismo.* Torino: [No publisher], 1922.

Saury, [No initial]. Du cocainisme. Contribution a l'étude du foli-toxique, with a discussion by Leglas, Pichon, et al. *Ann. Méd.-Psychol.*, Ser.7, 9: 439, 1889; see also *Arch. Neurol.* 20: 272, 1890.

Scherer, J. Zur Kasuistik der Kokainpsychosen. In: A. Dietrich, Ed., *Extracts from the Dissertations in the Faculty of Medicine, University of Cologne, 1919/20.* Bonn: Marcus & Weber, 1921.

Schinz, H.R. and Slotopolsky, B. Histologisches zur Steinachunterbindung. *Z. Mikrosk. Anat. Forsch.* 2: 225, 1925.

Schinz, H.R. and Slotopolsky, B. Grundsätzliches zur Steinachoperation. *Dtsch. med. Wochenschr.* 51: 518 and 557, 1925.

Schleich, C.L. *Kokainismus.* Diary 2, No. 43. Berlin: Rowohlt, 1921.

Schnyder, H. Ein Fall von Cocainvergiftung. *Corr.-Bl. Schweiz. Aerzte* 17: 161, 1887.

Schröder, P. In Aschaffenburg's *Handbuch der Psychiatrie*. Section III, Part 1: Intoxikationspsychosen. Leipzig and Wien: Deuticke, 1912.

Schroff, [No initial]. Vorläufige Mitteilung über Kokain. *Wien. med. Wochenbl.* [No vol.] Number 34: [No page], 1862.

Schultze, E. In Hoche's *Handbuch der gerichtliche Medizin,* 2nd edition. Berlin: Hirschwald, 1909.

Schultze, E. Kokainismus. In: Binswanger and Siemerling, Eds., *Lehrbuch der Psychiatrie,* 5th edition, p. 315. Jena: Fischer [No year].

Schultze, E. Der Entwurf zu einem Deutschen Strafgesetzbuch 1919 vom Standpunkte des Psychiaters. *Arch. Psychiat.* 66: 161, 1922.

Schürmayer, C.B. [No title]. *Jenaische Z. Med. Naturwissensch.* 24: 438, 1890.

Schwaeblé, R. *La Coco à Montmartre.* Paris: Editions Modernes [No year].

Seifert, [No initial]. Über Kokain und Kokainismus. *Proc. Würzb. physik. med. Ges.* [No vol., page], 1886.

Sicard, A. Injection sous-arachnoïdienne de cocaïne chez le chien. *C.R. Soc.Biol. (Paris)* 51: 408, 1899.

Simon, [No initial]. Narcotic Habit Under Control. *N.Y. Tribune* [No page], Jan. 18, 1924.

Simonton, T.G. The increase of the use of cocaine among the laity in Pittsburgh. *Philadelphia Med. J.* 11: 556, 1903.

Slayter, [No initial]. Ein Fall von Kokainvergiftung. *Dtsch. med. Wochenschr.* [No vol.]: 17, 18. [Original error]

Slotopolsky, B. and Schinz, H.R. Histologische Hodenbefunde bei Sexualverbrechern. *Virchows Arch. Pathol. Anat. Physiol.* 257: 294, 1925.

Smidt, H. Über Kokainismus und neue Erfahrungen über Kokainwirkung bei der Morphiumentziehung. *Naturforsch.-Vers. Berlin* [No vol., page], 1886.

Smidt, H. and Rank, C. Über die Bedeutung des Cocain bei der Morphiumentziehung. *Berlin. klin. Wochenschr.* 22: 592, 1885.

Smith, R.P. Case of cocainism. *J. Ment. Sci.* 38: 408, 1892.

Sollier, P. Un cas remarquable de cocaïnomanie. *J. Med. Paris* 22: 40, 1910.

Sollier, P. and Arnaud, [No initial]. Un cas de délire maniaque de longue durée chez un toxicomane à intoxications multiples (héroïne, morphine, cocaïne, alcohol). *Encéphale* 2: 73, 1910.

Steck, H. Neurologische Untersuchungen an Schizophrenen. *Z. ges. Neurol. Psychiat.* 82: 292, 1923.

Stein, A. Ein Fall von Kokainvergiftung. *Prag. med. Wochenschr.,* [No vol., page], 1889.

Stein, A. Über Paraffininjektionen. [No journal, publisher, etc.], 1904.

Steiner, P. *Étude spectrographique des alcaloïdes végétaux.* Lons le Saumiers: Declume, 1924.

Stoddard, C.F. *Where stands the question of prohibition and drug addiction in the United States?* Westerville, Ohio: The American Issue Publishing Company, 1923.

Straub, W. Über Kokainismus. *Frankfurter Ztg.* [No vol.]Number 462: [No page], April 25, 1919.

Tatum, A.L. A study of the action of cocaine on the splanchnic and cervical sympathetic neuromuscular mechanisms. *J. Pharmacol. Exp. Ther.* 16: 109, 1920.

Thomsen, R. Zur Casuistik der kombinierten Morphium-Cocain-Psychosen. *Charité-Ann.* 12: 405, 1887.

Tirelli, V. Morfina e cocaina. *Arch. Antropol. Crim. Psichiatr. Med. Leg. Sci. Affini* 40: 209, 1920.

Tobias, E. and Kroner, K. Zur Frage der Cocain-idiosynkrasie. *Berl. klin. Wochenschr.* 55: 163, 1918.

Tomasini, S. Sulla psicosi cocainica. *Il Manicomio* 20: 67, 1904.

Traube, J. Über die Wirkung von Basen und basischen Salzen auf Alkaloidsalze. *Biochem. Z.* 42: 470, 1912.

Trisolini, F. *Cocaina e sua Ebbrezza*. Napoli: De Gaudio, 1921.

Underhill, F.P. and Black, C.L. The influence of cocaine upon metabolism with special reference to the elimination of lactic acid. *J. Biol. Chem.* 11: 235, 1912.

Vallon, C. and Bessière, R. Les troubles mentaux d'origine cocaïnique. *Encéphale* [No vol.]: 136 and 232, 1914. See also *J. Méd. int. (Paris)* 18: 72, 1914.

Vervaeck, L. Quelques aspects médicaux et psychologiques de la cocaïnomanie. *Scalpel* 76: 741-749, 769-780, 797-806, 1923.

Vioux, M. *Une enlissée.* Paris: Charpentiers, 1920.

Völcker, F. Die Verwendung des Psikains in der Urologie. *Münch. med. Wochenschr.* 71: 851, 1924.

von Anrep, B. Über die physiologische Wirkung des Cocain. *Pflügers Arch. ges. Physiol. Mensch. Tiere* 21: 38, 1880.

von Bakody, A. Die Wirkung des Kokains auf das vegetative Nervensystem bei Schizophrenie. *Dtsch. Z. Nervenheilkd.* 77: 316, 1923.

von Bibera, E. [No title] *J. Pharmakodynamik* 4: [No page], 1857.

von Korczynski, A. *Die Methoden der exakten, quantitativen Bestimmung der Alkaloide,* p. 19. Berlin: Borntraeger, 1913.

von Krafft-Ebing, R. Belastung, Cocainismus; zweifelhafte Berufsfähigkeit als Arzt. Gerichtsärztliches Gutachten. *Friedrichs Bl. gerichtl. Med.* 40: 332, 1889. See also *Wien. med. Bl.* 12: 711, 1889.

von Lendenfeld, R. Experimentelle Untersuchungen über die Physiologie der Spongien. *Biol. Zbl.* 10: 102, 1890/91.

von Tschudy, J.J. *Peru: Reiseskizzen aus den Jahren 1832-1842.* Vol. 2, p.299. St. Gallen, 1846.

von Tschudy, J.J. *Reisen durch Südamerika.* Vol. 7, p. 37. Leipzig: Brockhaus, 1869.

Vulpian, A. Expériences sur le chlorhydrate de cocaïne. *Compt. rend. Acad. Sci. (Paris)* 99: 836 and 885, 1884.

Wagler, T. Über die Coca, ihre Geschichte, geographische Verbreitung und wirtschaftliche Bedeutung. *Tropenpflanzer*, Supplement to volume 17 [No page]. Berlin, 1917.

Wallé, [No initial]. Aphoristische Mittheilungen über Gegengifte der Opiate mit besonderer Berücksichtigung der Stellung des Cocaïns gegenüber dem Morphium. *Dtsch. Med.-Ztg.* 1: 25, 1885.

Wallé, [No initial]. Die Morphiumsucht und die Physiologie der Heilungsvorgänge. *Dtsch. Med.-Ztg.* 1: 469, 481 and 493, 1885.

Wedell, H.A. *Voyage dans le Nord de la Bolivie.* Paris & London: [No publisher], 1853.

Wiechowski, W. Ueber das Schicksal des Cocains und Atropins im Thierkörper. *Arch. exp. Pathol. Pharmakol.* 46: 155, 1901.

Wilbert, M.J. and Motter, M.G. *Digest of Laws and Regulations in Force in the United States Relating to the Possession, Use, Sale and Manufacture of Poisons and Habit-Forming Drugs.* Washington: Treasury Department, 1912.

Wildenrath, R. Die Cocain vergiftung vom gerichtsärztlichen Standpunkt. *Friedrichs Bl. gerichtl. Med.* 62: 215, 1911.

Williams, [No initial]. Morphine and alcohol affect brain cells. *W. Virginia Med. J.* [No vol., page], 1917.

Willstätter, R. Über die Synthese des Psikains. *Münch. med. Wochenschr.* 71: 849, 1924.

Winterstein, E. and Trier, G. *Die Alkaloide.* Berlin: Borntraeger, 1910.

Wolfensberger, M. Der Alkoholwahnsinn (akute Halluzinose der Trinker) und seine Beziehungen zu den Schizophrenien. *Z. ges. Neurol. Psychiat.* 82: 385, 1923.

Wolfer, P. Das Kokain, seine Bedeutung und seine Geschichte. *Schweiz. Med. Wochenschr.* 52: 674, 1922.

Wollenberg, [No initial]. In Hoche's *Handbuch der gerichtliche Medizin,* 2nd edition. Berlin: Hirschwald, 1909.

Zangger, H. Der Handel mit giftigen Stoffen und seine Gefahren. Reference to the fourth "Sanitätsdirektoren-Konferenz", June, 1921. Supplement to *Bull. d. eidg. Gesundheitsamtes,* No. 13, Bern, 1922.

Zangger, H. Diskussionsbemerkung zu dem Vortrag von Maier über Kokainismus. *Schweiz. Arch. Neurol. Psychiatr.* 11: 144, 1922.

Zangger, H. Vergiftungen. In: J. Schwalbe, Ed., *Diagnostische und therapeutische Irrtümer und deren Verhütung, Volume 15*. Leipzig: Georg Thieme, 1924.

Zangger, Th. Ein Fall von chronischem Cocainmissbrauch. *Corr.-Bl. f. Schweiz. Aerzte* 27: 427, 1897.

INDEX

Roman numerals refer to pages in the Introduction

T